WHEN ZIPPO WENT TO WAR

For Margaret—

First published in Great Britain in 2021 by
Pen and Sword History
An imprint of
Pen & Sword Books Ltd
Yorkshire—Philadelphia

ISBN 978 1 526777 690

A CIP catalogue record for this book is available from
the British Library.

Printed and bound in India,
by Replika Press Pvt. Ltd.

Pen & Sword Books Limited incorporates the imprints
of Pen & Sword Archaeology, Atlas, Aviation,
Battleground, Discovery, Family History, History,
Maritime, Military, Naval, Politics, Railways, Select,
Transport, True Crime, Fiction, Frontline Books, Leo
Cooper, Praetorian Press, Seaforth Publishing,
Wharncliffe and White Owl.

For a complete list of Pen & Sword titles please contact

PEN & SWORD BOOKS LIMITED
47 Church Street. Barnsley, South Yorkshire,
S70 2AS, England
E-mail: enquiries@pen-and-sword.co.uk
Website: www.pen-and-sword.co.uk

Or

PEN AND SWORD BOOKS
1950 Lawrence Rd, Havertown, PA 19083. USA
E-mail: uspen-and-sword@casematepublishers.com
Website: www.penandswordbooks.com

The crew of *Idiot's Delight*, an Eighth U.S. Army Air Force B-17 bomber based in England in the Second World War, The men just back from a raid on Berlin and are being interrogated by an Army Air Force intelligence officer.

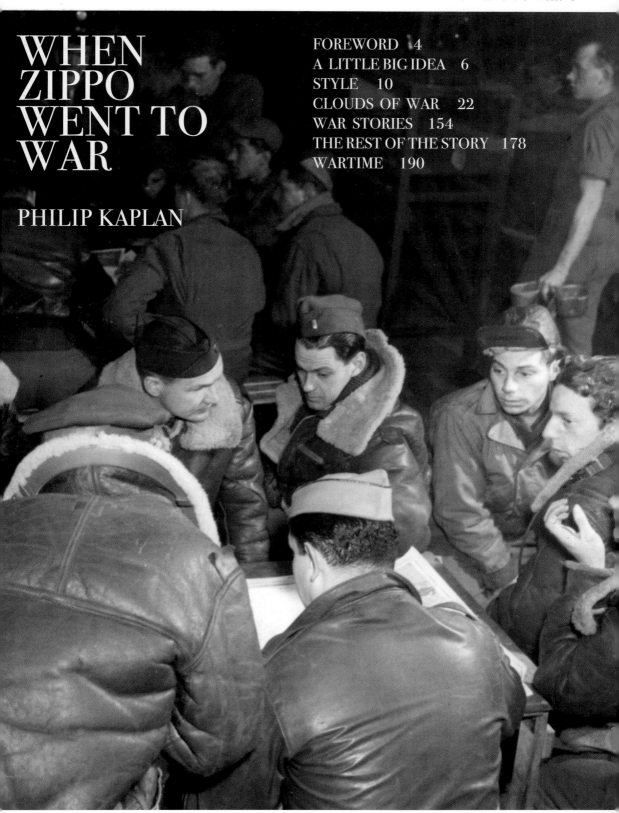

WHEN ZIPPO WENT TO WAR

PHILIP KAPLAN

The 1930s, 40s and 50s was a period when it seemed that most people were smokers. Magazine and newspaper advertisements for cigarettes and other tobacco-related products were commonplace. In that pre-television age movie audiences were virtually swamped with images of film star role models–men and women–with a cigarette, in every imaginable situation.

Legend has it that the great movie actress Bette Davis–often referred to as The First Lady of the American Screen–was once asked by an interviewer if she smoked after sex. Her response: 'To tell you the truth I've never looked.' That may be apocryphal, but it seems like something she might well have said.

Davis died in 1989. She is remembered today for her exceptional talents as a motion picture actress as well as her ability to employ the cigarette as a prop in some of her film appearances, to convey aspects of the role she was playing. Moviegoers and especially fans of the actress recall the style and facility she brought to the scenes in which she used that cigarette in a wide range of affectations to show the audience something of the nature of her fictional character. In talk show interviews she frequently lit up a cigarette to the dismay of hosts such as David Letterman, Johnny Carson, Dick Cavett and others, reassuring them with 'If I did not smoke a cigarette–they would not know who I was.'

A few Bette Davis quotes: On the Sydney Opera House: 'What a dump.' From her Oscar-winning film *All About Eve*: 'Fasten your seatbelts. It's going to be a bumpy night.' On the anti-smoking movement: 'I resent it more than I can tell you. I do not wish to be told what to do! Who has the right to say 'You can't smoke?'''

July 1955

Linnwood
Knolls
MARION, IOWA

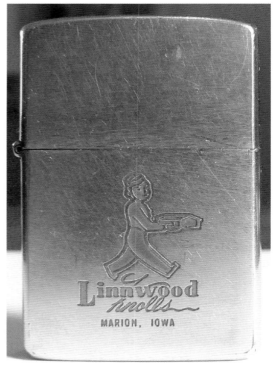

top: Zippo founder George Blaisdell with the original Austrian lighter that inspired him to create the first Zippo; above: An example of the Zippo as a corporate advertising display item.

In the 1930s a little cigarette lighter, first made in Bradford, Pennsylvania, became a phenomenal international success story. What made it such a hot product? What was it about the amazing little item that brought it such enormous fame and fortune in the next decade? This then is the story of when Zippo went to war.

The Zippo pocket lighter has always been known for and recognized by the distinctive 'clink clop' sound it makes when you open and close it, the familiar subtle scent it delivers when you use it and the elegant art deco design of this simple little machine. And in addition to all it offers, the unique lighter has always been brilliantly marketed with the world-famous Zippo lifetime guarantee: THIS PRODUCT, OR ANY ZIPPO, WILL BE PUT IN FIRST-CLASS MECHANICAL CONDITION FREE OF CHARGE, FOR WE HAVE YET TO CHARGE A CENT FOR THE REPAIR OF A ZIPPO REGARDLESS OF AGE OR CONDITION–THE ZIPPO MANUFACTURING COMPANY, BRADFORD, PA.

No one has ever had to pay for repairs to their Zippo. Frequently, owners include money when they send their lighter to the Zippo Manufacturing Company for repair. Their lighter is always returned to them, usually within two weeks, repaired, postage-paid and their remittance enclosed. Such a service is obviously expensive and adds to the company's overheads, but it continues to operate the Zippo Repair Clinic on that basis, for the immeasurable goodwill it has always generated. Upwards of half a million Zippos a year were being mended in the clinic by the 1960s. Nowadays, loyal and appreciative Zippo fans send about 1,000 lighters a day to the clinic for repair.

The Zippo lighter continues to offer these features and more. It is, of course, compact enough to fit comfortably into a small pocket. It is truly windproof and in some of its advertising, the company has invited prospective customers to stop by and test the windproof performance of the Zippo to see for themselves how efficiently it works. It is designed and engineered to be easily used with one hand. The Zippo is among the most reliable products most people will ever own.

All of its qualities and characteristics readily positioned the Zippo to be the dependable companion of millions of American Army, Navy and Air Force personnel with their entry into the Second World War early in the 1940s. The little lighter accompanied them wherever they went in those troubled and uncertain times.

The central theme of this book is the unique phenomenon of a handsome little device that went along to War with many millions of military service men and women around the globe, becoming much more than simply a commercial success story. Zippo was a loyal companion that helped most of them get through the horrors, the danger, the loneliness and the monotony of that terrible experience. The ugly reality of being at war and in the war caused a majority of these soldiers, sailors, airmen and women to smoke. They felt that a cigarette helped calm their nerves; helped them relax a bit and cope with whatever situations they might encounter. Zippo served them well.

It would be several years before the medical world and the general public would finally become aware of the other, darker aspects of the smoking habit.

The economy of the town of Bradford in the foothills of the Allegheny Mountain Range, near the Pennsylvania border with New York state, hummed along relatively quietly thanks mainly to the local timber industry, until 1871. It was then that a large reserve of petroleum was discovered beneath a farm near Bradford. The find was part of the major oil exploration effort in Pennsylvania in that time and it led to the addition of more than 7,000 new residents to the town which is located some 78 miles south of Buffalo, New York.

The great oil rush of the 1870s resulted in prosperity for Bradford, which is still home to the American Refining Group (formerly the Kendall Oil Company, makers of the world-famous Kendall Racing Oils).

Another famous Bradford resident was the Taylor Brothers Aircraft Corporation which designed and built the Taylor Cub aeroplane in the 1930s. Following a fire in the factory, the company was purchased by Piper Aircraft of Lockhaven, Pennsylvania. Piper soon redesigned the Taylor Cub and produced a new version, the enduring, well-known Piper Cub trainer, in which many famous aviators had their early flights. This author, in fact, experienced an unforgettable flying lesson in just such an ancient yellow Cub when my old and jaded instructor finally reached the end of his tether with the lack of progress I had displayed one day. He took his hand off the stick, folded his arms across his chest and growled 'You've got it.' And down we went. No natural flier I, and it was quickly obvious that he was going to have to resume control if we were to avoid becoming a blot on the landscape. I was later fortunate to hook up with a more patient and forgiving instructor who graduated me to a far more pleasant and sophisticated learning experience in the Piper Cherokee, an all-metal, low-wing monoplane that was just as forgiving as my new teacher.

As well as playing host to Taylor Aircraft, Bradford would become home to the Zippo Manufacturing Company, which established itself there in 1932. Zippo has been making its world-renowned pocket lighter in its Bradford factory for more than eight decades. The company celebrated the production of its 500-millionth lighter in 2012. The Zippo lighter has been described as a 'legendary and distinct symbol of America'.

It was in the 1930s that our story really began. Early in the twentieth century one Philo Blaisdell, an enterprising manufacturer of oil drilling equipment in Bradford, was thriving in the oil boom. After two years in military school, his young son, George, returned to the family home in Bradford and went to work as an apprentice in his father's factory where he laboured fifty-nine hours a week, for the princely sum of ten cents an hour. George did well in his apprenticeship and then moved into sales. By the beginning of the First World War he had taken over the management of the company and in 1920 he sold the business and went into oil drilling with his brother.

The brothers Blaisdell prospered in oil drilling until the coming of the Great Depression at the end of the decade. George was attending a function at the Bradford Country Club on a warm summer evening in 1931 and there he is believed to have met Dick Dresser, a well turned-out businessman who was having a cigarette on the porch of the club. George couldn't resist asking him why such a dapper fellow would be lighting up with what was the ugliest lighter he had ever

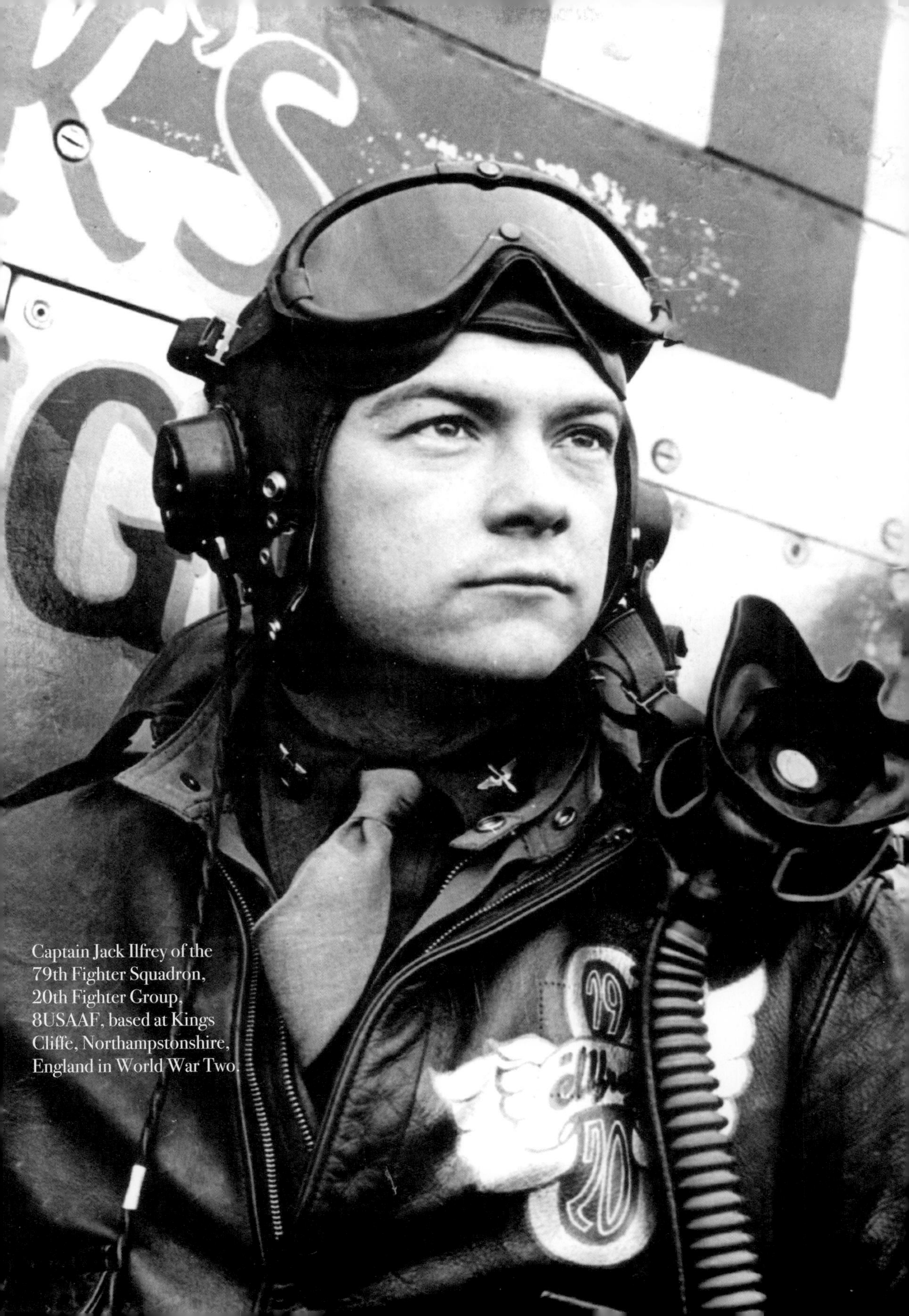

Captain Jack Ilfrey of the 79th Fighter Squadron, 20th Fighter Group, 8USAAF, based at Kings Cliffe, Northampstonshire, England in World War Two.

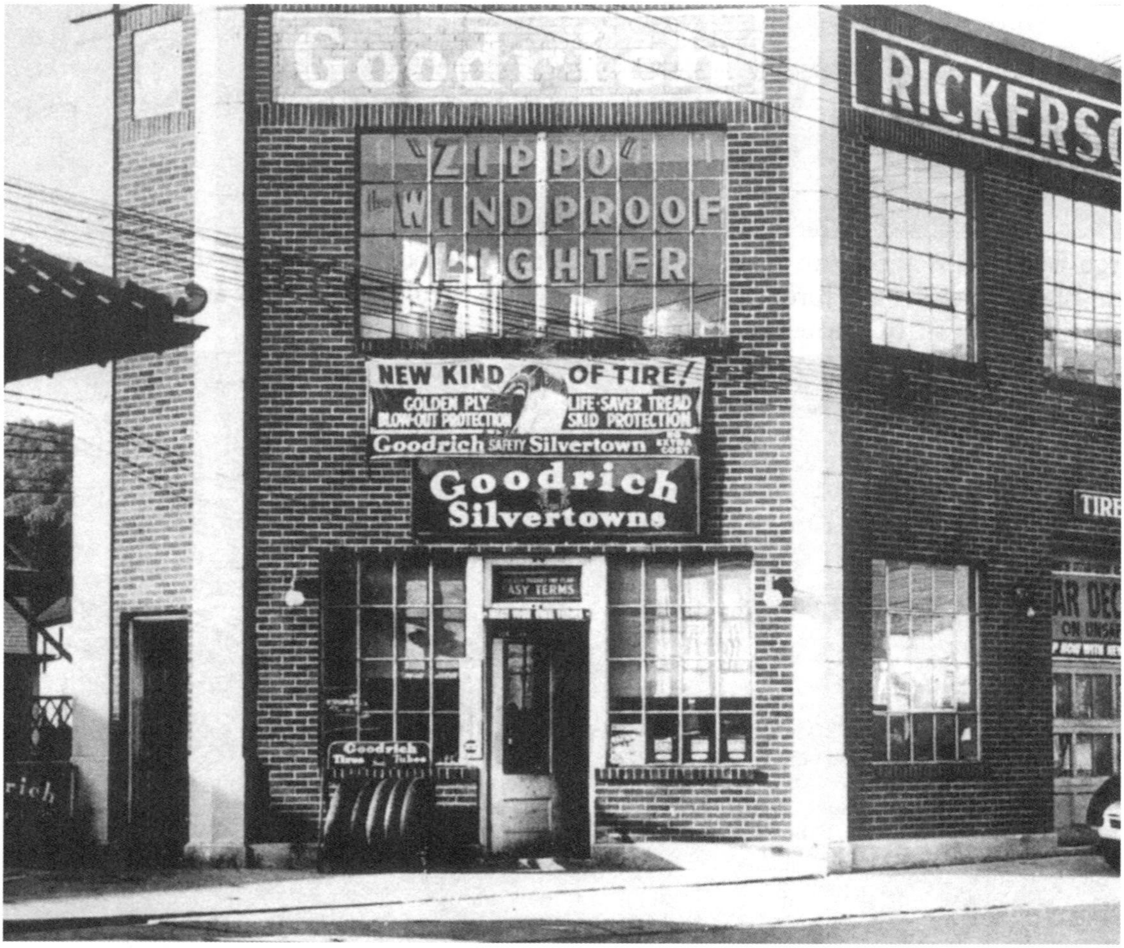
"ZIPPO"
WIND PROOF
LIGHTER
NEW KIND OF TIRE!
GOLDEN PLY
BLOW-OUT PROTECTION
LIFE-SAVER TREAD
SKID PROTECTION
Goodrich SAFETY Silvertown
Goodrich
Silvertowns

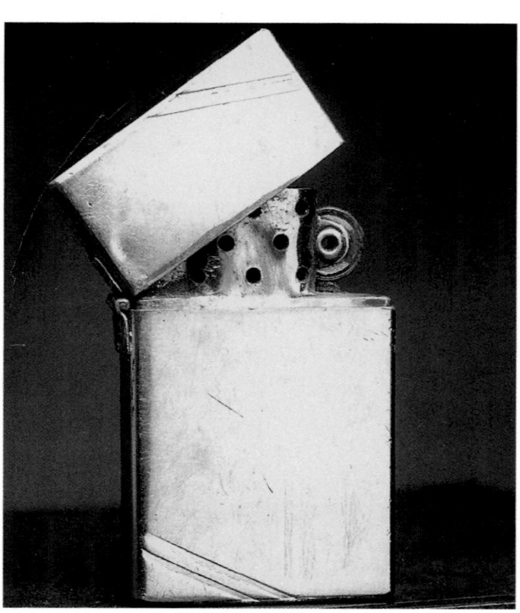

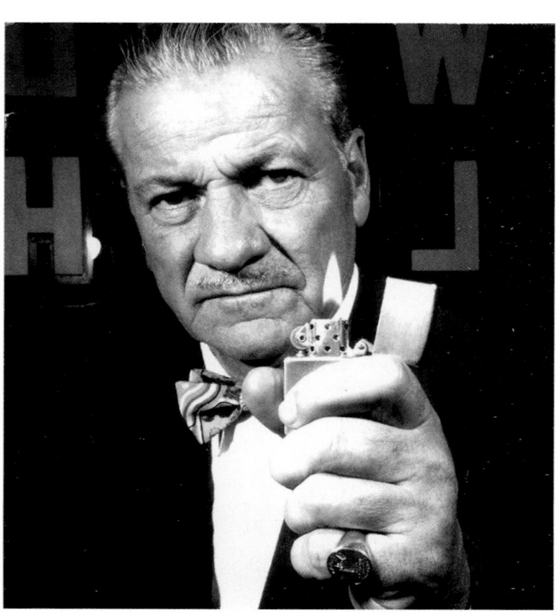

seen. Dresser replied, 'Well, it works.' He told Blaisdell that the crude, clumsy looking device had been made in Austria and he had bought it for one dollar. Interested, George went after and was granted the American distribution rights for the unattractive but apparently reliable lighter. He then managed to persuade its Austrian maker to improve the look of the thing by chrome plating the casing. Sales, however, were meagre and he later decided to give up the distribution rights. He then rented a small workshop, the first Zippo factory, on the second floor of the Rickerson and Pryde building in Bradford, over an automobile garage for $10 a month. He had 'ZIPPO' WINDPROOF LIGHTER painted on the front window of the workshop and hired his first three employees. He set about designing and manufacturing his own lighter, one that was to be compact and fit comfortably in the palm of a hand. It had to be attractive, and perhaps most importantly, operable with just one hand. So pleased was Blaisdell with the design, fabrication and operation of his new lighter, he decided it would not be changed as long as he lived, and, apart from only a few relatively minor improvements and the introduction of new technologies that increased production and reliability, little has changed about the product since George's original 1933 Zippo.

Why did he call it Zippo? It was a matter of timing, really. Just prior to the release of George Blaisdell's original lighter in the early 1930s, the Talon Company—another Pennsylvania enterprise—had introduced its revolutionary new sliding fastener, calling it the zipper. Blaisdell liked the sound of that word. He thought it catchy and thus inspired, he chose to call his new product, Zippo. The name and the noise would both become world famous; the 'clink clop' sound of a thumb flipping the lighter top open and shut has become universally recognizable and is known everywhere as 'the Zippo Click.' The Zippo Click supposedly still alerts quality-control inspectors in the manufacturing plant at Bradford to the passing or failing of the products they examine at the end of the assembly process. That, of course, is only a rumour. What is fact, however, is the domestic sales of the lighter have fallen dramatically since the 1990s, with the efforts in the United States to curb cigarette smoking. China, however, with more than 300 million smokers, provides a continuing market for Zippo. Before the decline of cigarette smoking in the U.S., Zippo was one of the top 100 brands in the world. Its annual sales of the windproof lighter peaked at 17.3 million units in 1996. But that was a very different time.

Let us now pause briefly to draw a long, slow smoke-free breath while we consider the reality of cigarette smoking: surely, one must have better and safer things to do with one's life. There, now that we have cleared the air, let's continue.

From the 1930s through the 1940s and into the 1960s, lighting a cigarette with a Zippo in the movies exuded glamour, sophistication and being downright cool. Doing so in that time and context was simply unmatchable. Here are some examples of the parts played by the cigarette, often with Zippo in a key supporting role.

top left: The first Zippo factory shop ; far left: The first Zippo; left: George Blaisdell, the founder.

below: John Mills in the 1945 film *The Way To The Stars*; bottom: Jack Hawkins in *The Cruel Sea*.

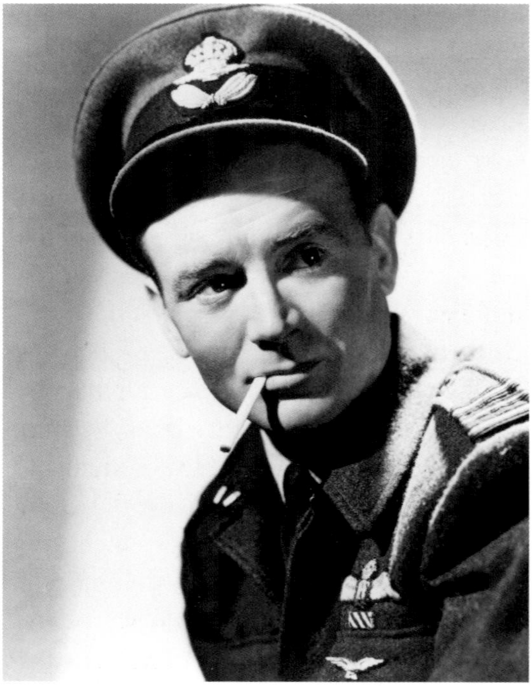

In the 1930s the appearance of the new and unique Zippo cigarette lighter with its fashionable art deco design, its comfortable and easy-to-use feel, its one-hand operation, its windproof performance, its streamlined appeal and its 'clink clop' opening and closing sounds got it a lot of attention from the general public and specifically from the motion picture industry.

Many prominent film directors realized that cigarette smoking was seen as a glamourous activity and, with growing frequency, were finding room for it in their movies. More and more film stars of the '30s and '40s were filmed with a cigarette and more and more movie fans were impressed and influenced by what they saw as stylish, sophisticated and cool. Stars such as Humphrey Bogart, Bette Davis, Gregory Peck, Fred Astaire, Noel Coward,

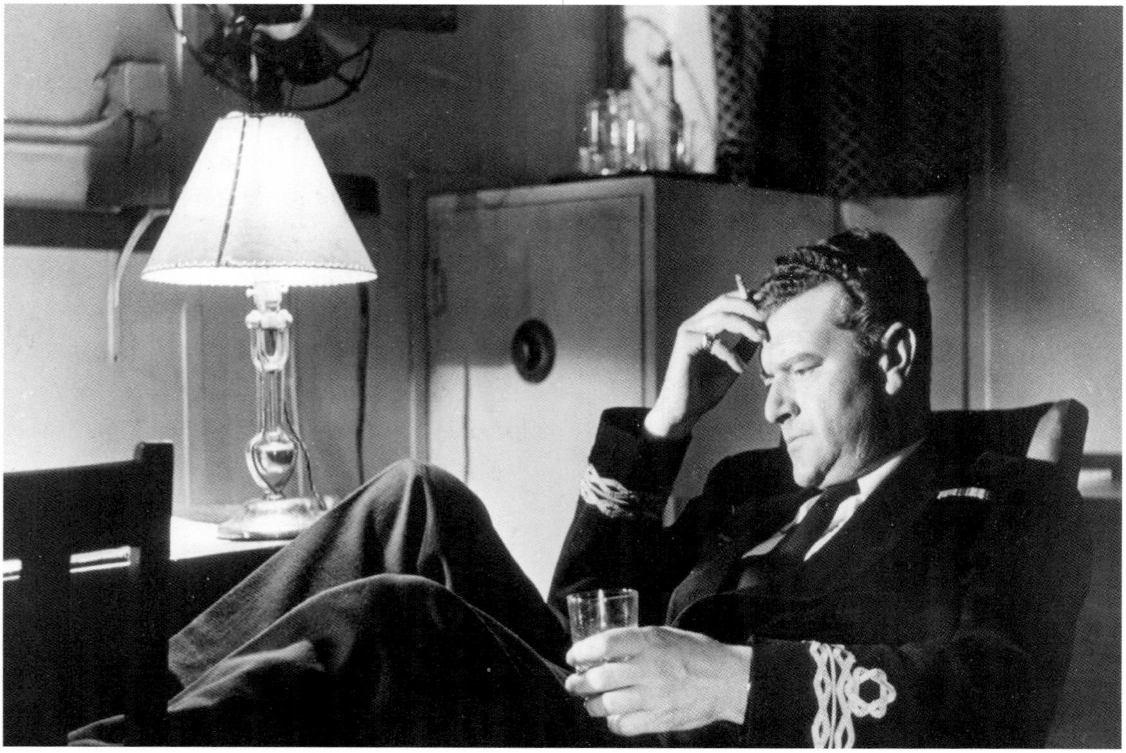

below: Two iconic views of the inimitable movie star Marlene Dietrich.

John Barrymore, William Powell, Peter Lorre, Jack Hawkins, Paul Muni, James Cagney, John Garfield, Fredric March, John Wayne, Rudolph Valentino, Marlene Dietrich, Alice Faye, Greta Garbo, Rita Hayworth, Virginia Mayo, Lauren Bacall who lit up the silver screen, were often seen lighting up with a stylish, impressive Zippo. For most of these stars, the employment of a cigarette as a featured prop in a film scene—sometimes supported by a Zippo lighter—could actually be a career booster.

It was a level of product promotion never imagined by the little Pennsylvania lighter maker. And other rather well-known people who were considered sophisticated and admirable, including war correspondents Edward R. Murrow and Ernie Pyle, as well as U.S. President Franklin D. Roosevelt, were frequently photographed with a cigarette. And British Prime Minister Winston Churchill was almost always photographed with a cigar.

How times have changed. In a (London) *Daily Telegraph* article of 2 April 2016, film critic Robbie Collin refers to a class action lawsuit filed in California in March of that year. The complaint against the Motion Picture Association of America, six major studios, and the Association of Theatre Owners alleged that 'smoking in films since 2003 had led 4.6 million under-16s to become smokers themselves.

'A recent example from the World Health Organisation, quoted extensively in the law suit, notes that "films can provide [the tobacco industry] the opportunity to convert a deadly consumer product into a cool, glamourous and desirable lifestyle necessity.

"In the Thirties and Forties, 33 of the era's top 50 box office stars, including Clark Gable, Joan Crawford, Bette Davis and John Wayne—all prolific screen smokers—were paid millions

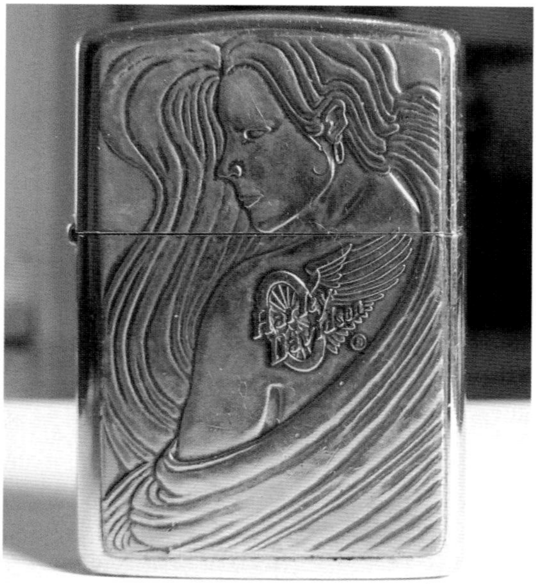

above: A Harley-Davidson Zippo

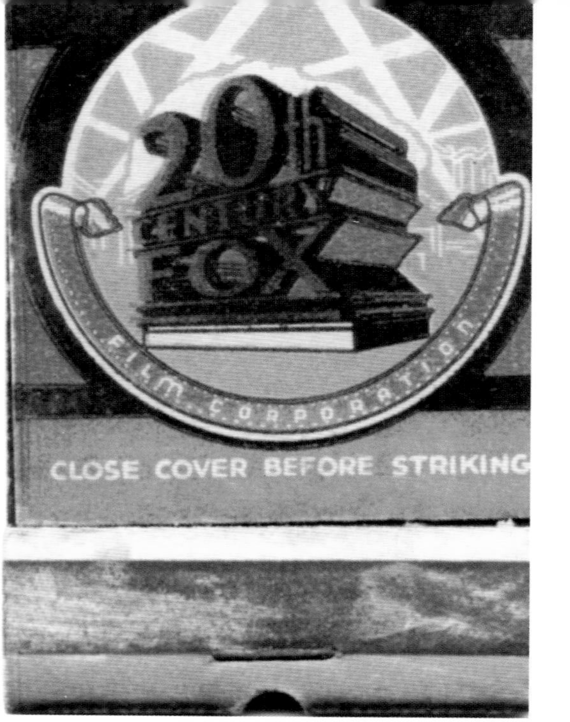
FILM CORPORATION
CLOSE COVER BEFORE STRIKING

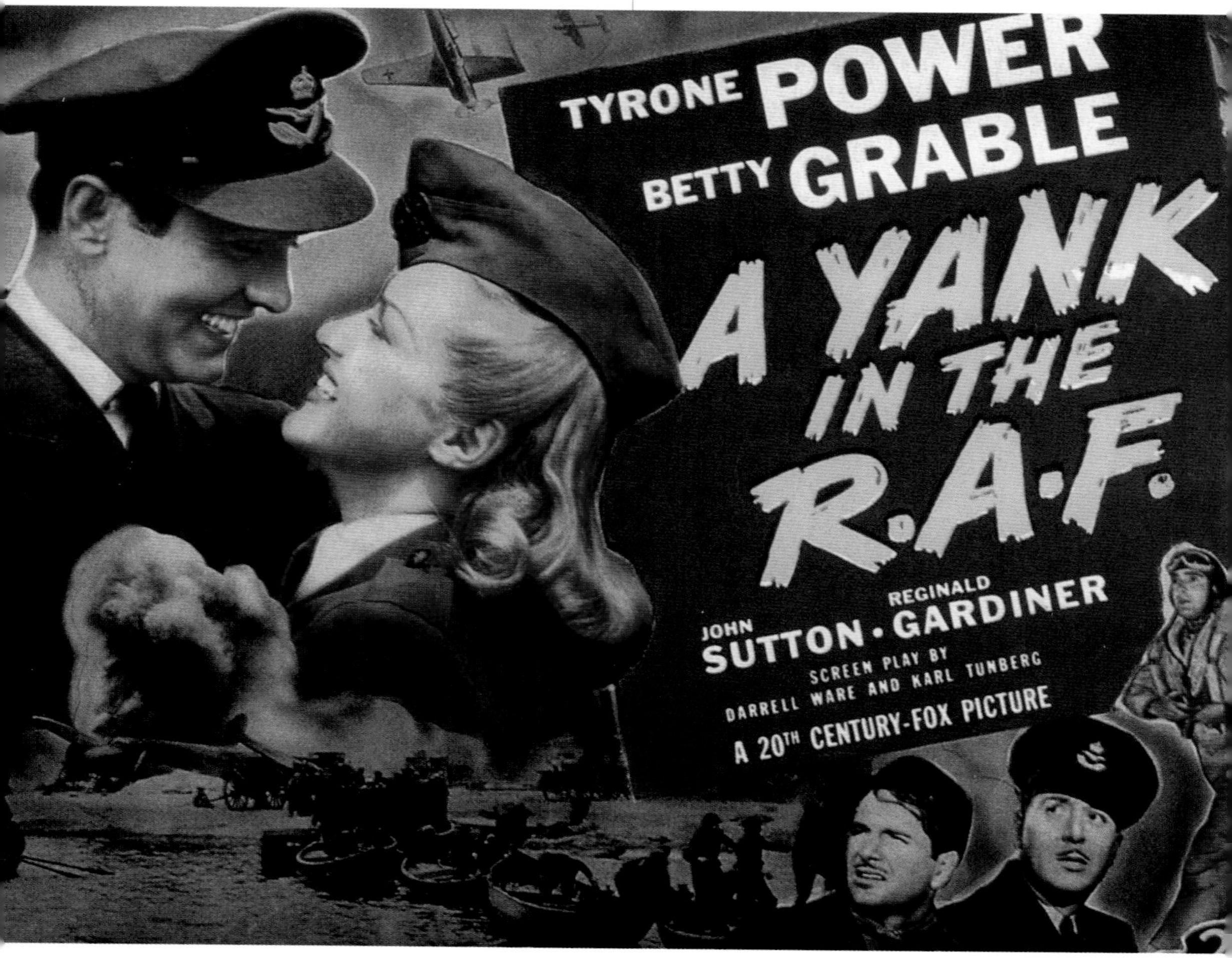
TYRONE POWER
BETTY GRABLE
A YANK IN THE R.A.F.
JOHN SUTTON · REGINALD GARDINER
SCREEN PLAY BY DARRELL WARE AND KARL TUNBERG
A 20TH CENTURY-FOX PICTURE

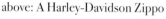

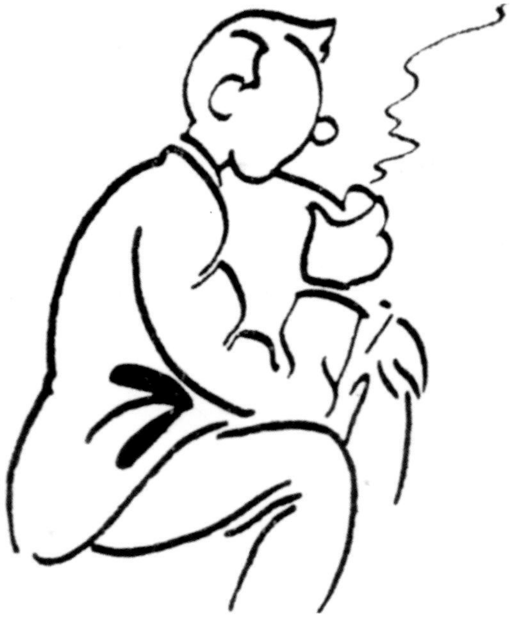

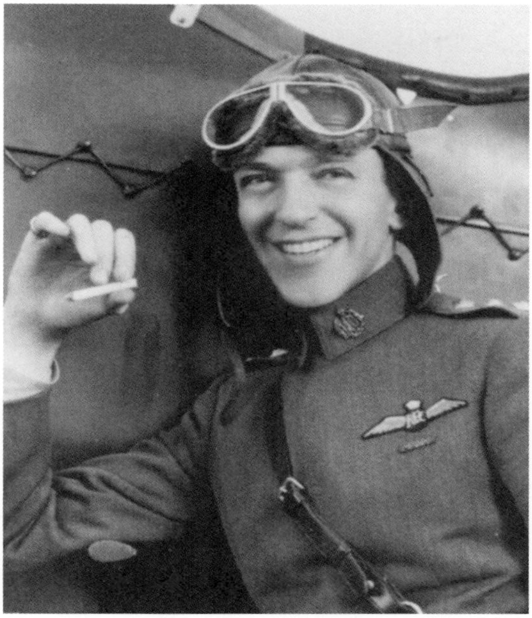

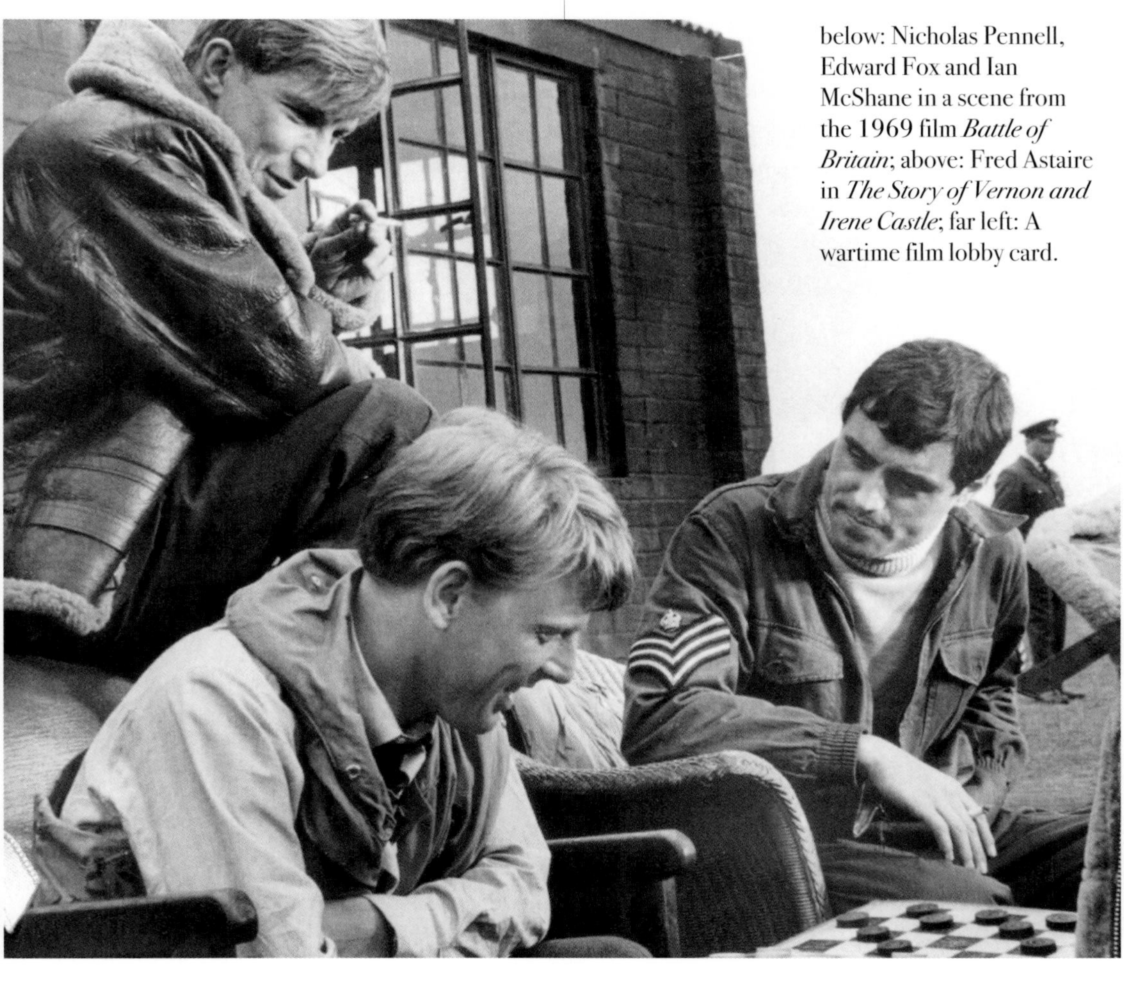

below: Nicholas Pennell, Edward Fox and Ian McShane in a scene from the 1969 film *Battle of Britain*; above: Fred Astaire in *The Story of Vernon and Irene Castle*; far left: A wartime film lobby card.

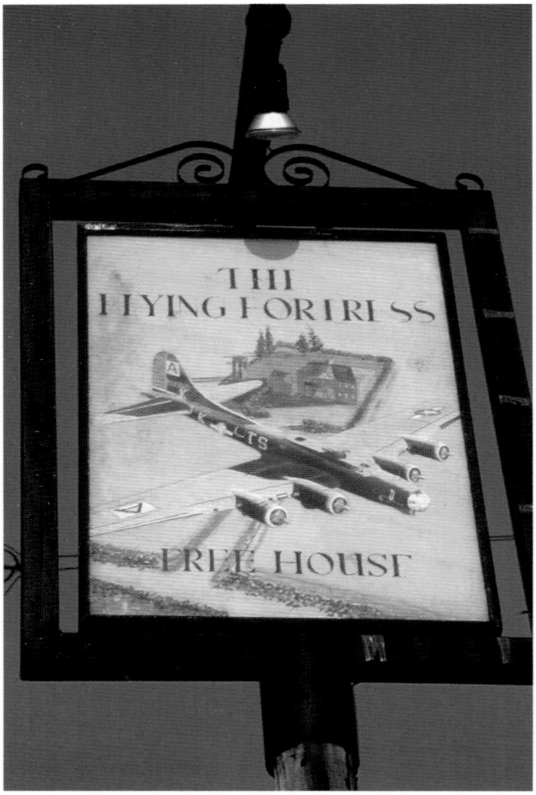
THE FLYING FORTRESS
FREE HOUSE

of dollars to personally endorse particular brands of cigarettes. In the Fifties, the tobacco companies' marketing budgets were lured away from cinema by the homely glow of the television set." '

When America entered the Second World War, Lucky Strike, a popular cigarette brand whose green package was printed with an ink made with something then declared a 'strategic material' by the U.S. Government, leading to a redesign of the package with an all white background. The new look enabled the cigarette maker to advertise that its famous product LUCKY STRIKE GREEN HAS GONE TO WAR!

It was not long before the war had created such a great demand and a hugely increased

left: An example of a commercial Zippo; below: Airmen of the 385th Bomb Group, 8USAAF enjoying Thanksgiving dinner at Great Ashfield, England, 1943; Pub sign near the 94th Bomb Group base at Rougham.

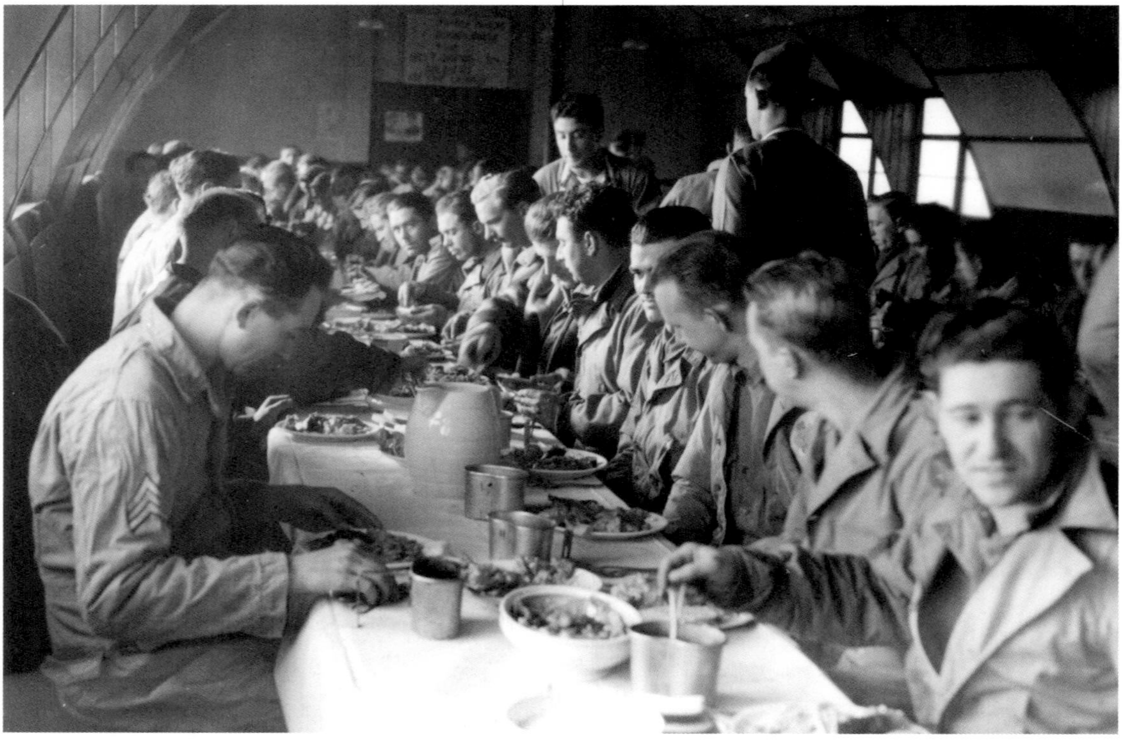

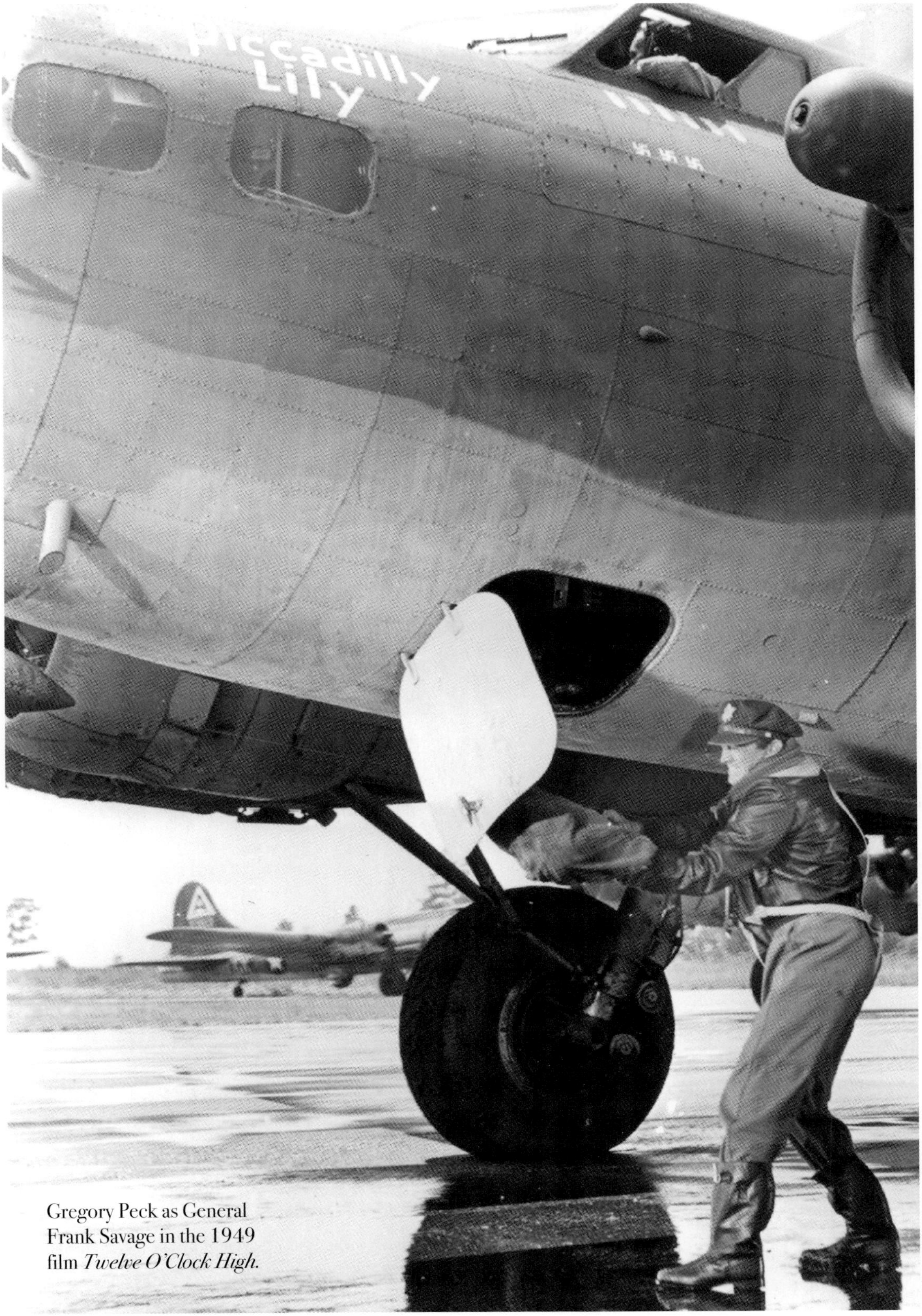
Piccadilly
Lily

Gregory Peck as General Frank Savage in the 1949 film *Twelve O'Clock High.*

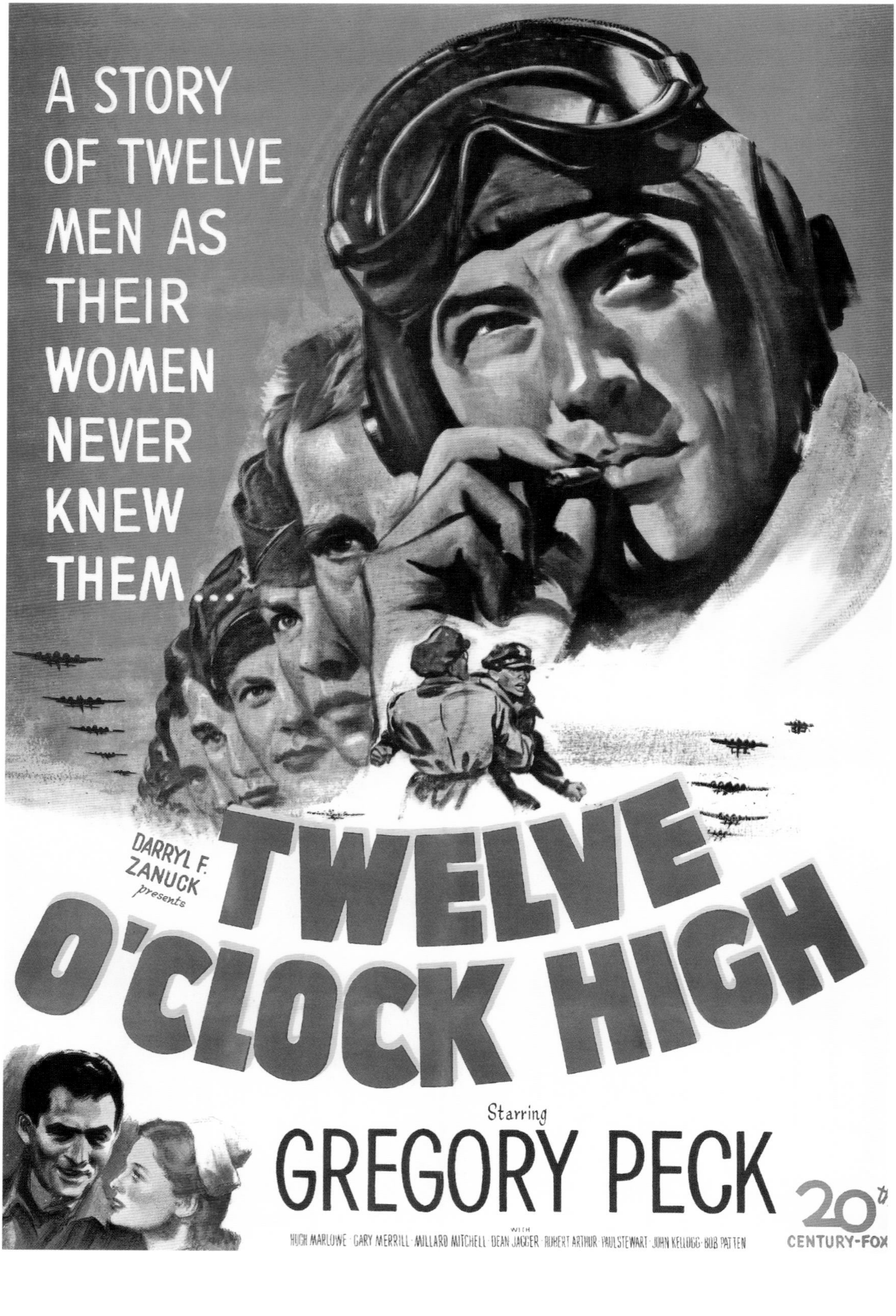
A STORY OF TWELVE MEN AS THEIR WOMEN NEVER KNEW THEM...
DARRYL F. ZANUCK presents
TWELVE O'CLOCK HIGH
Starring
GREGORY PECK
WITH
HUGH MARLOWE · GARY MERRILL · MILLARD MITCHELL · DEAN JAGGER · ROBERT ARTHUR · PAUL STEWART · JOHN KELLOGG · BOB PATTEN
20th CENTURY-FOX

market for the Zippo that its manufacturer found itself no longer able to supply the lighters in the enormous quantities required by post exchanges in the U.S. Shortly that demand was such that the company had to limit Zippo distribution of the lighters to post exchanges on overseas military bases only. No Zippos were available on U.S. domestic sale for the duration of the war. One of the magazine ads run by the Zippo company during the war was headed TAKE CARE OF YOUR ZIPPO. YOU CAN'T BUY A NEW ONE TODAY.

Collin continues: 'By 1990, when health concerns about smoking could no longer be ignored, the Cigarette Advertising and Promotion Code had been updated to rule out product placement (of cigarettes, at least) in both films and television.

'But there are crucial advantages to smoking in films . . . it gives actors a useful, subtle, non-verbal way to tell us something about their characters, from Michael Corleone's dead-calm manipulation of a Zippo in *The Godfather*, to Norma Desmond's talon-like cigarette-holder in *Sunset Boulevard*.

'There are, of course, lower-tar alternatives. Brad Pitt is a master of conveying character through eating. In *Moneyball*, he gets the same kind of dramatic mileage from a mouthful of popcorn that Humphrey Bogart would have done with a ten-pack.

'The second advantage—the very nature of the ritual of smoking, coupled with the smoke itself—is considerably trickier to get around. Because both, intrinsically and unavoidably, are—how best to put it?—cool. On screen, smoking adds movement to stillness, and pricks the dark with momentary flares of warmth and light. It's a catalyst for

ZIPPO
1932

PAPER DOLL
by JOHNNY BLACK
sung by the MILLS BROS.
on BRUNSWICK record Nº 03464
Featured by FRANK SINATRA
The Voice That is Thrilling Millions
1/-

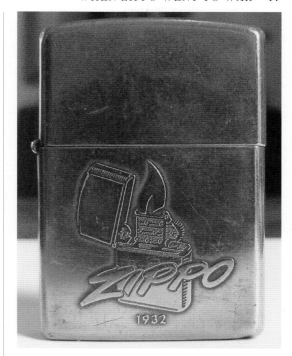

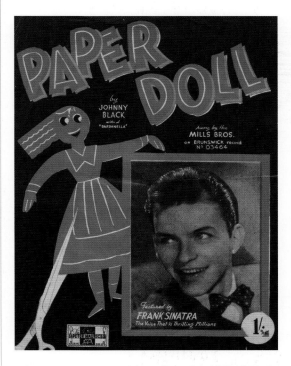

left: A poster for the release of *Twelve O'Clock High*, a great war film of the 1940s; top: A commemorative Zippo lighter celebrating the company's work on the first of the line; above: Sheet music for one of the hit songs of early in the swing era.

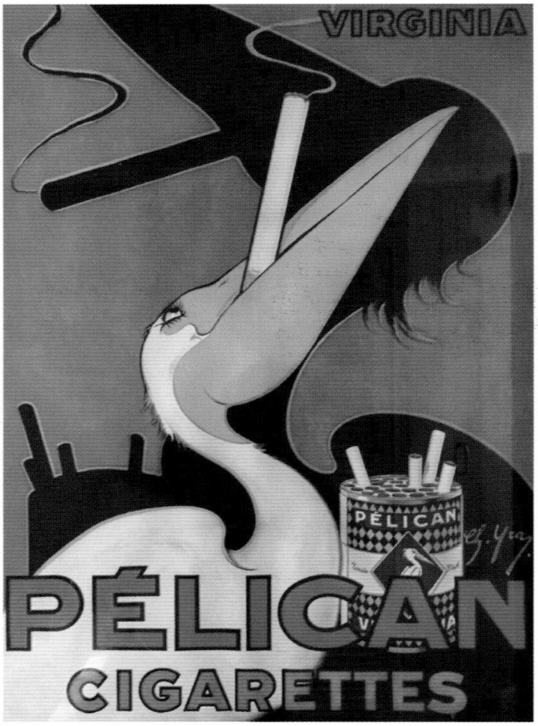
VIRGINIA
PÉLICAN
PÉLICAN
CIGARETTES

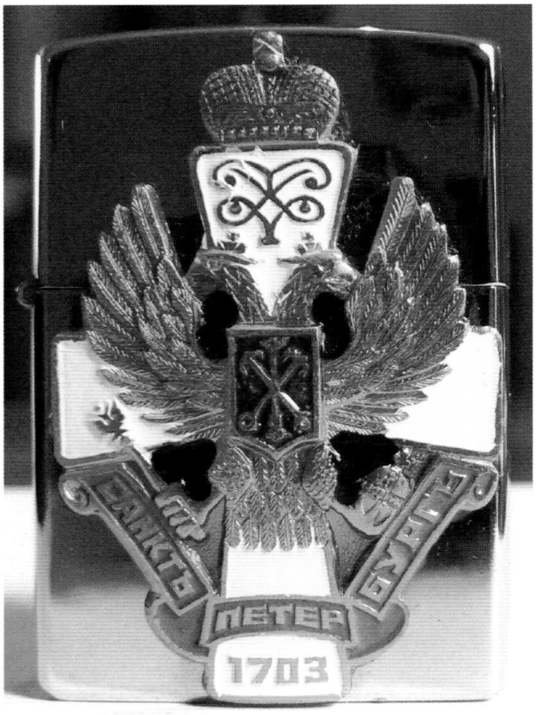
ПЕТЕР
1703

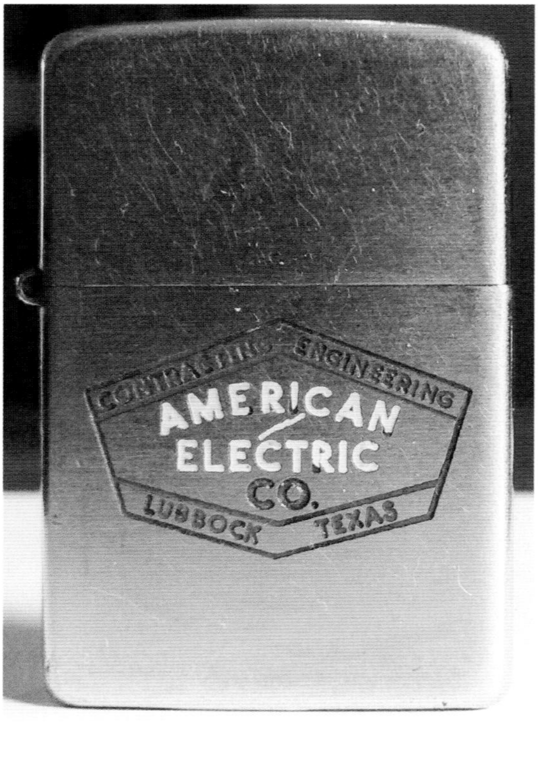
CONTRACTING ENGINEERING
AMERICAN
ELECTRIC
CO.
LUBBOCK TEXAS

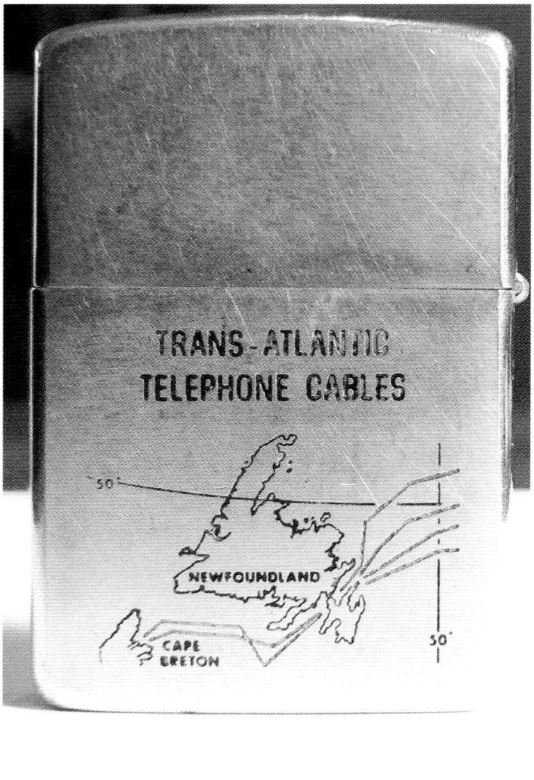
TRANS-ATLANTIC
TELEPHONE CABLES
NEWFOUNDLAND
CAPE
BRETON

A variety of Zippos.

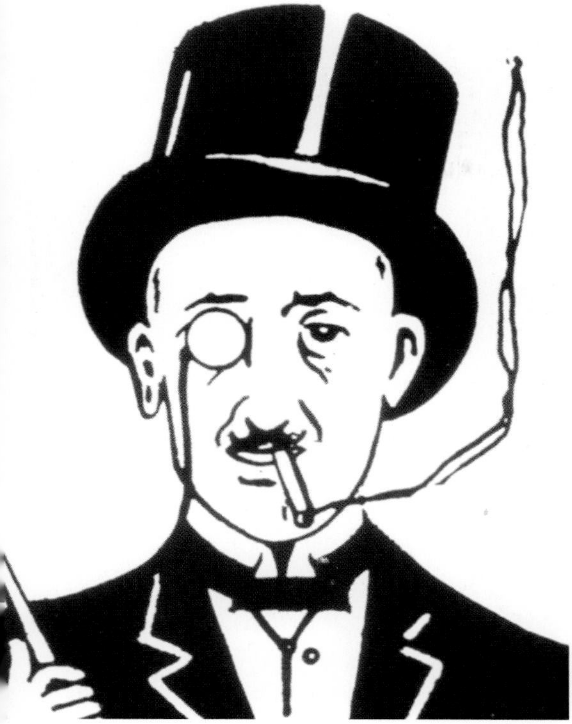

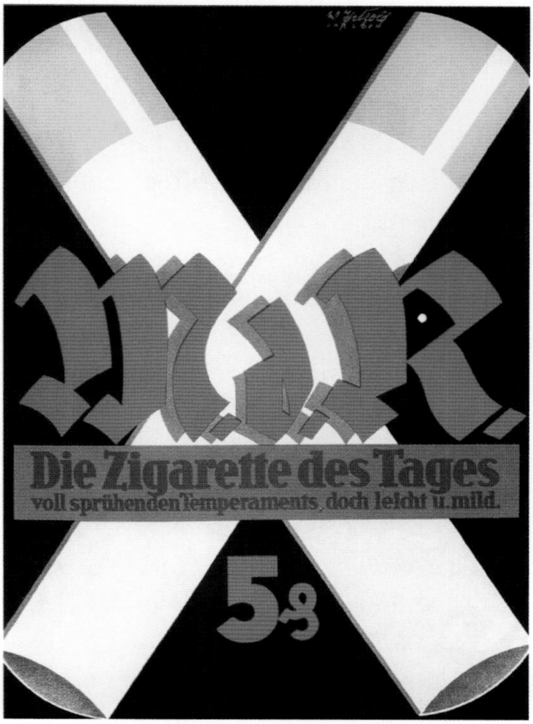
Die Zigarette des Tages
voll sprühenden Temperaments, doch leicht u. mild.
5

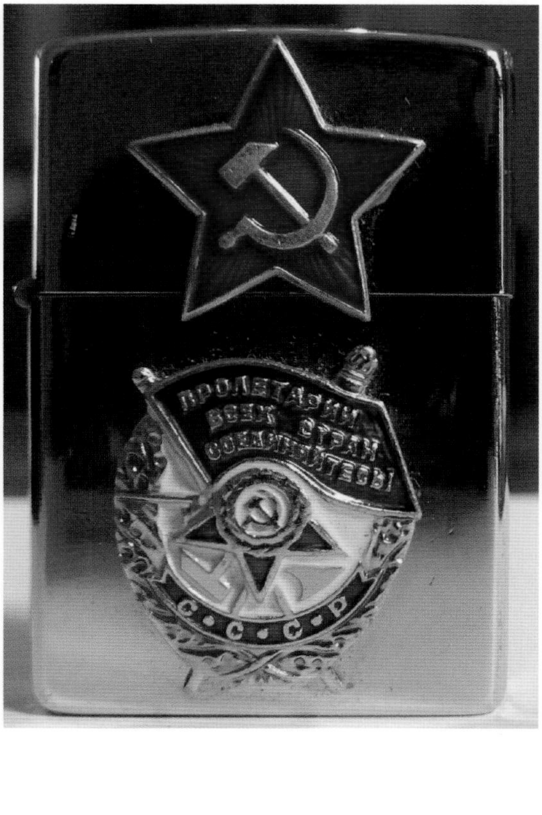
ПРОЛЕТАРИИ ВСЕХ СТРАН СОЕДИНЯЙТЕСЬ
С.С.С.Р

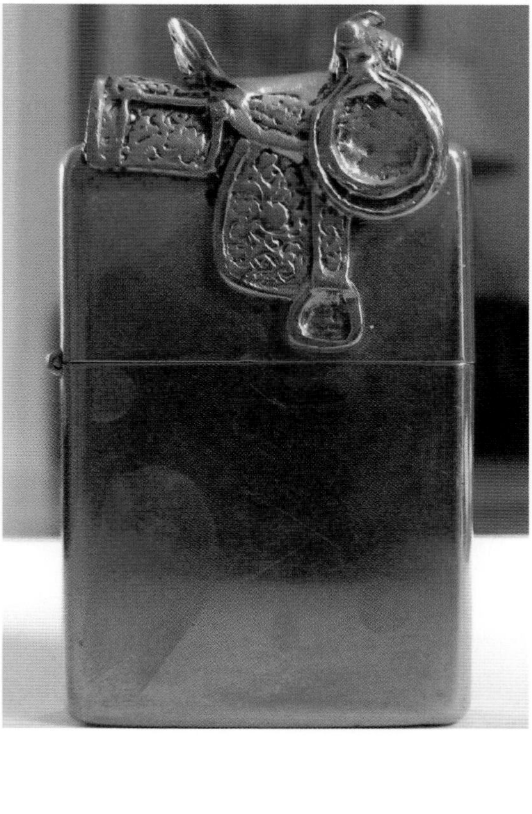

intimacy, and particularly in the film noir era, there was often no fire without it.

'Take Lauren Bacall's debut screen appearance in *To Have And Have Not*, Howard Hawks' noir-tinged romance from 1944.

' "Anybody got a match?' comes a purr from just out of shot: Bogart turns to see her in the doorway and obligingly tosses her his matchbox, which she snatches from the air with a cat-like swipe. Or try the opening sequence to Hawks' *The Big Sleep*. We see Bogart and Bacall in silhouette: he lights her cigarette, then his, while the credits drift past in a fug. Then the camera tilts down to a crystal ashtray, where two hands place the still-smouldering coffin-nails side by side but separate, like lovers in a motel bed. Never mind the cliché of the post-coital cigarette. Sometimes a cigarette alone was all it took to get the job done.

Collin: "Smoke came to Hollywood in style from Germany in the Thirties, when directors like GW Pabst, Fritz Lang and Josef von Sternberg used its satiny visual texture to fill their films with luxury and intrigue. It's no coincidence that Marlene Dietrich, the greatest star of Weimar cinema, was also cinema's greatest smoker. Kenneth Tynan called Dietrich 'Sex without gender' and there's no question cigarettes endowed her with an androgynous potency. In von Sternberg's *The Blue Angel* (1930), Dietrich's cabaret singer, Lola Lola, coolly whips a cigarette from its case before passing the box to her flustered admirer, Professor Rath (Emil Jannings), who drops it on the carpet. He gets down on his hands and knees and the camera cuts underneath Lola's dressing table—and we see Jannings fumbling on the left of the frame, and Dietrich's bare

legs tantalisingly on the right. " When you're done," she smiles while taking a drag, "send me a postcard." '

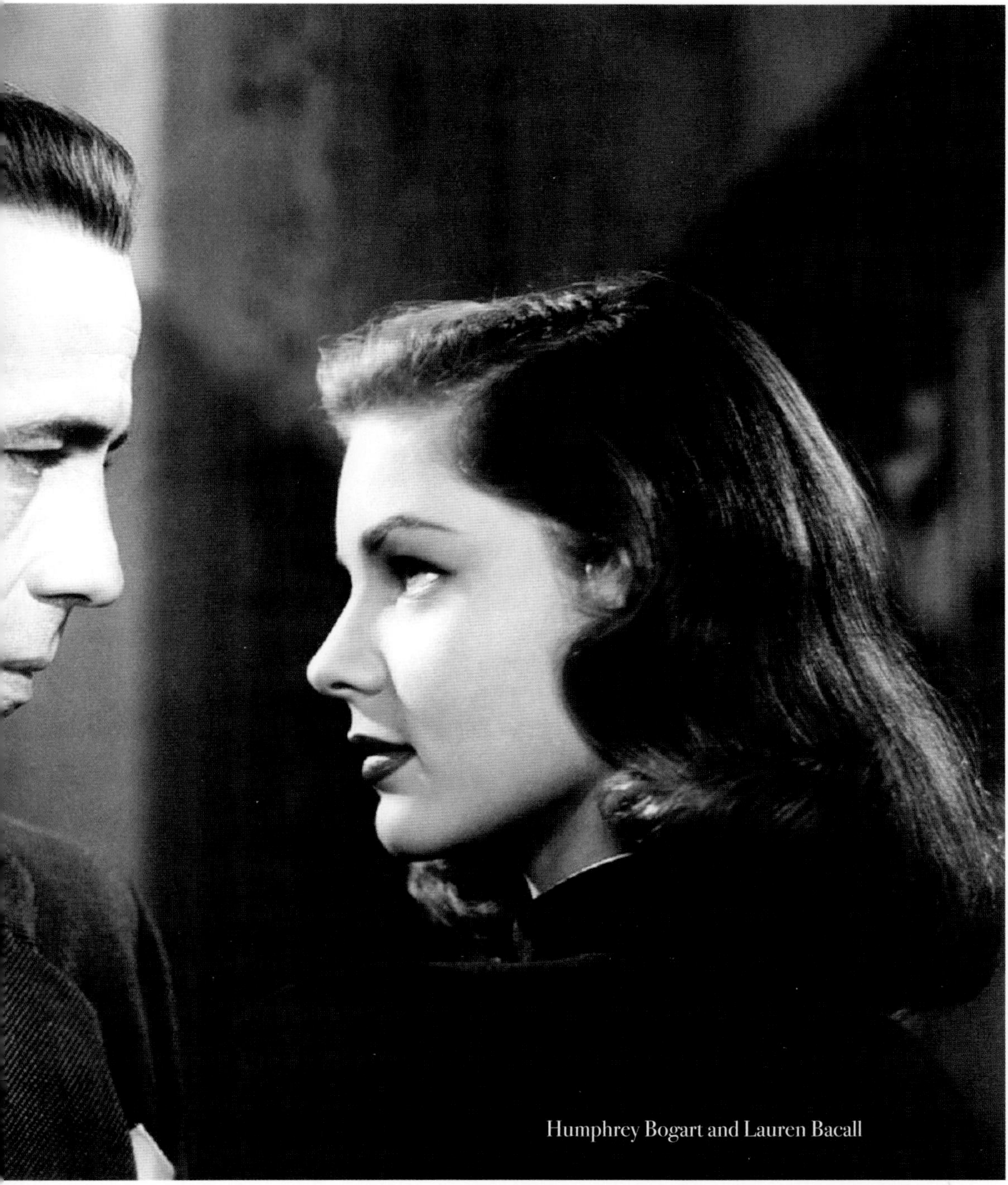

Humphrey Bogart and Lauren Bacall

A cigarette that bears a lipstick's traces . . .
–*These Foolish Things* (Remind me of you)
Music: Jack Strachey; Lyrics: Eric Maschwitz

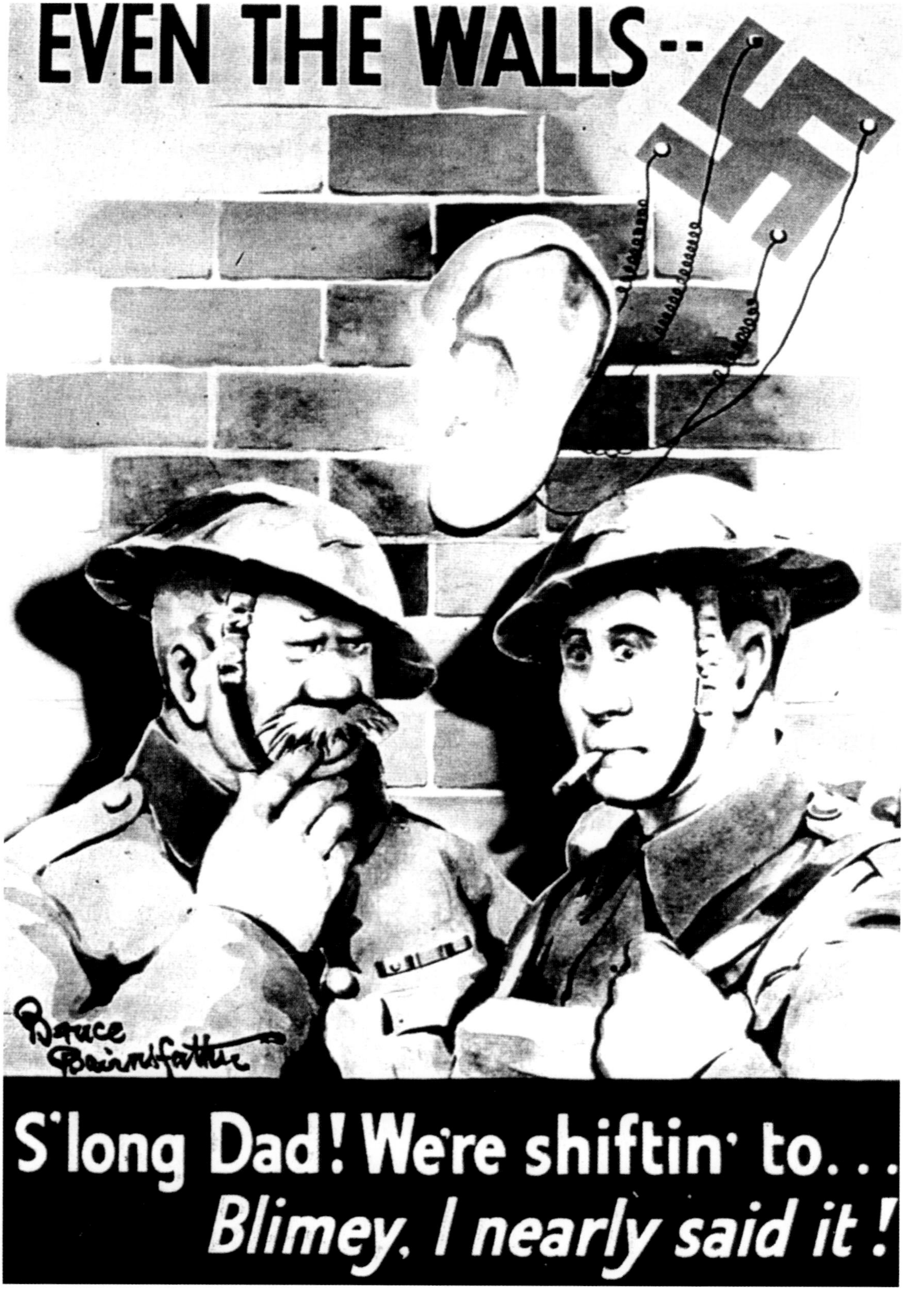
EVEN THE WALLS--
Bruce Bairnsfather
S'long Dad! We're shiftin' to...
Blimey, I nearly said it!

Between September 1939 and August 1945 a global conflict—the deadliest in human history—raged, involving more than thirty countries and the participation of more than 100 million people. When it ended more than eighty million had died with the majority of the casualties in China and the Soviet Union. Most of these deaths resulted from starvation; disease; strategic bombing; land, sea and air combat; genocide, the Holocaust; and the nuclear bomb attacks on Hiroshima and Nagasaki, Japan.

By the 1940s there was war all over the world. In the Western Pacific region, the progress of the Japanese military in its rapid conquests was considered by many in Asia as a form of liberation from the curse of western domination. But with the sea change of the Battle of Midway in June 1942, barely six months after the Japanese surprise attack on the U.S. naval base at Pearl Harbor, Hawaii, which had temporarily crippled the capital ships of the American Pacific Fleet, Japan was defeated in an historic air and sea fight that changed the course of the Pacific war. She was never again able to mount the sort of large-scale offensives at sea that had enabled her forces to take so much territory. With that tide-turning event, the way cleared for the Allied island-hopping campaign that led to victory in the Pacific in summer 1945.

Meanwhile the war in Europe and elsewhere continued with unprecedented fury as the preparations progressed for the opening of a second front on the continent by means of Operation Overlord, the Allied invasion of the Normandy coast of France in June 1944. From that point until Germany was defeated in May 1945, and Japan in August, and the gathered clouds of war finally dispersed, the harsh realities of the conflict for all on both sides, the combatants, the support personnel, and the many war industry workers and civilians in other capacities—wore on bringing deprivation, tragedy and countless hardships.

Around the world, wherever there was combat, American soldiers continued the fight. They gobbled the grub and griped about the mud, gaped at the gals and were usually referred to as GIs (Government Issue) or Dogfaces. One of their favourite smokes during the war years was the Lucky Strike and one of the better ad campaigns of the period was headlined by that famous slogan 'Lucky Strike Green Has Gone To War'. As noted earlier, the cigarette maker had to eliminate the solid green background colour formerly used on its cigarette packages, when a part of the green ink was declared a strategic war material. It was a patriotic decision in wartime that led to a huge sales advance for Lucky Strike and a big rise in demand in 1942.

Throughout the 1930s Zippo Manufacturing Company had prospered on the success of its incomparable little lighter. But with the coming of the Second World War there was a dramatic adjustment for everyone in the combatant nations. In the United States, brass, which formed the basic structure of the Zippo lighter, was also declared to be a strategic material. The U.S. Government now needed enormous quantities of the metal for the production of hundreds of millions of shell and cartridge casings for the armed forces. Almost overnight the brass was unobtainable in the amounts required by the Zippo company and had to be replaced by steel. But steel can corode, so the company decided to protect its wartime pocket lighters with a new black paint finish

Polish pilots who flew and fought with the British Royal Air Force in the Second World War.

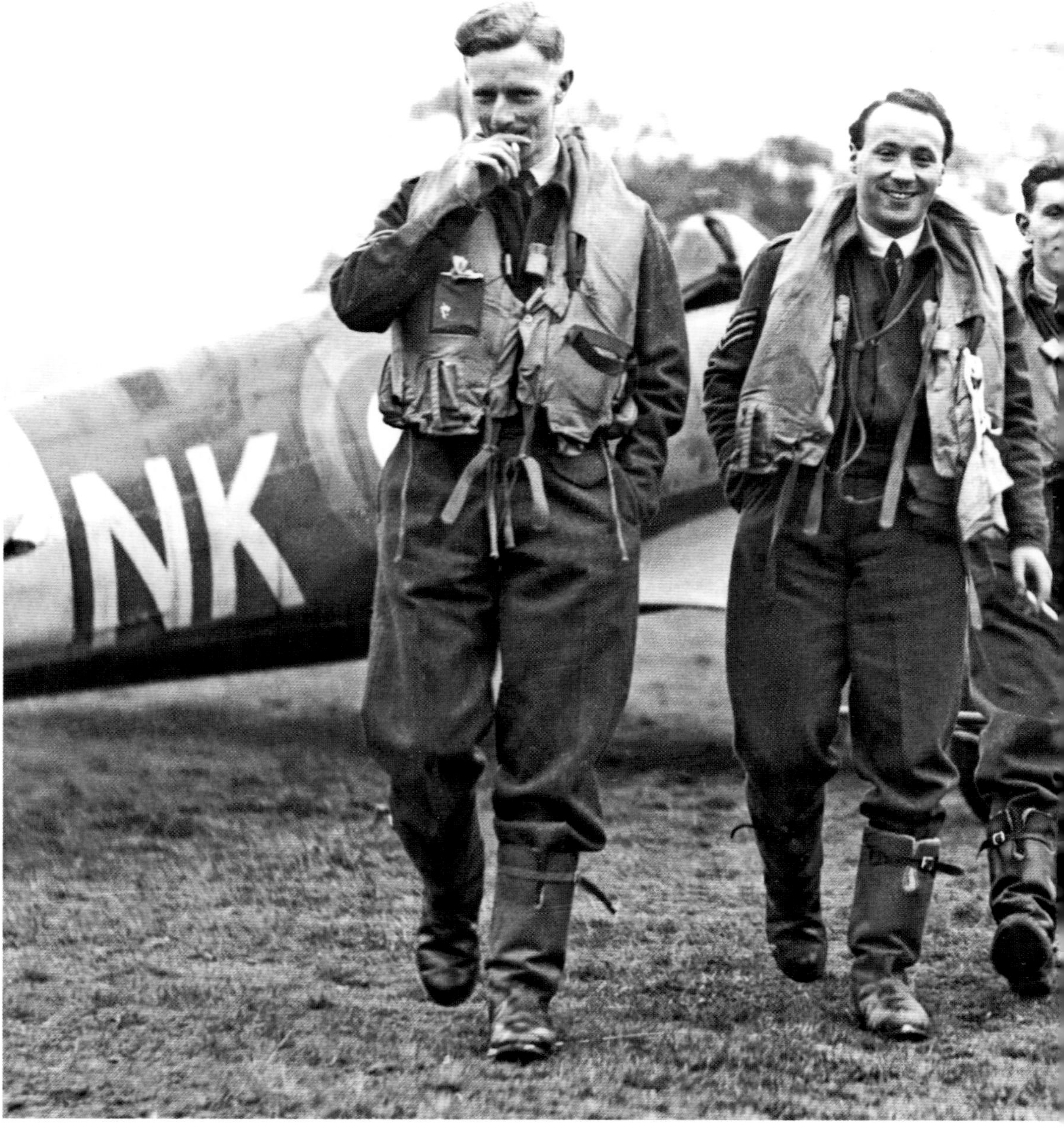

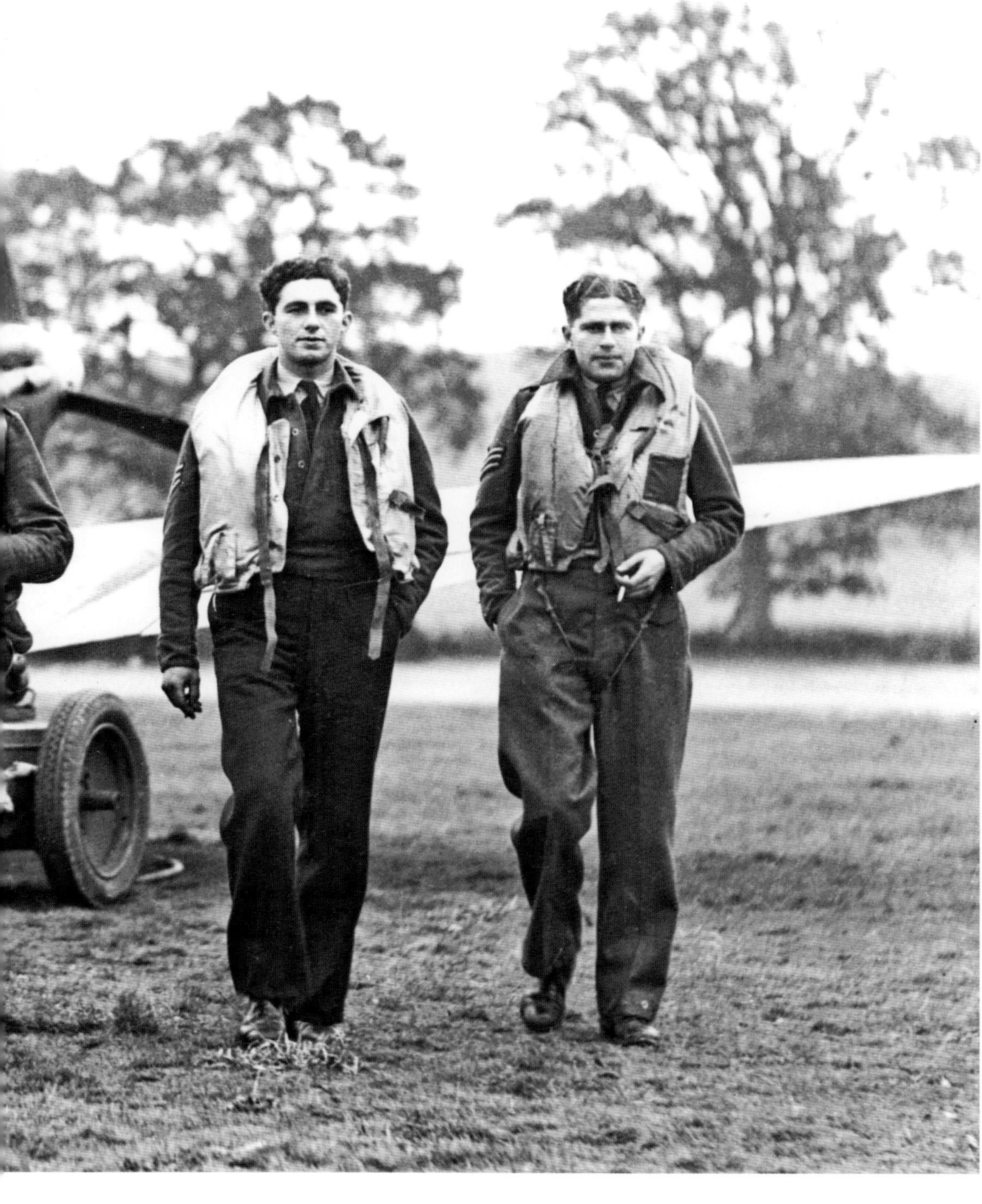

In the Second World War, women comprised a major part of the American aircraft, ship-building and armaments industries; right: A German submarine returns to its pen shelter base on the Brittany coast of France at the end of a successful patrol.

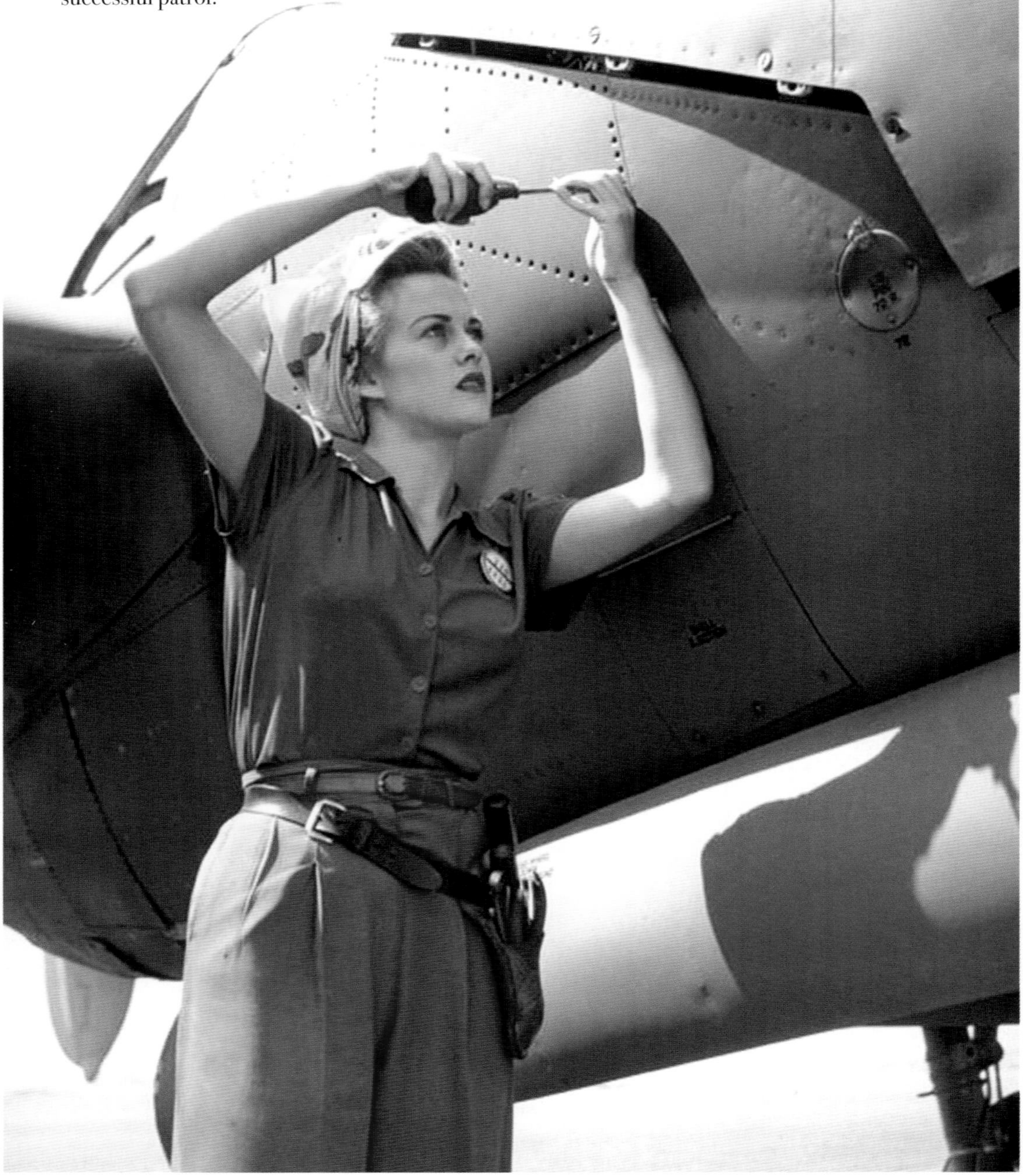

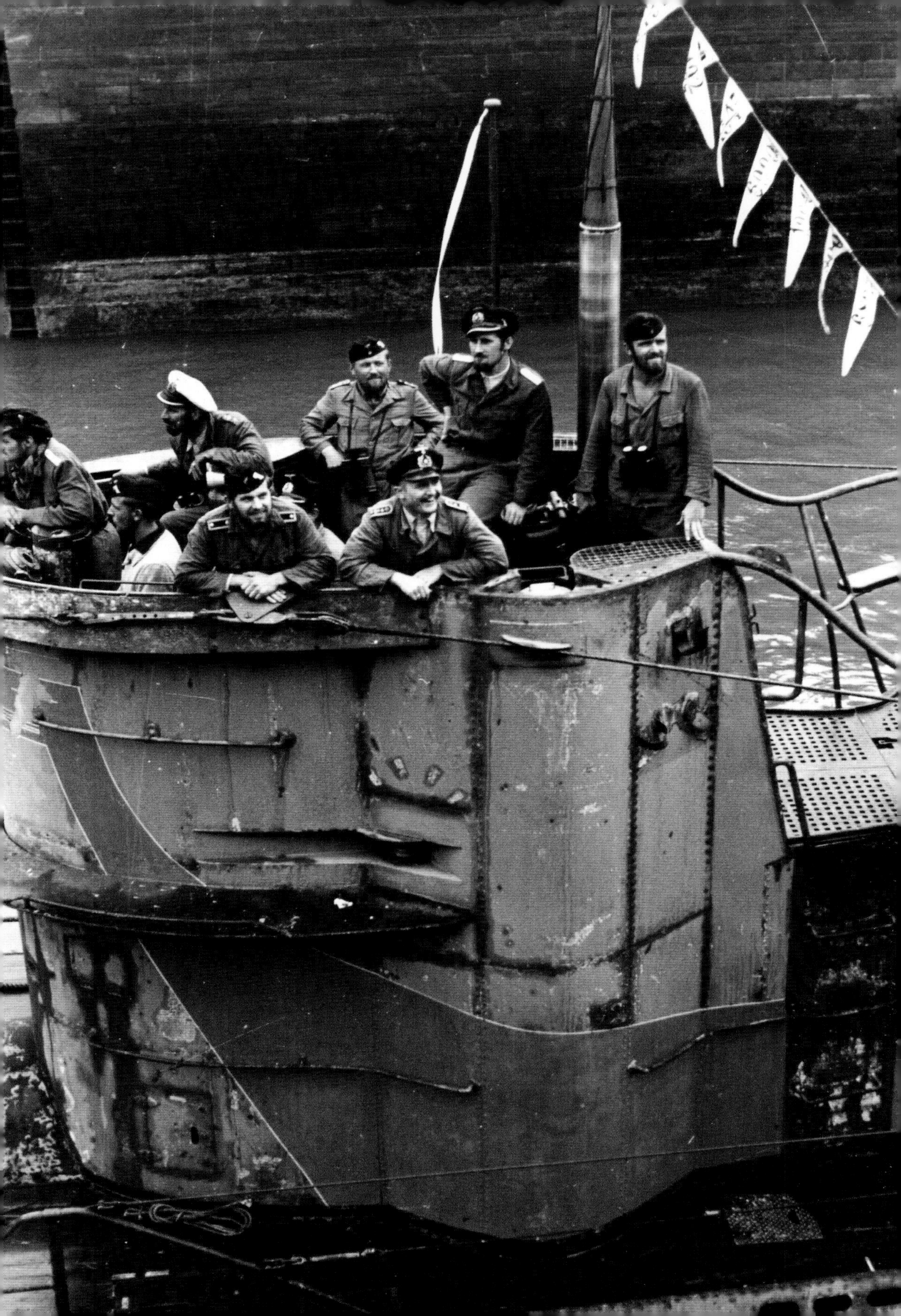

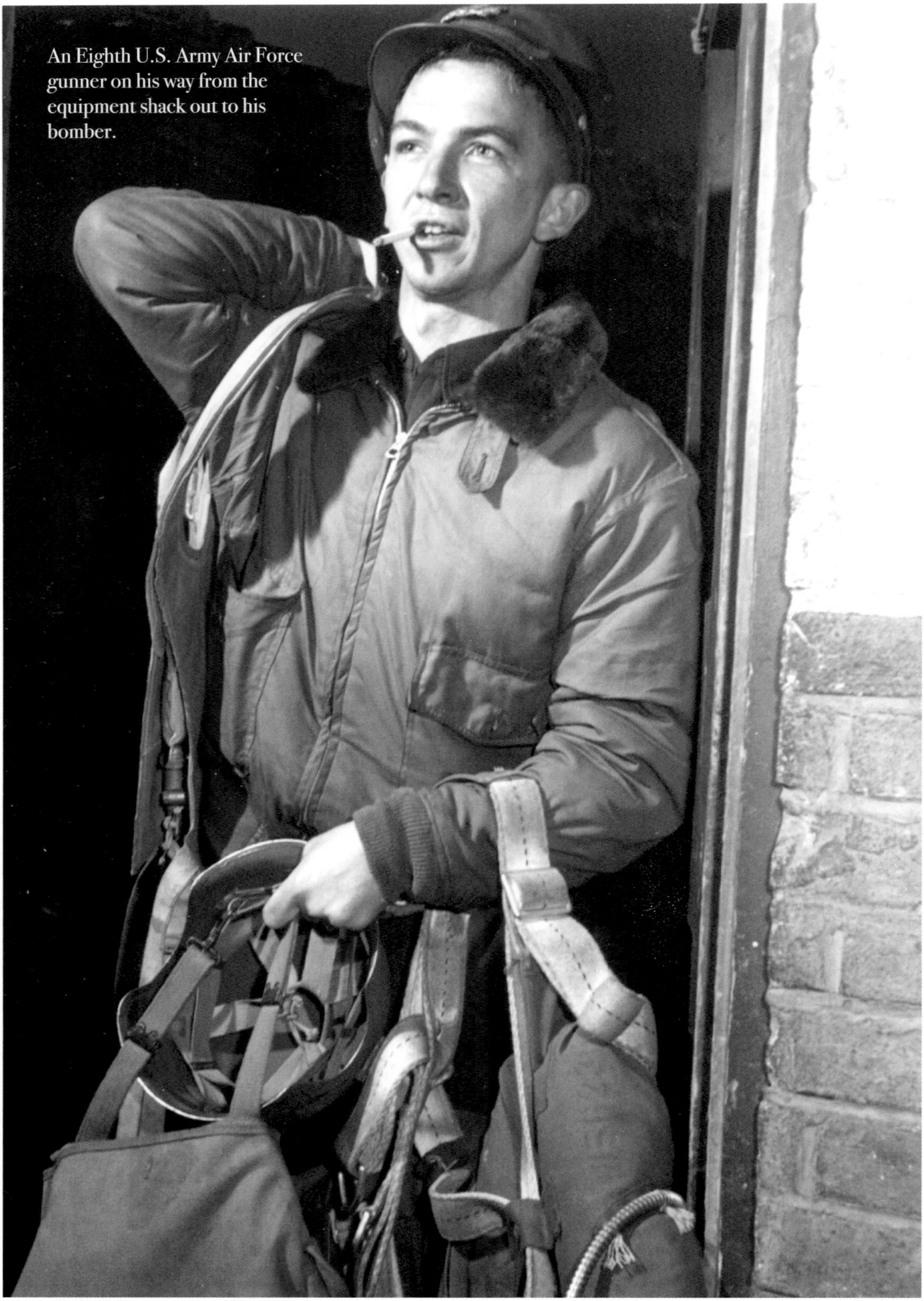

An Eighth U.S. Army Air Force gunner on his way from the equipment shack out to his bomber.

which, when baked on the surface of the casing, resulted in a unique 'crackle effect'. Not only did the new 'black crackle' finish protect and preserve the lighters wherever they served in action around the globe, the company received thousands of letters from GIs praising the non-reflective characteristic of their Zippos in the field.

Throughout the war, the company had to limit production of the lighters to the black crackle finish model with only a small quantity made in plain steel. A wartime ad run by the company proclaimed: 'Out there, Zippo is a Friend Indeed. The boys fighting in the tropics know that the ever-reliable Zippo Windproof lighter means more than a sure light for pipe or fag. Mid winds that blow and blow, and rains that never seem to cease, the windproof, waterproof Zippo comes in mighty useful, for lighting lanterns. That's why sales at Zippo Lighters are limited to our fighting forces on the high seas and outside the continental U.S.A. Keep your Zippo in perfect order'

Another ad read: 'She gave me her Zippo . . . and I Married Her. Pretty swell gal, to part with her precious Zippo–she can't buy a new one. I'll remember her every time I light up. In a Nor' easter I'll know the Zippo will be as dependable as the gal who gave it. You can't buy a new Zippo, so keep yours in good order.'

The Zippo was not officially adopted by the American armed forces during the Second World War, but George Blaisdell had shipped many thousands of the lighters to U.S. post exchanges around the United States. Such was the demand for them that they sold out almost as soon as they arrived at the PXs. When American troops got to their overseas

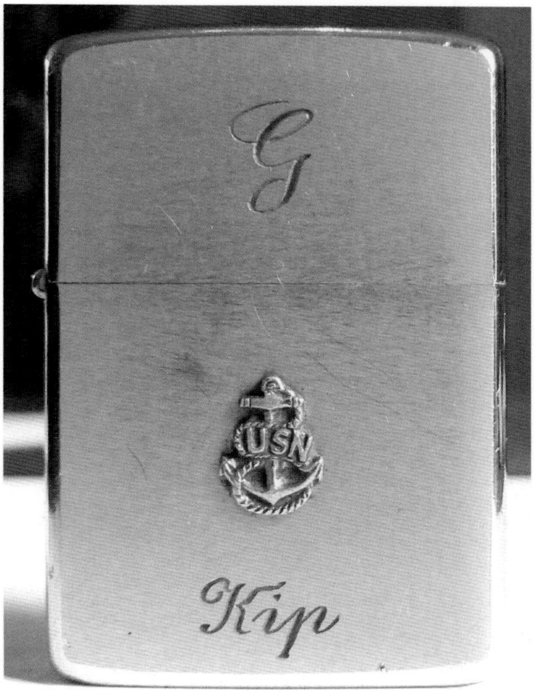
G
USN
Kip

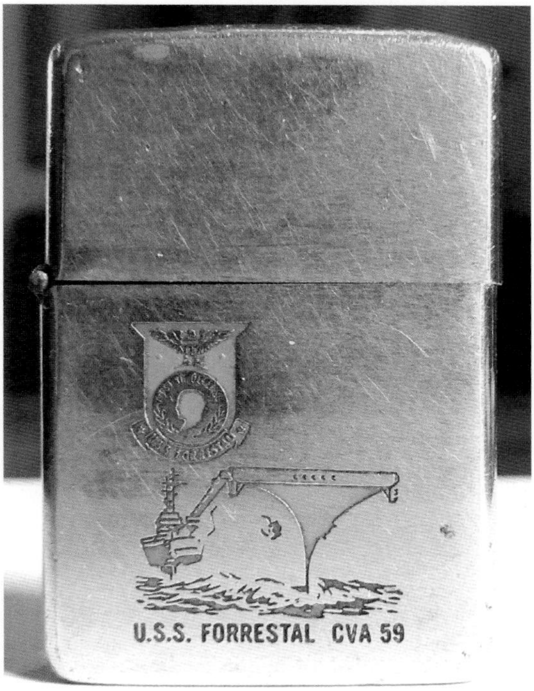
U.S.S. FORRESTAL CVA 59

United States Navy Zippos that went to war at sea.

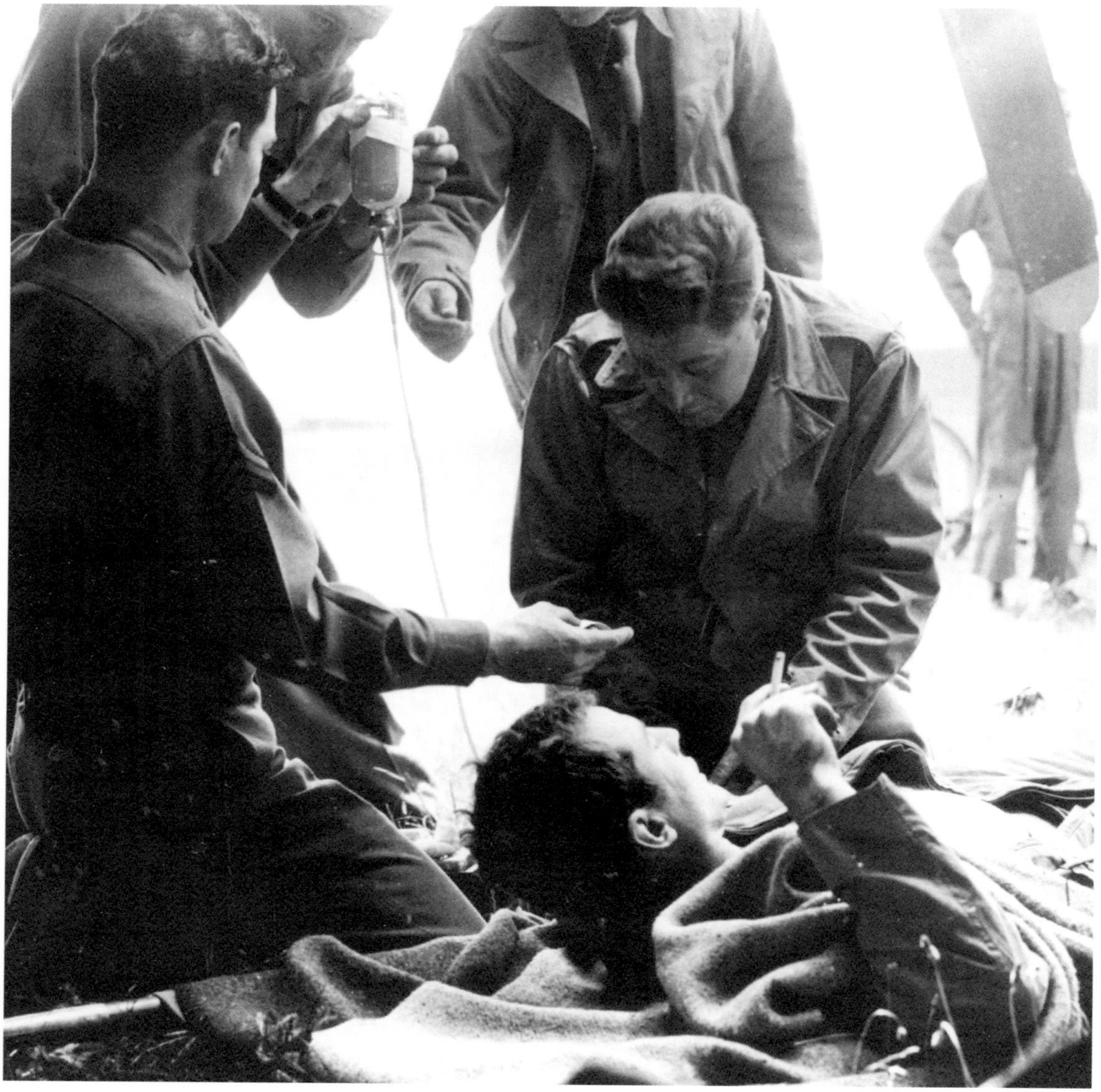

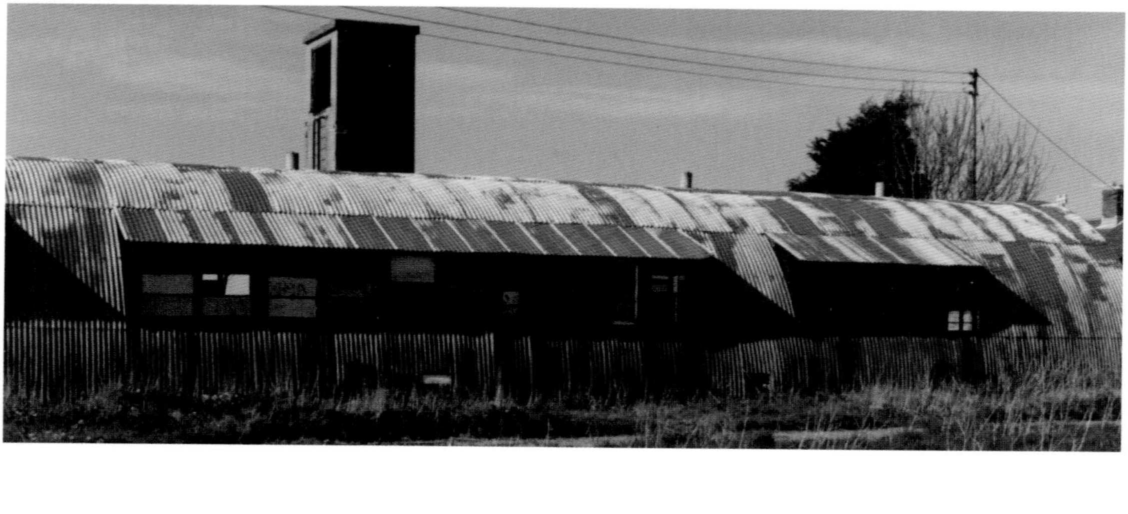

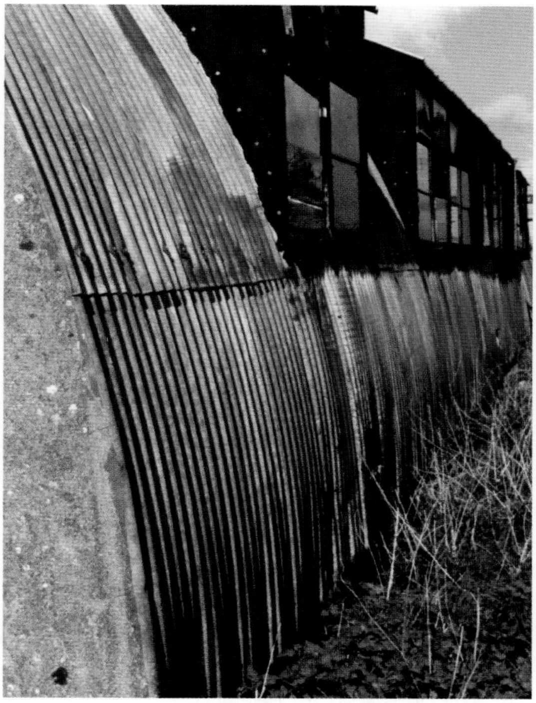

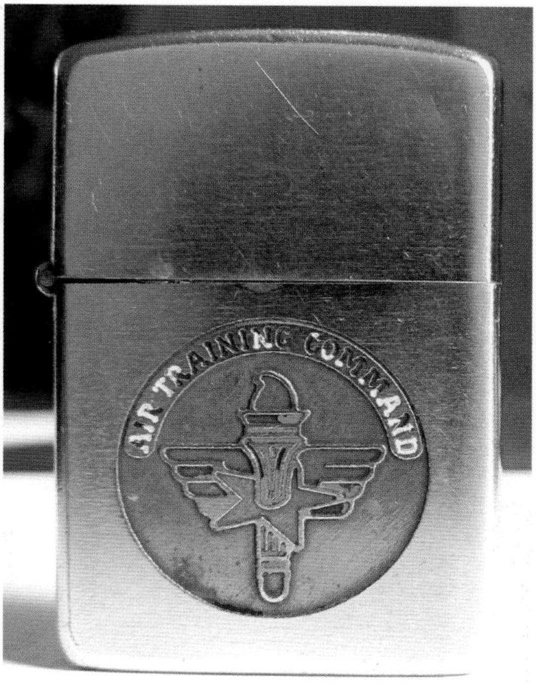
AIR TRAINING COMMAND

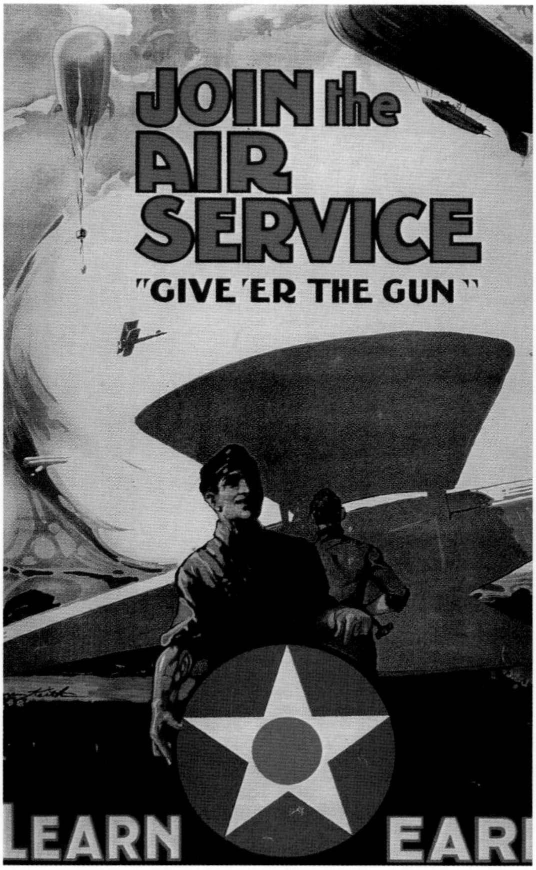
JOIN the
AIR
SERVICE
"GIVE 'ER THE GUN"
LEARN
EAR

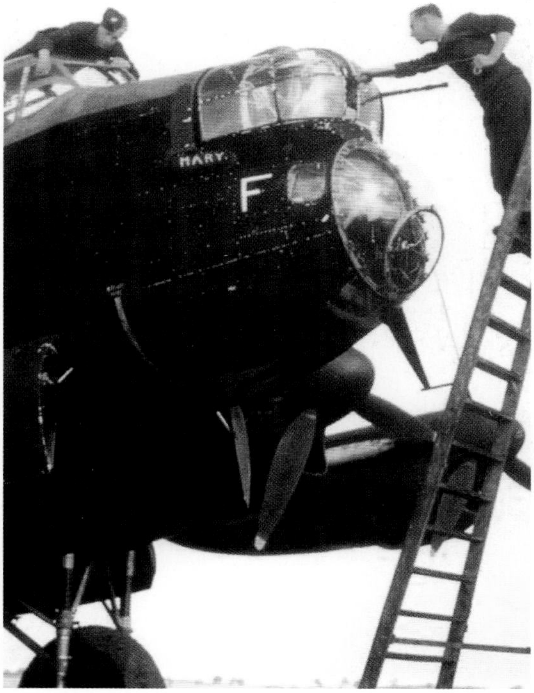
MARY.
F

top left: A medic of the Kimbolton-based 379th Bomb Group tending a wounded B-17 gunner; bottom left and at top: A large Nissen hut at Winkleigh, Devon; top: A World War Two Zippo; above: A Lancaster bomber.

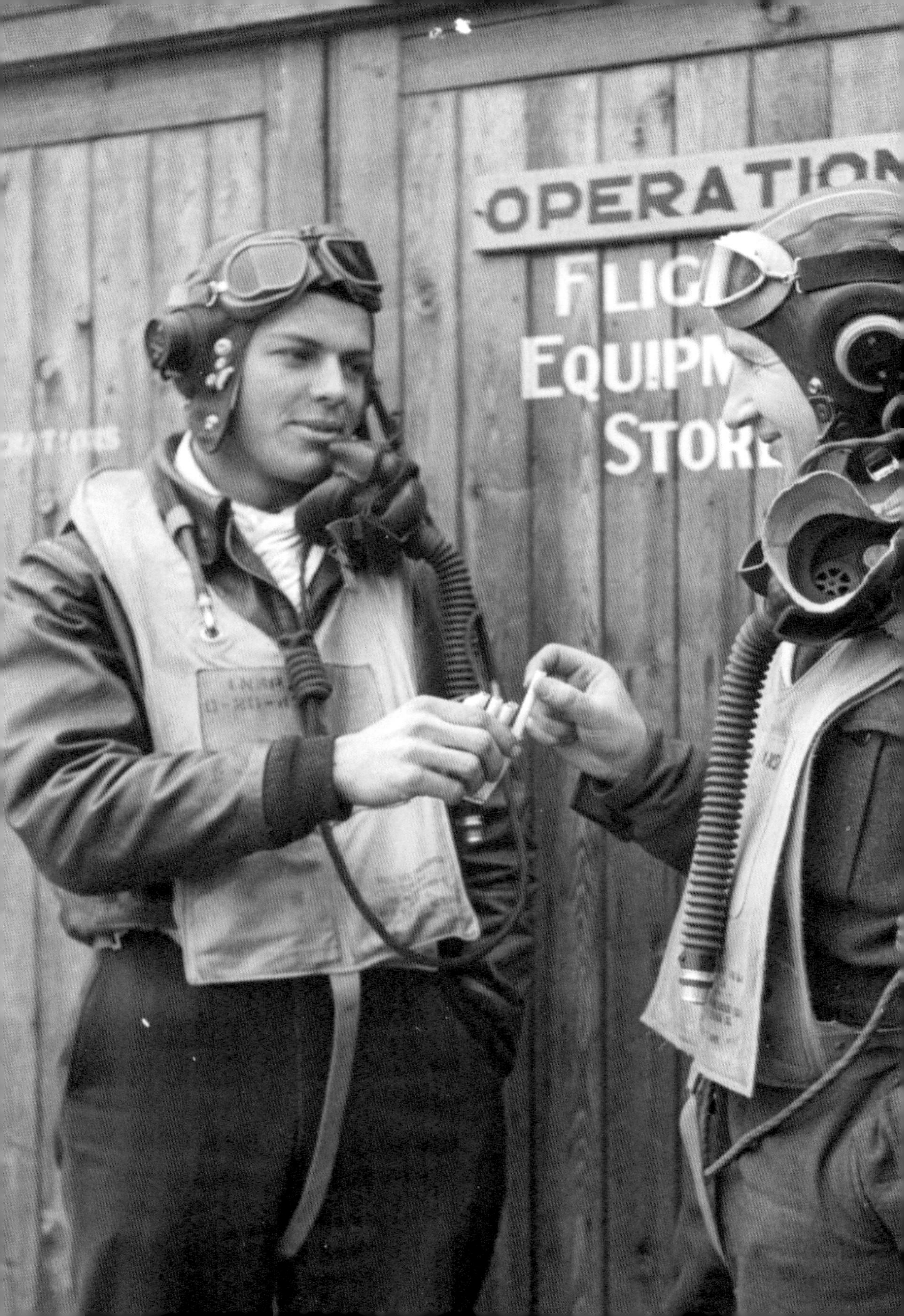
OPERATION
STORE

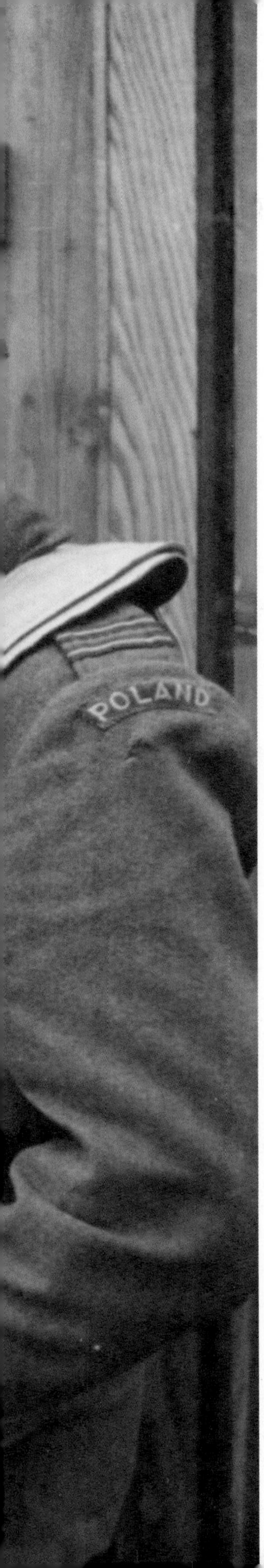
POLAND

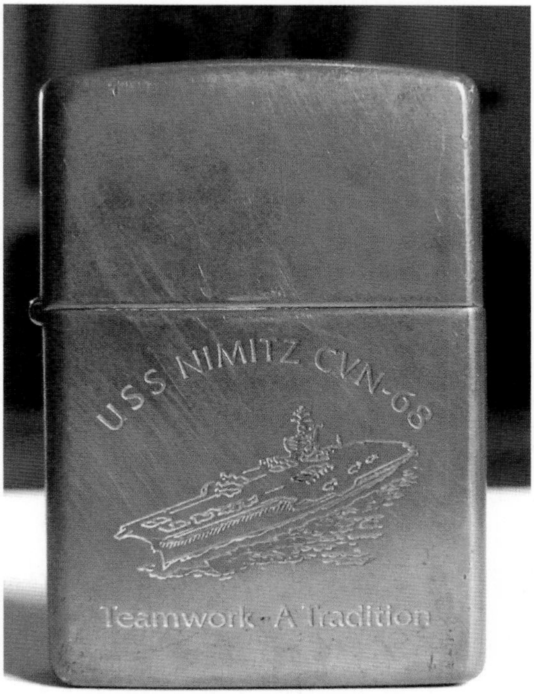
USS NIMITZ CVN-68
Teamwork - A Tradition

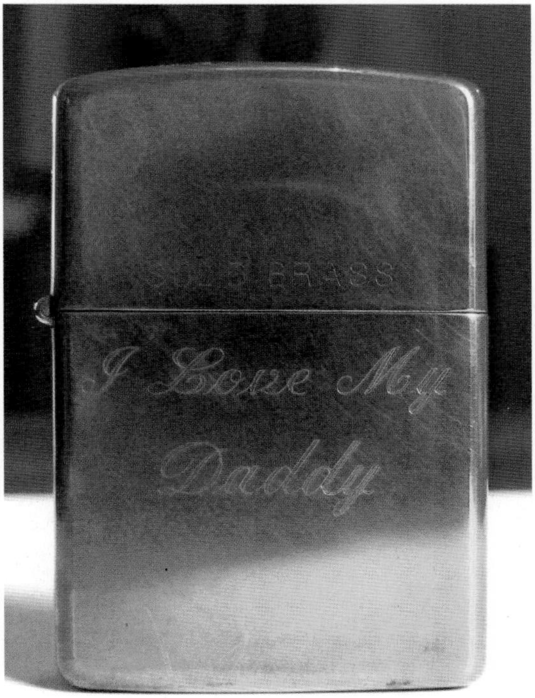
I Love My
Daddy

left: Fighter pilots on an RAF air base in the Second World War; right: Brass wartime Zippos.

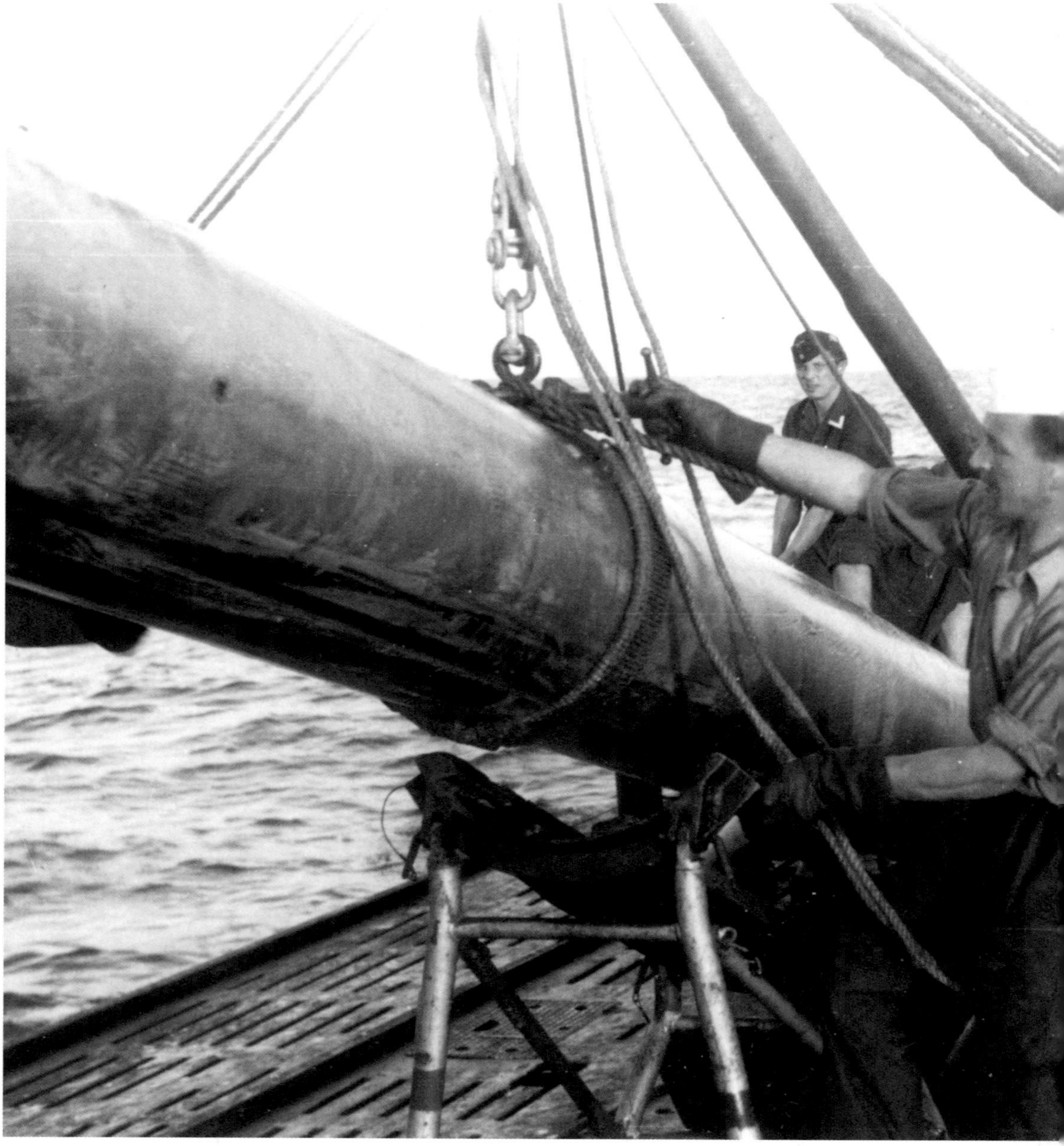

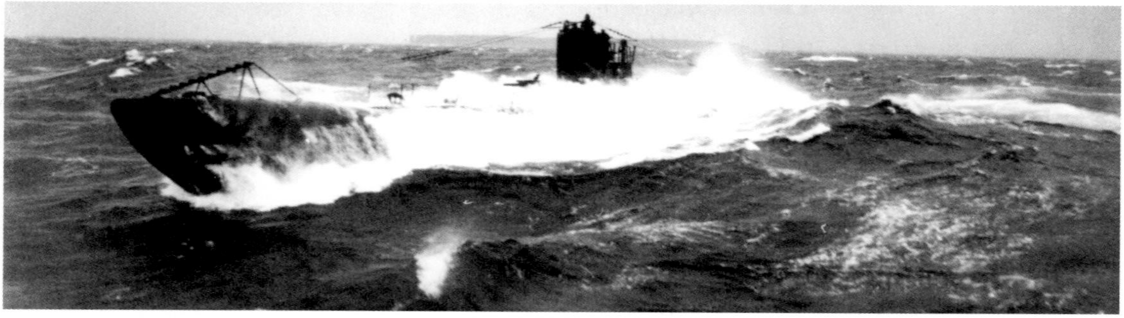

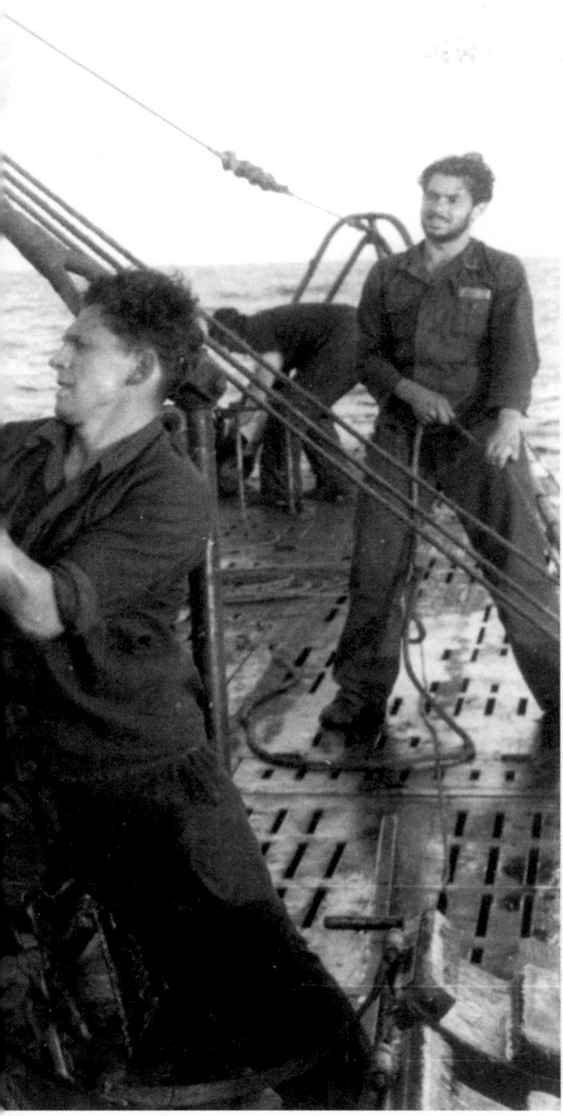

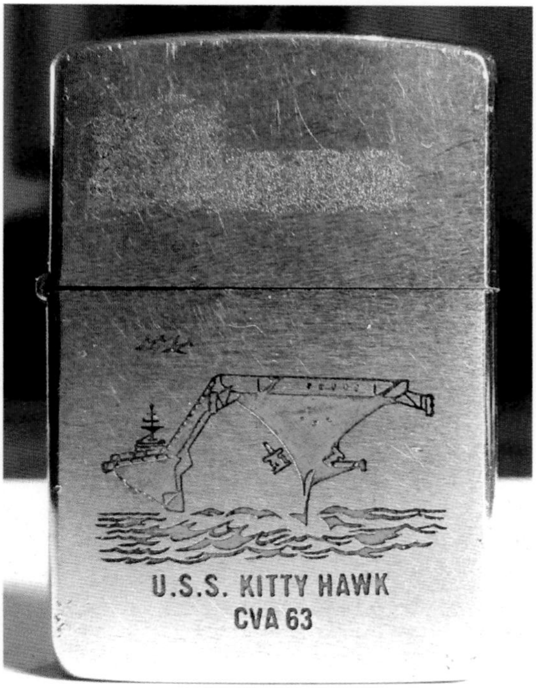
U.S.S. KITTY HAWK
CVA 63

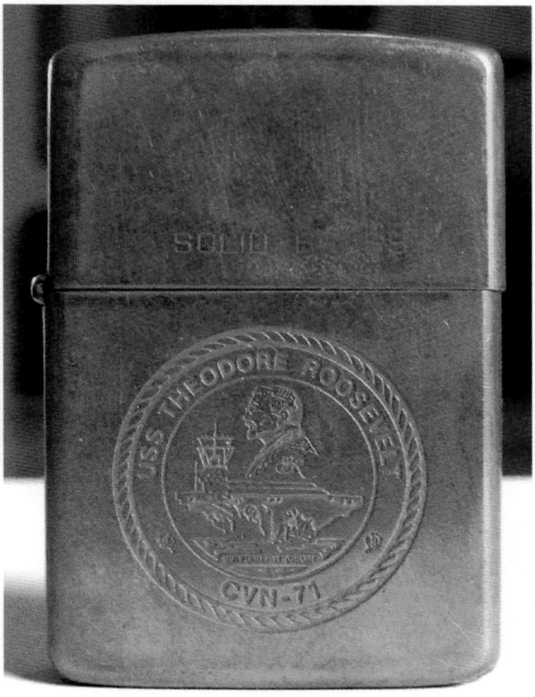
USS THEODORE ROOSEVELT
CVN-71

above: Crew members of a German submarine loading a weapon into the forward torpedo room of their boat during World War Two; below left: A U-boat in a rough sea in the war; right: Examples of wartime Zippo memorablilia saved by their owners.

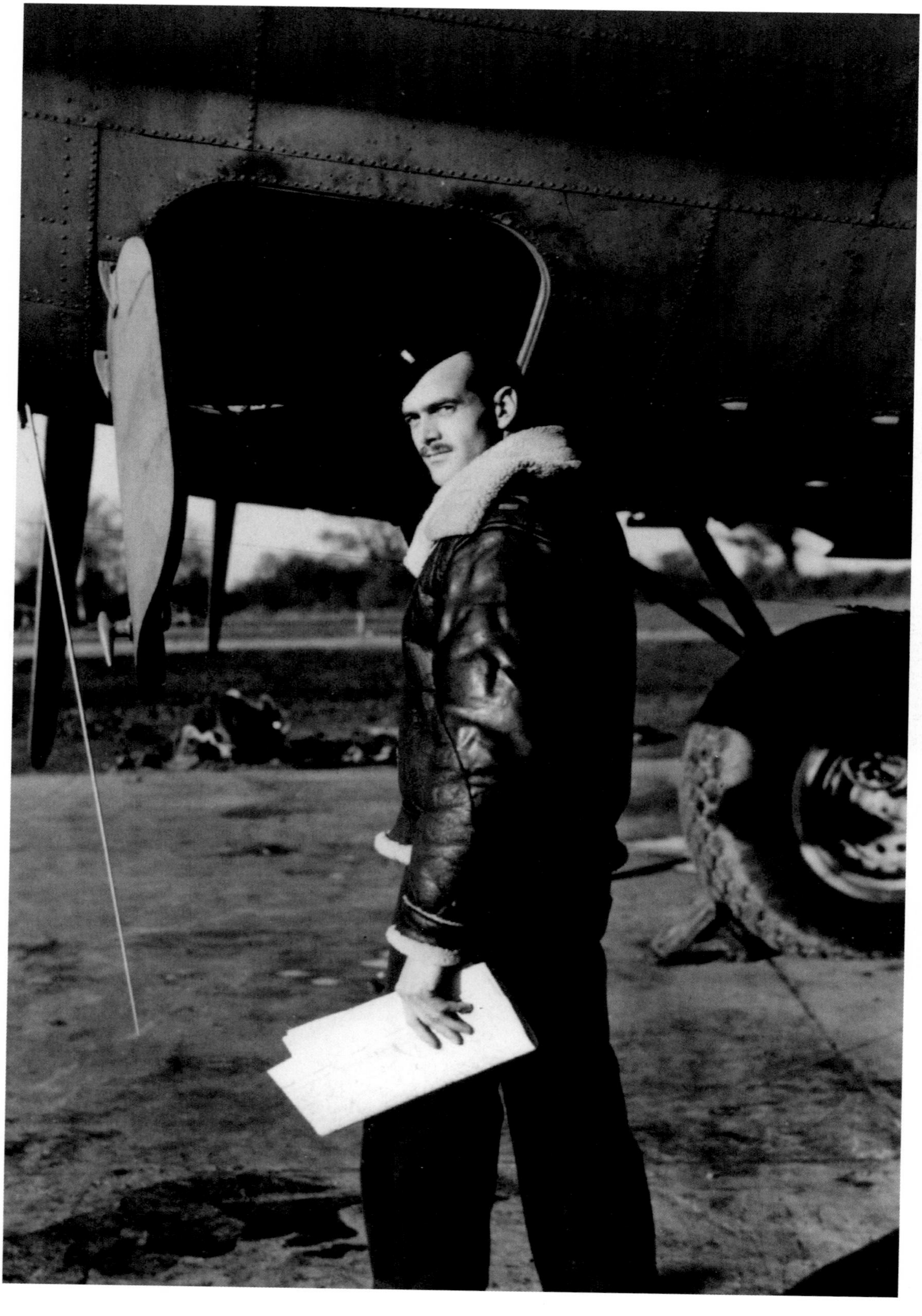

above: A British Merchant sailor on a smoke break; left: 2nd Lt R.E. Bennett at the 385th Bomb Group base, Great Ashfield.

assignments, they were happy to find that they could buy Zippos virtually everywhere. The lighter was so popular among military personnel the world over that Zippo Manufacturing's entire production for the duration of the war was soon given over to the armed forces. From that point on, wartime Zippos were only provided to the overseas Post Exchanges.

The Zippo company began its tenth year of production in 1942 and celebrated by shipping its one millionth lighter. The demand among the armed forces alone was so intense that by the end of the war several million of the wartime lighters had been

sold. And even with the extremely limited wartime availability of materials for the manufacture, the people of Zippo were able to design and make nine different styles of their hot little lighter in the black crackle and steel versions.

Everywhere the American soldiers, sailors, marines and airmen went during the war years, they were part of a fast-growing trend of personalizing their lighters by engraving the names or initials of their wives or their sweethearts, military emblems or other types of ornamentation on the casings of their Zippos. They applied these decorations themselves or had them done by professional

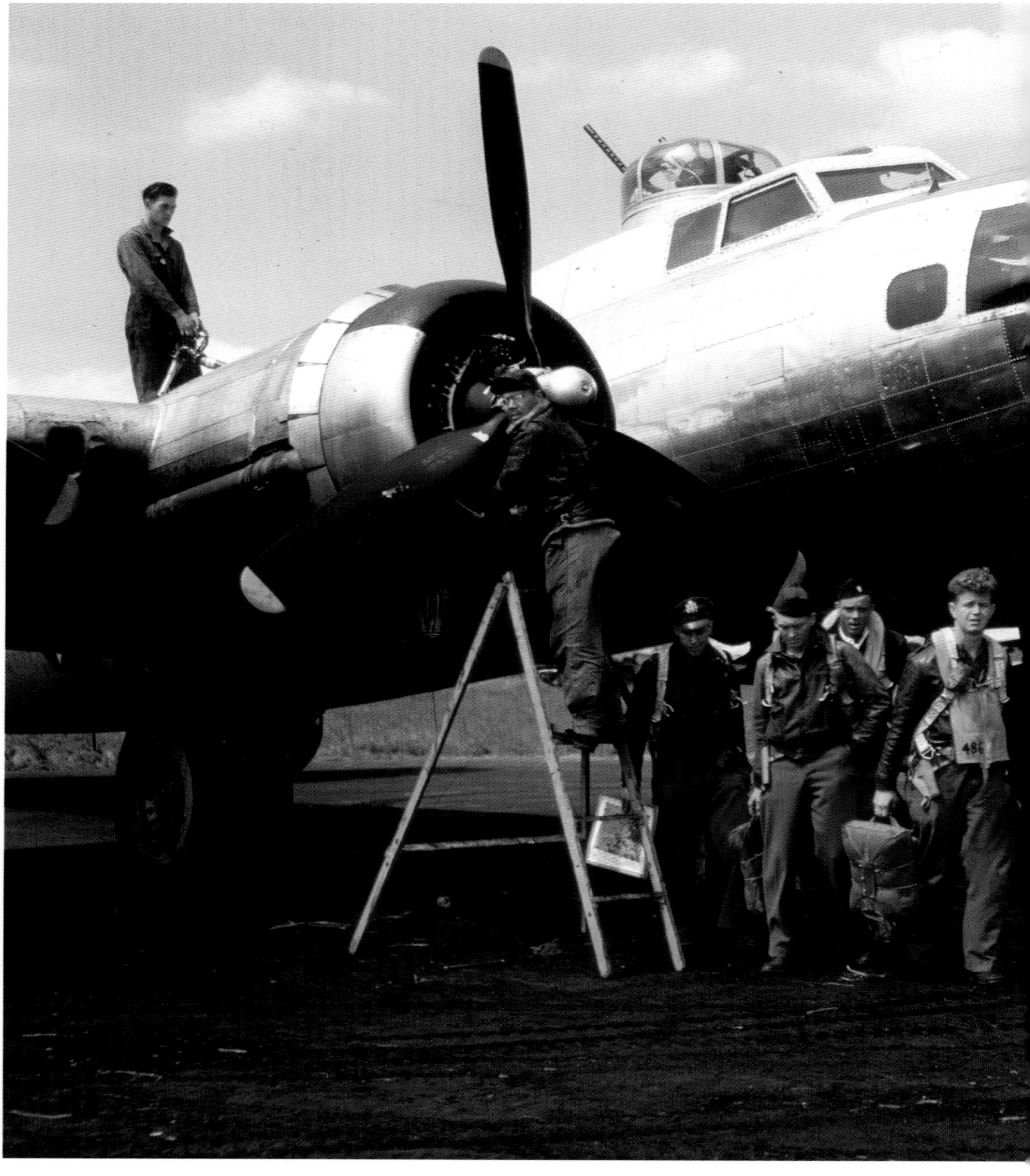

A Boeing B-17G Flying Fortress bomber and crew.

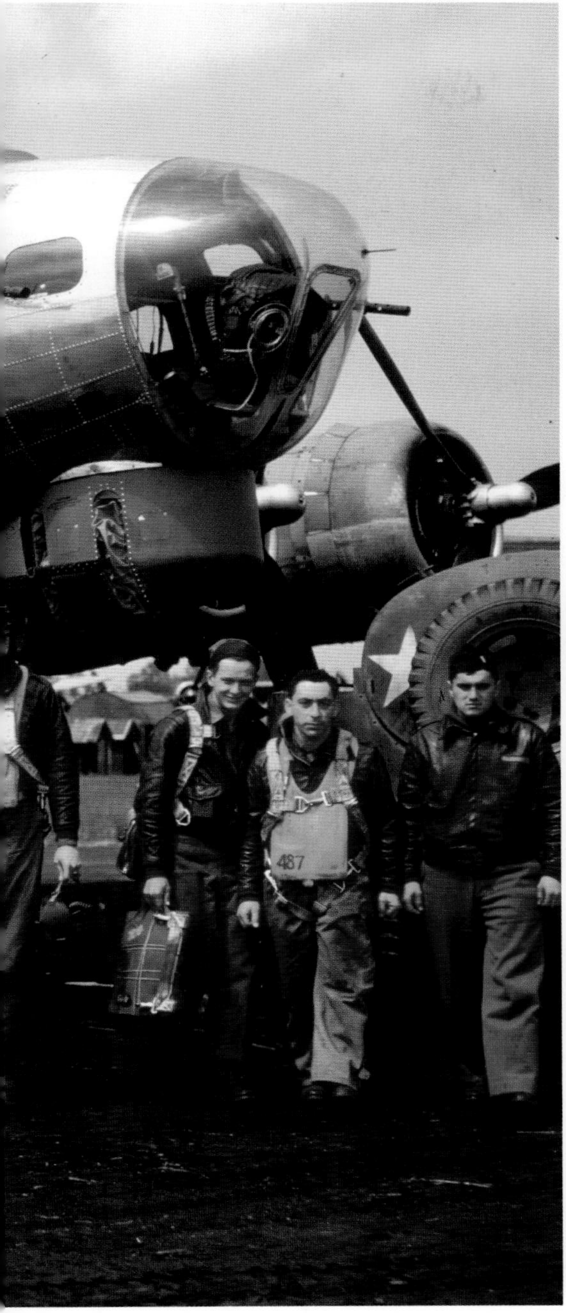
487

jewellers. Most servicemen and women who owned a Zippo in that time carried, used and displayed it with pride, satisfaction and considerable sentiment. Many such items are still kept and displayed in the homes of Second World War veterans or their descendants as objects of memorabilia in remembrance of a long-past adventure in a difficult and tragic time; part of a memory that survives the years.

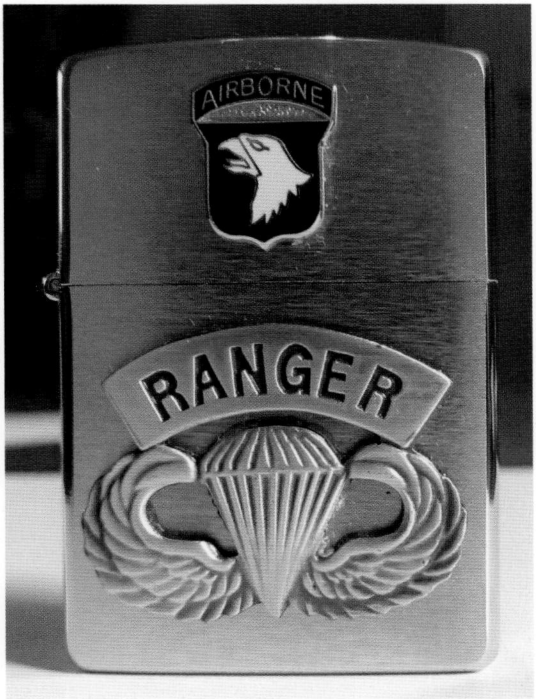
AIRBORNE
RANGER

There have been United States military units called Rangers since the American Revolutionary War. During the Second World War, the 2nd Ranger Battalion scaled the 90-foot cliffs of Pointe du Hoc, west of Omaha Beach in Normandy, France. Their mission included the capture and destruction of the enemy 155mm guns there. But the weapons had been removed. While under continuing gunfire, as they climbed they eventually found the missing guns in trees at the rear of the Point area. The Rangers disabled and destroyed the guns and held the main road for another two days before a relief force arrived. The 29th Ranger Battalion was reinforced by substantial personnel from the 5th Ranger Battalion who had arrived by sea on D-Day, 6 June 1944. Their famous motto was 'Rangers lead the way.'

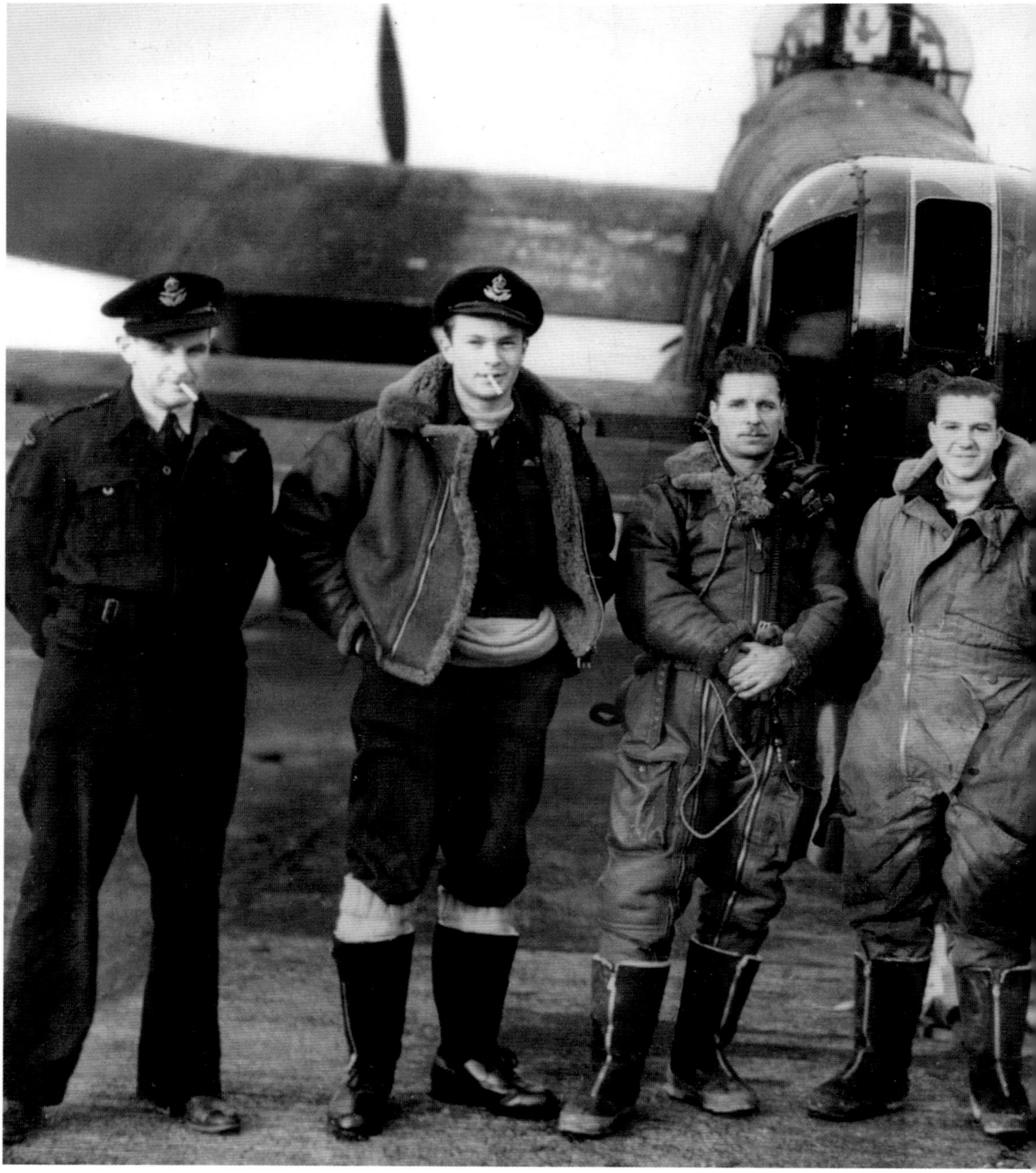

Jack Currie (second from left) and his Lancaster crew at RAF Wickenby, Lincolnshire, England.

Reflecting the loneliness, the longing and the lack of loving of the war years were the incomparable songs and thoughtful classics that helped so many folks get through some very rough times. In no particular order tunes of the 1920s through the 1940s included I'LL BE SEEING YOU

I'LL GET BY
I'LL BE AROUND
BLUES IN THE NIGHT
DON'T SIT UNDER THE APPLE TREE
THE WHITE CLIFFS OF DOVER
WHITE CHRISTMAS
SENTIMENTAL JOURNEY

I'LL BE WITH YOU IN APPLE
  BLOSSOM TIME
YOU'LL NEVER KNOW
PAPER DOLL
SMOKE GETS IN YOUR EYES
I'LL WALK ALONE
SWINGIN' ON A STAR
I'LL NEVER SMILE AGAIN
I LOVE YOU FOR SENTIMENTAL
  REASONS
SMOKE DREAMS
AS TIME GOES BY
HARBOR LIGHTS
AT LAST
MY DEVOTION
YOU STEPPED OUT OF A DREAM
A NIGHTINGALE SANG IN BERKELEY
  SQUARE
WE'LL GATHER LILACS
BUT NOT FOR ME
DON'T GET AROUND MUCH ANYMORE
EV'RY TIME WE SAY GOODBYE
I'LL STRING ALONG WITH YOU
I'M BEGINNING TO SEE THE LIGHT
IT'S BEEN A LONG LONG TIME
LONG AGO AND FAR AWAY
MY FUNNY VALENTINE
THE VERY THOUGHT OF YOU
THERE'S A SMALL HOTEL
WE'LL MEET AGAIN
WHERE OR WHEN
EMBRACEABLE YOU
IT HAD TO BE YOU
DADDY
A FOGGY DAY IN LONDON TOWN
TAKING A CHANCE ON LOVE
THAT OLD BLACK MAGIC
DON'T FENCE ME IN
THERE ARE SUCH THINGS
BLUE SKIES
I HAD THE CRAZIEST DREAM

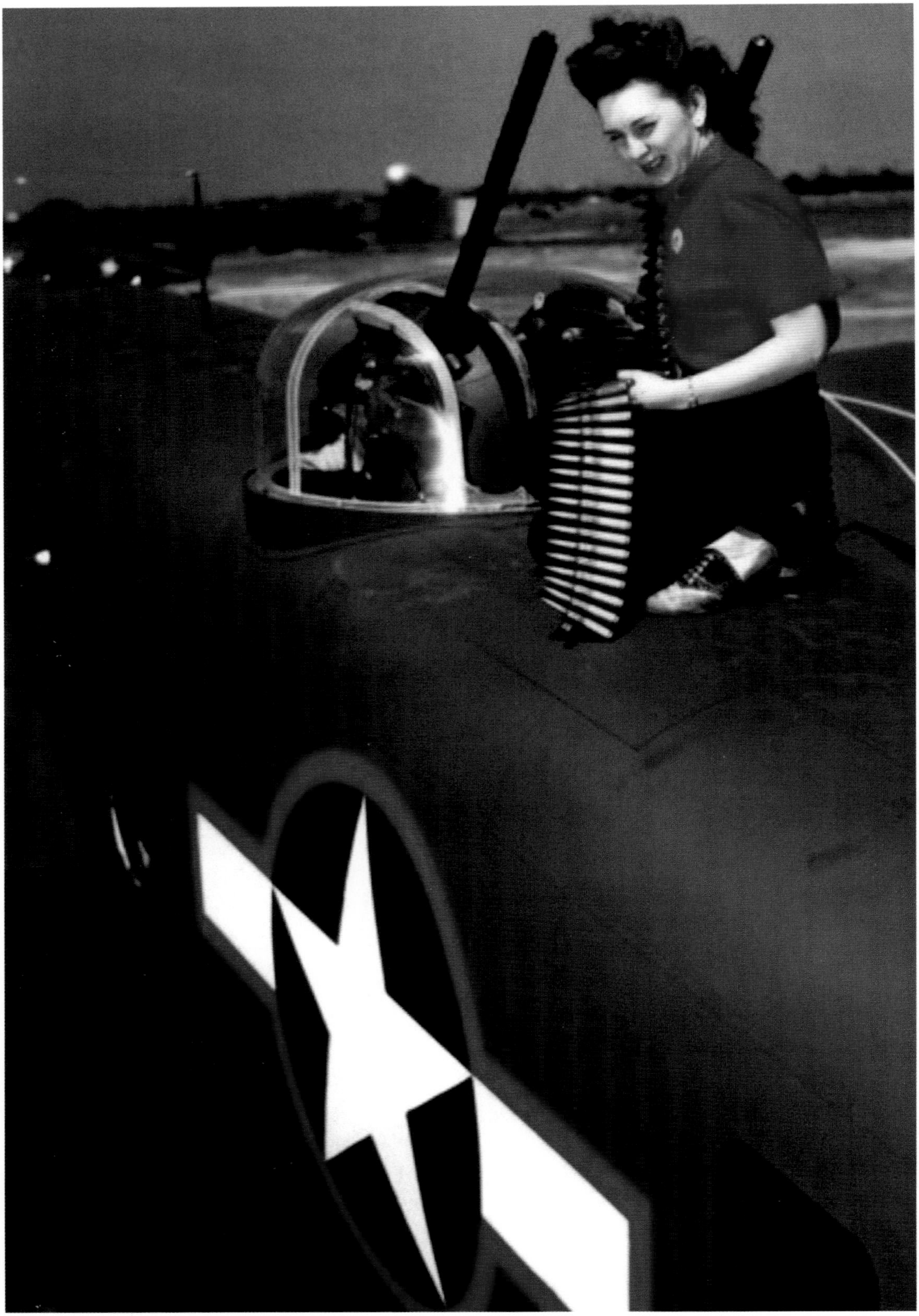

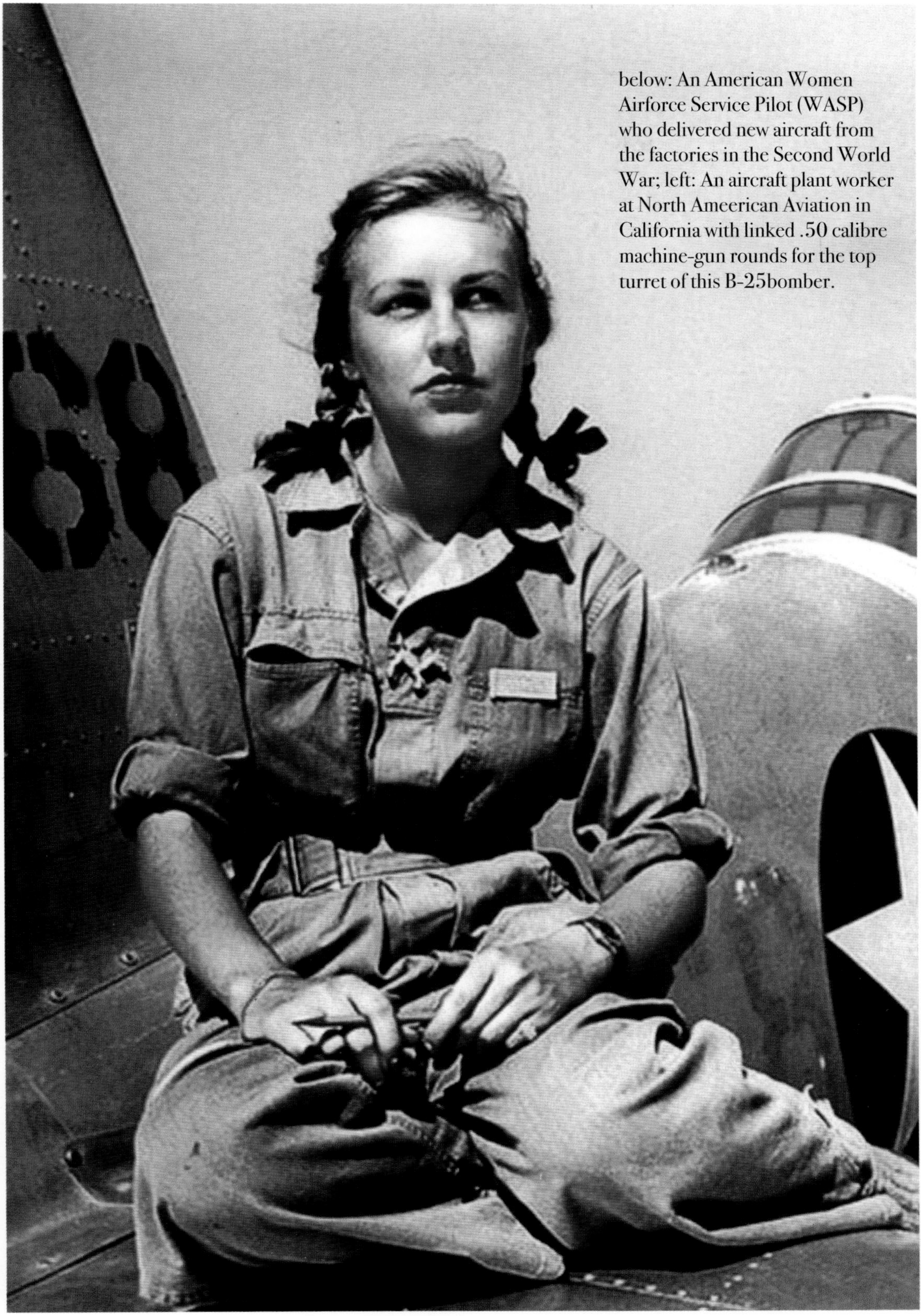

below: An American Women Airforce Service Pilot (WASP) who delivered new aircraft from the factories in the Second World War; left: An aircraft plant worker at North Ameerican Aviation in California with linked .50 calibre machine-gun rounds for the top turret of this B-25bomber.

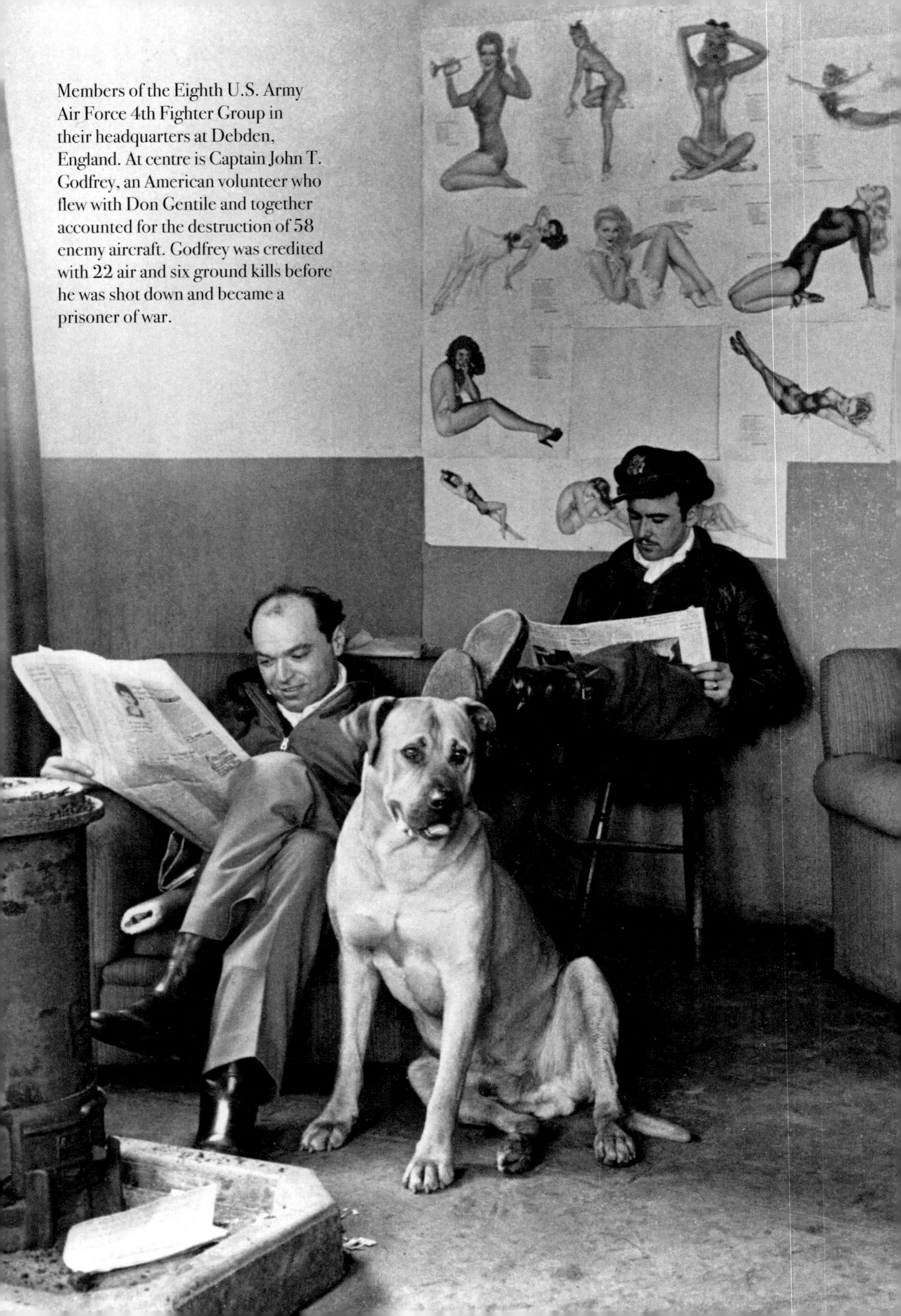

Members of the Eighth U.S. Army Air Force 4th Fighter Group in their headquarters at Debden, England. At centre is Captain John T. Godfrey, an American volunteer who flew with Don Gentile and together accounted for the destruction of 58 enemy aircraft. Godfrey was credited with 22 air and six ground kills before he was shot down and became a prisoner of war.

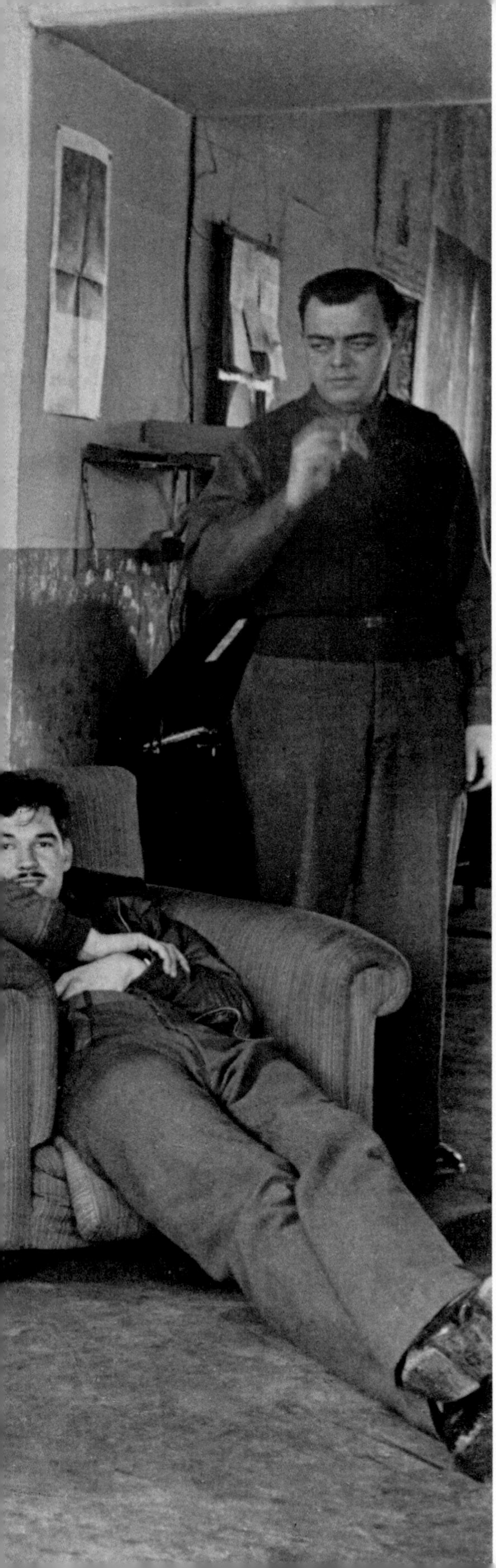

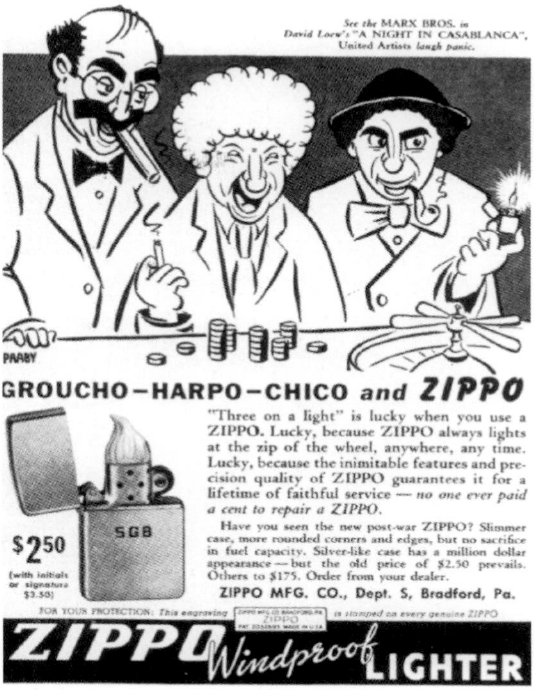
See the MARX BROS. in
David Loew's "A NIGHT IN CASABLANCA",
United Artists laugh panic.
PAABY
GROUCHO–HARPO–CHICO and ZIPPO
"Three on a light" is lucky when you use a ZIPPO. Lucky, because ZIPPO always lights at the zip of the wheel, anywhere, any time. Lucky, because the inimitable features and precision quality of ZIPPO guarantees it for a lifetime of faithful service — no one ever paid a cent to repair a ZIPPO.
Have you seen the new post-war ZIPPO? Slimmer case, more rounded corners and edges, but no sacrifice in fuel capacity. Silver-like case has a million dollar appearance — but the old price of $2.50 prevails. Others to $175. Order from your dealer.
SGB
$2.50
(with initials or signature $3.50)
ZIPPO MFG. CO., Dept. S, Bradford, Pa.
FOR YOUR PROTECTION: This engraving
is stamped on every genuine ZIPPO
ZIPPO Windproof LIGHTER

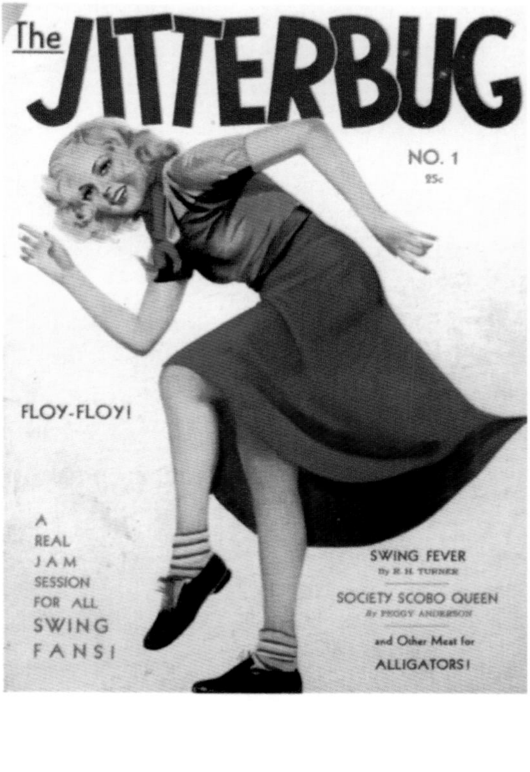
The JITTERBUG
NO. 1
25c
FLOY-FLOY!
A REAL JAM SESSION FOR ALL SWING FANS!
SWING FEVER
SOCIETY SCOBO QUEEN
and Other Meat for
ALLIGATORS!

at top: A Zippo lighter ad from 1946; above: The first issue of *The Jitterbug* magazine.

The huge demand for Zippos during the war years caused a massive rise in the creation and production of fake Zippos. These imitations invariably gave themselves away when they failed to produce the well-known, characteristic 'Zippo Click' sound and failed to match the refined styling and manufacturing quality of the real thing. That copycat practice has continued over the years since the Second World War. Many thousands of phoneys appeared during and after the Korean and Vietnam wars and are frequently available to purchase at swapmeets, boot sales and on Ebay. The Zippo company has always taken a strong stance in opposition to the presence of imitation lighters on sale in the United States, by warning prospective Zippo buyers to be wary of the possibility of being taken in by fakes and reminding them that the actual Zippo felt 'right' in the hand and when operated produced the readily recognizable Zippo 'clink clop' sound . . . a sound that also came to be used in the war as a signal between troops. As noted GIs worldwide looked for and found thousands of ways to personalize their Zippo lighters, whether through the application of unique artwork, signatures, initials or other personal graphics by the owners themselves or through the skill and artful craftsmanship of others. The names of wives, children, sweethearts, pets, friends, military units, aircraft, ships, tanks and many other objects and subjects duly decorated the Zippos of armed forces members in ships, aircrews and far-flung bases and ports the world over. In combat environments everywhere in that hellish conflict, the American military personnel met others, as well as

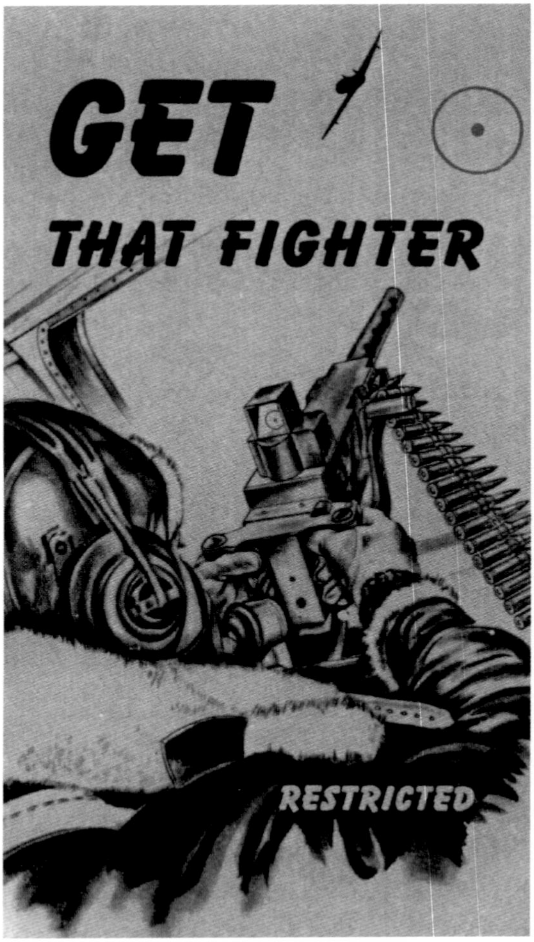
GET
THAT FIGHTER
RESTRICTED

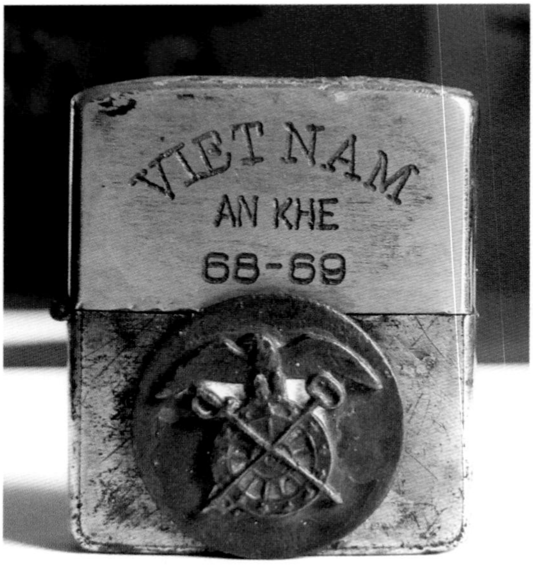
VIET NAM
AN KHE
68-69

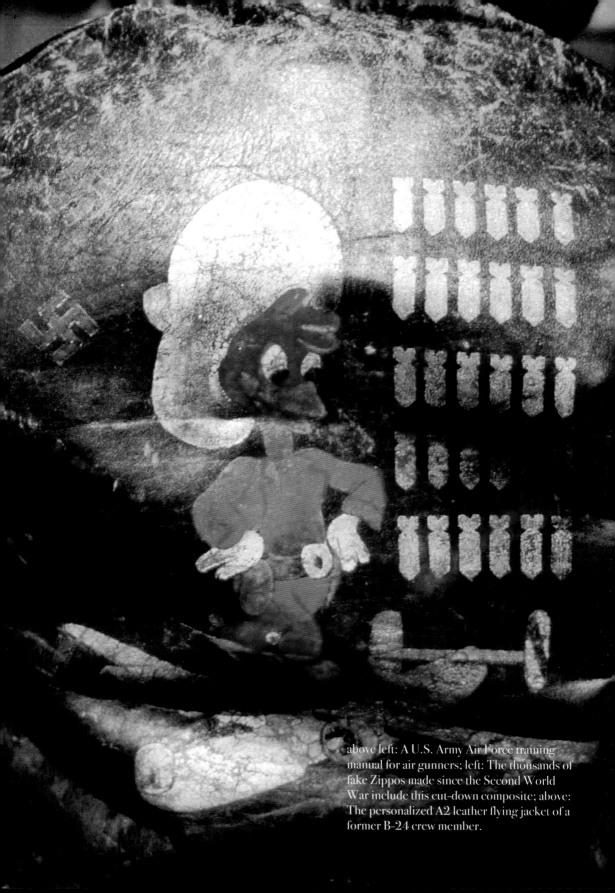

above left: A U.S. Army Air Force training manual for air gunners; left: The thousands of fake Zippos made since the Second World War include this cut-down composite; above: The personalized A2 leather flying jacket of a former B-24 crew member.

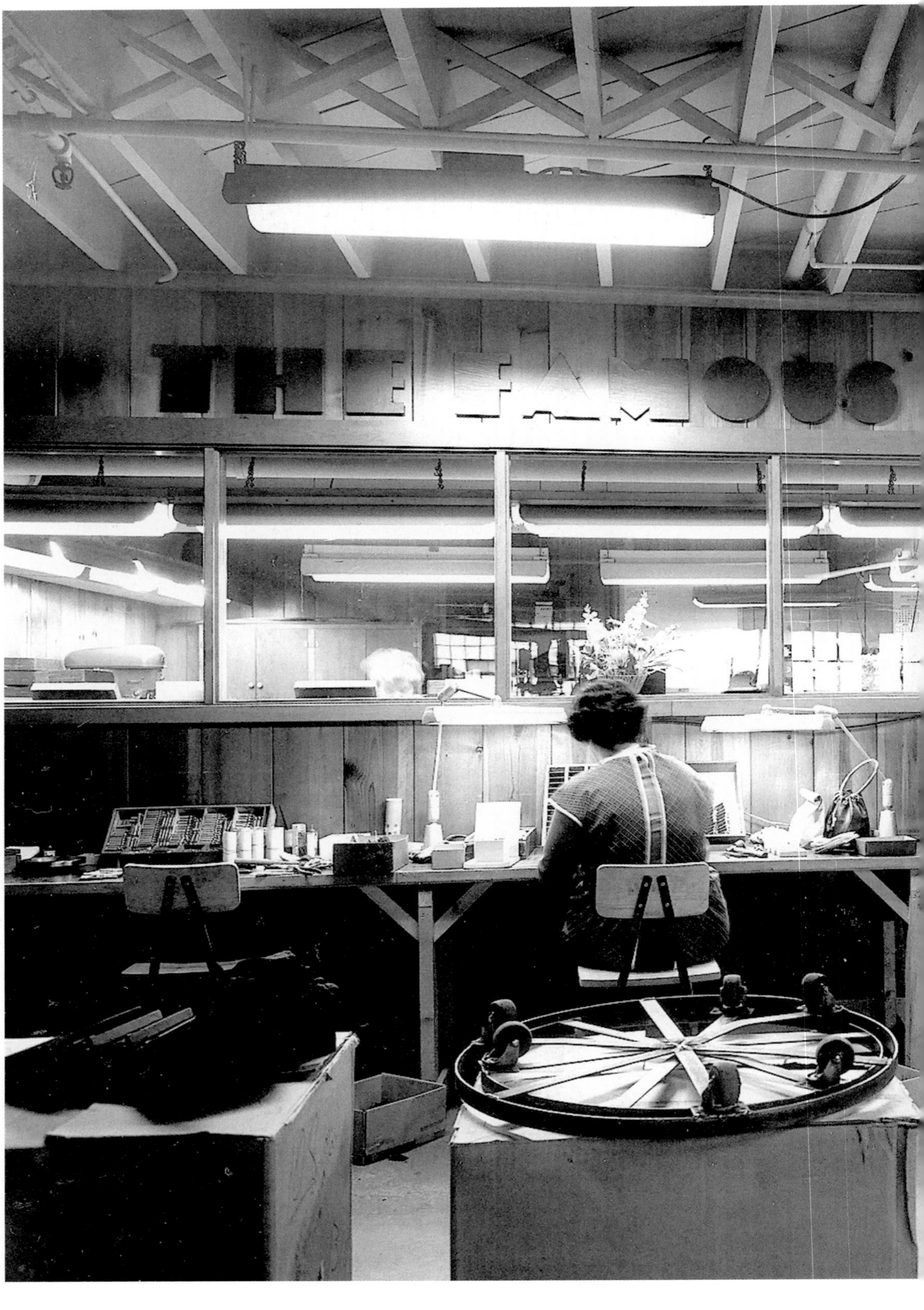
THE FAMOUS

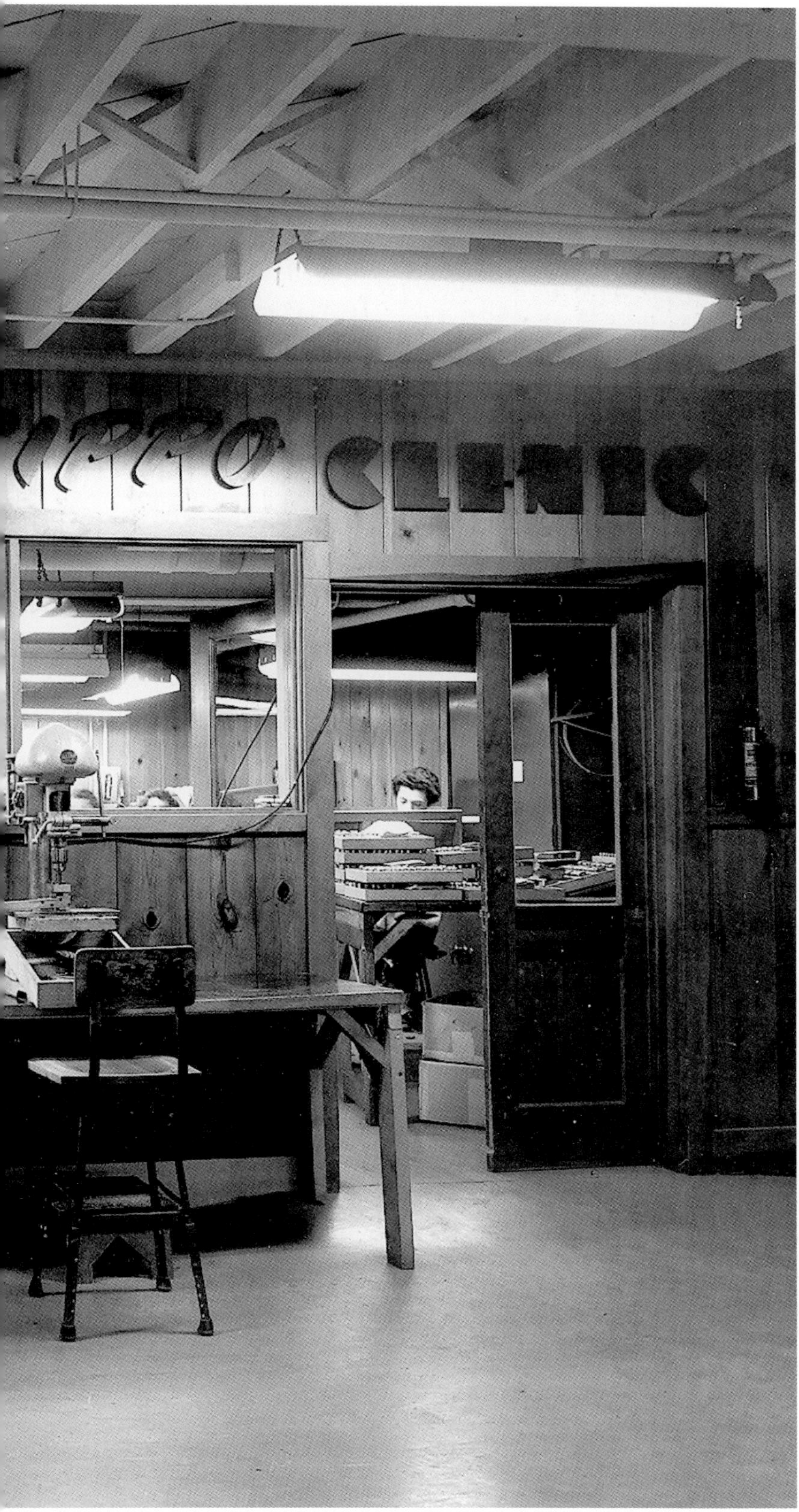
ZIPPO CLINIC

Employees of the Zippo Manufacturing Company have been carefully and quickly repairing lighters that customers have sent to the Bradford, PA. plant to take advantage of the famous Zippo guarantee. No Zippo lighter repair is ever charged to the customer. Zippo Clinic technicians restore Zippo lighters to first-class mechanical condition and return them to their owners for many more years of reliable service.

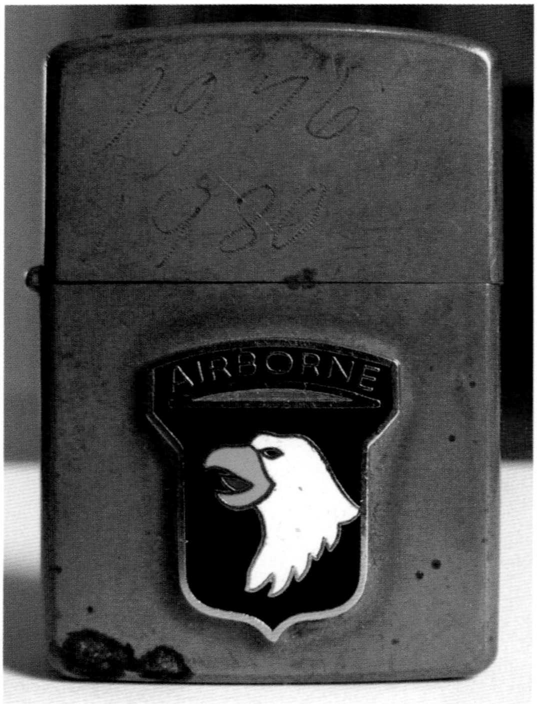
AIRBORNE

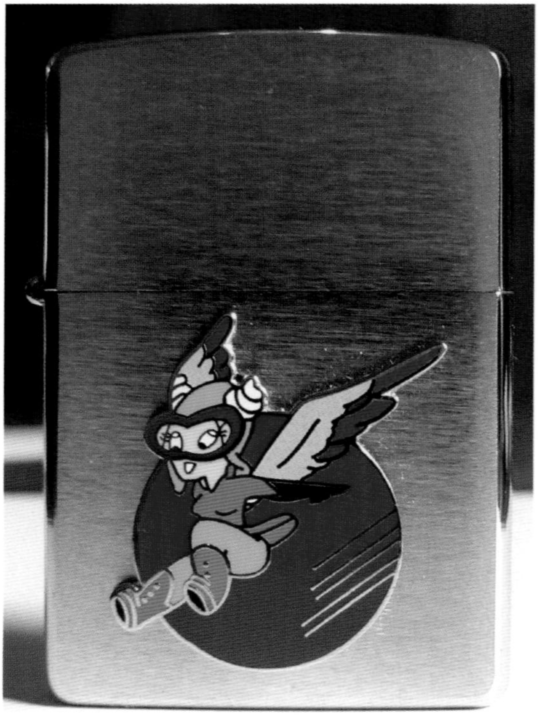

soldiers, sailors and airmen of other nations, who would become lasting friends and recipients of such gifts in the form of an engraved or embellished Zippo. It was a token of remembrance from a new and lasting comrade who had been there with them in that strange, stressful and wholly unforgettable time.

In that period of war, when so many of the participants smoked as one way of easing the tension and relaxing for a moment or two in a tough, demanding situation, there were significant numbers of American and Allied war correspondents, photographers and other newsmen and women on the scene covering events of the day for their bureaus, networks and other employers back home. Prominent among them were Edward R. Murrow, Ernie Pyle, William L. Shirer, John Hersey, Howard K. Smith, John Gunther, Vincent Sheean, Drew Middleton, H.V. Kaltenborn, Walter Cronkite, Quentin Reynolds, Bob Post, Gladwin Hill and Toni Frissell. Of these superb, high-achieving reporters of that twentieth century conflict it is known that Pyle and Murrow were serious smokers. Of the habit Ed Murrow said: 'I doubt I could spend a half hour without a cigarette with any comfort or ease.' In his book *Brave Men*, Ernie Pyle wrote: 'The Zippo Manufacturing Company, of Bradford, Pennsylvania, makes Zippo cigarette lighters. In peacetime they are nickel-plated and shiny. In wartime they are black, with a rough finish. They are not available at all to civilians. In Army PXs all around the world, where a batch comes in occasionally, there are long waiting lists.'

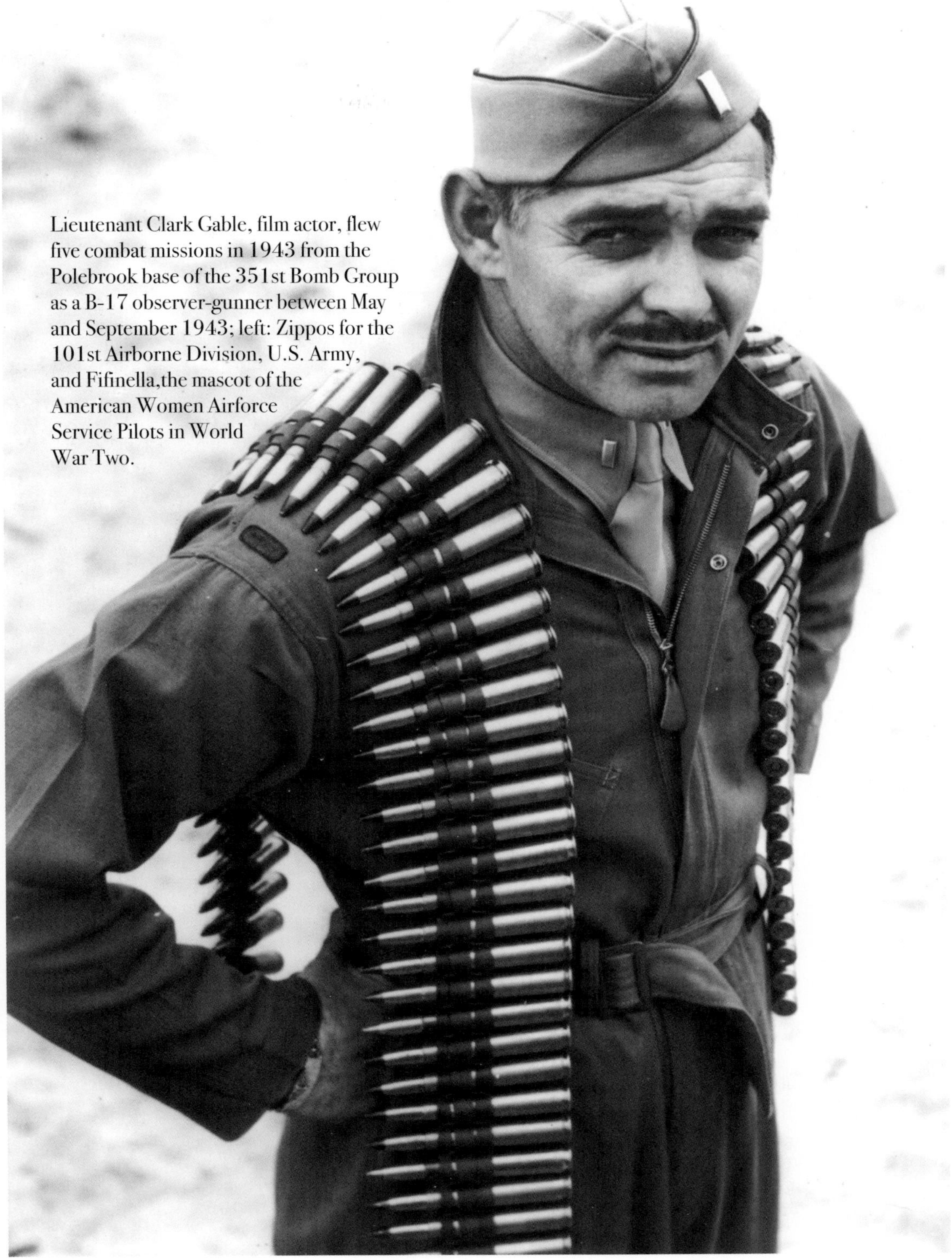

Lieutenant Clark Gable, film actor, flew five combat missions in 1943 from the Polebrook base of the 351st Bomb Group as a B-17 observer-gunner between May and September 1943; left: Zippos for the 101st Airborne Division, U.S. Army, and Fifinella,the mascot of the American Women Airforce Service Pilots in World War Two.

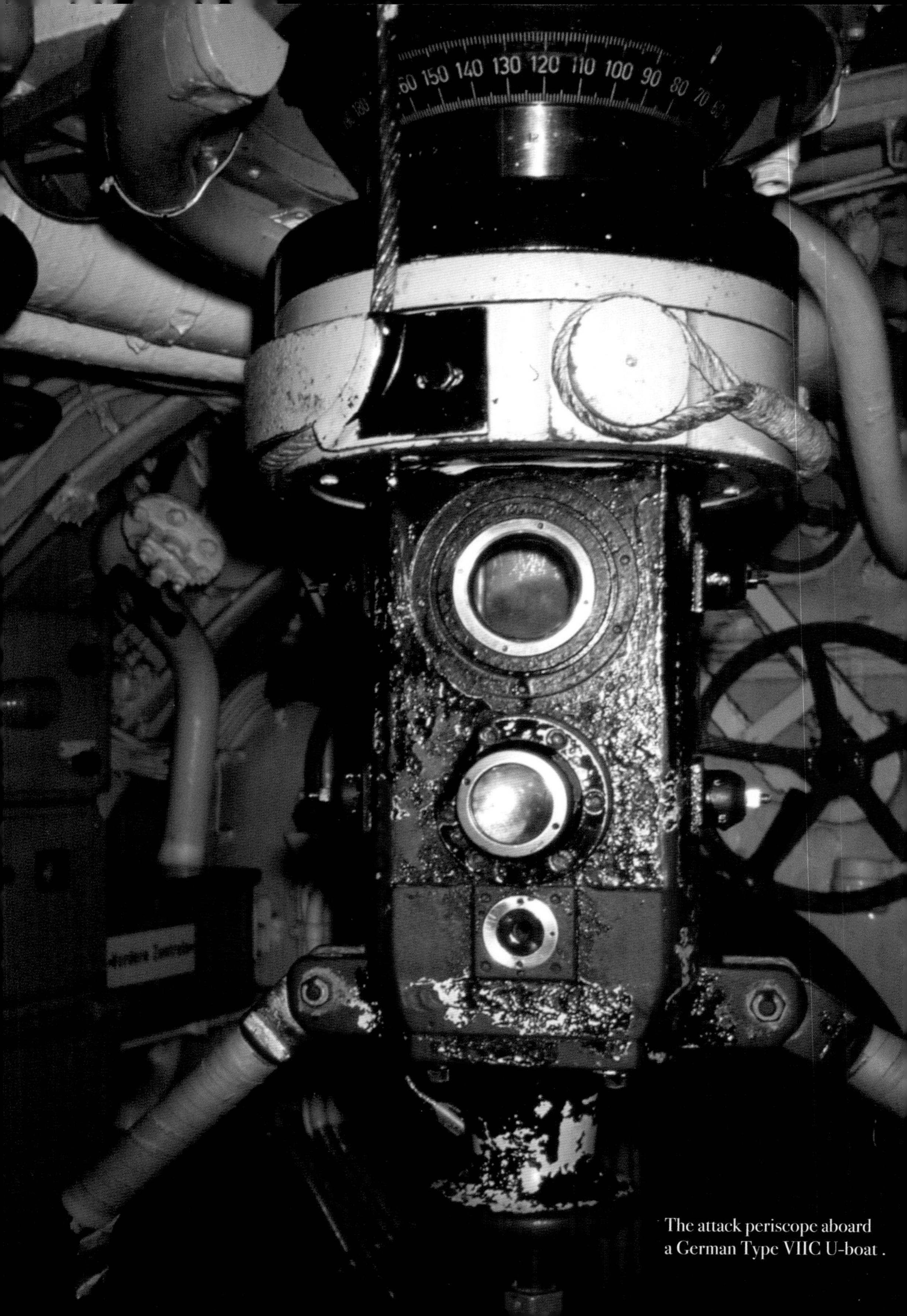
150 140 130 120 110 100 90 80 70

The attack periscope aboard
a German Type VIIC U-boat .

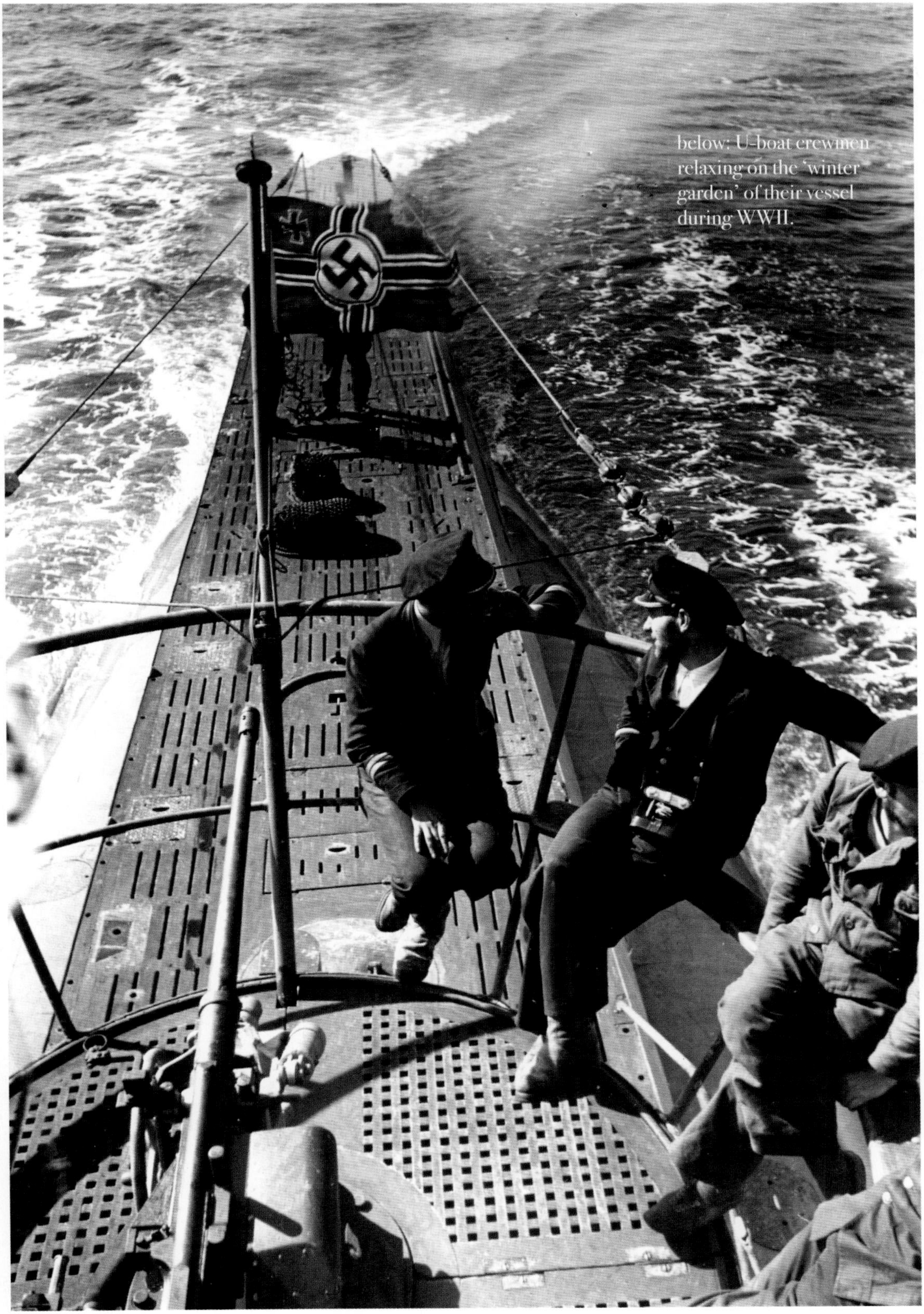

below: U-boat crewmen relaxing on the 'winter garden' of their vessel during WWII.

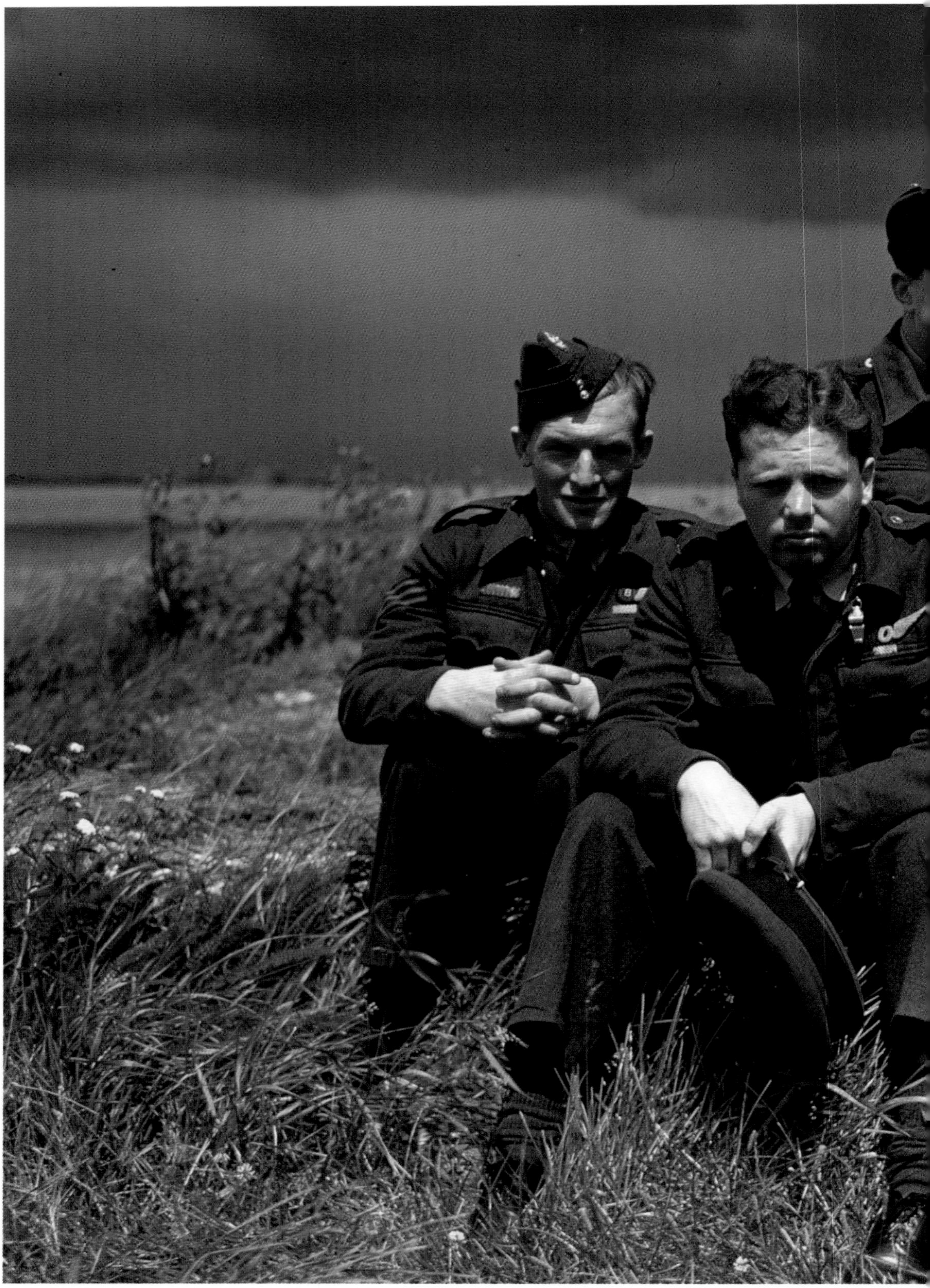

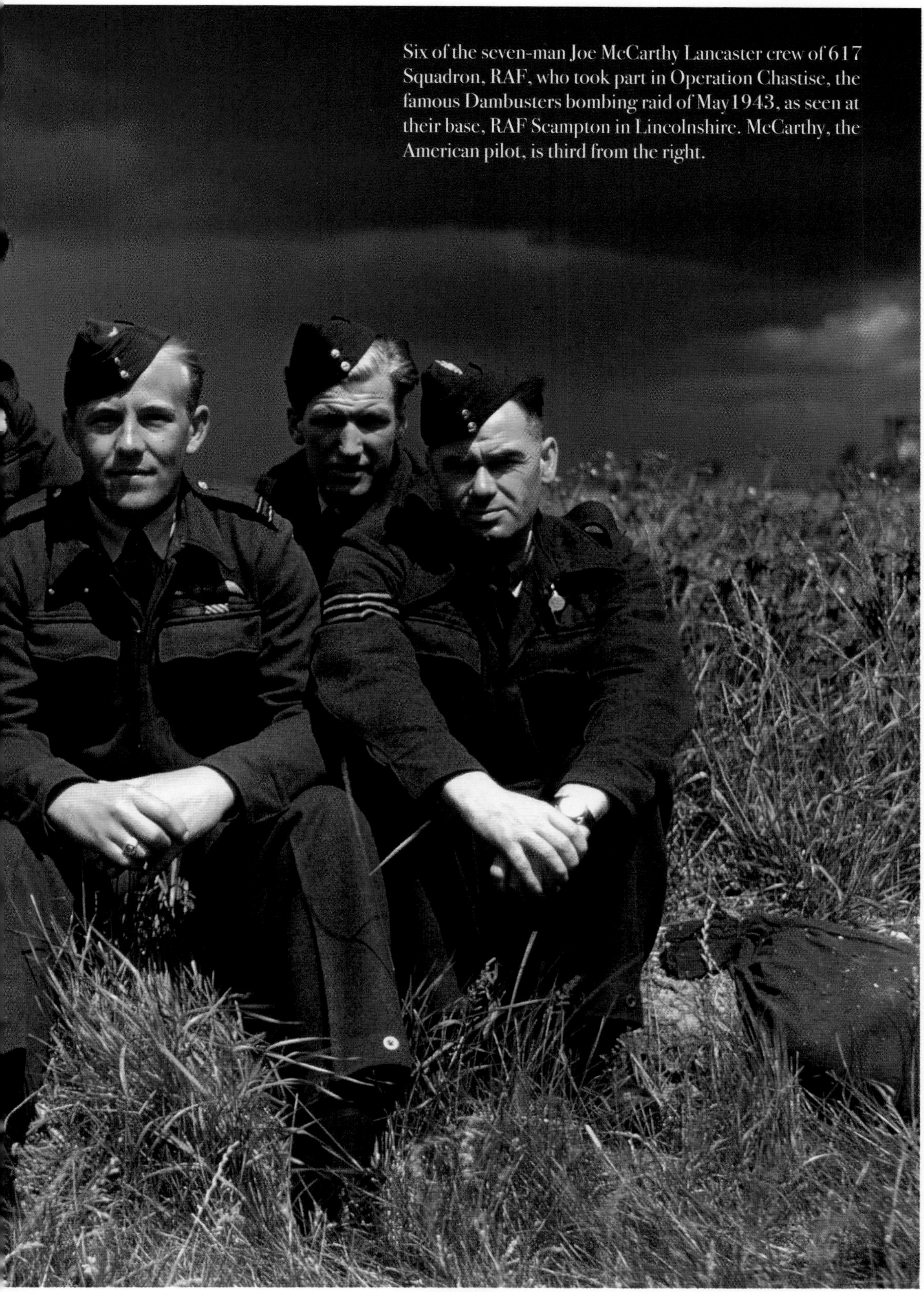
Six of the seven-man Joe McCarthy Lancaster crew of 617 Squadron, RAF, who took part in Operation Chastise, the famous Dambusters bombing raid of May1943, as seen at their base, RAF Scampton in Lincolnshire. McCarthy, the American pilot, is third from the right.

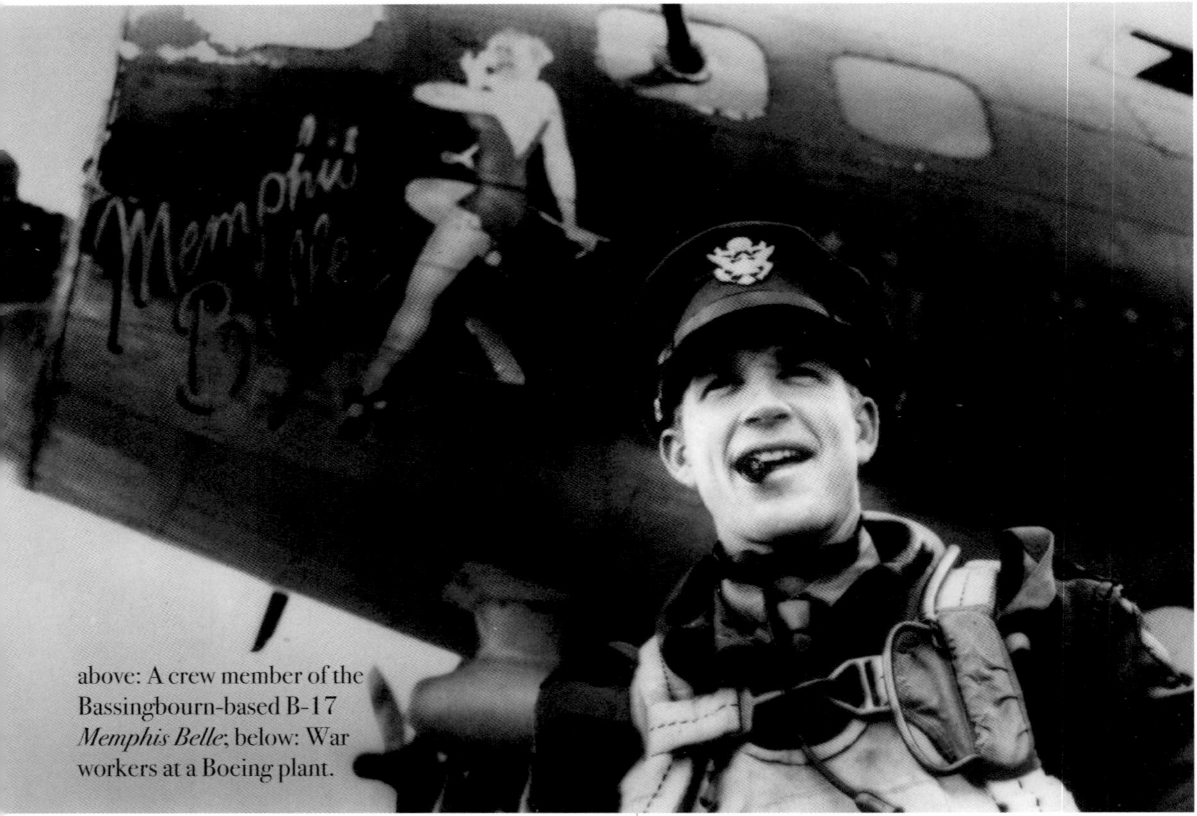
Memphis Belle

above: A crew member of the Bassingbourn-based B-17 *Memphis Belle*; below: War workers at a Boeing plant.

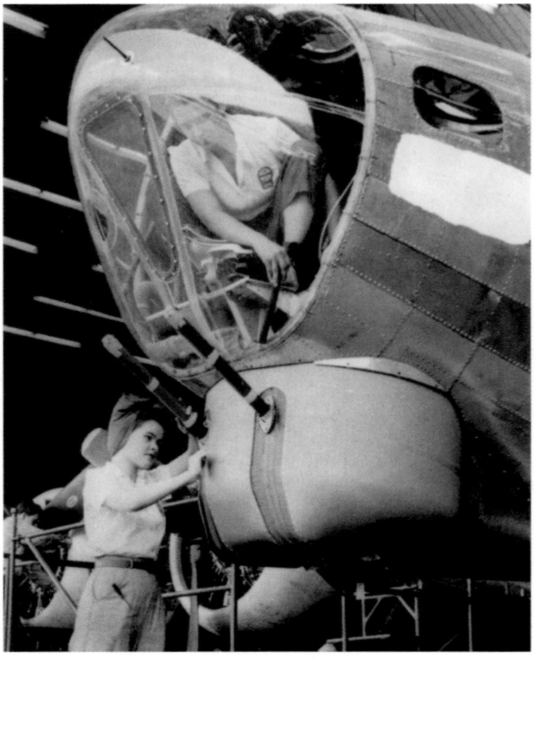

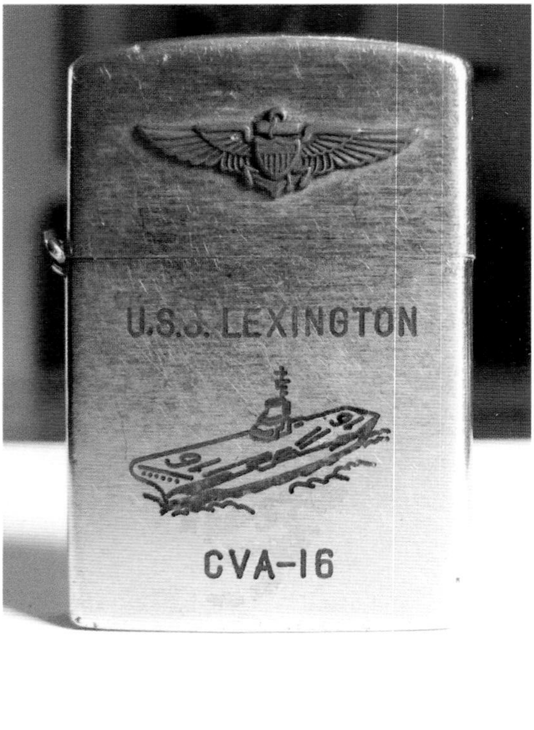
U.S.S. LEXINGTON
CVA-16

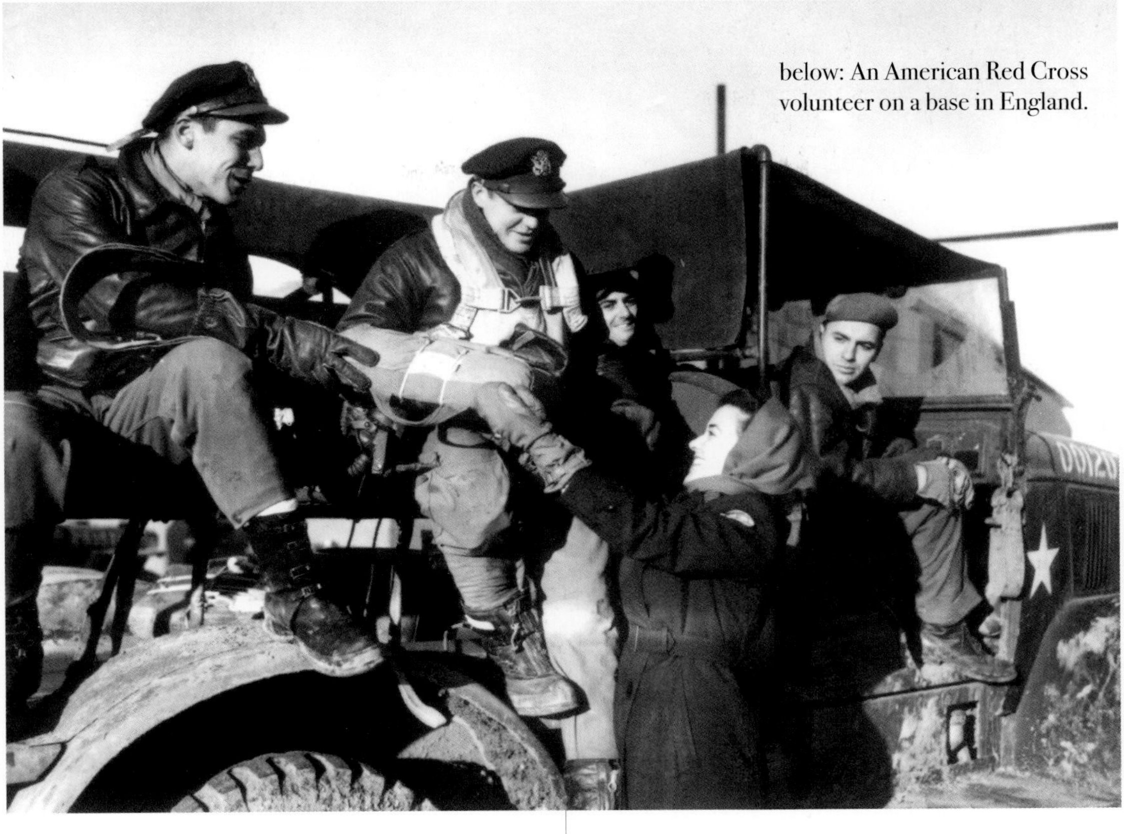

below: An American Red Cross volunteer on a base in England.

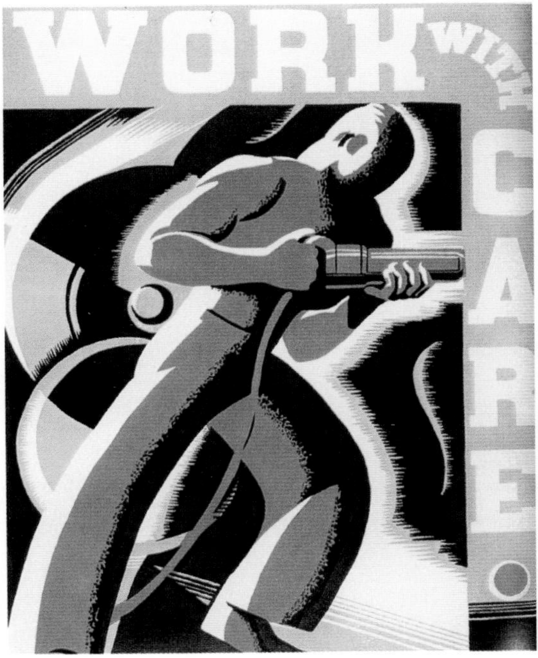
WORK
WITH
CARE

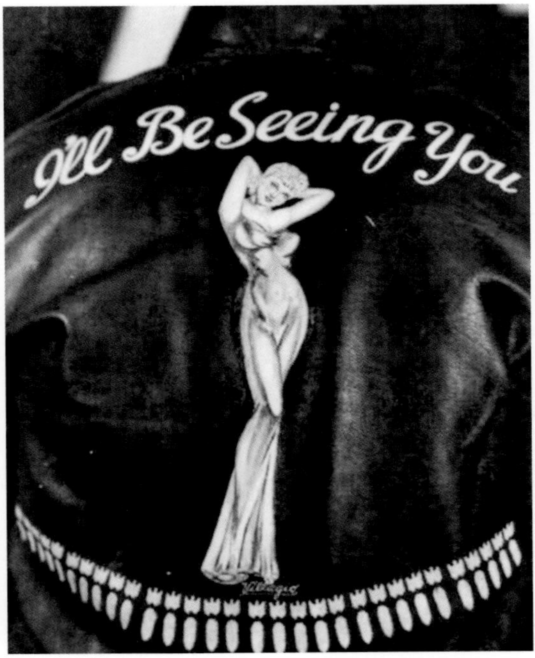
I'll Be Seeing You

F.

Police Notice

AIR RAID DANGER

CONCEAL YOUR LIGHTS—Precautions to be taken immediately by all concerned

PRIVATE DWELLINGS

All windows, skylights, glazed doors, or other openings must be completely screened after dusk, so that no light is visible from outside.

If blinds are used alone, they must be of stout material and dark in colour and must cover the window completely.   If curtains are used they must be dark and thick.

Dark blankets or carpets or thick sheets of brown paper can be used to cover windows temporarily.

Special care must be taken to cover completely skylights and other windows directly visible from the air.

All lights near a door leading outside the building must be screened so that no light can be seen when the door is opened.

SHOPS, FACTORIES, BUSINESS PREMISES AND PLACES OF ENTERTAINMENT

All windows, skylights, glazed doors, pavement lights, etc., must be completely screened after dusk with thick dark material, so that no light is visible from outside.

All advertising signs and other external lights on such premises must be extinguished, without exception.

Doors admitting to shops and other business premises must be screened, so that the opening and shutting of the door does not cause light to be thrown on the street outside. Also shades—which can be improvised for the purpose—should be fixed to all lights near the door, to ensure that all light is thrown on the floor.

ROAD VEHICLES

A separate leaflet describing the lighting restrictions for motor vehicles may be obtained at any police station.

No car may be on any road during the hours of darkness until the measures prescribed in that leaflet have been complied with.

KEEP YOUR HOUSE DARK
If a Raid takes place—REMAIN INDOORS

These instructions are issued for the public safety, as a matter of urgency, pending more detailed instructions regarding the extinction and screening of lights.

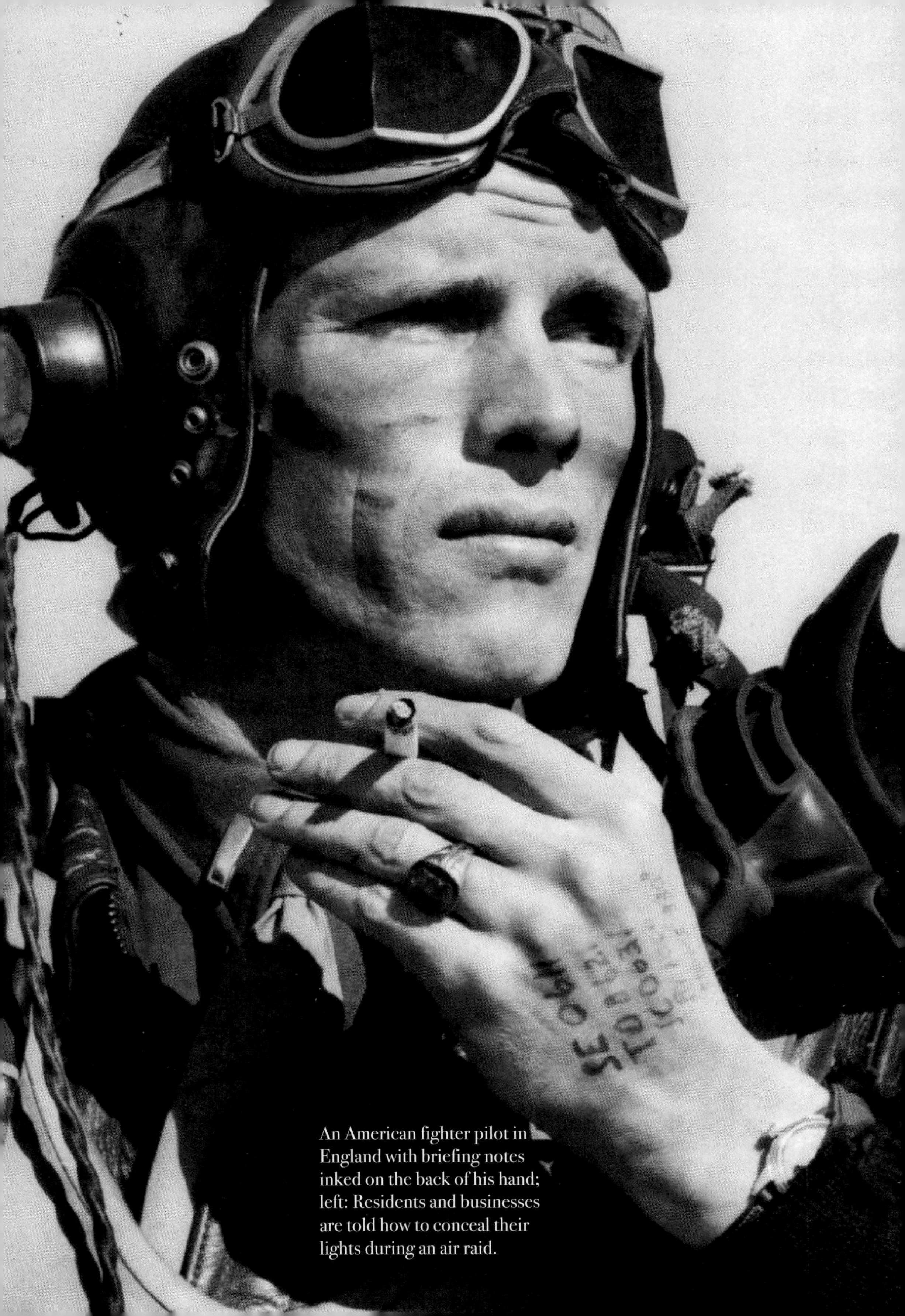

An American fighter pilot in England with briefing notes inked on the back of his hand; left: Residents and businesses are told how to conceal their lights during an air raid.

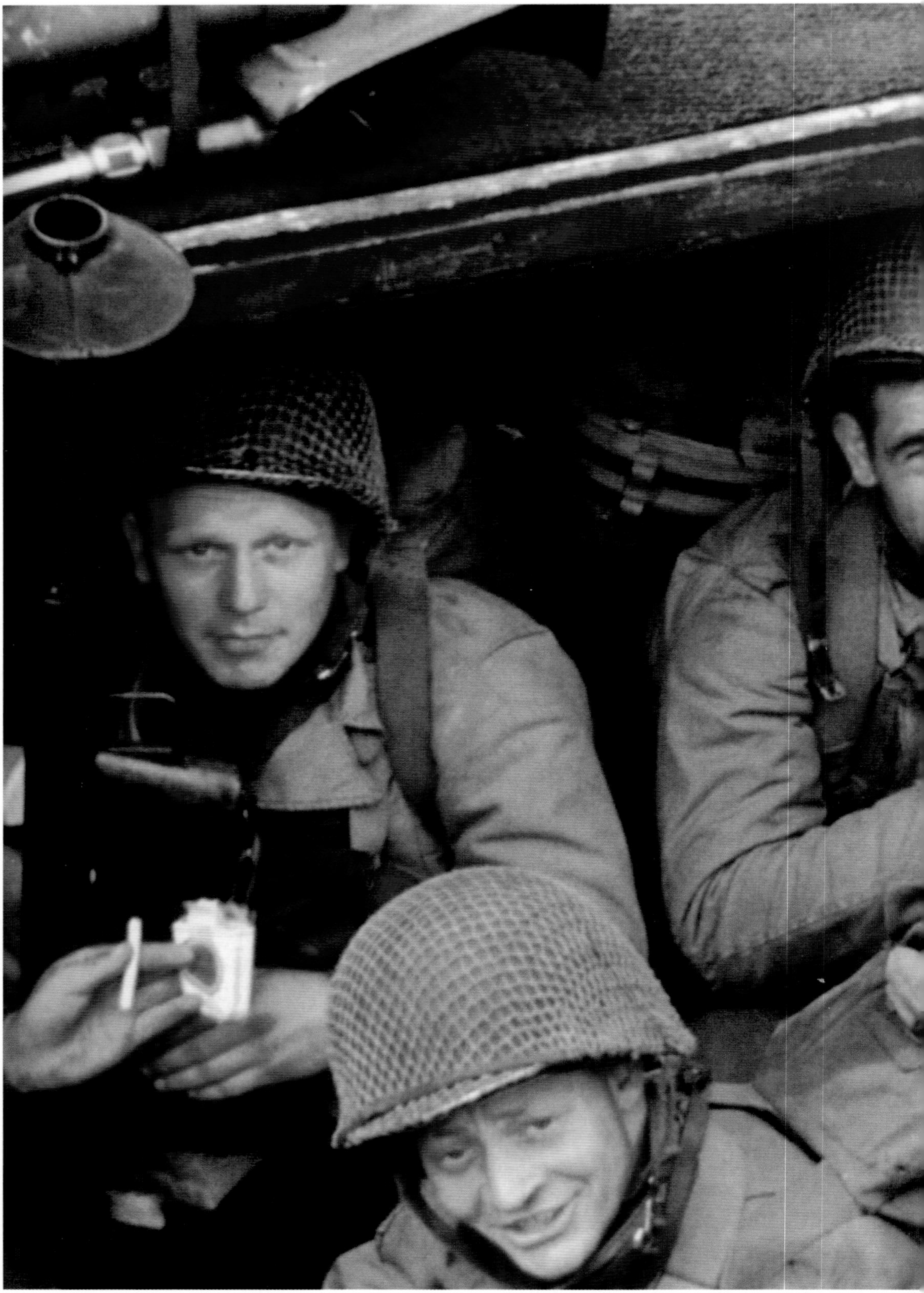

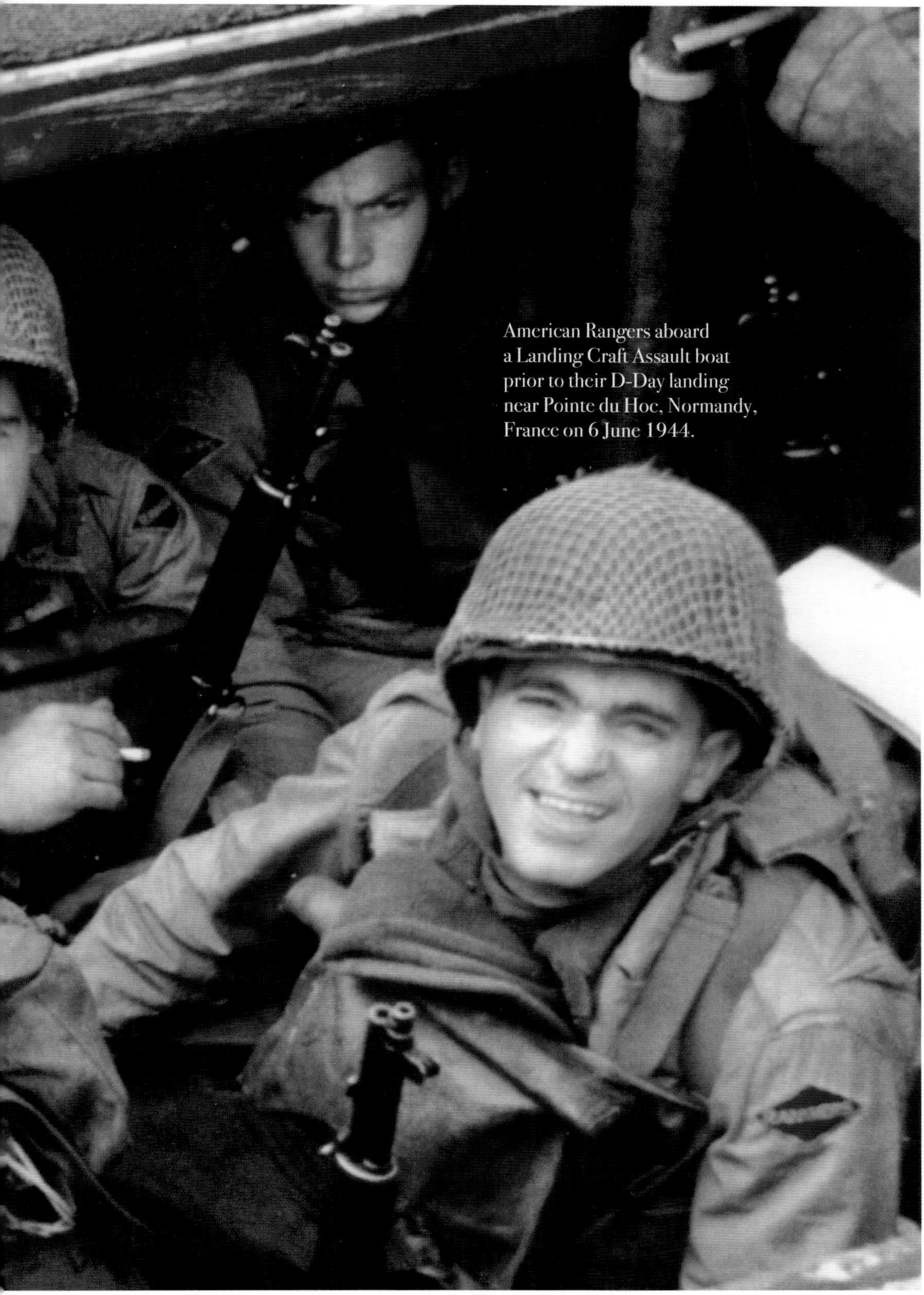

American Rangers aboard a Landing Craft Assault boat prior to their D-Day landing near Pointe du Hoc, Normandy, France on 6 June 1944.

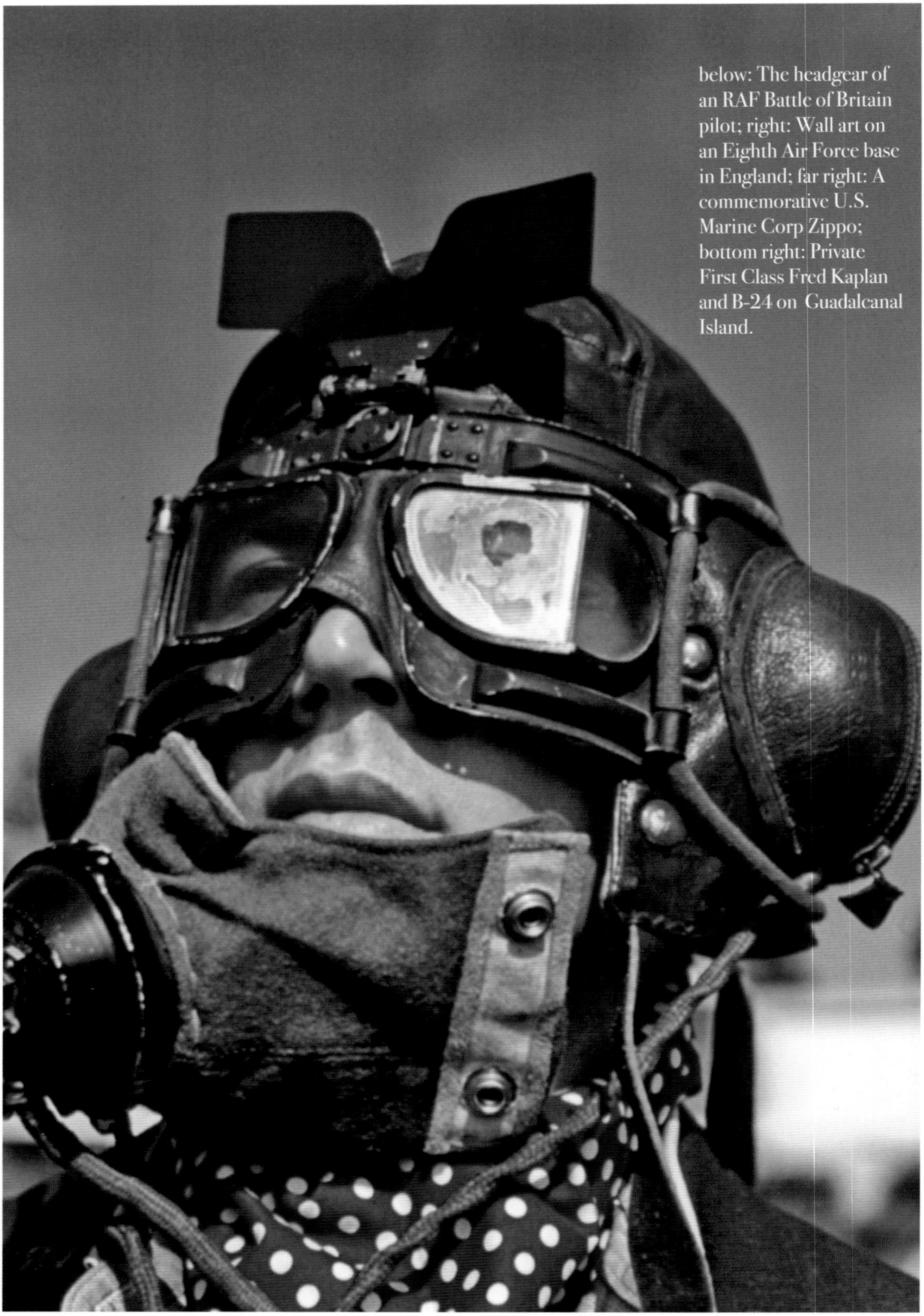

below: The headgear of an RAF Battle of Britain pilot; right: Wall art on an Eighth Air Force base in England; far right: A commemorative U.S. Marine Corp Zippo; bottom right: Private First Class Fred Kaplan and B-24 on Guadalcanal Island.

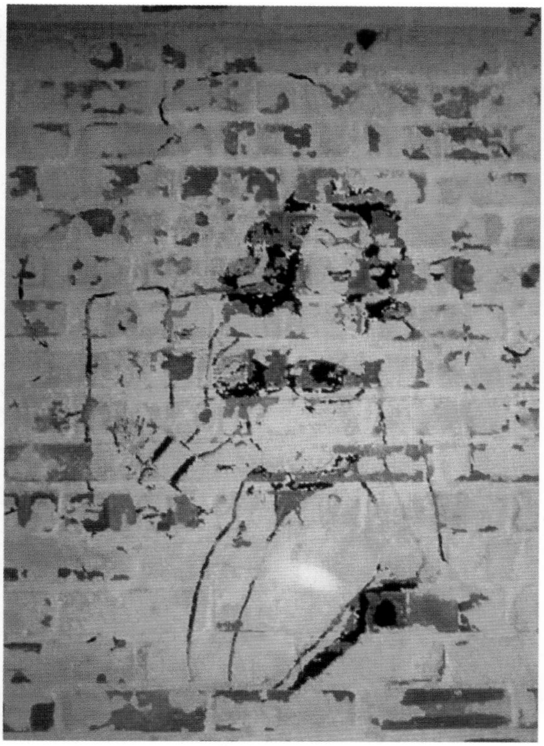

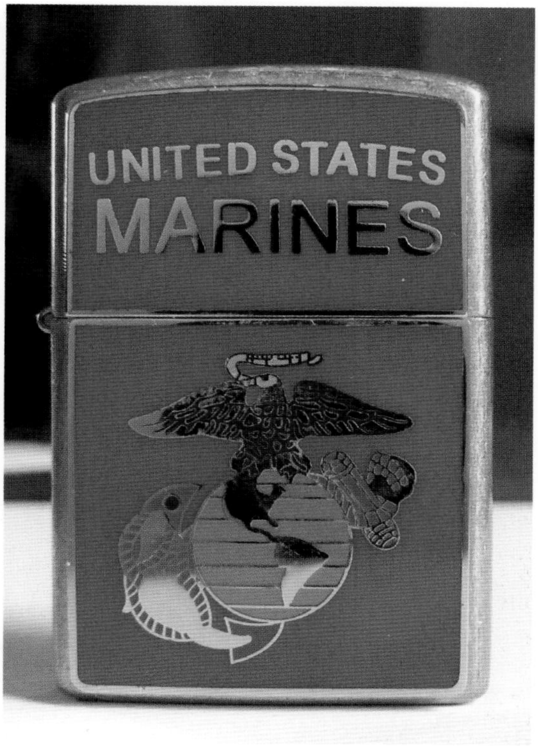
UNITED STATES
MARINES

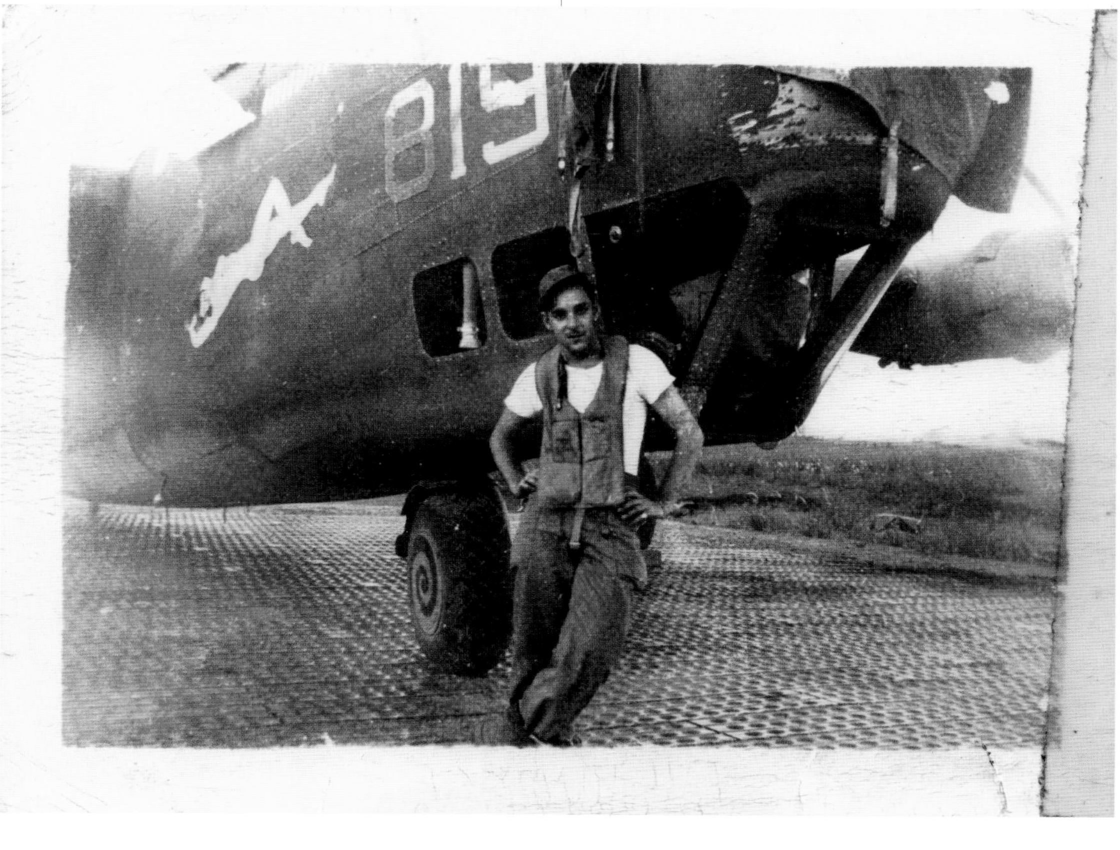
819

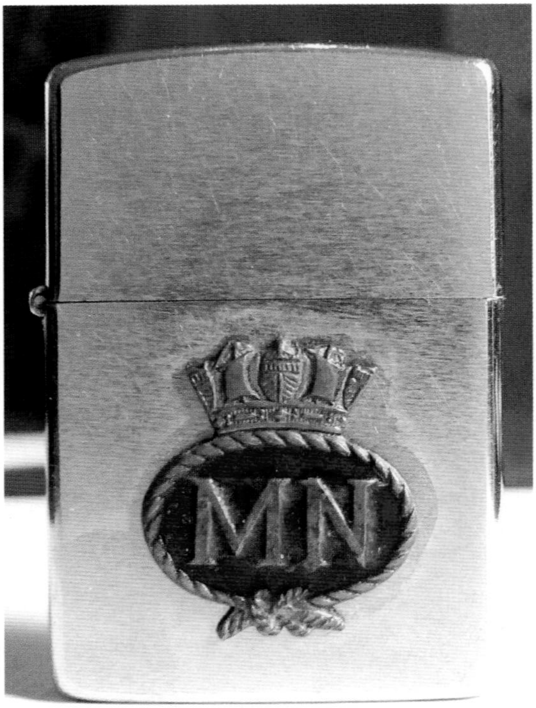
MN

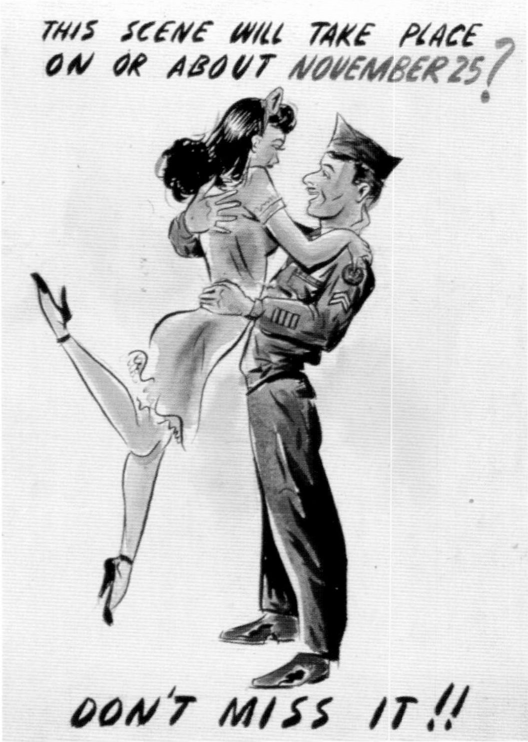
THIS SCENE WILL TAKE PLACE
ON OR ABOUT NOVEMBER 25?
DON'T MISS IT!!

above: A Zippo honouring the British Merchant Navy whose hard-working, dedicated seamen kept the United Kingdom supplied with ammunition, fuel, food, arms, raw materials and vital provisions in WW2.

above: Part of an American soldier's letter to his wife; below: Debden-based pilots John Godfrey, left, and Don Gentile; right: The original 34th Bomb Group memorial at Mendlesham, England.

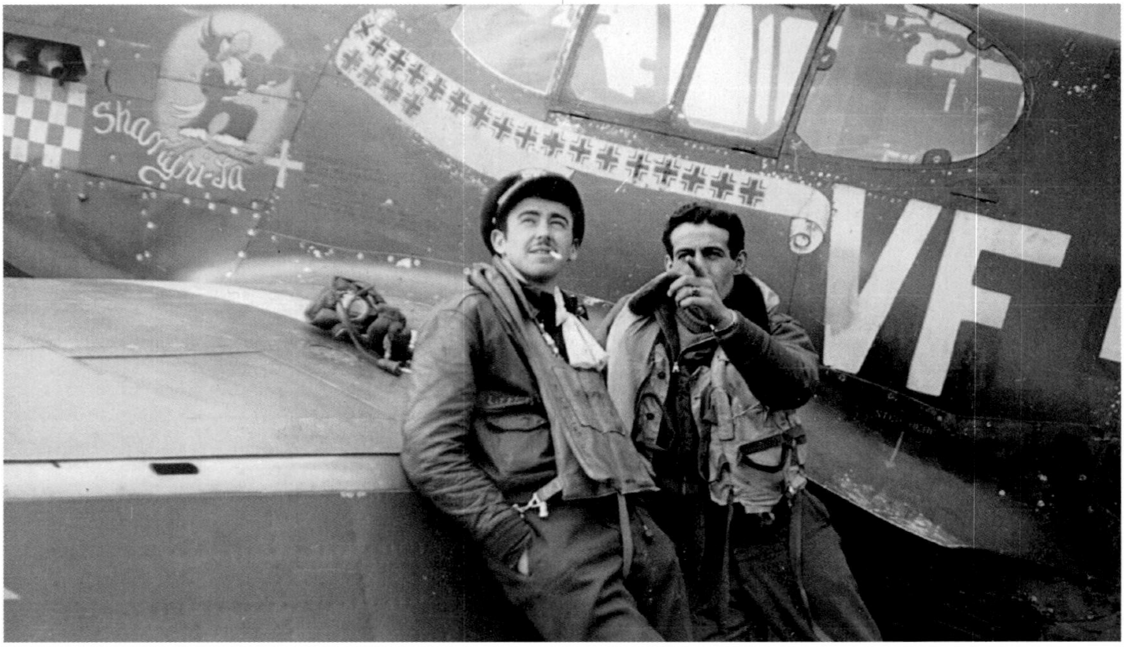
Shangri-La
VF

TO THE AMERICAN AIRMEN
OF THE '34TH' WHO, IN VALOR
GAVE THEIR LIVES TO THE VICTOR
THAT MADE REAL THE CHALLENG
FOR WORLD PEACE AND UNIT

HE 34TH HEAVY BOMBARDMENT GROUP
A UNIT OF THE UNITED STATES
EIGHTH AIR FORCE
IN WORLD WAR II
APRIL 1944 TO JUNE 1945
MENDLESHAM AERO
DROME SUFFOLK

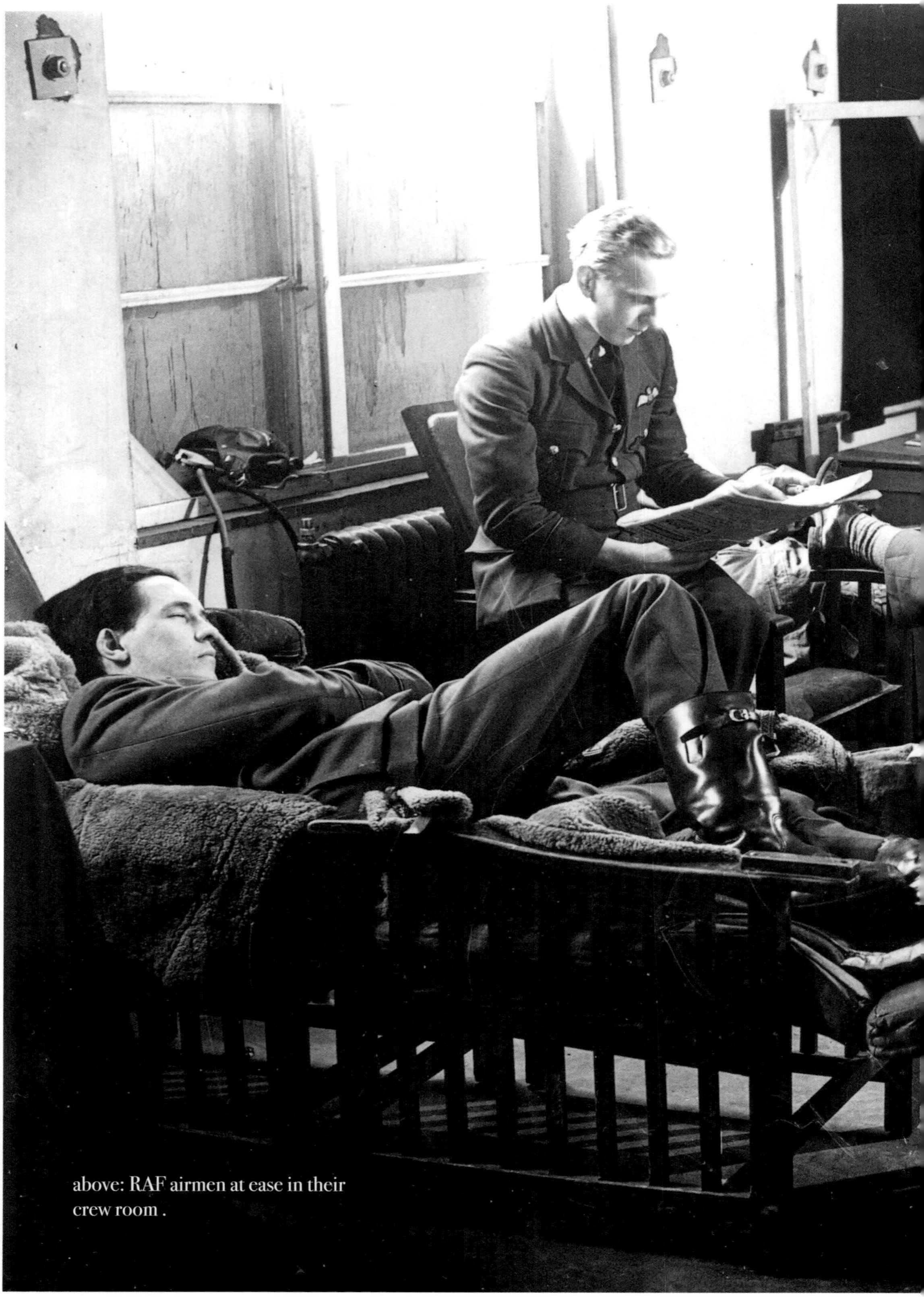

above: RAF airmen at ease in their crew room .

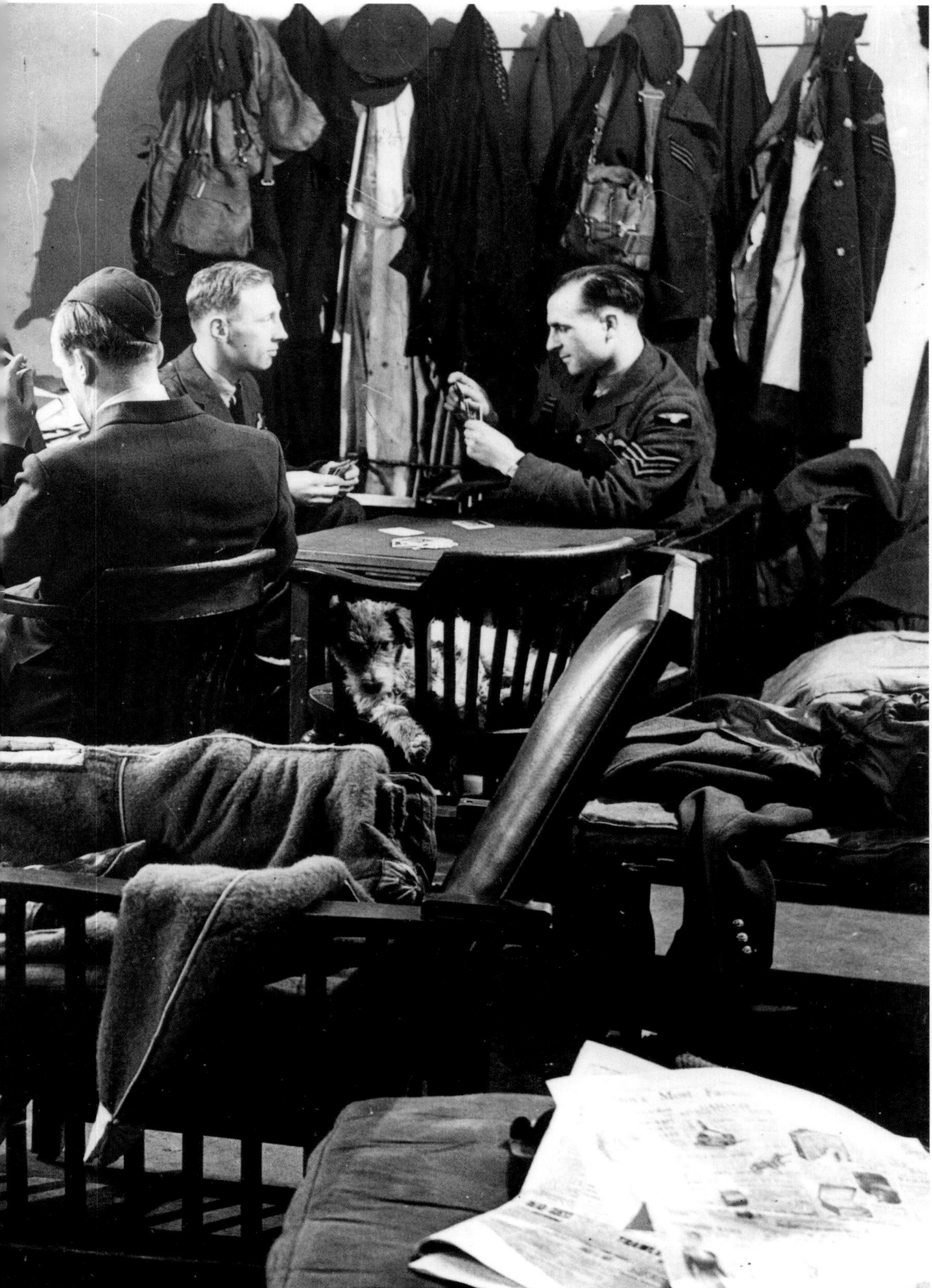

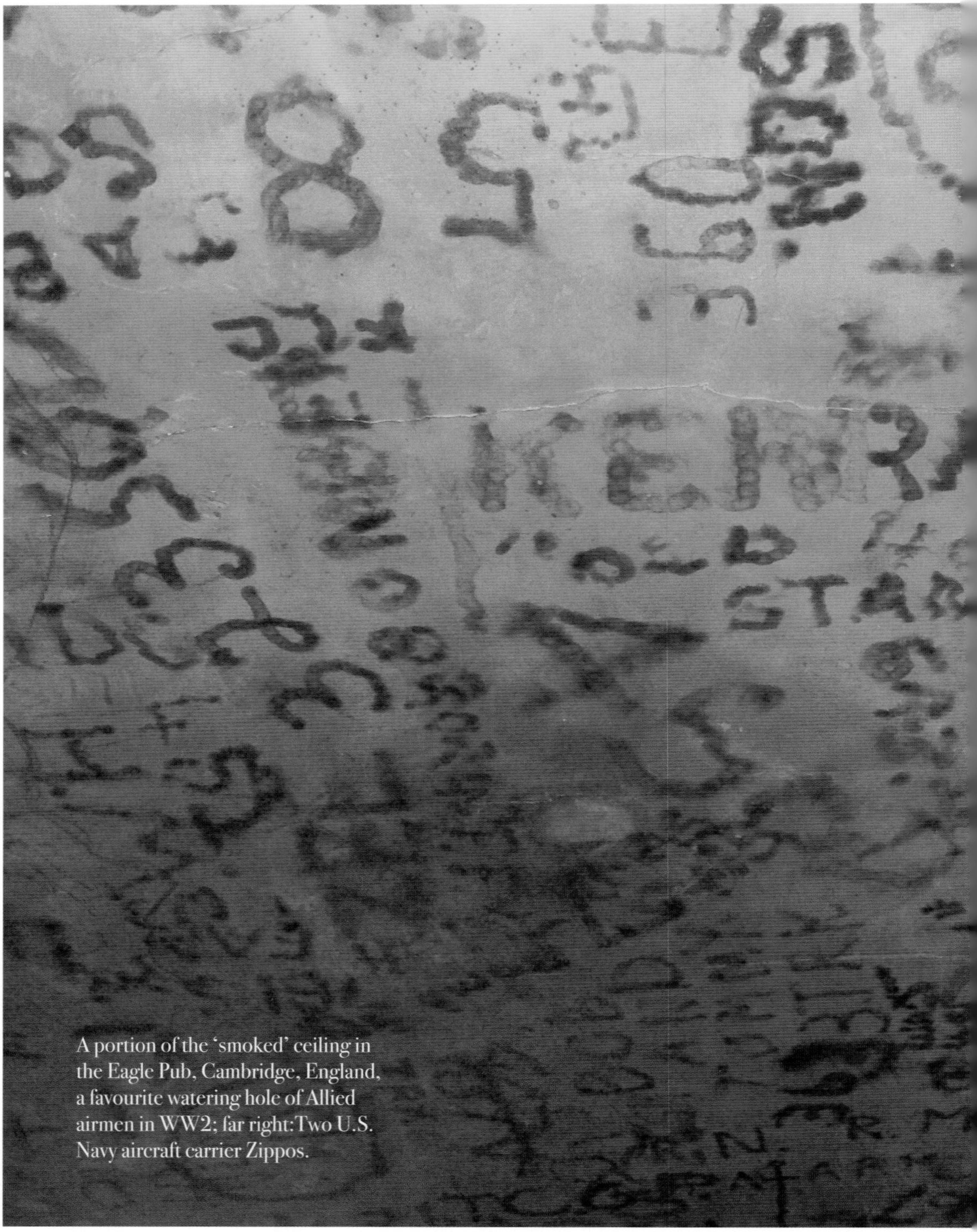

A portion of the 'smoked' ceiling in the Eagle Pub, Cambridge, England, a favourite watering hole of Allied airmen in WW2; far right: Two U.S. Navy aircraft carrier Zippos.

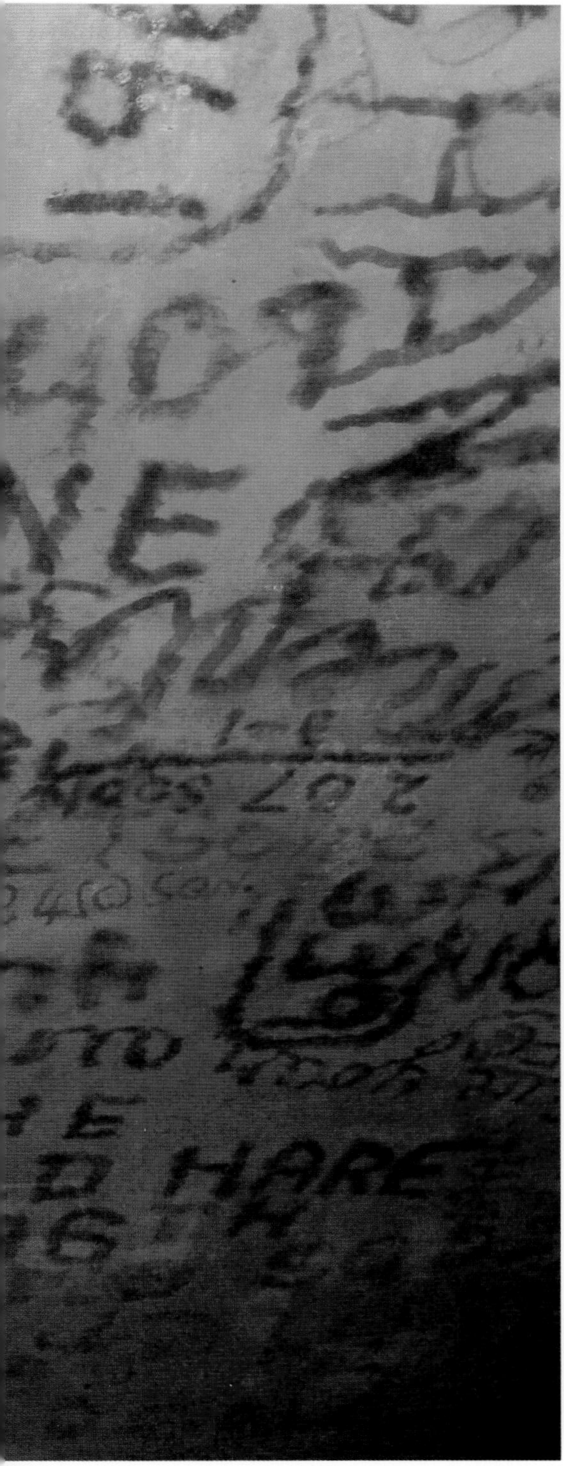

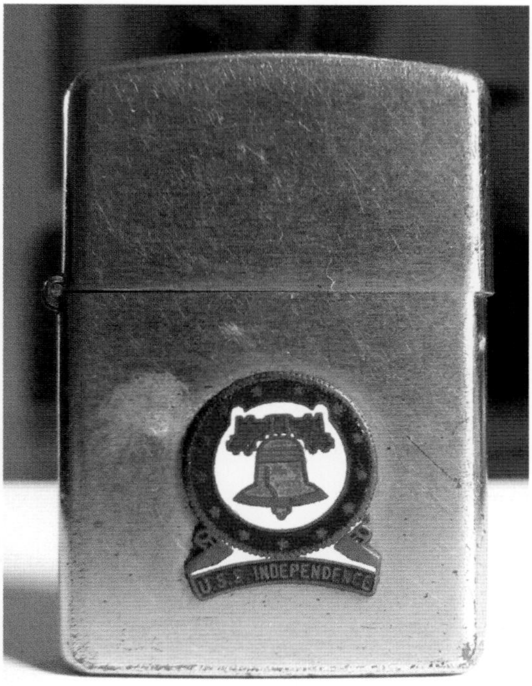
U.S.S. INDEPENDENCE

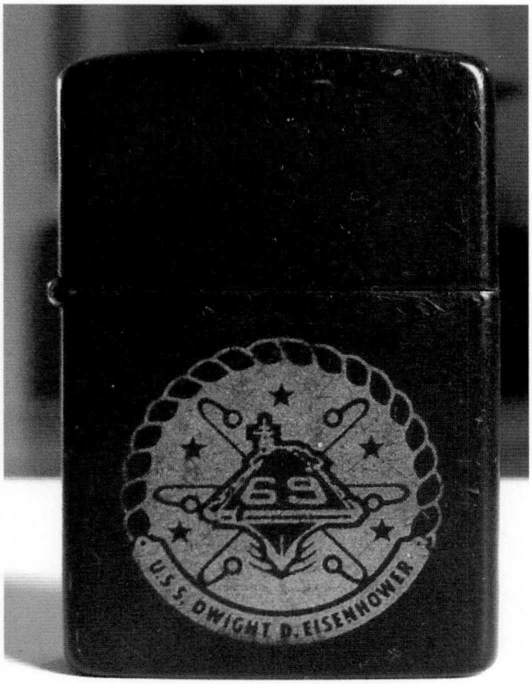
69
U.S.S. DWIGHT D. EISENHOWER

German prisoners, sailors captured by the Americans during the Second World War. Here, three on a butt.

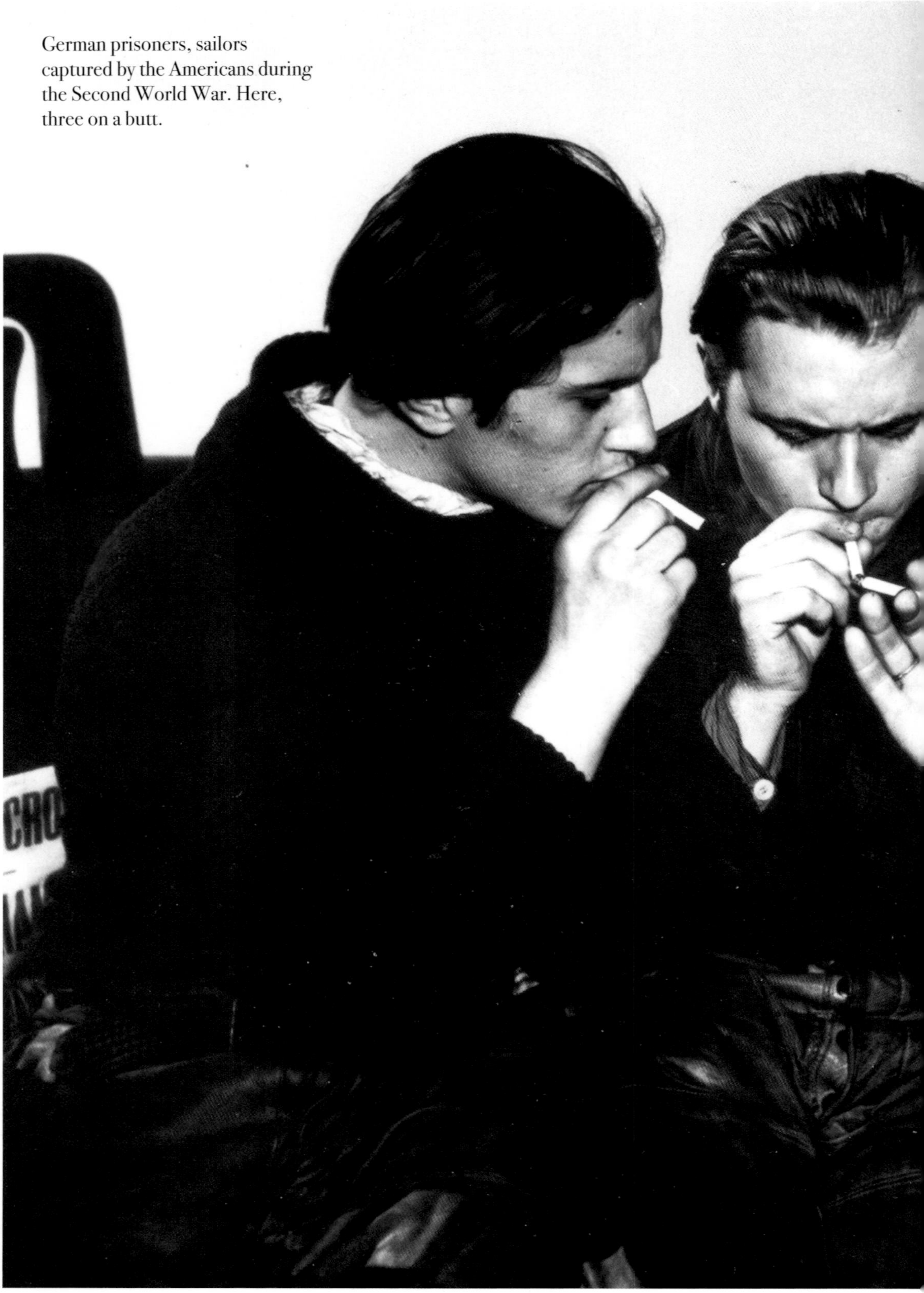

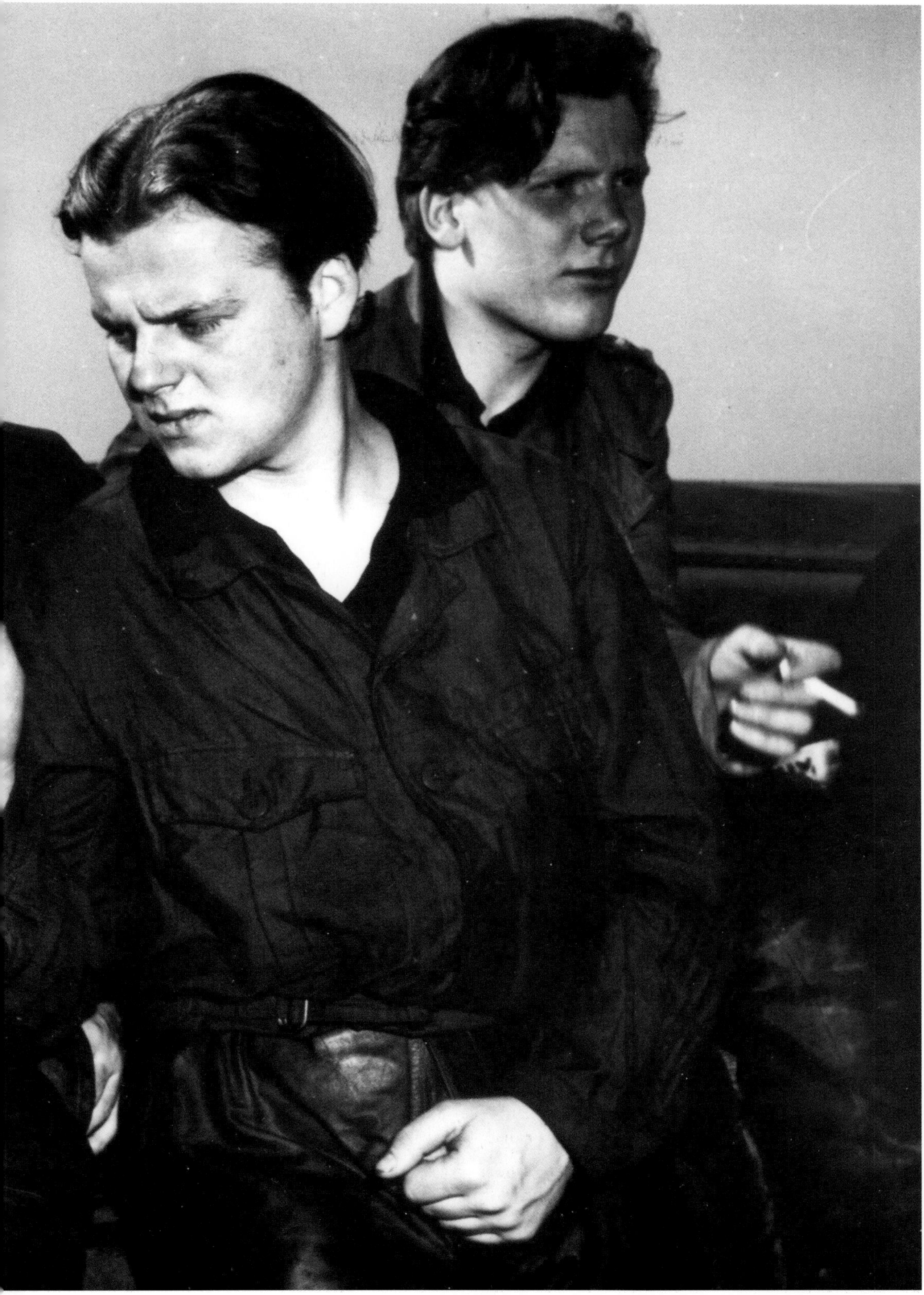

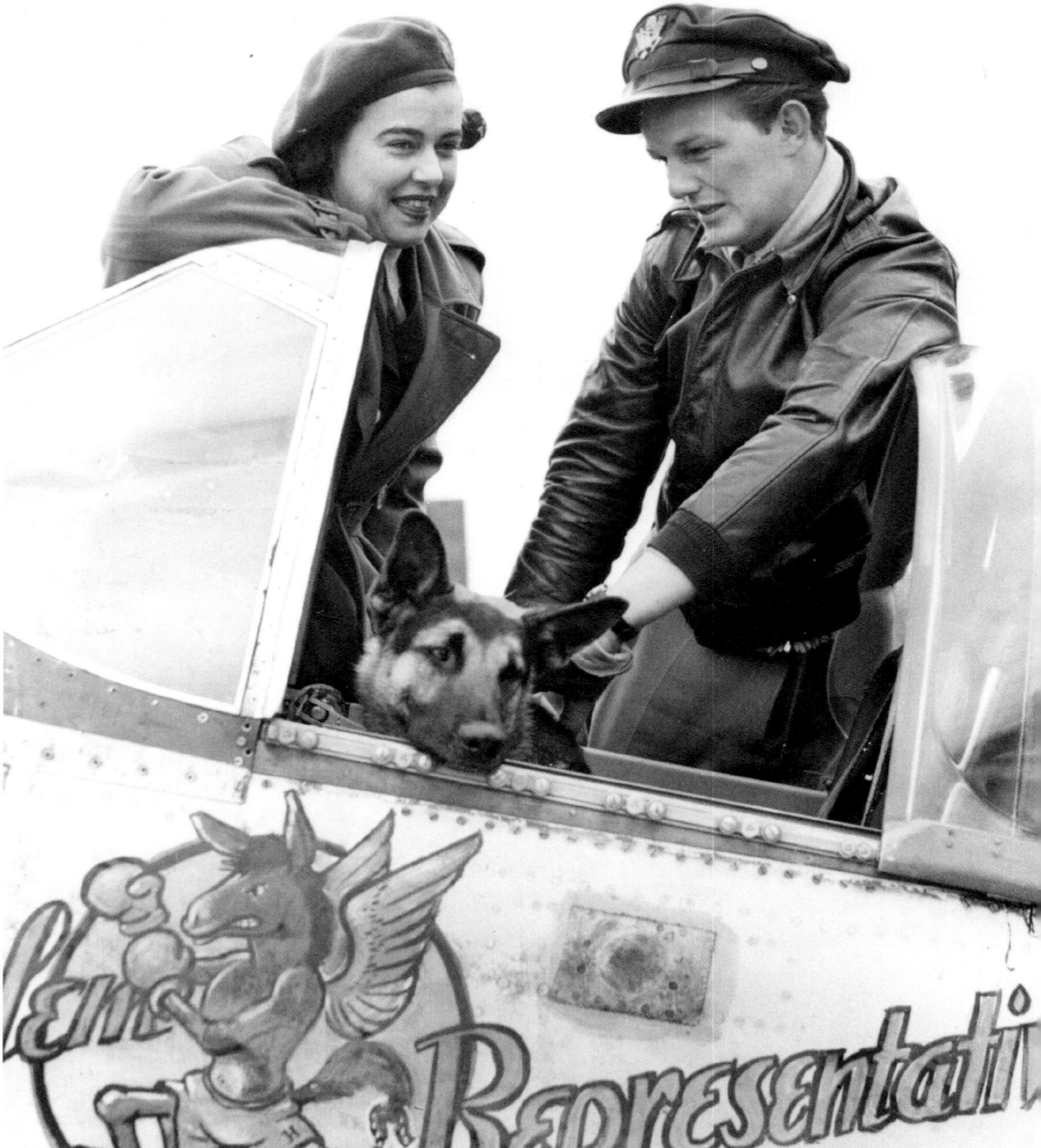
Representati

right: A Zippo commemorating the USS *New Jersey*, one of the most important capital ships in the history of the American Navy; above: Virginia Irwin of the *St Louis Post-Dispatch* interviews Ralph 'Kid' Hofer, a Missouri-born pilot with the Debden-based 4th Fighter Group,

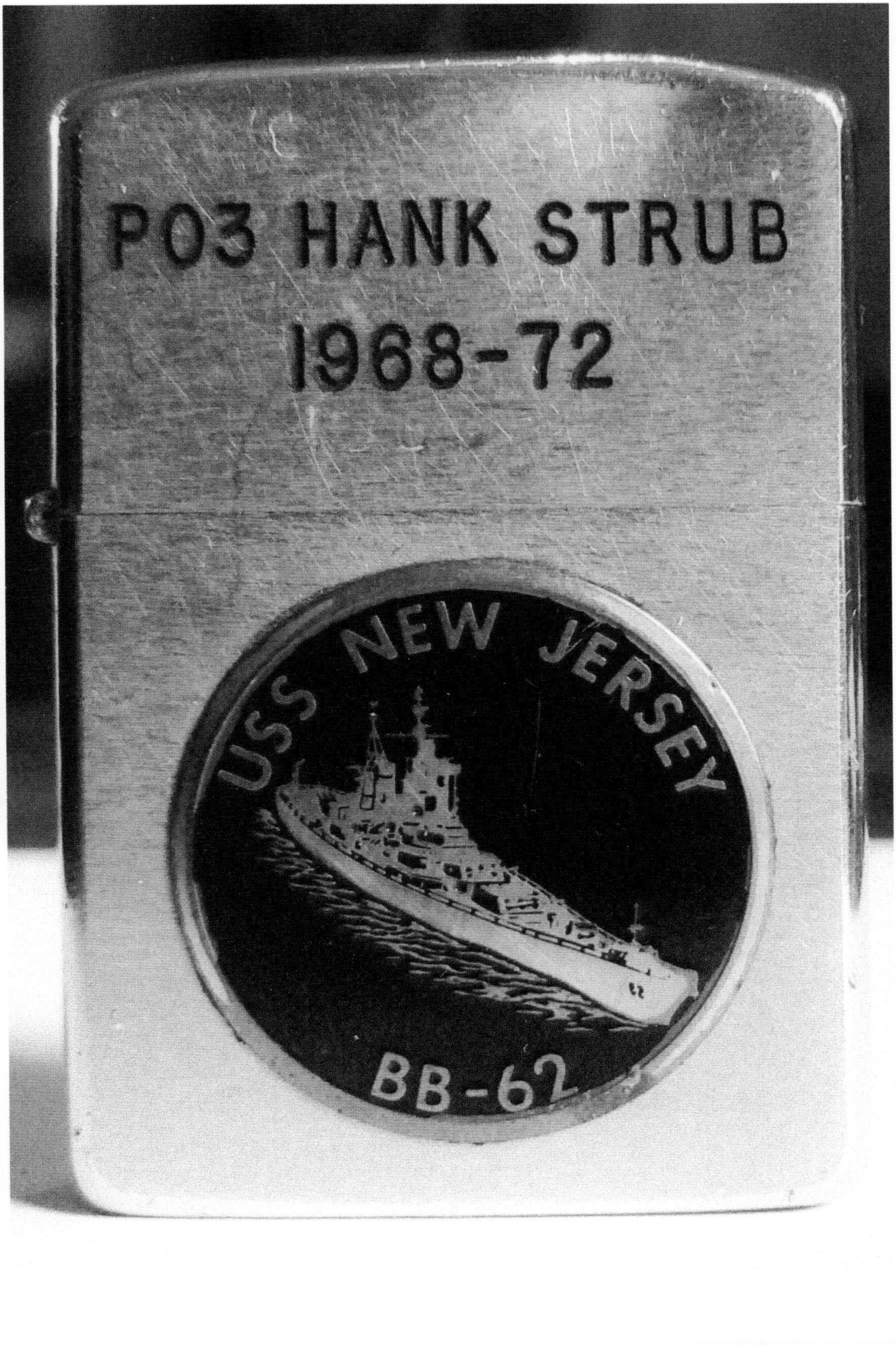
PO3 HANK STRUB
1968-72
USS NEW JERSEY
BB-62

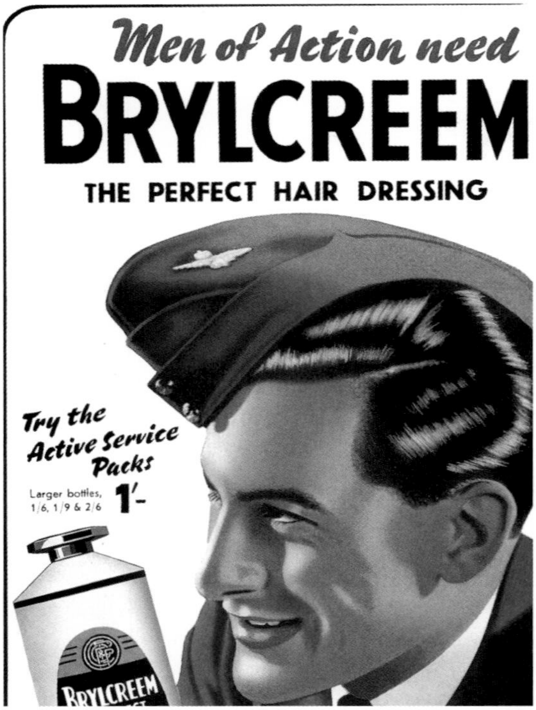
Men of Action need
BRYLCREEM
THE PERFECT HAIR DRESSING
Try the Active Service Packs
Larger bottles, 1/6, 1/9 & 2/6
1/-
BRYLCREEM

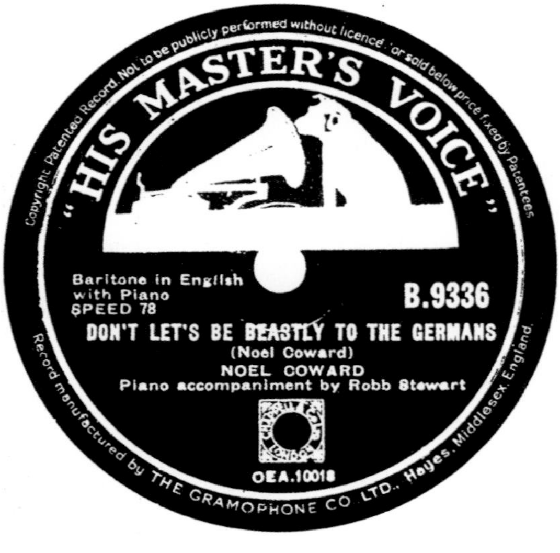
Copyright Patented Record. Not to be publicly performed without licence, or sold below price fixed by Patentees.
"HIS MASTER'S VOICE"
Baritone in English with Piano
SPEED 78
B.9336
DON'T LET'S BE BEASTLY TO THE GERMANS
(Noel Coward)
NOEL COWARD
Piano accompaniment by Robb Stewart
OEA.10018
Record manufactured by THE GRAMOPHONE CO LTD., Hayes, Middlesex, England.

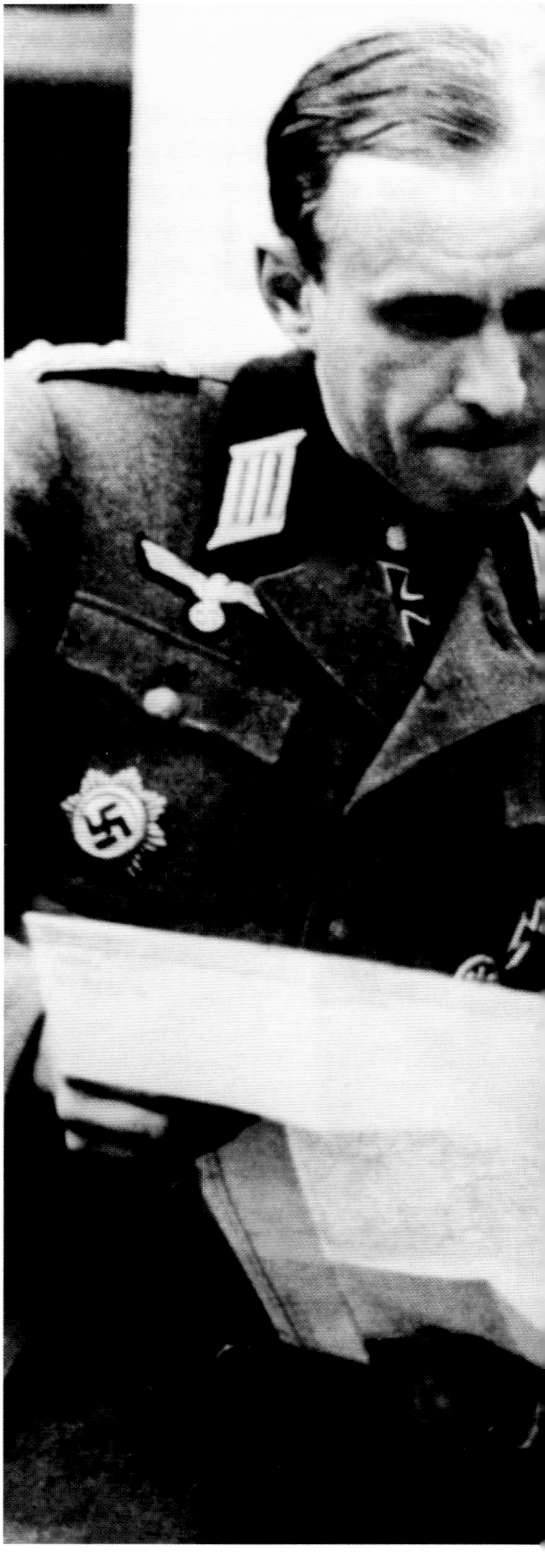

right: German officers studying a map during the war; at top: A Brylcreem hair dressing ad of the war years.

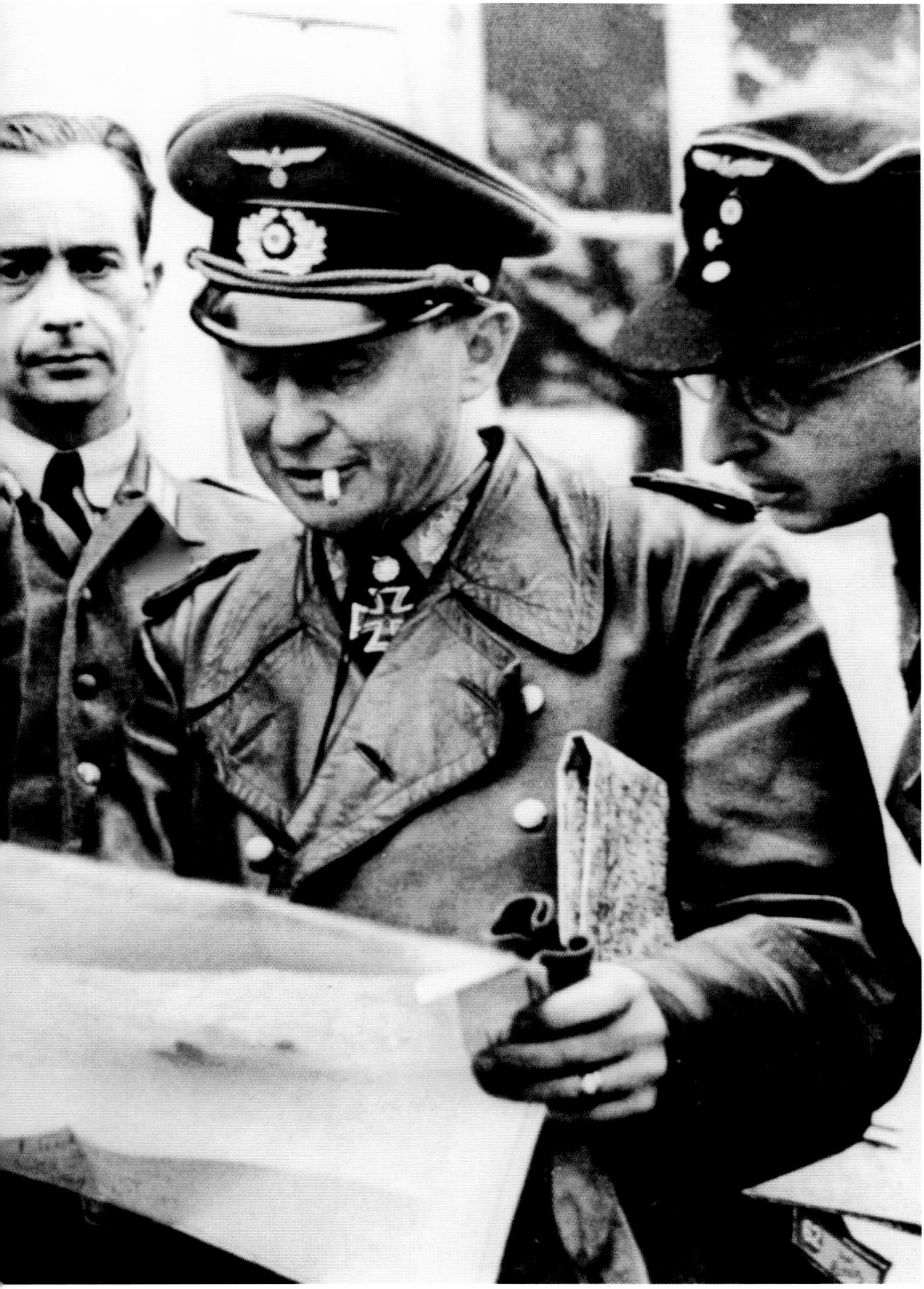

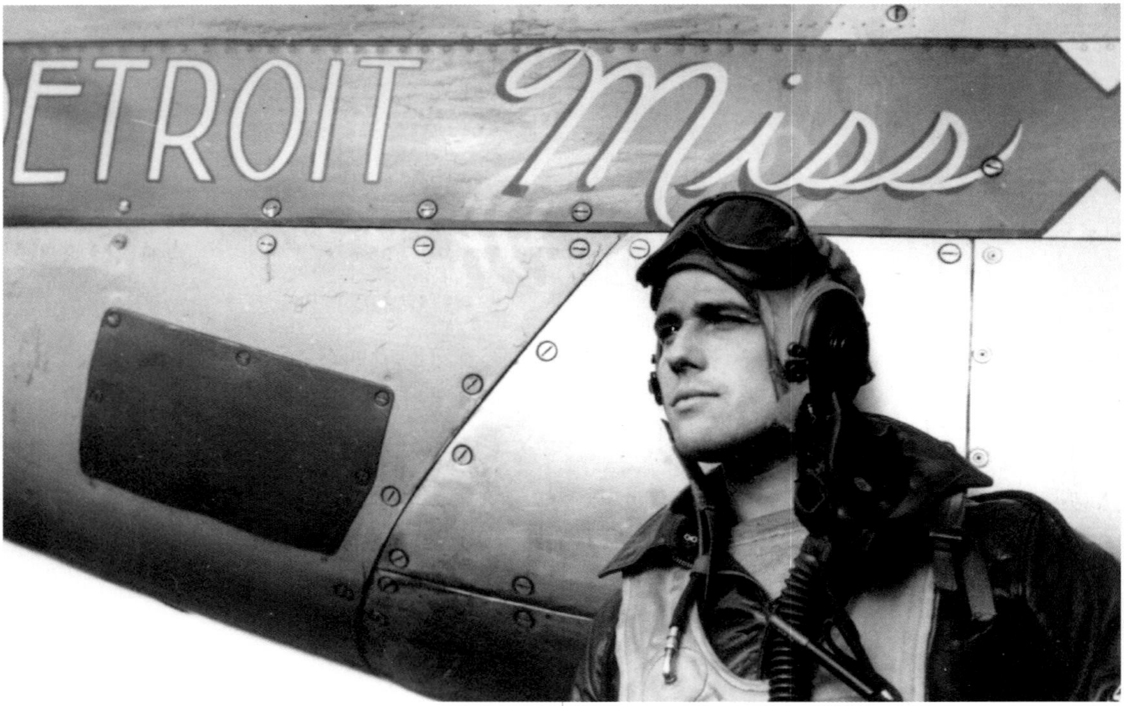
ETROIT Miss

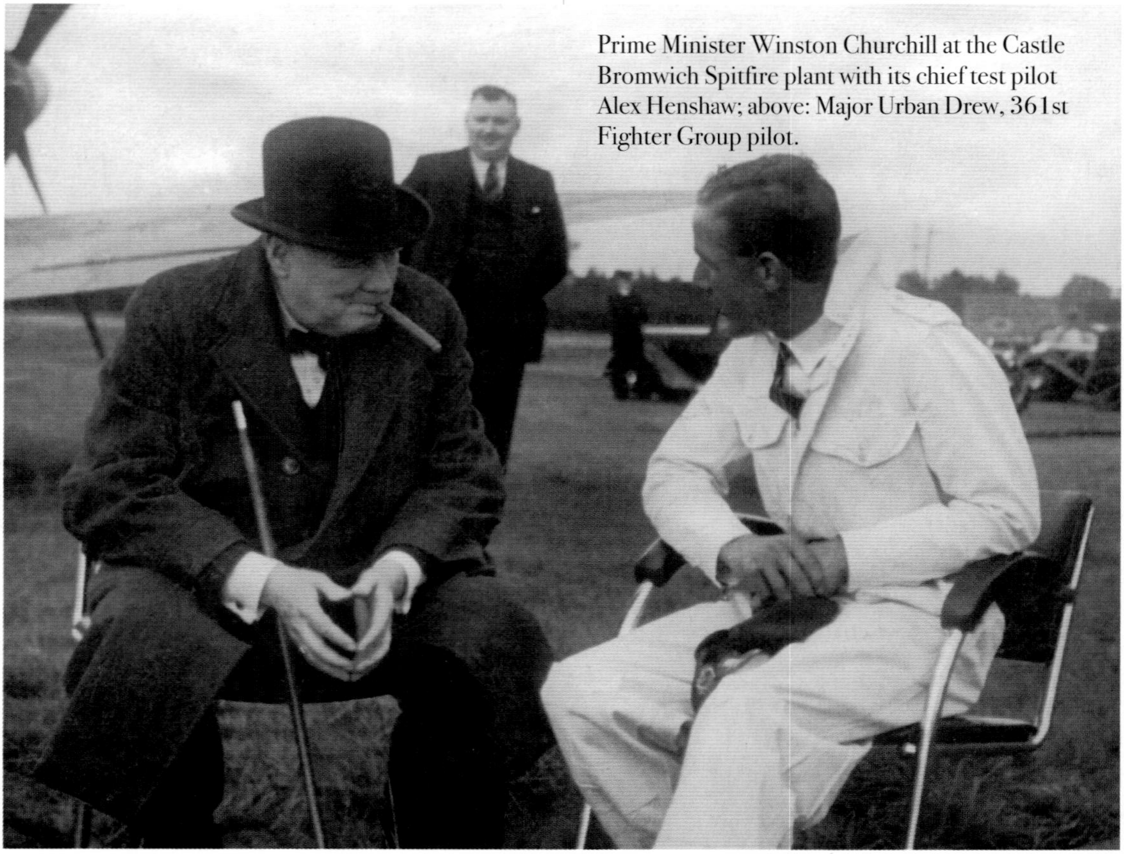

Prime Minister Winston Churchill at the Castle Bromwich Spitfire plant with its chief test pilot Alex Henshaw; above: Major Urban Drew, 361st Fighter Group pilot.

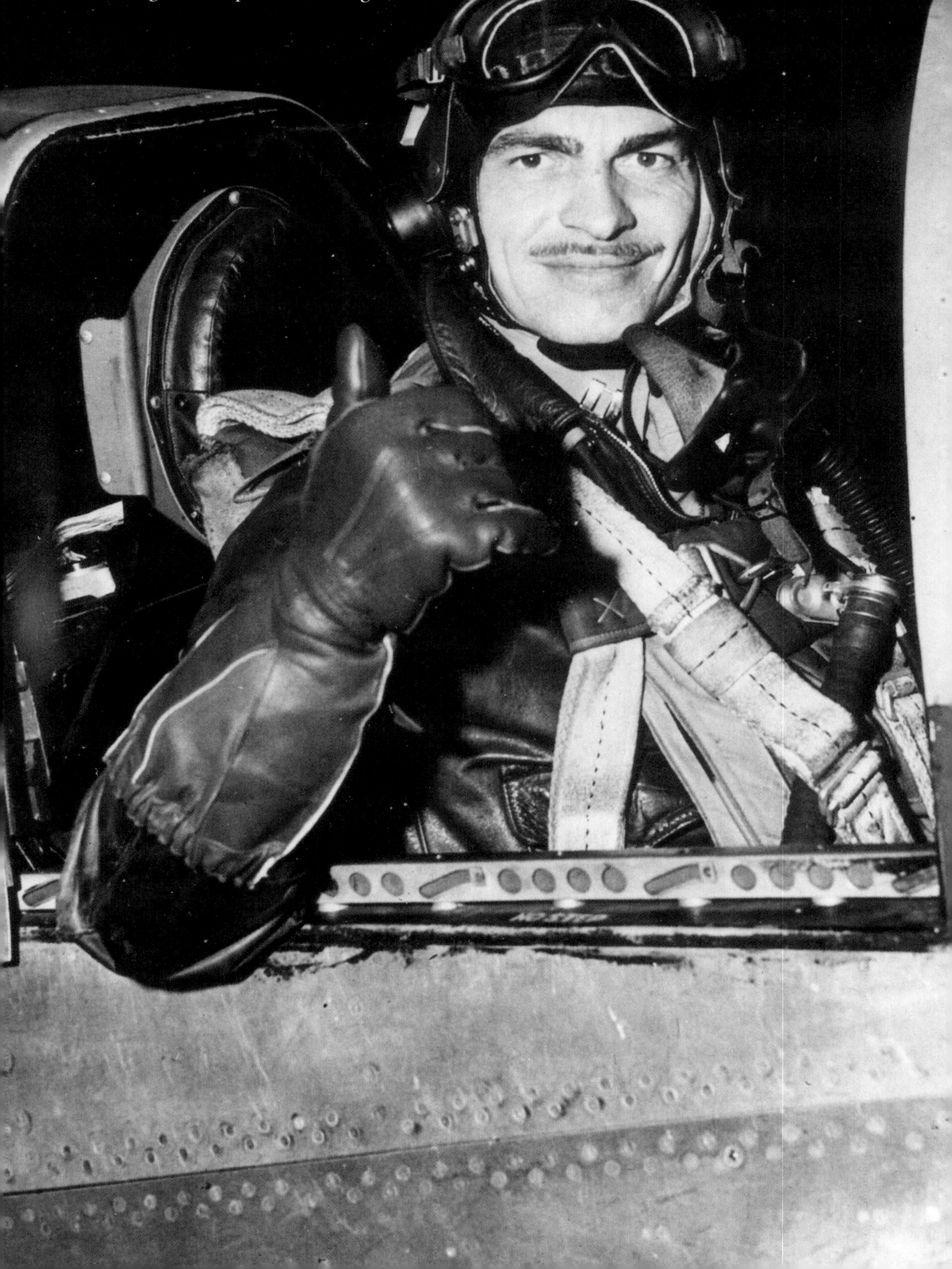

Major Howard 'Deacon' Hively of the Eighth U.S. Army Air Force 4th Fighter Group at Debden, England.

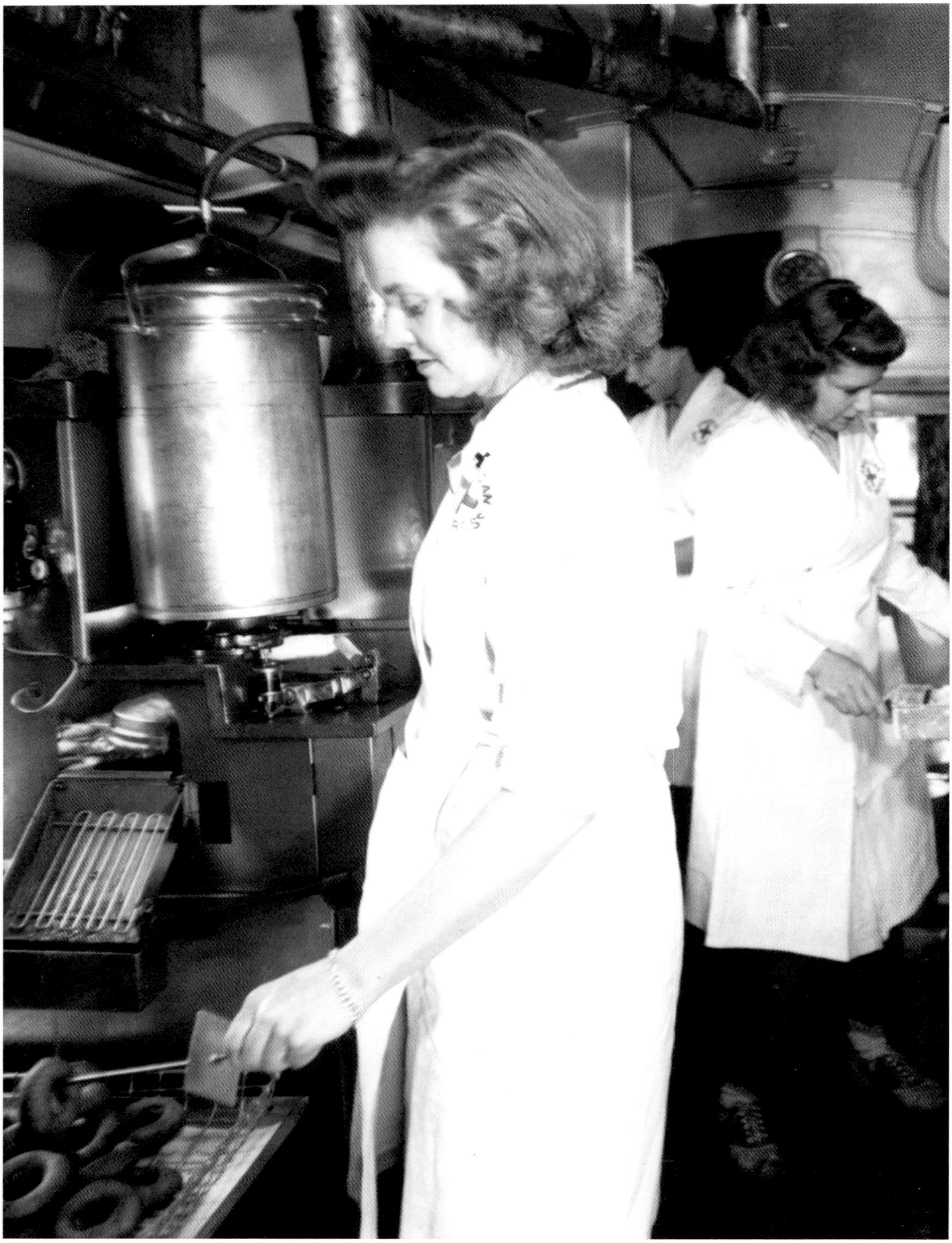

American Red Cross mobile van workers preparing coffee and doughnuts for personnel on an air base in World War Two England and bringing a little of the U.S.A. with them; right: A Zippo for the *Resolution*-class nuclear ballistic missile submarine (SSBN) *Repulse*, in Royal Navy service from 1968 to 1996.

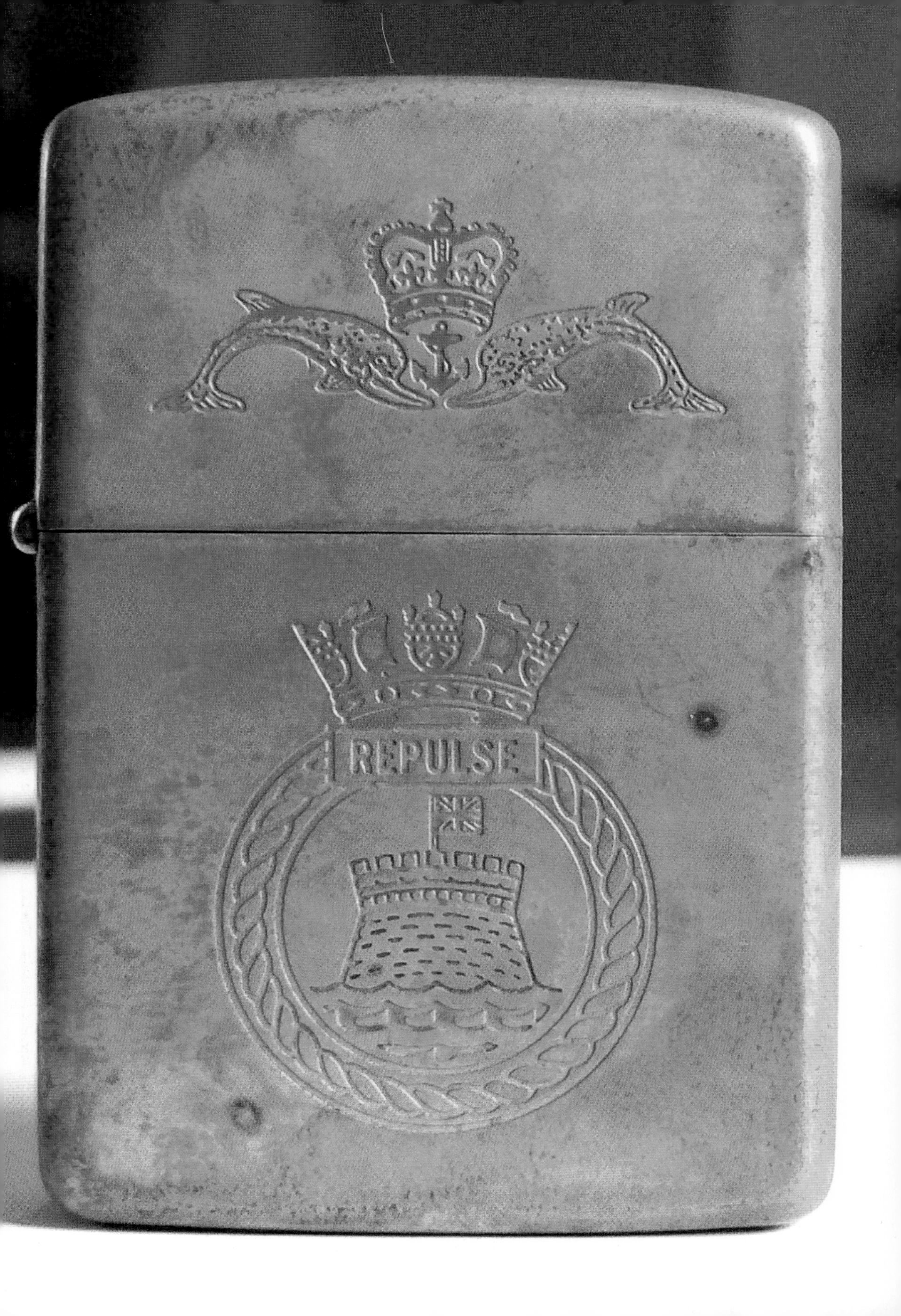
REPULSE

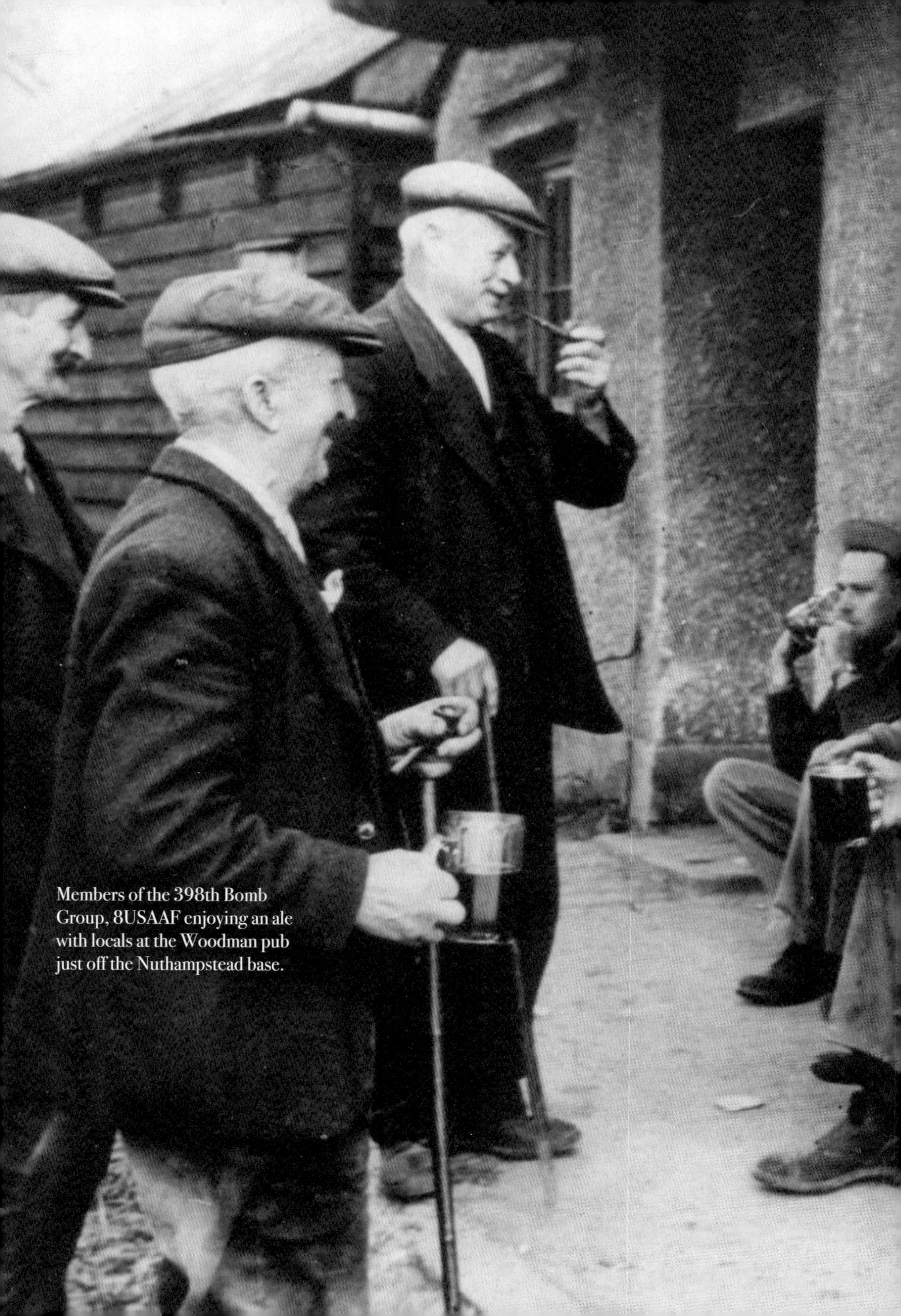

Members of the 398th Bomb Group, 8USAAF enjoying an ale with locals at the Woodman pub just off the Nuthampstead base.

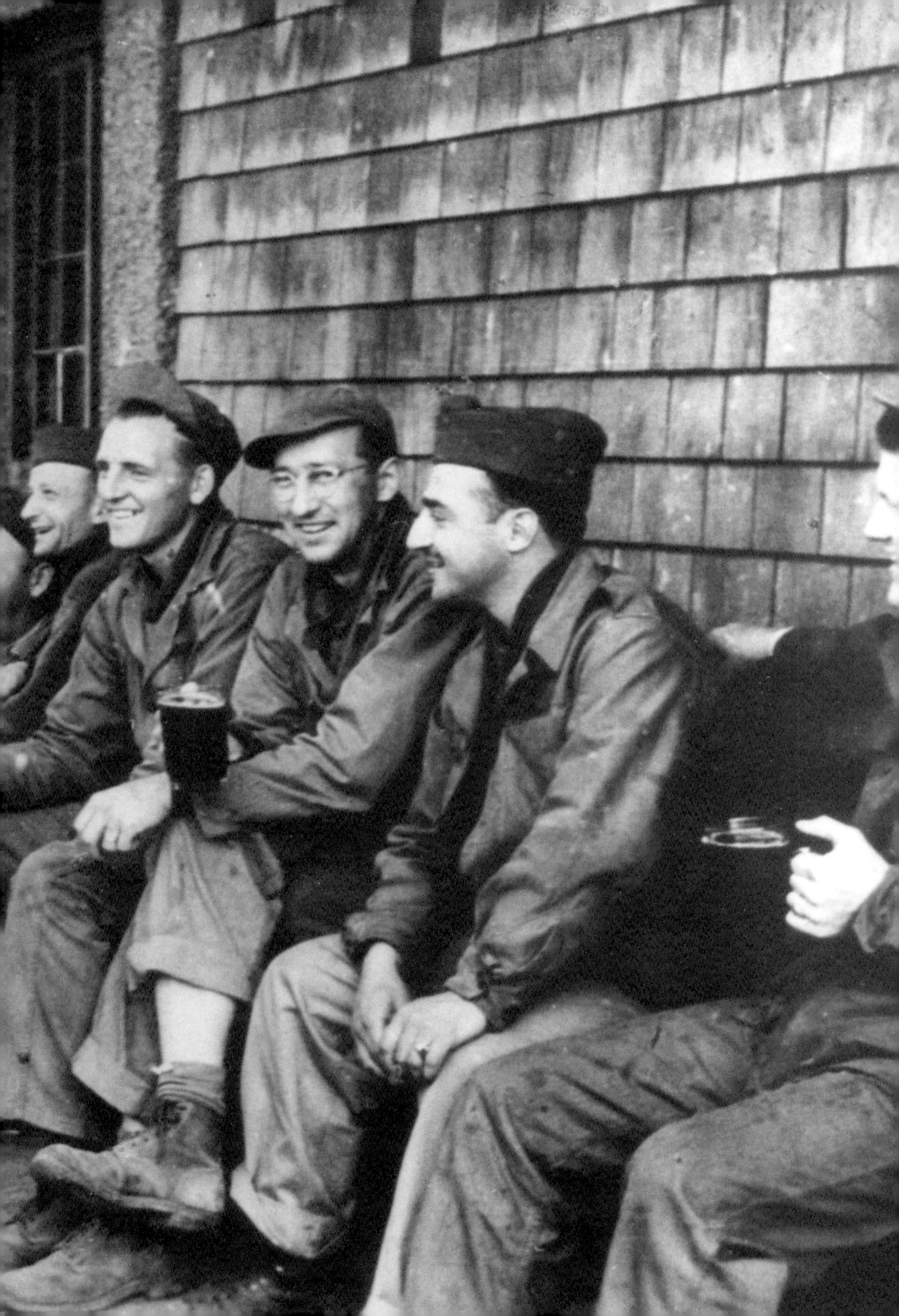

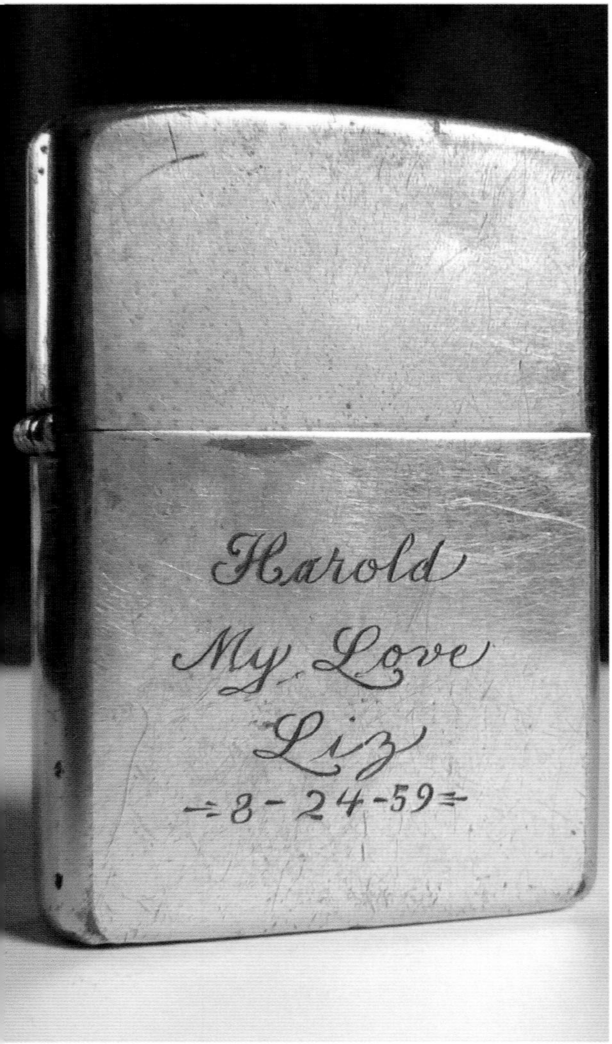
Harold
My Love
Liz
8-24-59

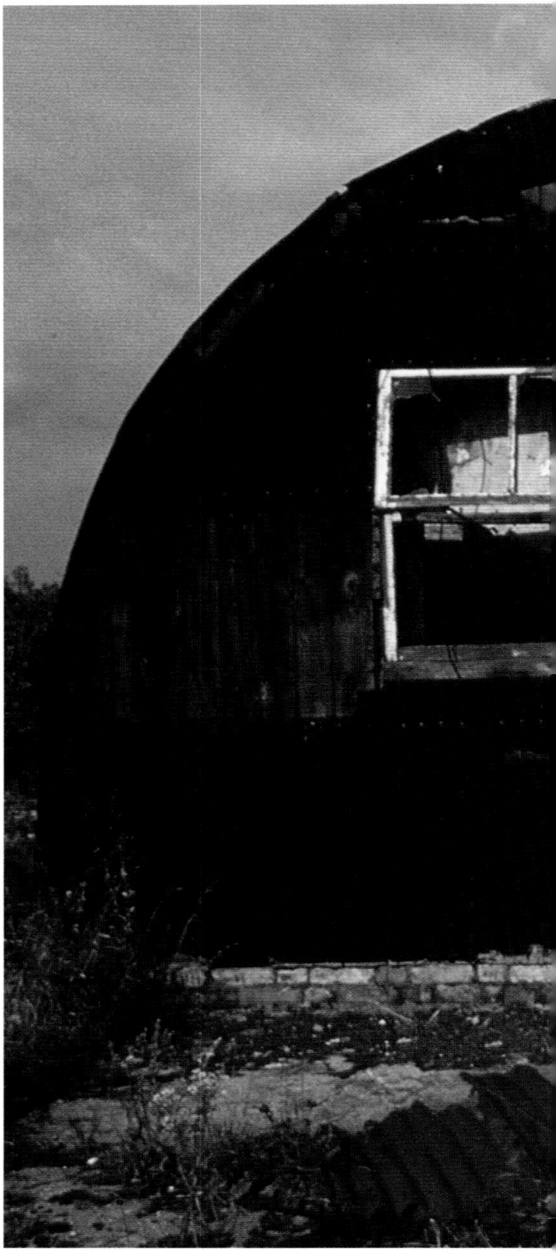

right: All that remains of a typical Nissen hut on an English air base of the Second World War; above: An engraved Zippo displays the feeling between two postwar sweethearts.

'She was just part of the gang. She drifted around with a lot of different guys, buddies with everyone. There wasn't any ending. We just went away on the train to the staging area.

'She was there at the finish, with somebody else most of the time. I waved to her when we went by, and she yelled she'd write to me, and I figured she was probably out of my life now and a good thing too.

'We staged at Grand Island. They turned us loose every night. I got a taste for sparkling burgundy. We had a couple of quarts between four of us and were pretty well through them our second night there, I think it was. I looked

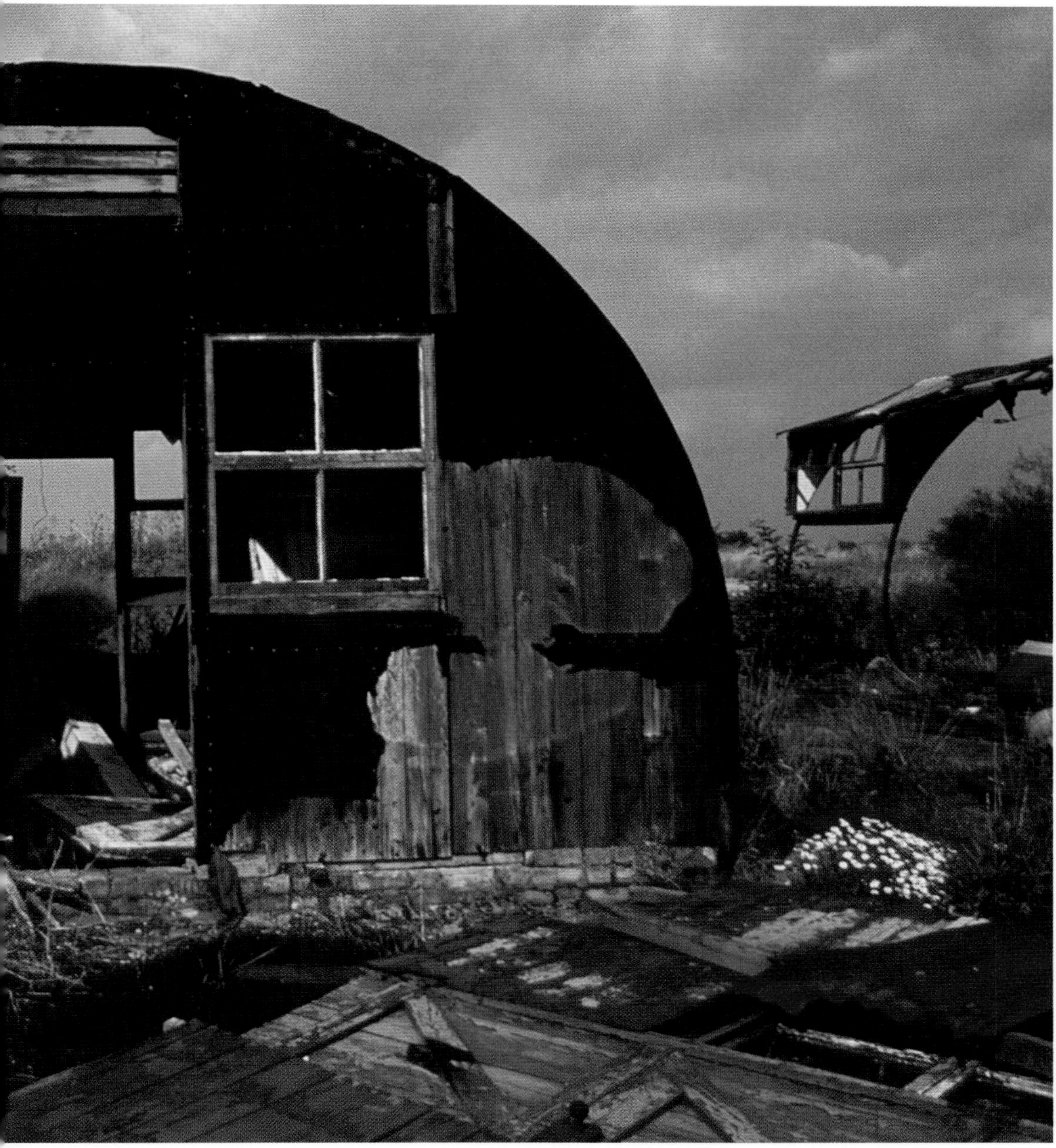

up and there walking across the floor was this August dame. I wasn't sure it was her. I didn't see how it could be. But she came over and it was. "Hello", she said. "How the hell did you get here?", I said. She had come with somebody's wife. So she was there. She was with another guy then, but we danced, and somewhere halfway around the floor she told me she came to see me. "Sure," I said. "Have another big one." "Okay", she said. "Don't believe me." 'I won't." And I didn't. She walked out on me a couple of times, but she always turned up again later.'

–from *Serenade To The Big Bird* by Bert Stiles

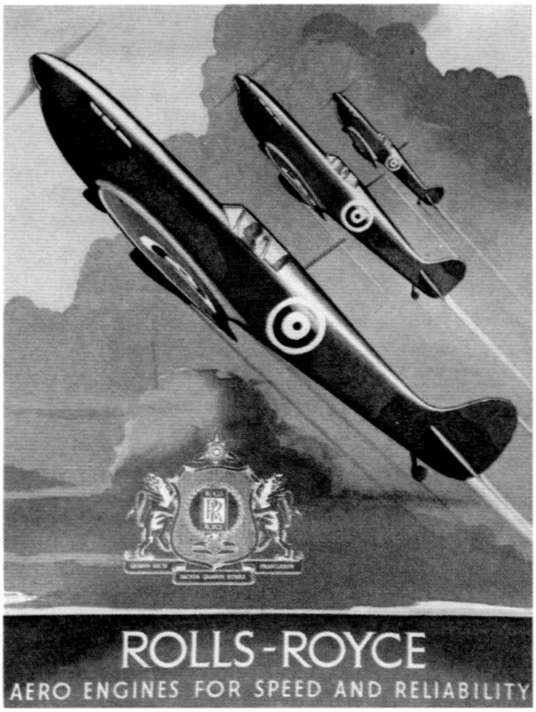
ROLLS-ROYCE
AERO ENGINES FOR SPEED AND RELIABILITY

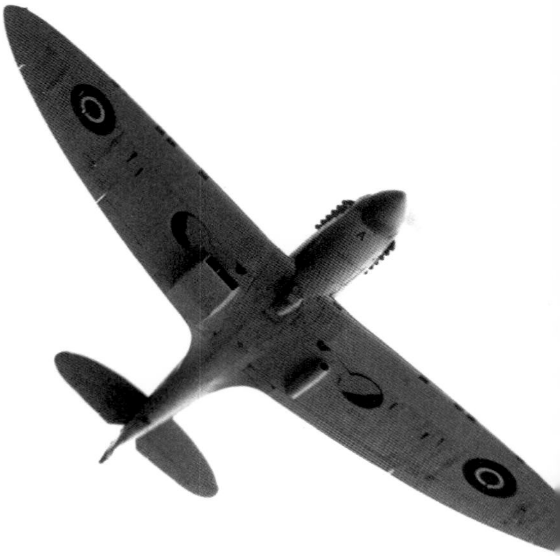

above and left: Supermarine Spitfire; below: Winslow 'Mike' Sobanski of the U.S. 4th Fighter Group; right: Eighth U.S. Army Air Force bomber aircrew men.

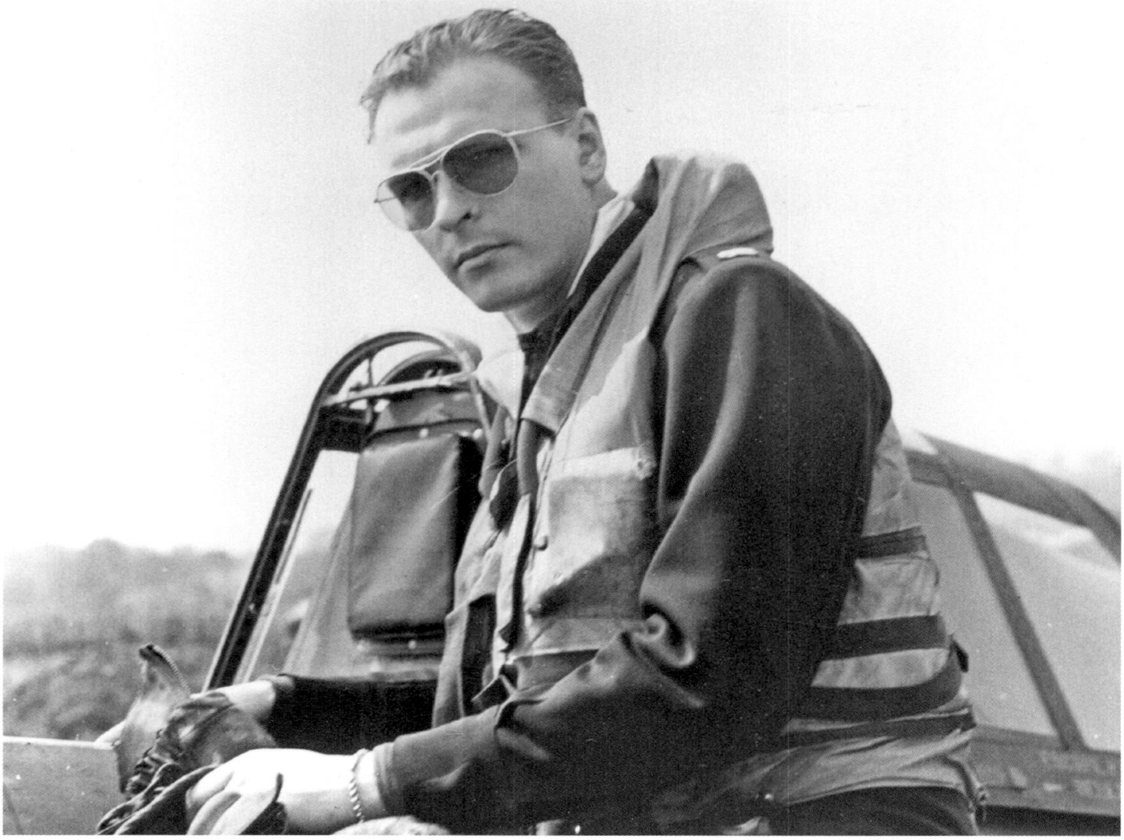

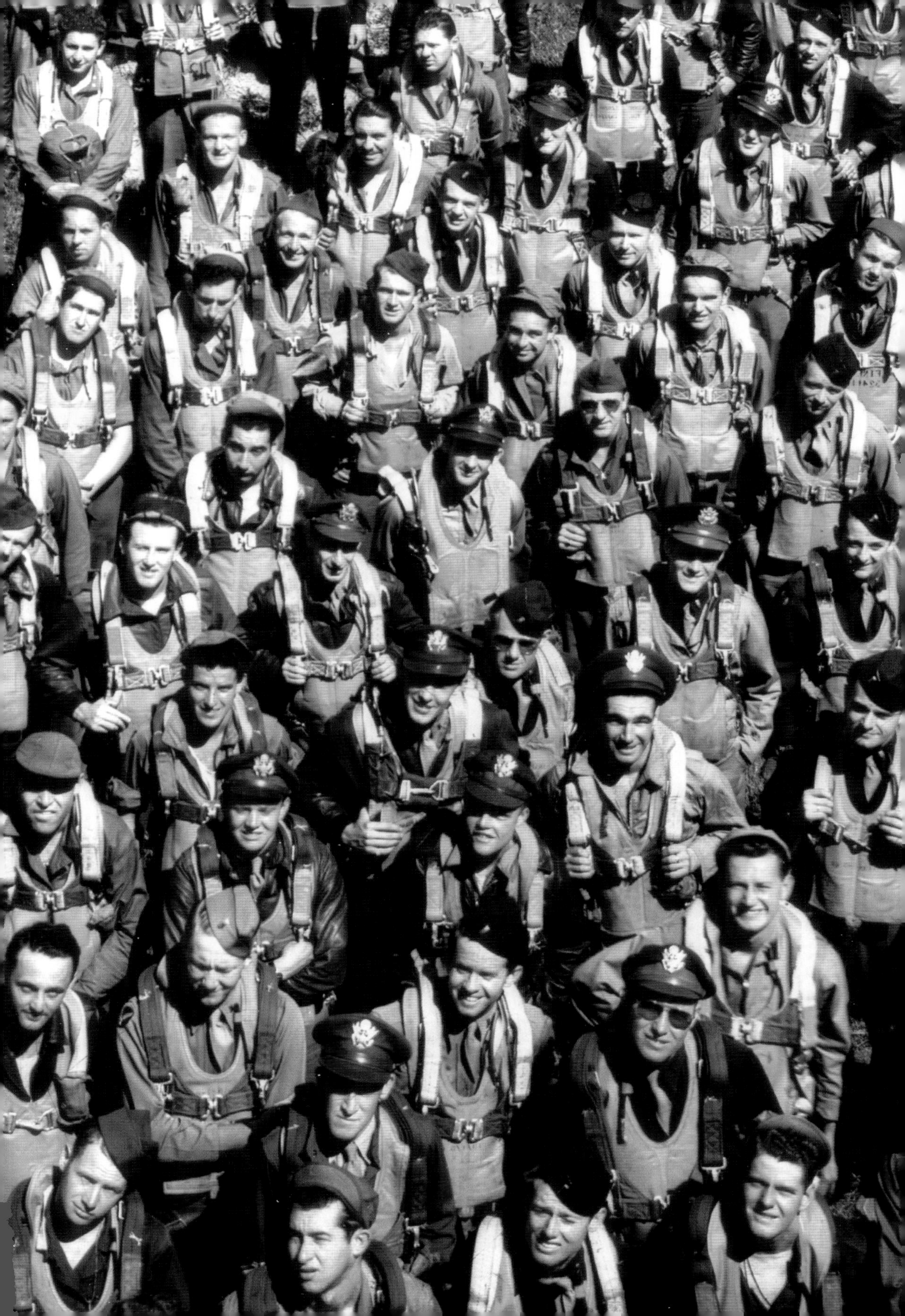

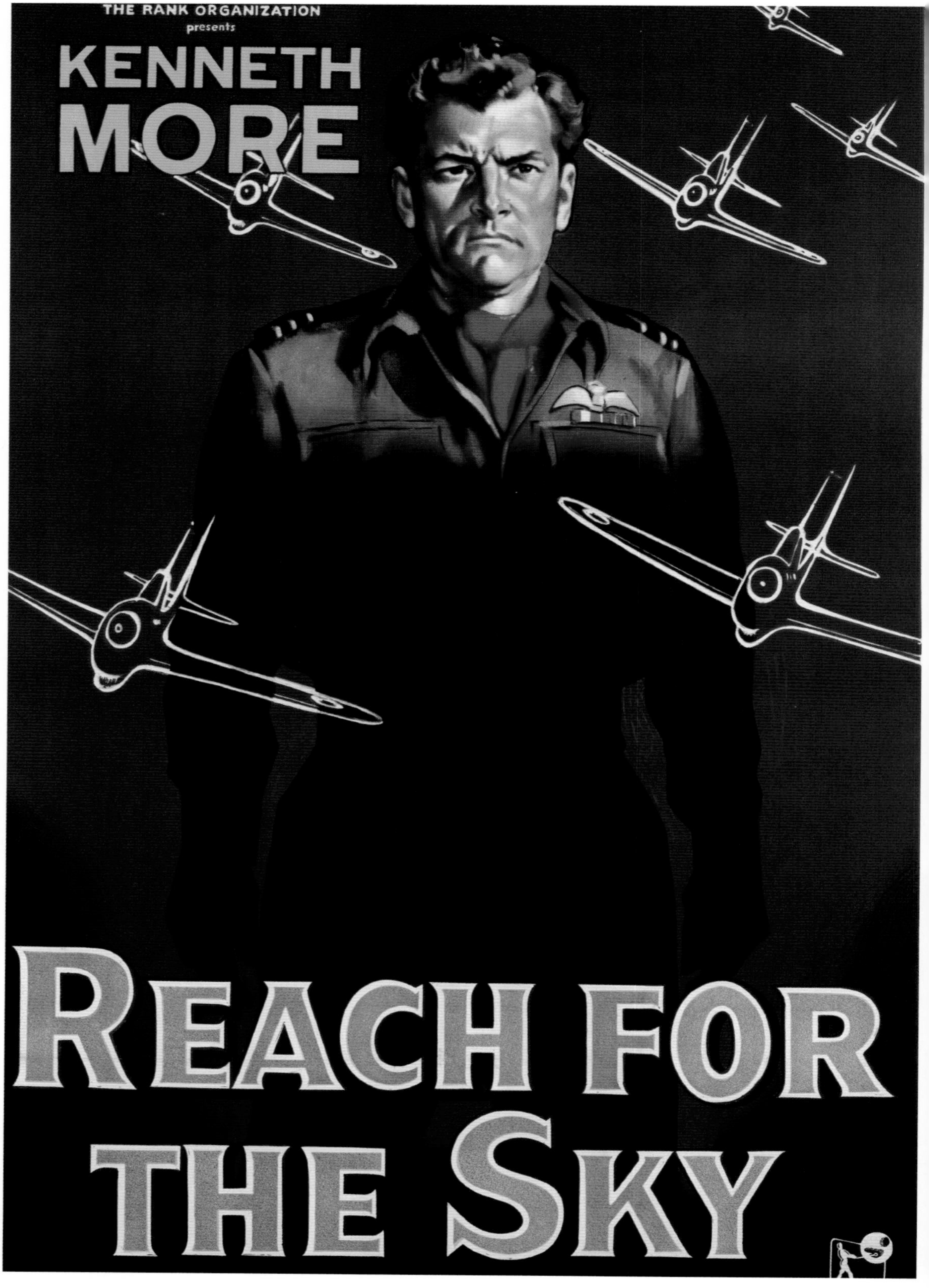
THE RANK ORGANIZATION
presents
KENNETH
MORE
REACH FOR
THE SKY

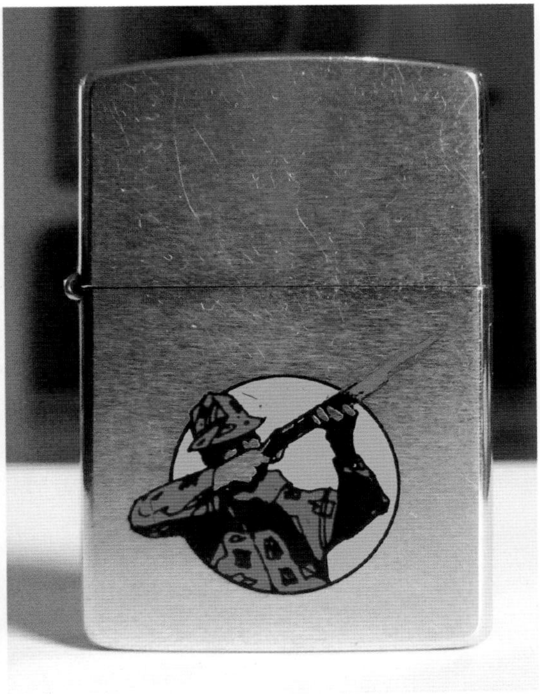

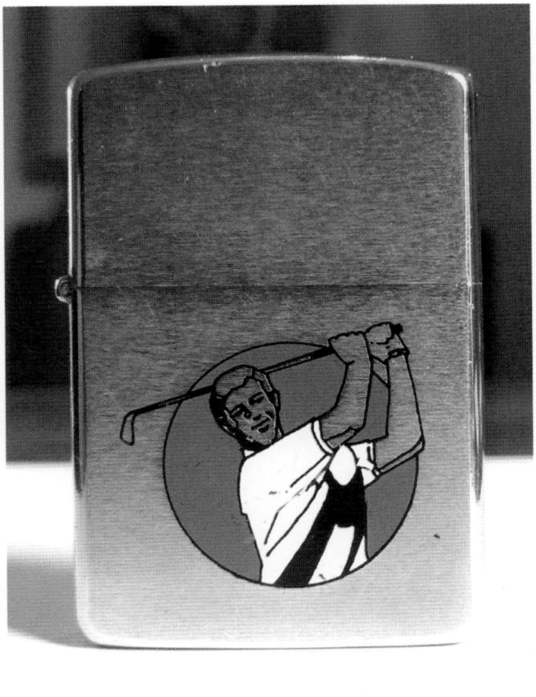

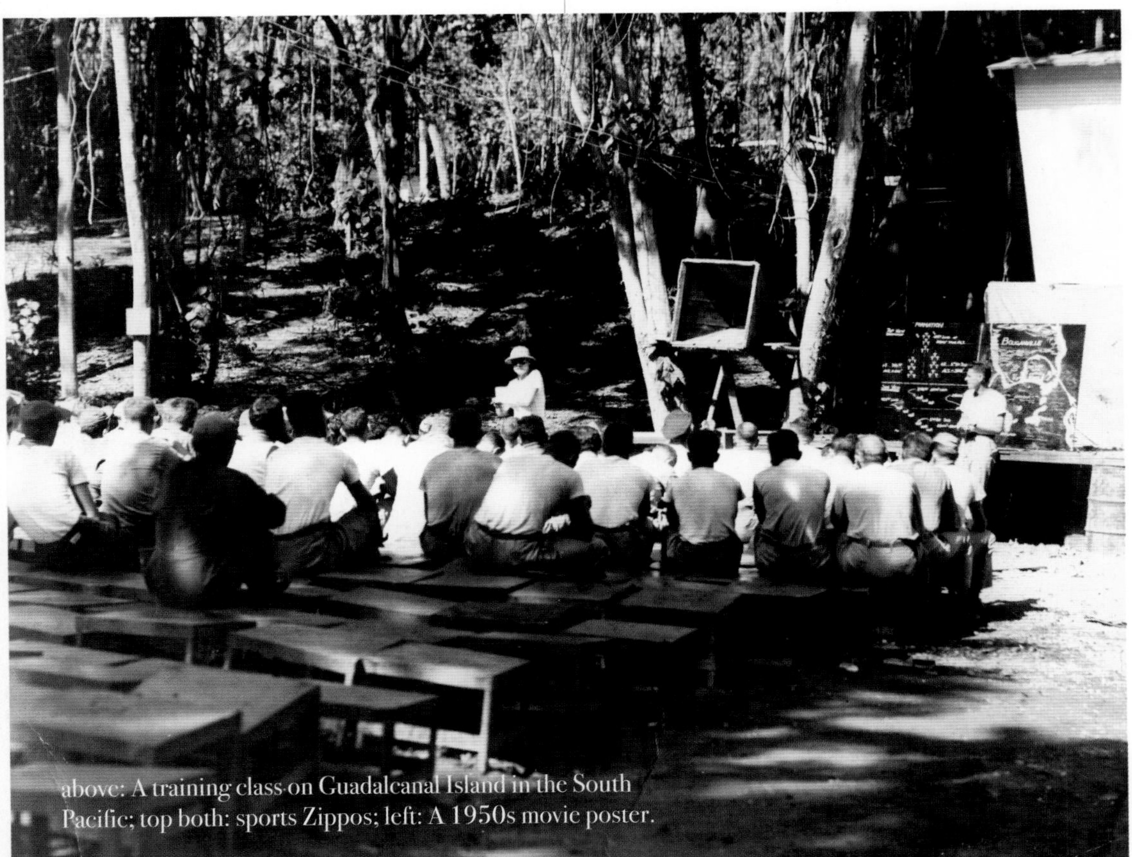

above: A training class on Guadalcanal Island in the South Pacific; top both: sports Zippos; left: A 1950s movie poster.

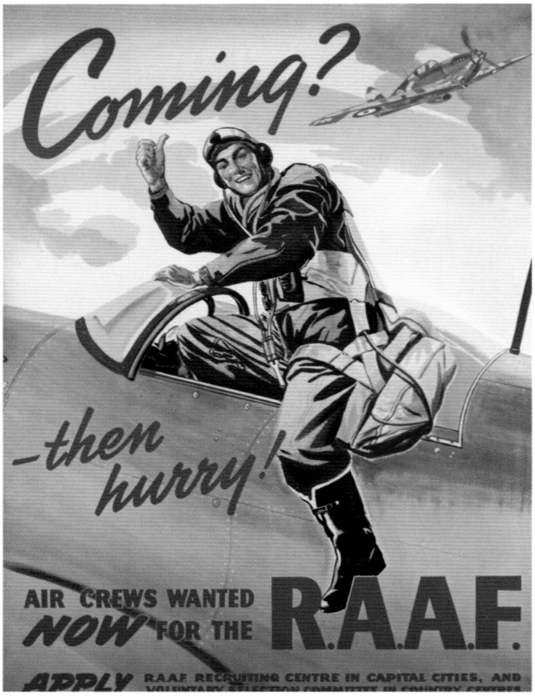
Coming?
—then hurry!
AIR CREWS WANTED
NOW FOR THE
R.A.A.F.
APPLY RAAF RECRUITING CENTRE IN CAPITAL CITIES, AND

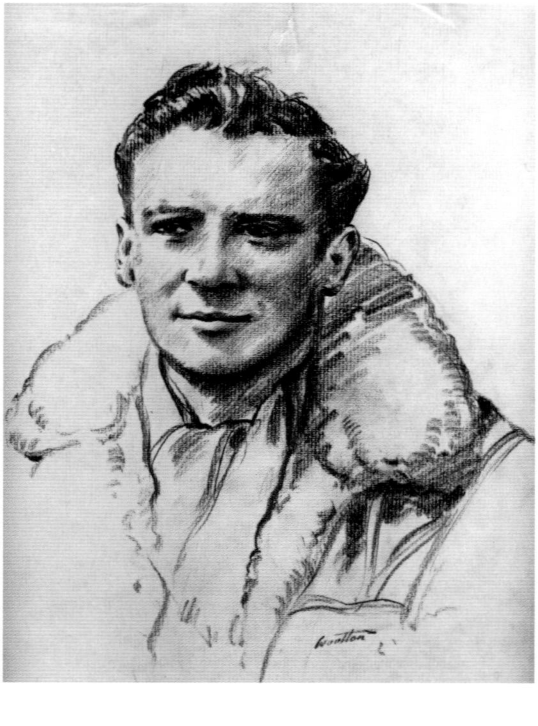

bottom left: Wing Commander Geoffrey Page of No 56 Squadron, RAF; right: The ten-man crew of the 91st Bomb Group B-17 bomber *Memphis Belle*, famous for being among the first B-17s to complete a 25-mission tour of duty. The *Belle* was based at Bassingbourn, England in WW2.

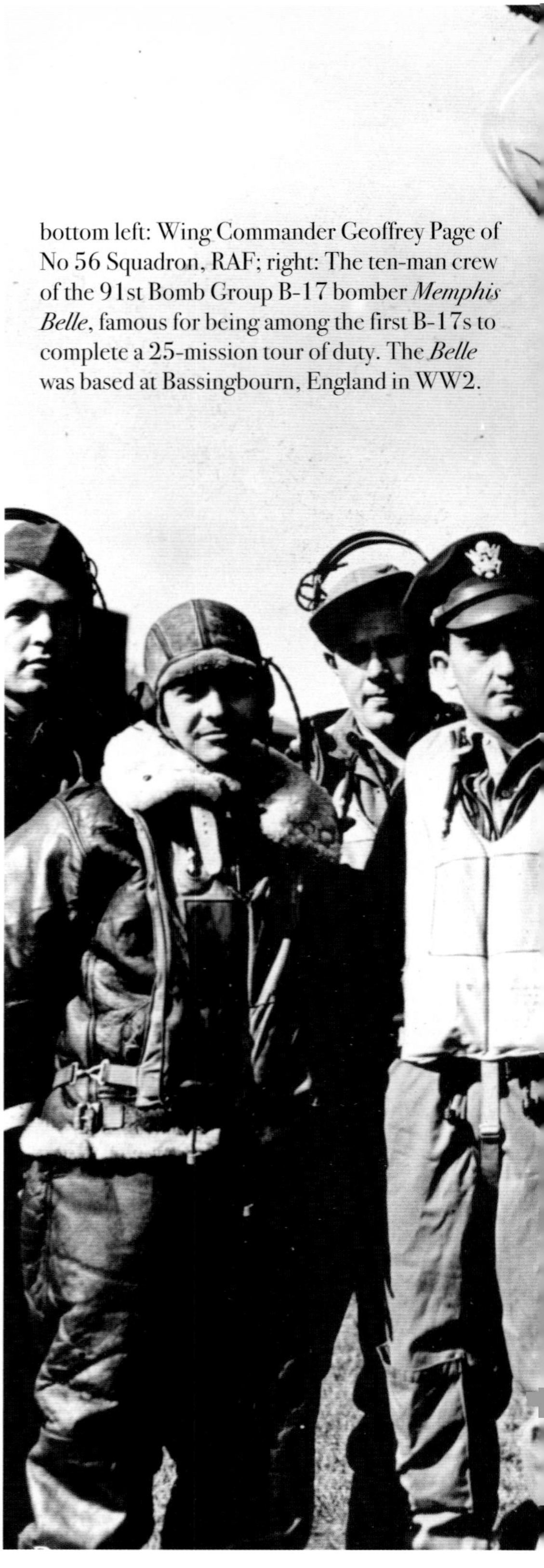

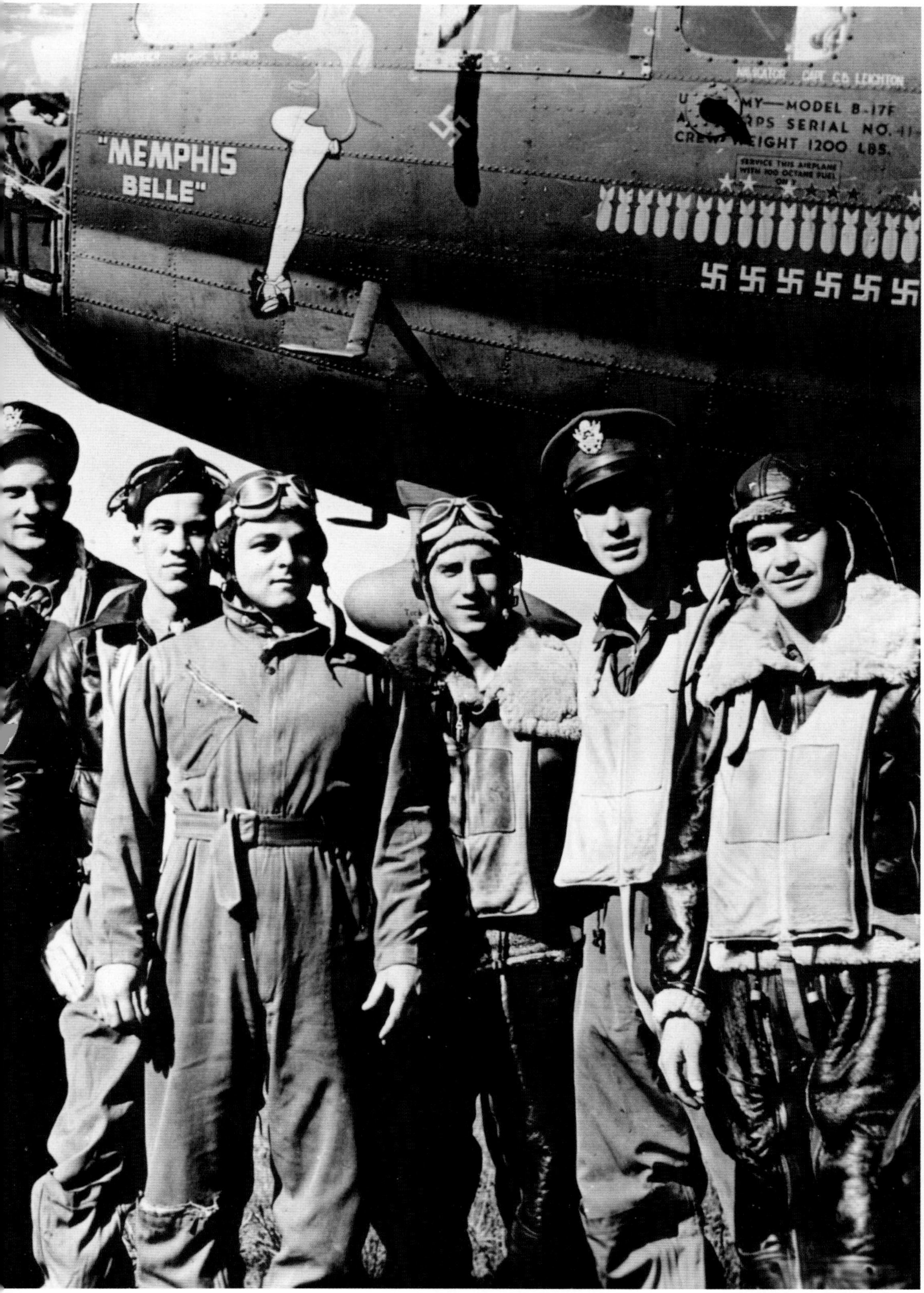
"MEMPHIS
BELLE"
MODEL B-17F
SERIAL NO.
1200 LBS.

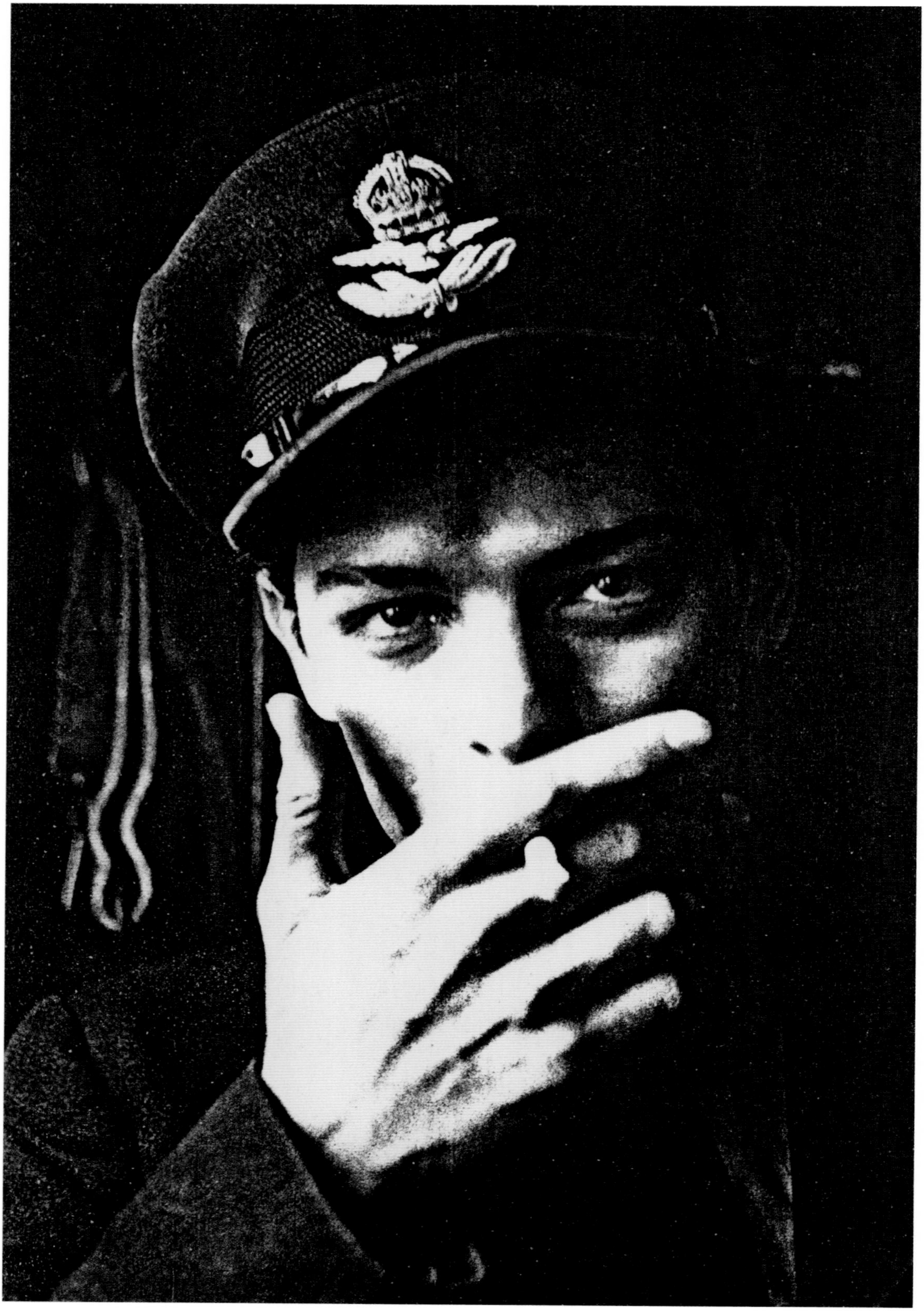

left: An RAF flyer; below: The *Wolf Wagon*, a bus that brought local girls to a U.S. Army Air Force base in England for wartime dances; bottom: U.S. Navy Zippos.

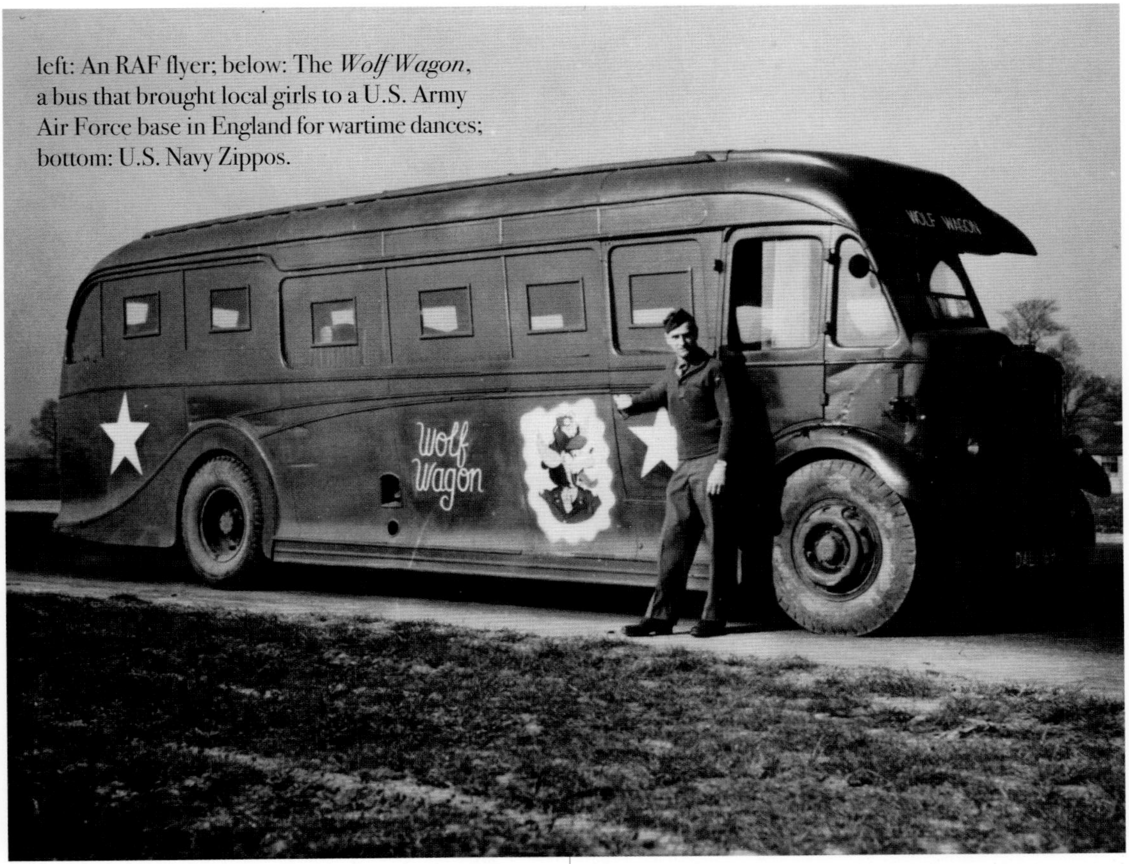
WOLF WAGON
Wolf Wagon

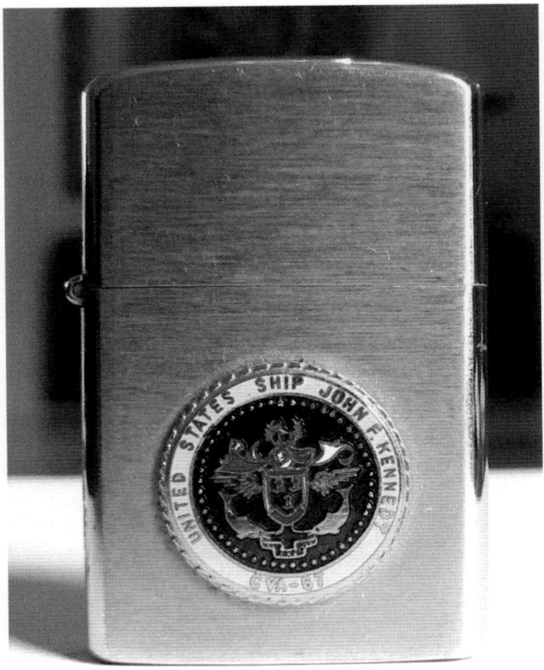
UNITED STATES SHIP JOHN F KENNEDY
CVA-67

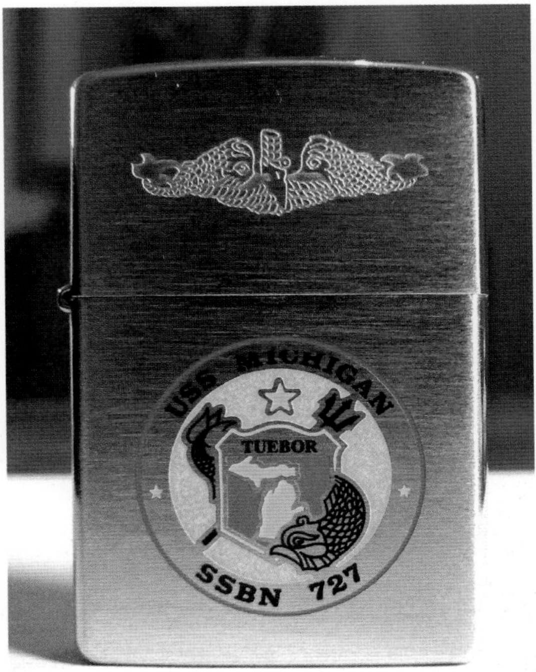
USS MICHIGAN
TUEBOR
SSBN 727

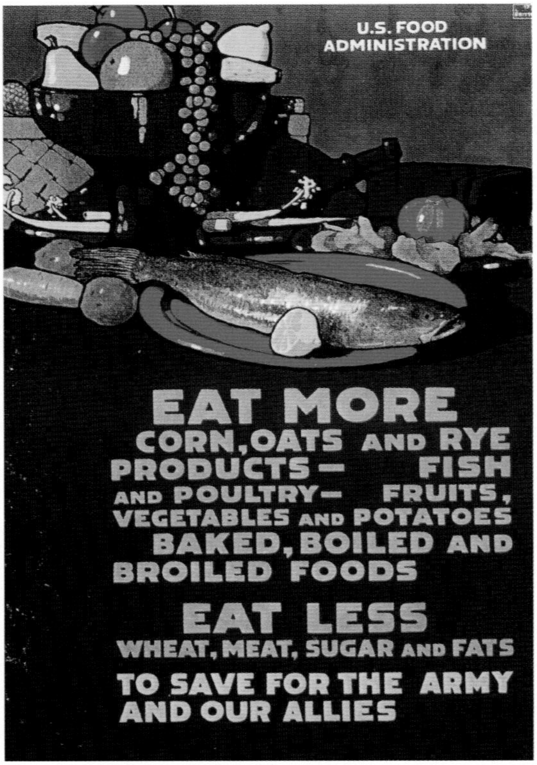
U.S. FOOD ADMINISTRATION
EAT MORE
CORN, OATS AND RYE PRODUCTS— FISH AND POULTRY— FRUITS, VEGETABLES AND POTATOES BAKED, BOILED AND BROILED FOODS
EAT LESS
WHEAT, MEAT, SUGAR AND FATS
TO SAVE FOR THE ARMY AND OUR ALLIES

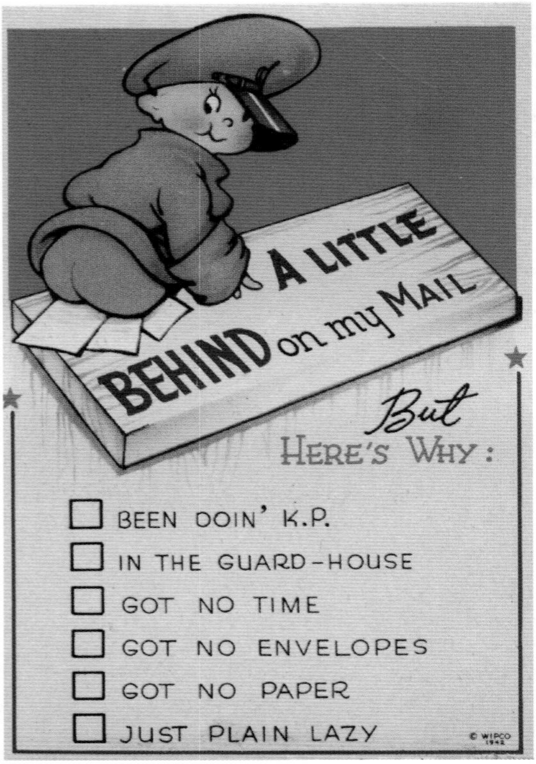
A LITTLE BEHIND on my MAIL
But
HERE'S WHY:
BEEN DOIN' K.P.
IN THE GUARD-HOUSE
GOT NO TIME
GOT NO ENVELOPES
GOT NO PAPER
JUST PLAIN LAZY
© WIPCO 1942

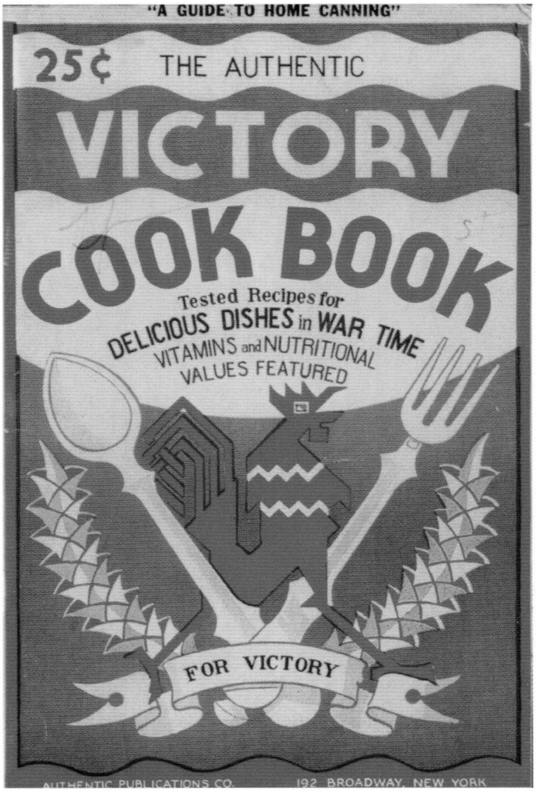
"A GUIDE TO HOME CANNING"
25¢ THE AUTHENTIC
VICTORY
COOK BOOK
Tested Recipes for
DELICIOUS DISHES in WAR TIME
VITAMINS and NUTRITIONAL VALUES FEATURED
FOR VICTORY
AUTHENTIC PUBLICATIONS CO. 192 BROADWAY, NEW YORK

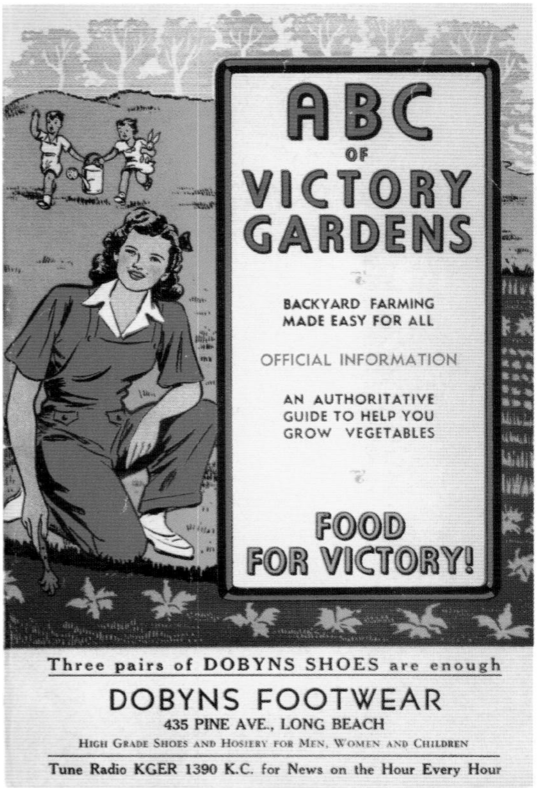
ABC OF VICTORY GARDENS
BACKYARD FARMING MADE EASY FOR ALL
OFFICIAL INFORMATION
AN AUTHORITATIVE GUIDE TO HELP YOU GROW VEGETABLES
FOOD FOR VICTORY!
Three pairs of DOBYNS SHOES are enough
DOBYNS FOOTWEAR
435 PINE AVE., LONG BEACH
HIGH GRADE SHOES AND HOSIERY FOR MEN, WOMEN AND CHILDREN
Tune Radio KGER 1390 K.C. for News on the Hour Every Hour

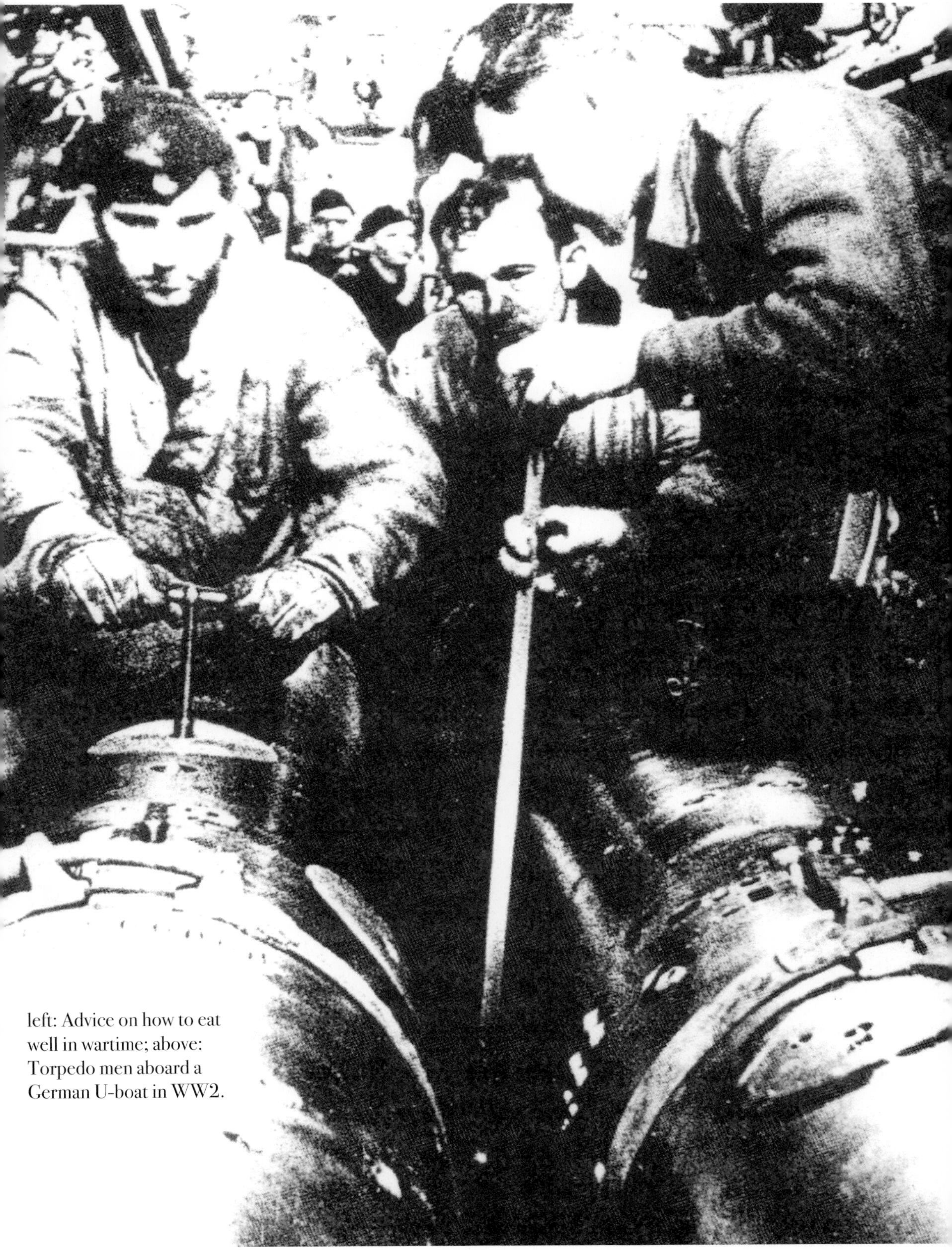

left: Advice on how to eat well in wartime; above: Torpedo men aboard a German U-boat in WW2.

Lt Allen Bunte, lean and mean-looking with the moustache of an Old West outlaw, was chasing five Me109s down towards the ground and began firing at them when 1,000 yards from the nearest one. He advanced to within 200 yards and his bullets found their mark. Just before Bunte lost sight of the enemy aircraft, it spun out and apparently crashed. Within minutes and while still flying low, the American came upon a small German training plane breezing slowly over the deeply wooded countryside. Determined not to allow the student to graduate, he fired on the light aircraft . . . and missed. Closing too rapidly on his intended victim, Bunte hopped over the German at the last second and turned back to see the trainer settling into the canopy of trees it had been skimming; below right: A U.S. Navy Zippo; right: A wartime Guinness ad.

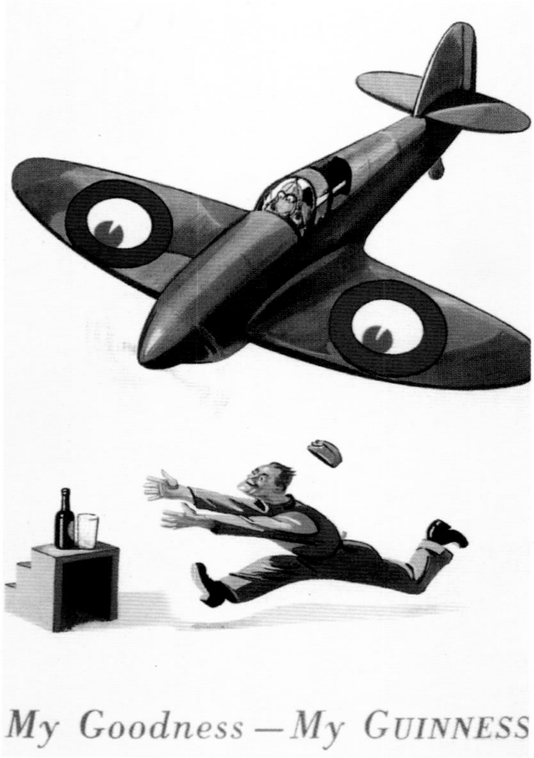
My Goodness—My GUINNESS

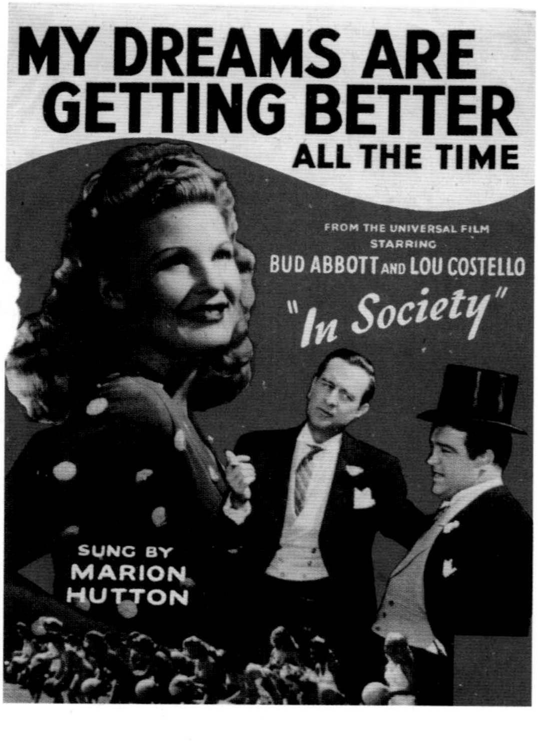
MY DREAMS ARE
GETTING BETTER
ALL THE TIME
FROM THE UNIVERSAL FILM
STARRING
BUD ABBOTT AND LOU COSTELLO
"In Society"
SUNG BY
MARION
HUTTON

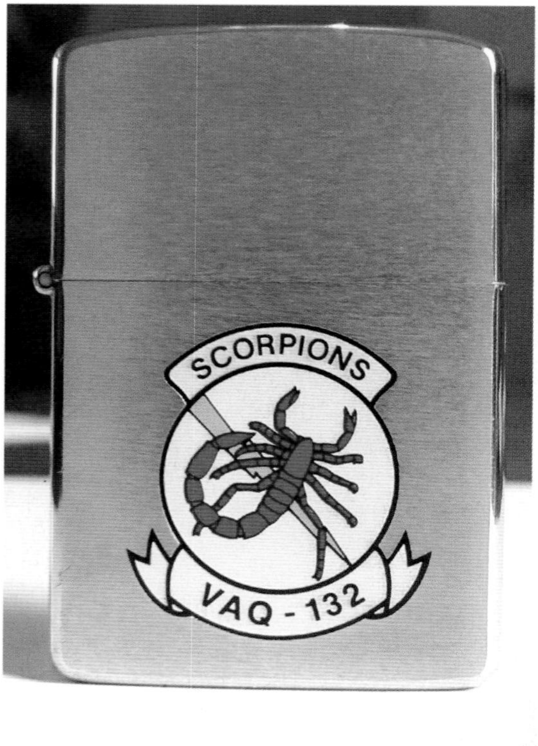
SCORPIONS
VAQ - 132

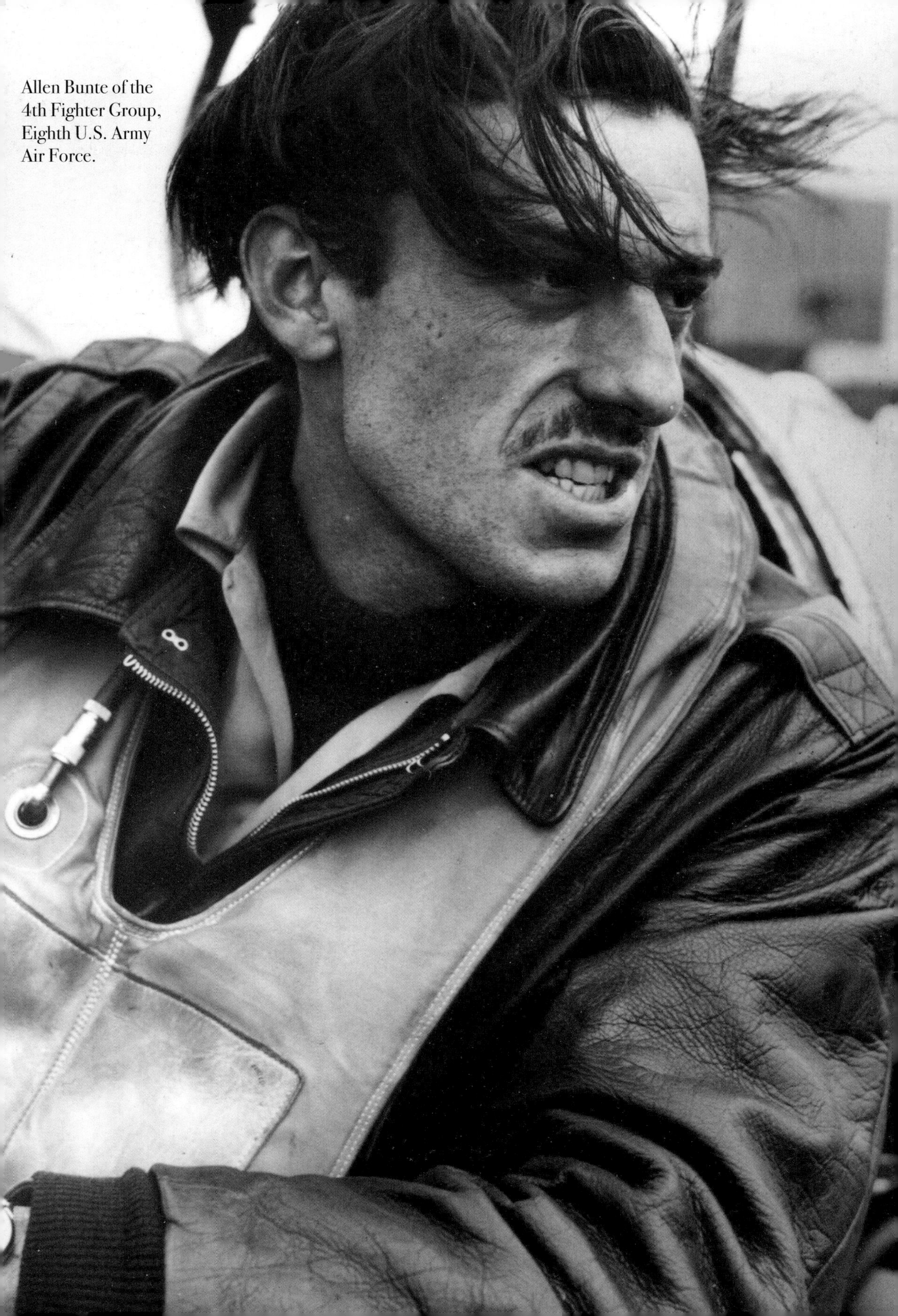

Allen Bunte of the
4th Fighter Group,
Eighth U.S. Army
Air Force.

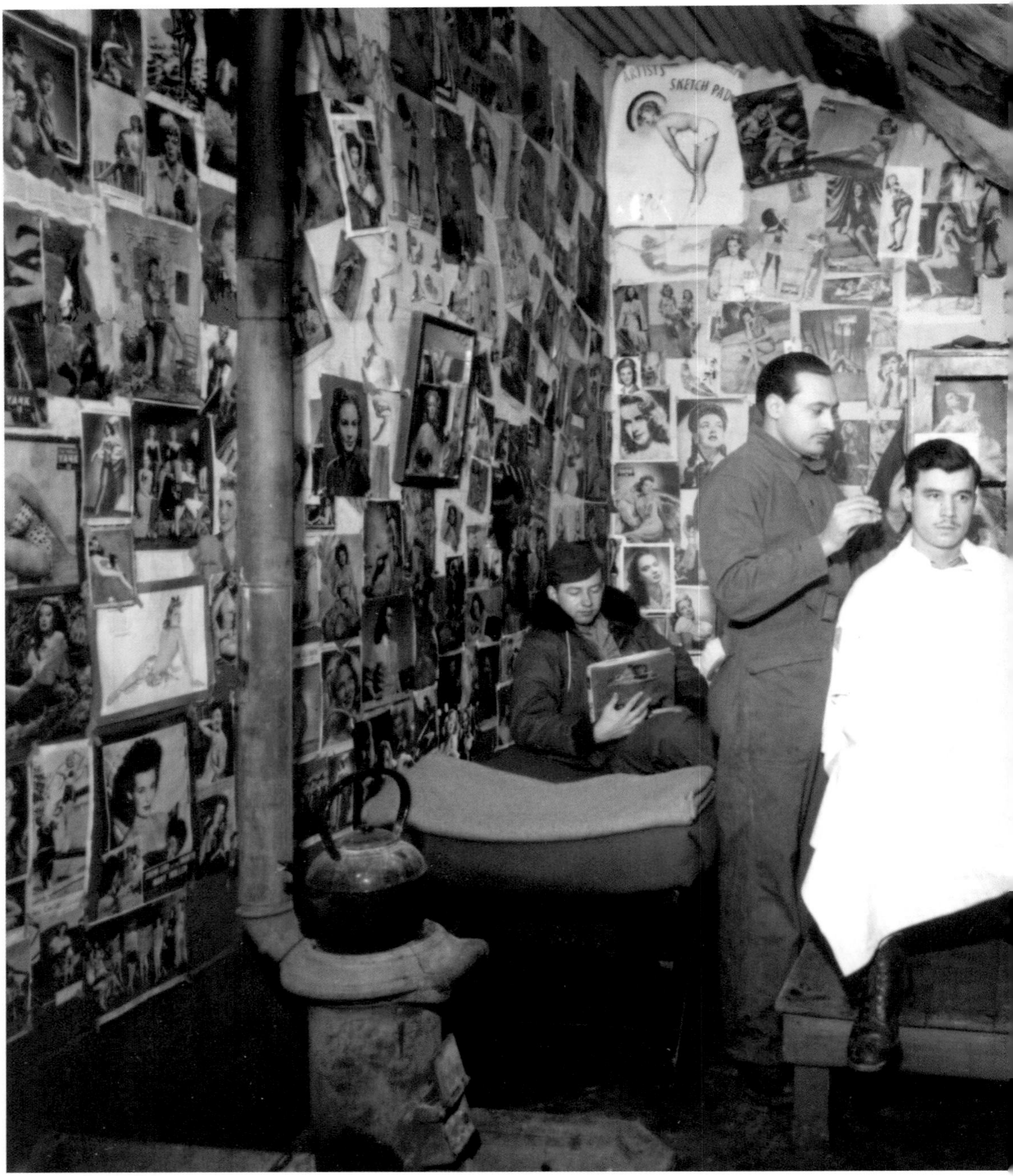
SKETCH PAD

above: A barber shop on an Eighth Air Force base in England; right: U.S. Navy lighter; above right: From a Zippo sports series.

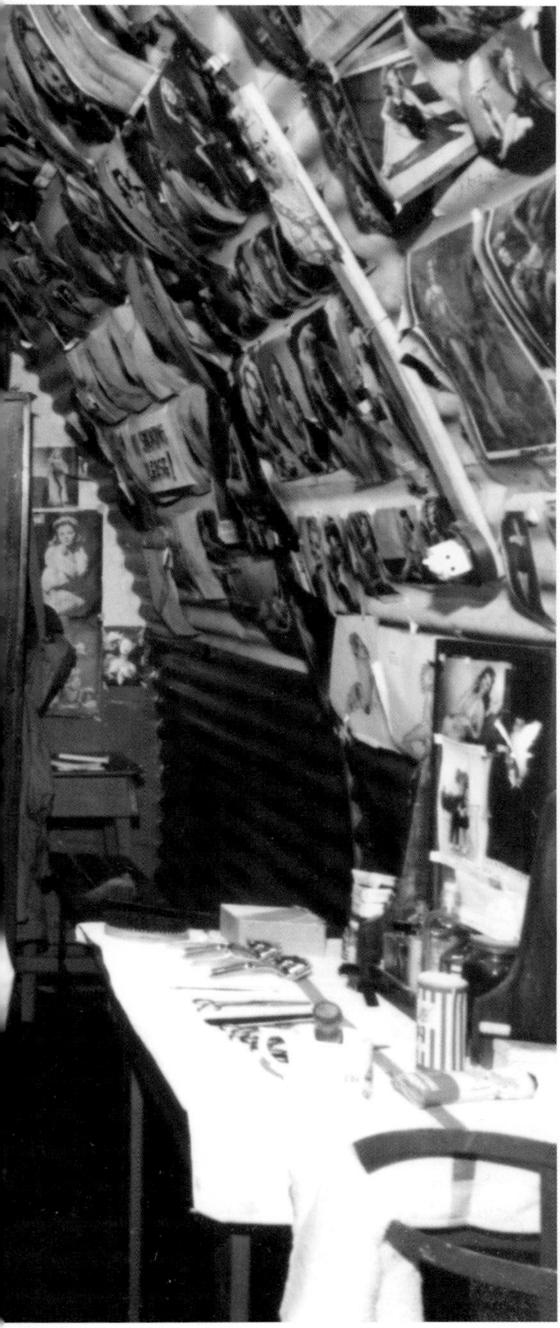

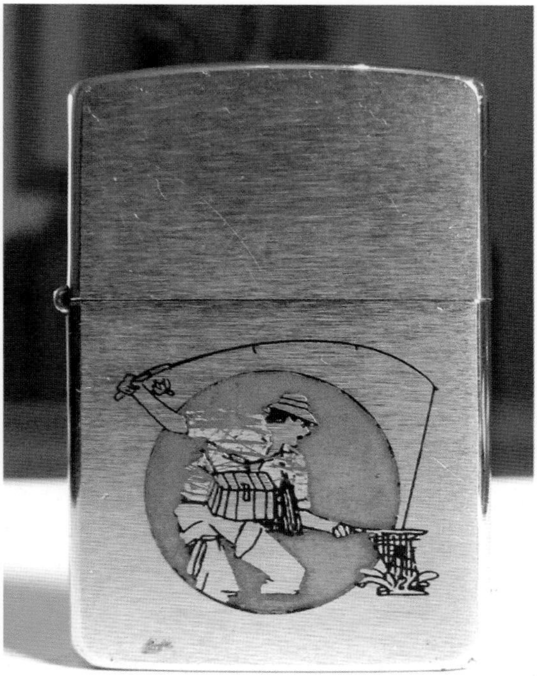

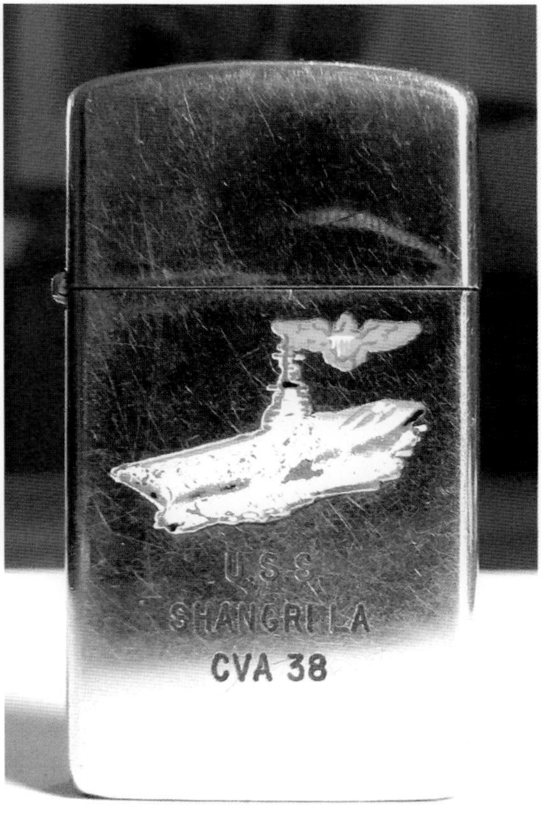
U.S.S.
SHANGRILA
CVA 38

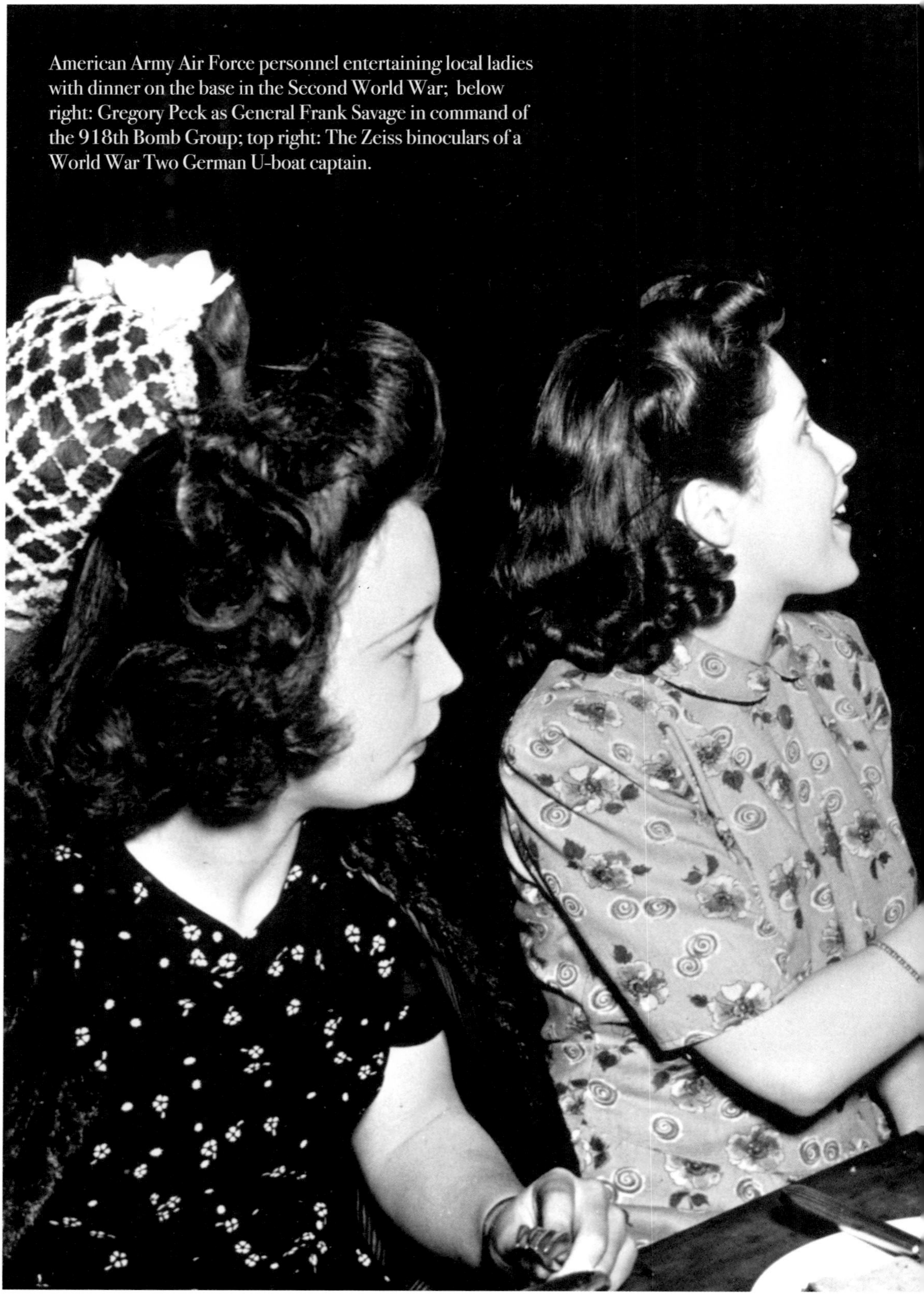

American Army Air Force personnel entertaining local ladies with dinner on the base in the Second World War; below right: Gregory Peck as General Frank Savage in command of the 918th Bomb Group; top right: The Zeiss binoculars of a World War Two German U-boat captain.

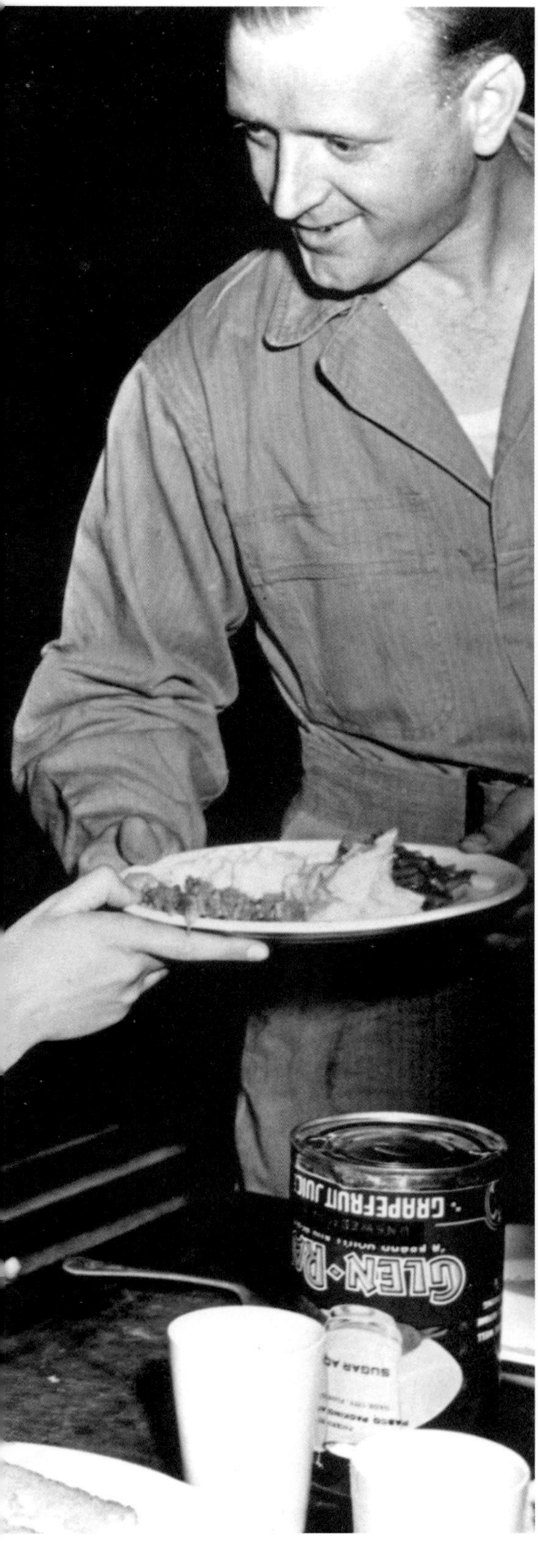

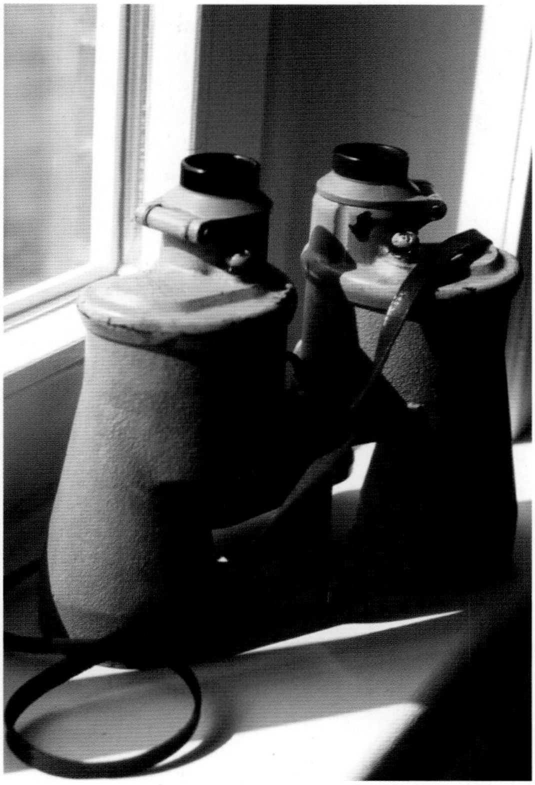

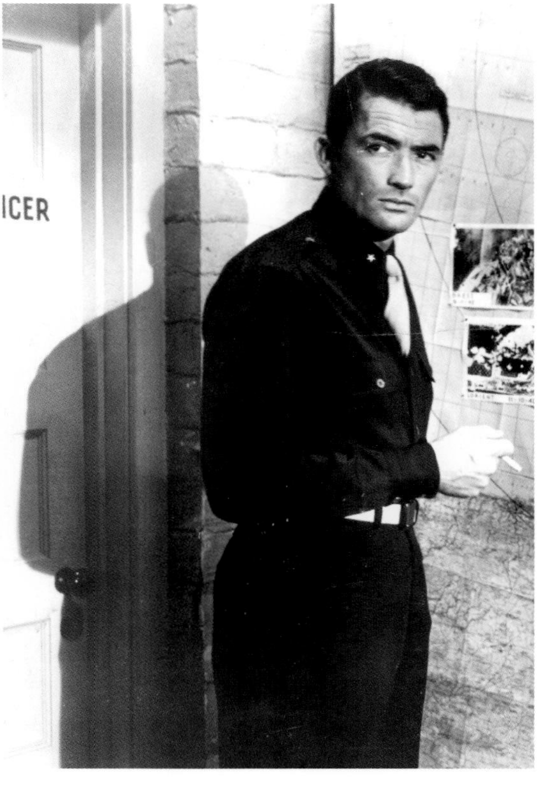

below: A pair of Second World War-vintage flying goggles; bottom left: The painted A2 flying jacket of a crew member of *Heavenly Body*, an 8USAAF heavy-bomber; bottom right: A Zippo commemorating the aircraft carrier USS *Constellation*.

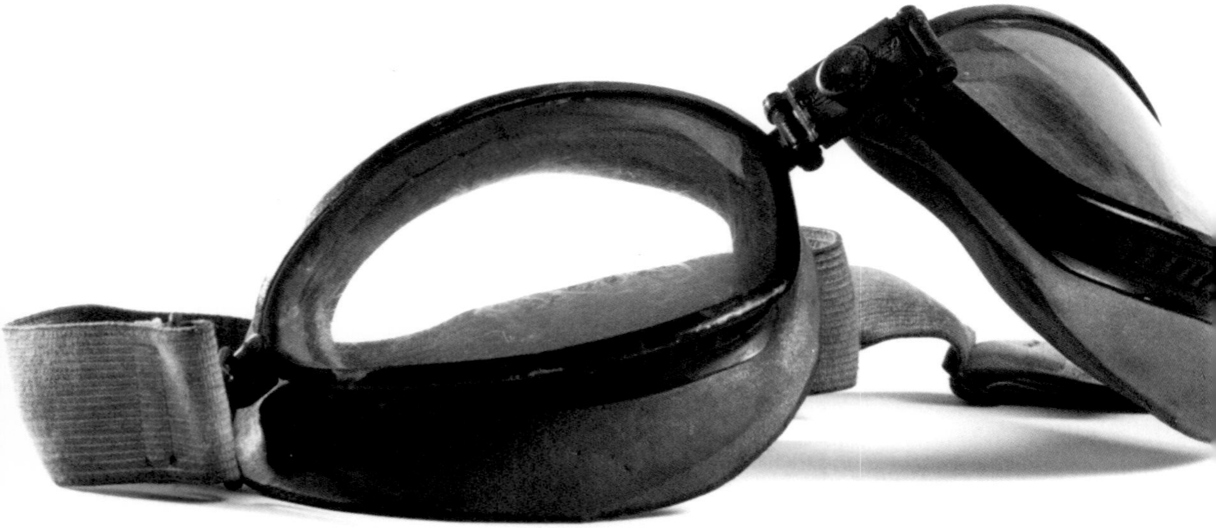

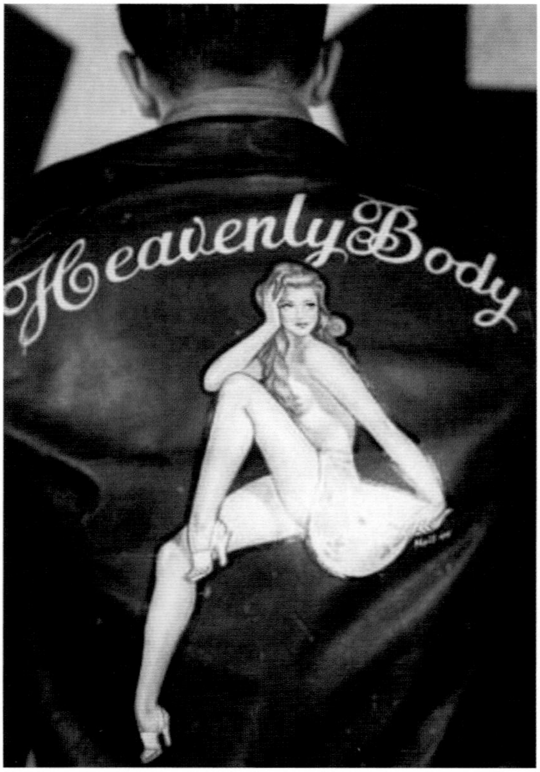
Heavenly Body

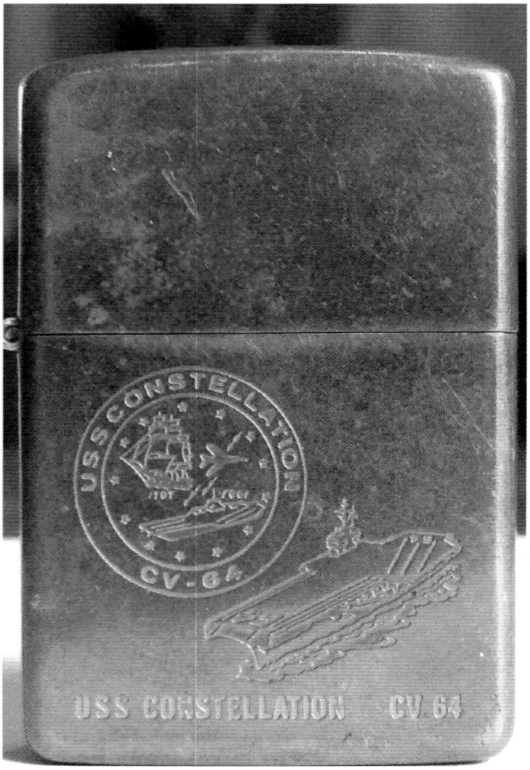
USS CONSTELLATION
CV-64
USS CONSTELLATION CV 64

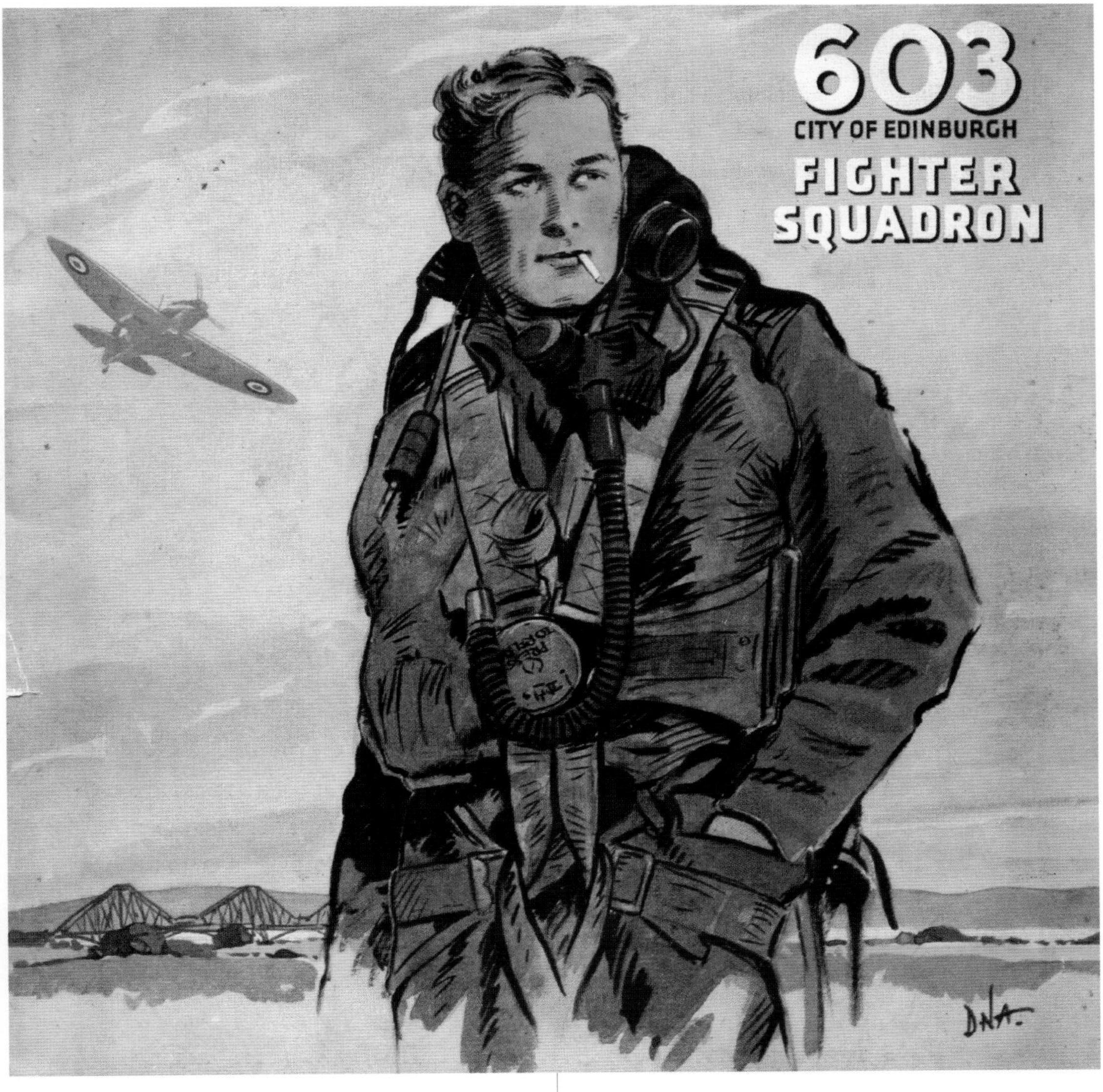
603
CITY OF EDINBURGH
FIGHTER
SQUADRON
DNA.

left: The USS *Constellation* aircraft carrier, a *Kitty Hawk*-class vessel, was commissioned in October 1961. During her operational life, the Connie took part in a range of assignments that included the Gulf of Tonkin off the coast of Vietnam in August 1964, as well as further operations off Vietnam in 1966 and 1967 and into the 1970s until the end of the Vietnam War.

Formed on 14 October 1925 No 603 'City of Edinburgh' RAF Squadron, flew Gladiator fighters until August 1939 when they transitioned into the Spitfire. Early in the Second World War, bombers of the German Air Force began targetting the Royal Navy Home Fleet then anchored in Scapa Flow, and 603 Squadron's Spitfire pilots, were assigned to intercept the enemy raiders. Following this action the squadron was moved south in August 1940 to RAF Hornchurch, Essex, and attached to No. 11 Group for the remainder of the Battle of Britain. Pilot Officer Richard Hillary was shot down on 3 September, badly burnt and hospitalized for three years during which he wrote the famous book *The Last Enemy*.

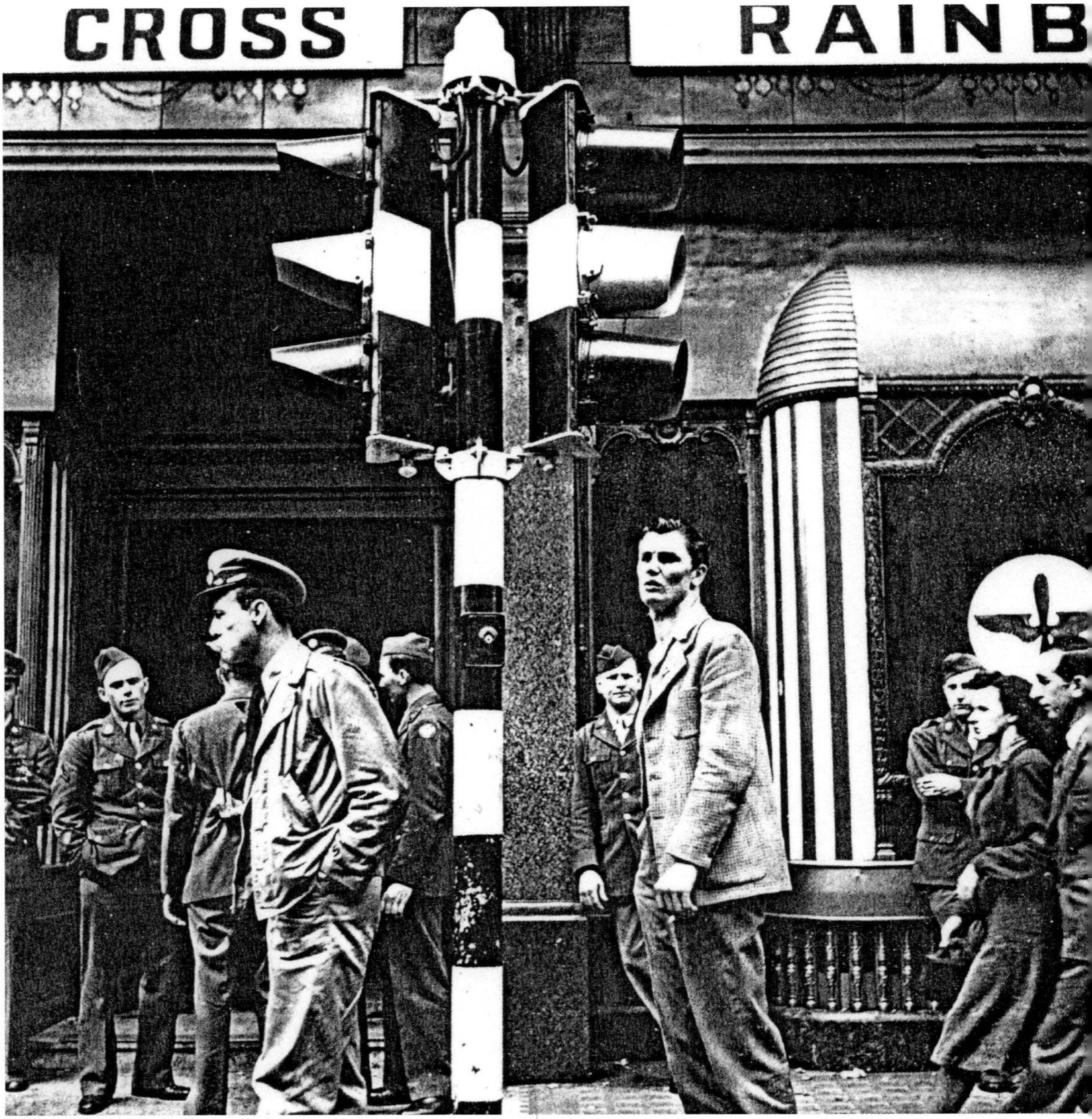
CROSS
RAINB

From November 1942 until January 1946, a wonderful club for American Army, Navy and Air Force personnel was open twenty-four hours a day. It was the American Red Cross Club, called Rainbow Corner, in London near Piccadilly Circus. It was established to bring some touches of the U.S. into the overseas lives of servicemen far from home. In style it was like a modern drugstore. It provided a range of activities including a gym, a library, pool tables, pin-ball machines, and a jukebox, as well as good food available in two large dining rooms. In addition to these there were cafés and a basement snack bar, Dunker's Den, serving hamburgers, waffles, coffee and doughnuts, and of course, Coca Cola. For the convenience of attendees the Den stayed open long after most British eateries closed. The most popular attraction of all

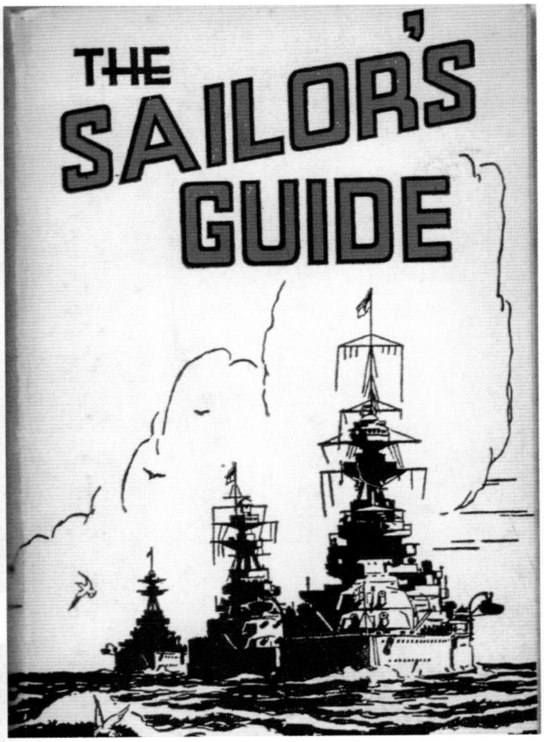
THE SAILOR'S GUIDE

far left: Service men and women flocked to the American Red Cross Club in central London; left: A publication that advanced the British war effor in WW2; below: Nothing goes to waste as a young girl donates homegrown leftovers to feeding animals; bottom left: Major Don Gentile, a top-scoring ace of the famous 4th Fighter Group which was based at Debden, Essex in the war.

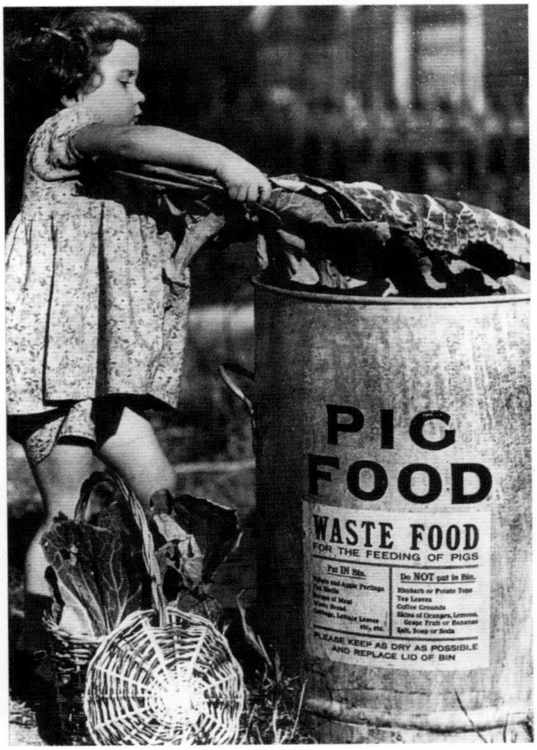
PIG
FOOD
WASTE FOOD
FOR THE FEEDING OF PIGS
Put IN Bin.
Do NOT put in Bin.
PLEASE KEEP AS DRY AS POSSIBLE
AND REPLACE LID OF BIN

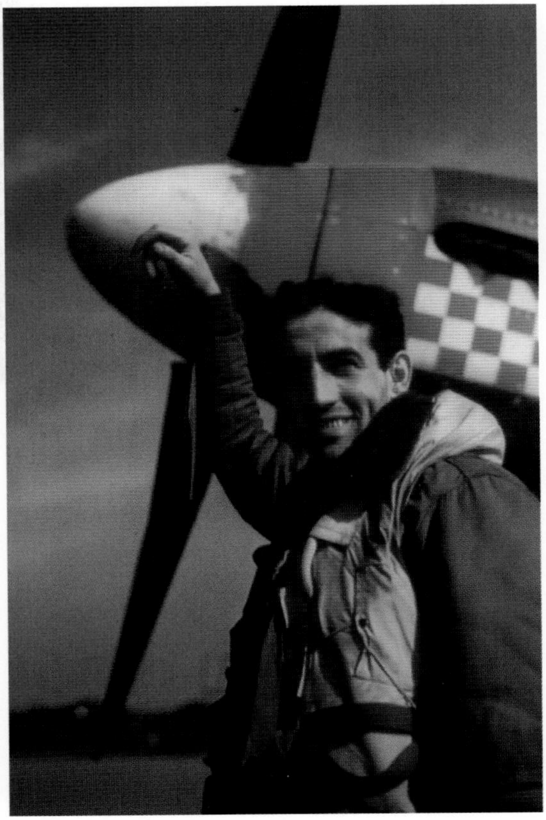

was the marvelous ballroom dancing which offered the great swing tunes of the day and a chance to dance with attractive, carefully vetted young women. The big bands playing regularly were the Skyliners, the Thunderbolts, the Flying Yanks and others. The military personnel turned up in their thousands to take full advantage of the facilities—barber shop, showers, a laundry, a bed for the night in London or an hour of bed rest before catching that train back to base. The Yanks were by no means the only patrons of the Rainbow Corner. It attracted many military personnel from Britain, Norway, Canada, France, Poland, Czechoslovakia, Belgium, the Netherlands and more. The Americans eagerly responded to requests from the girls there to teach them how to do the jitterbug. They soon mastered the intricacies of the dance. Celebrities dropped in occasionally adding a bit of charm and magic to the mood. They included James Stewart, George Raft, Fred Astaire's sister Adele, and other notables. Some of the greatest big bands of the time made what were called 'Eagle Broadcasts' from the Rainbow, including Glenn Miller's Army Air Force Band and the Navy Band of Artie Shaw.

Operating around the clock, the Rainbow Corner club was staffed by hundreds of enthusiastic, caring volunteers who helped give many thousands of service personnel a good time and distract them from the horrors of war.

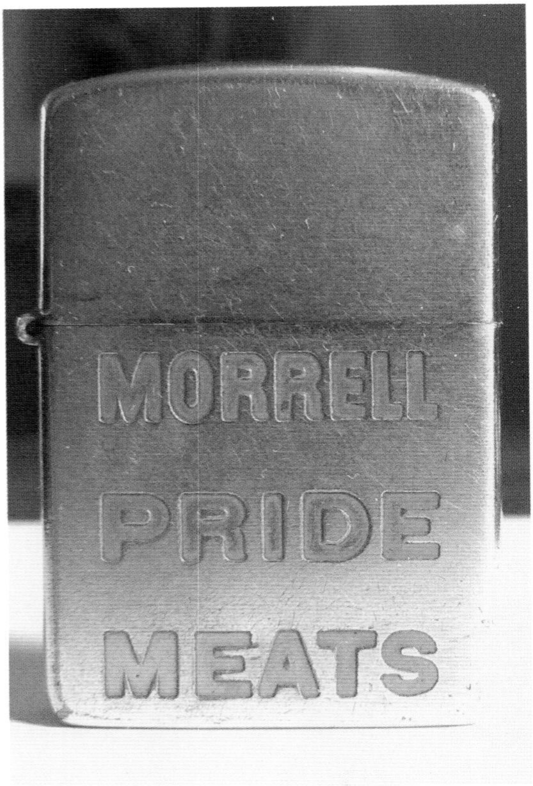
MORRELL
PRIDE
MEATS

above: A commerical example of a 1950s Zippo; below: A reminder of how to prepare for an air raid.

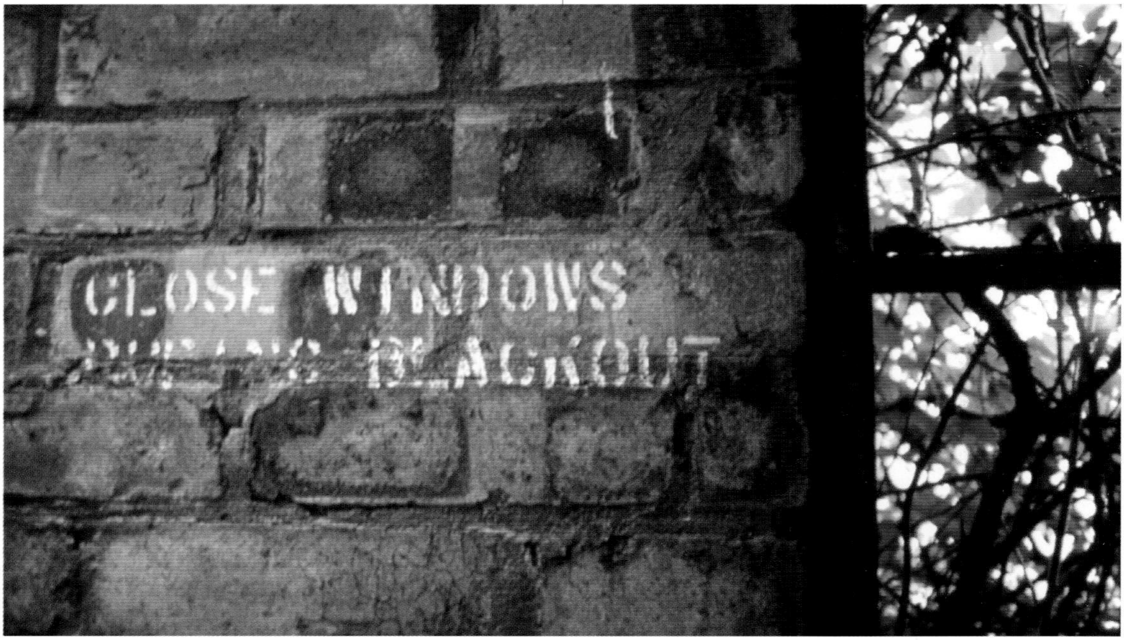
CLOSE WINDOWS

U.S. airmen pause for a break on this B-24 Liberator bomber base in World War Two England.

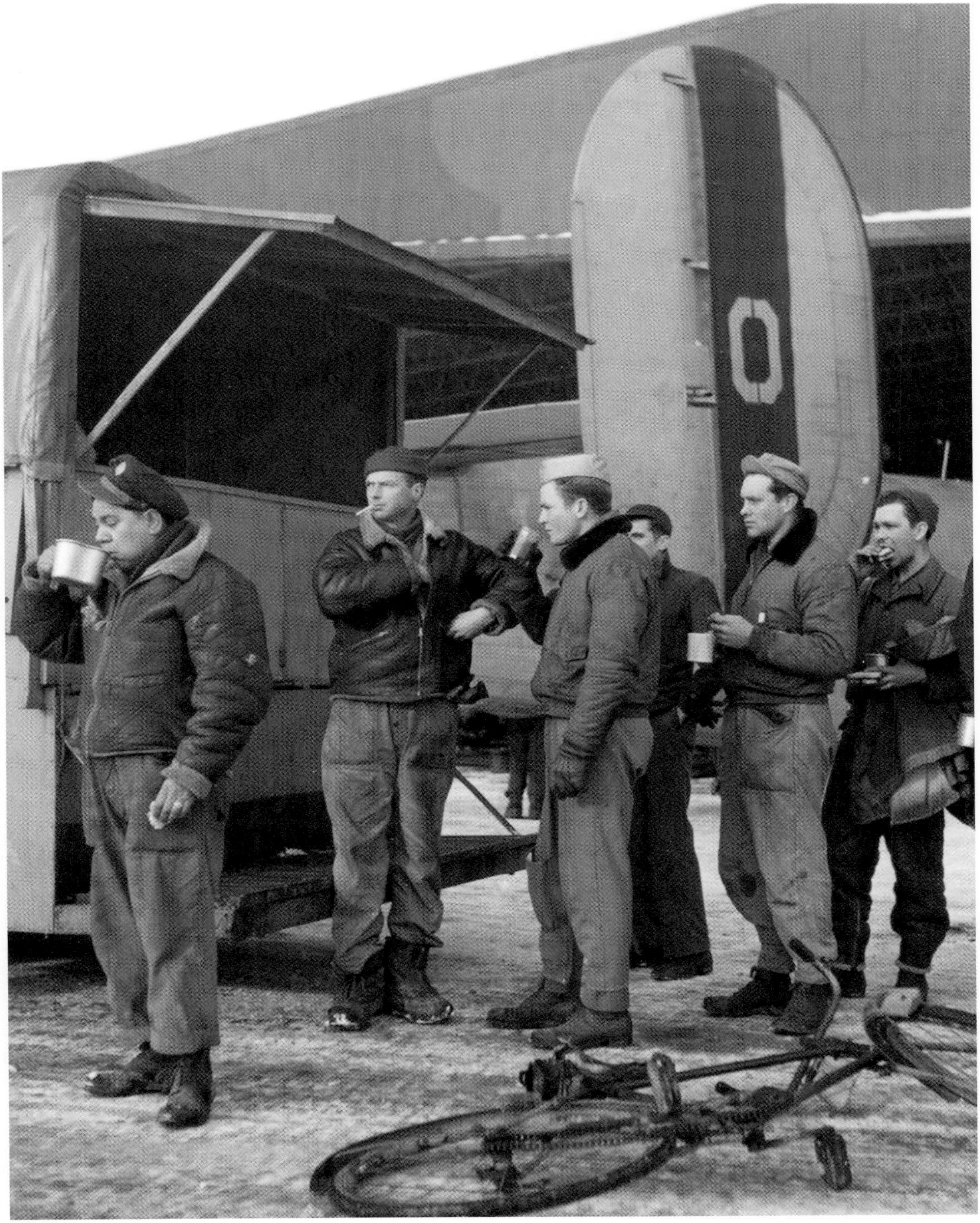

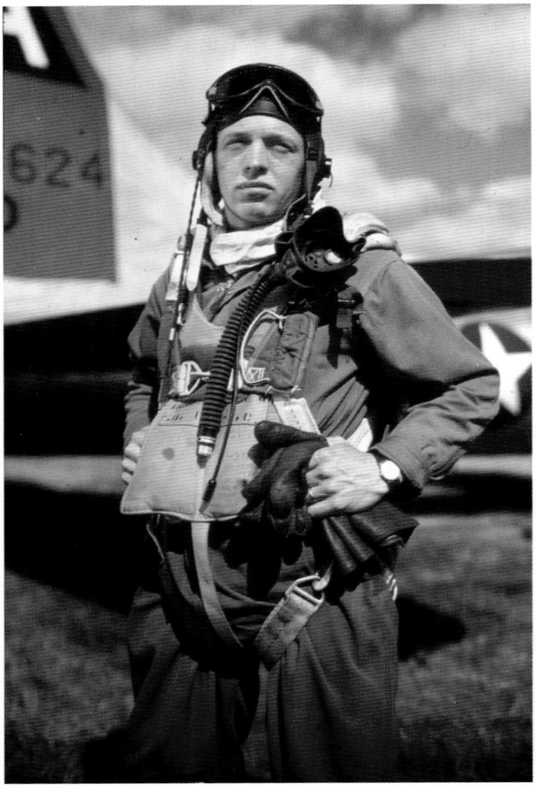

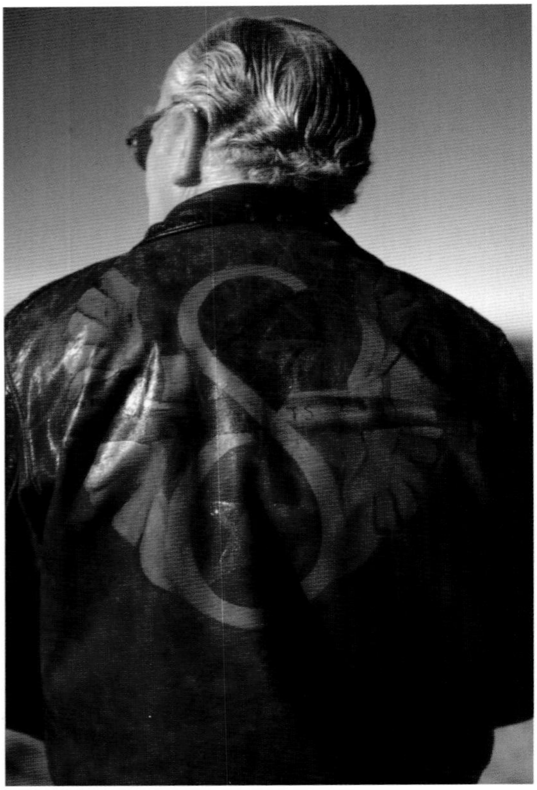

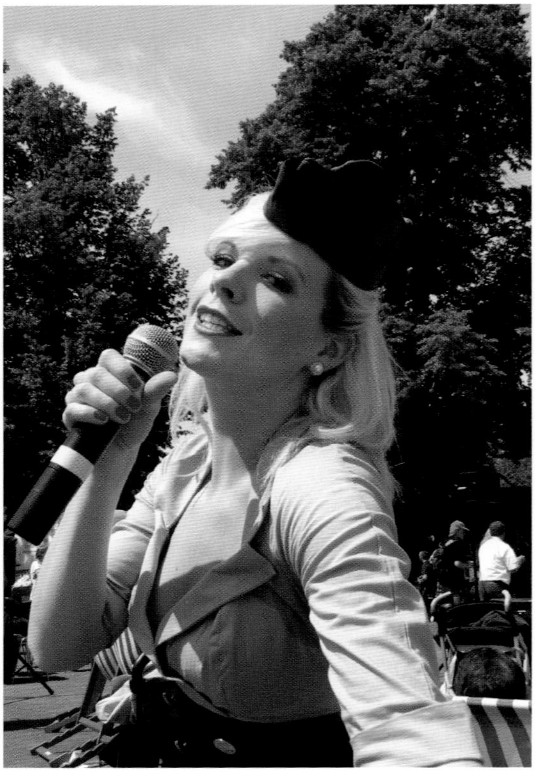

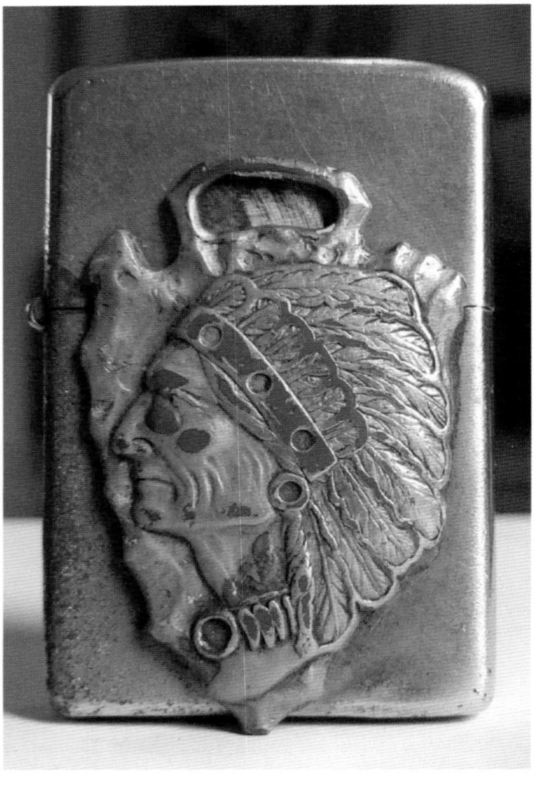

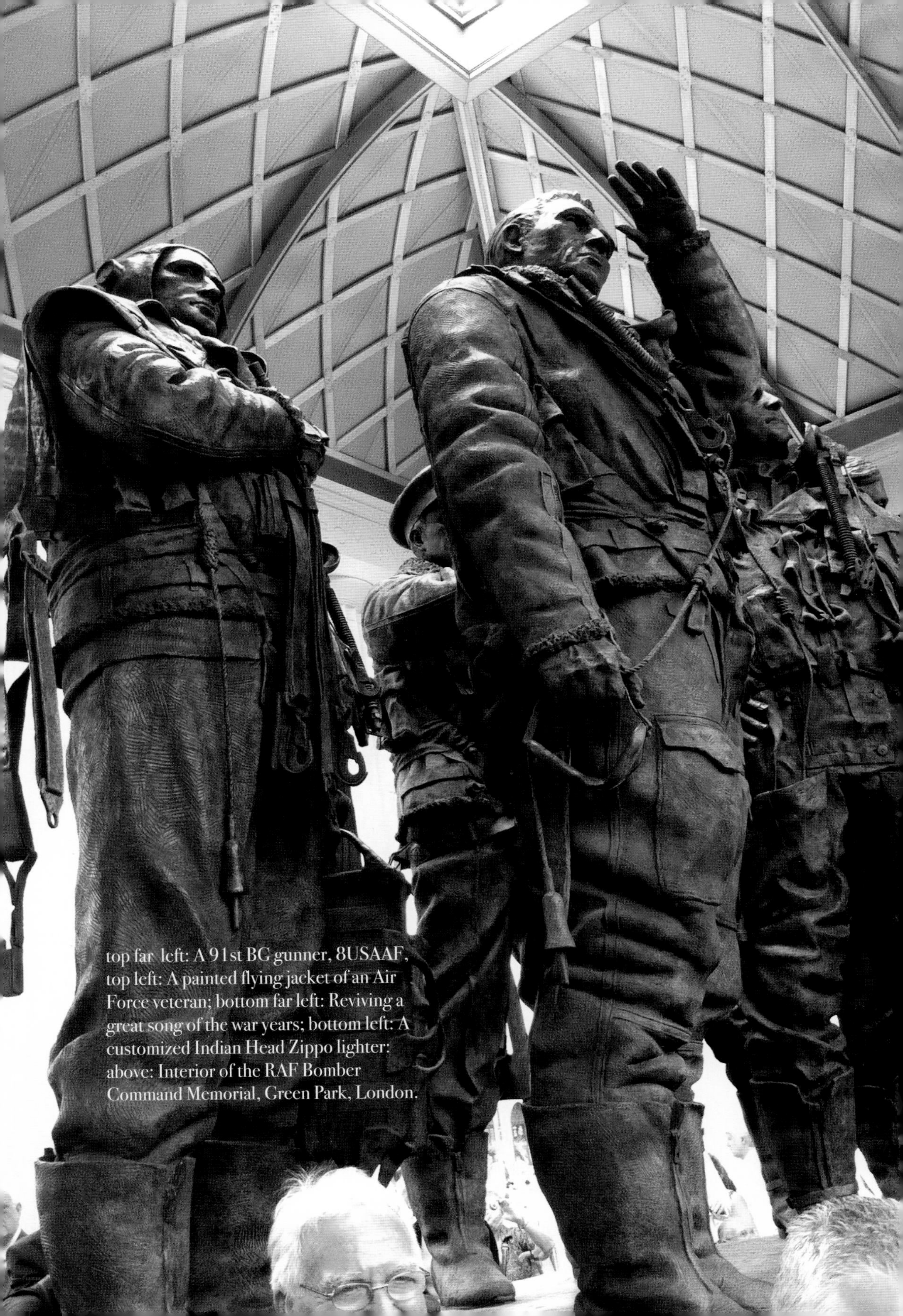

top far left: A 91st BG gunner, 8USAAF, top left: A painted flying jacket of an Air Force veteran; bottom far left: Reviving a great song of the war years; bottom left: A customized Indian Head Zippo lighter: above: Interior of the RAF Bomber Command Memorial, Green Park, London.

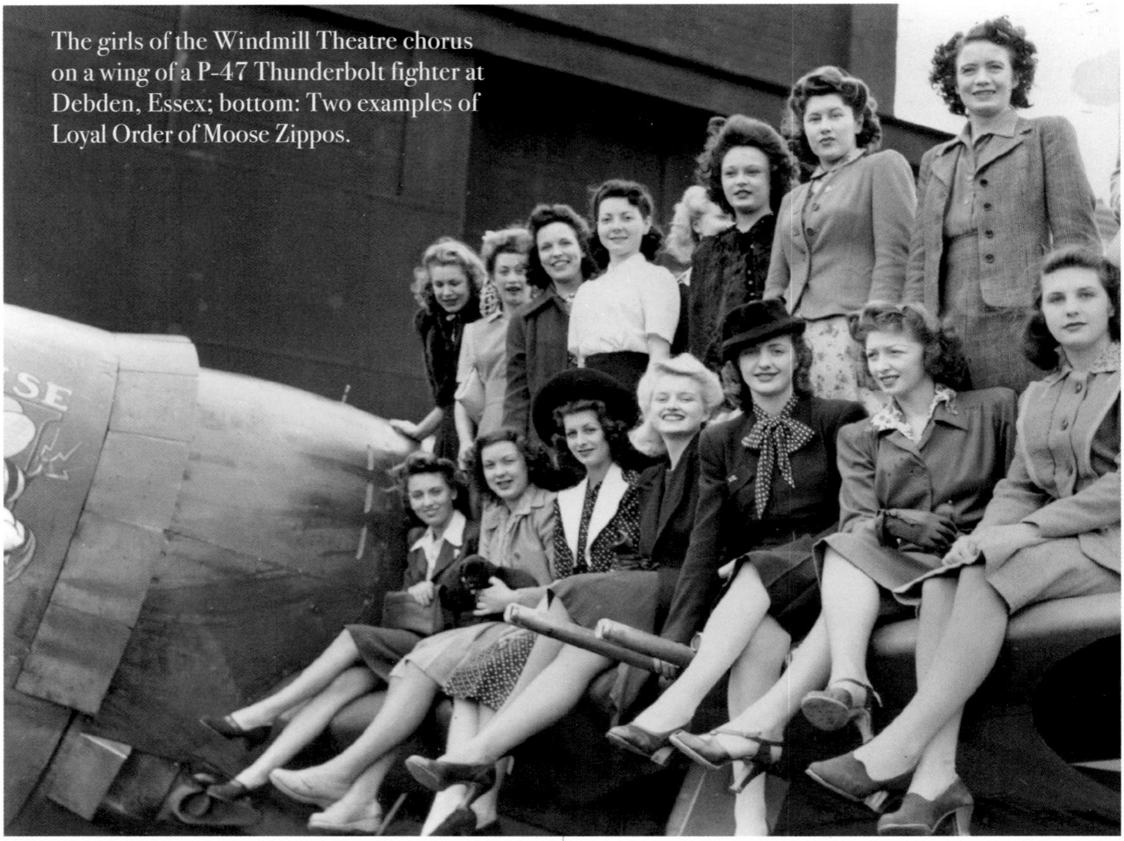

The girls of the Windmill Theatre chorus on a wing of a P-47 Thunderbolt fighter at Debden, Essex; bottom: Two examples of Loyal Order of Moose Zippos.

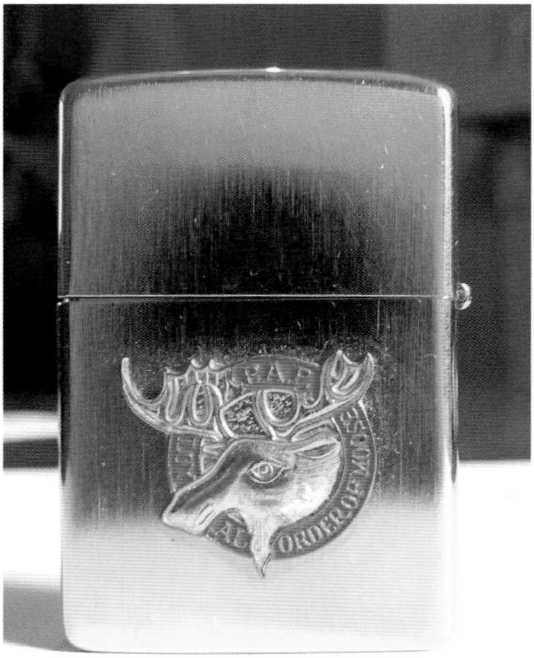
P.A.P.
AL ORDER OF MOOSE

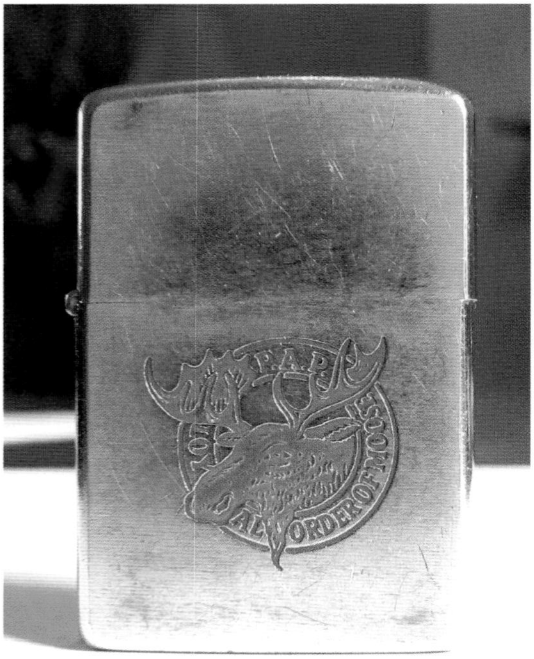
P.A.P.
AL ORDER OF MOOSE

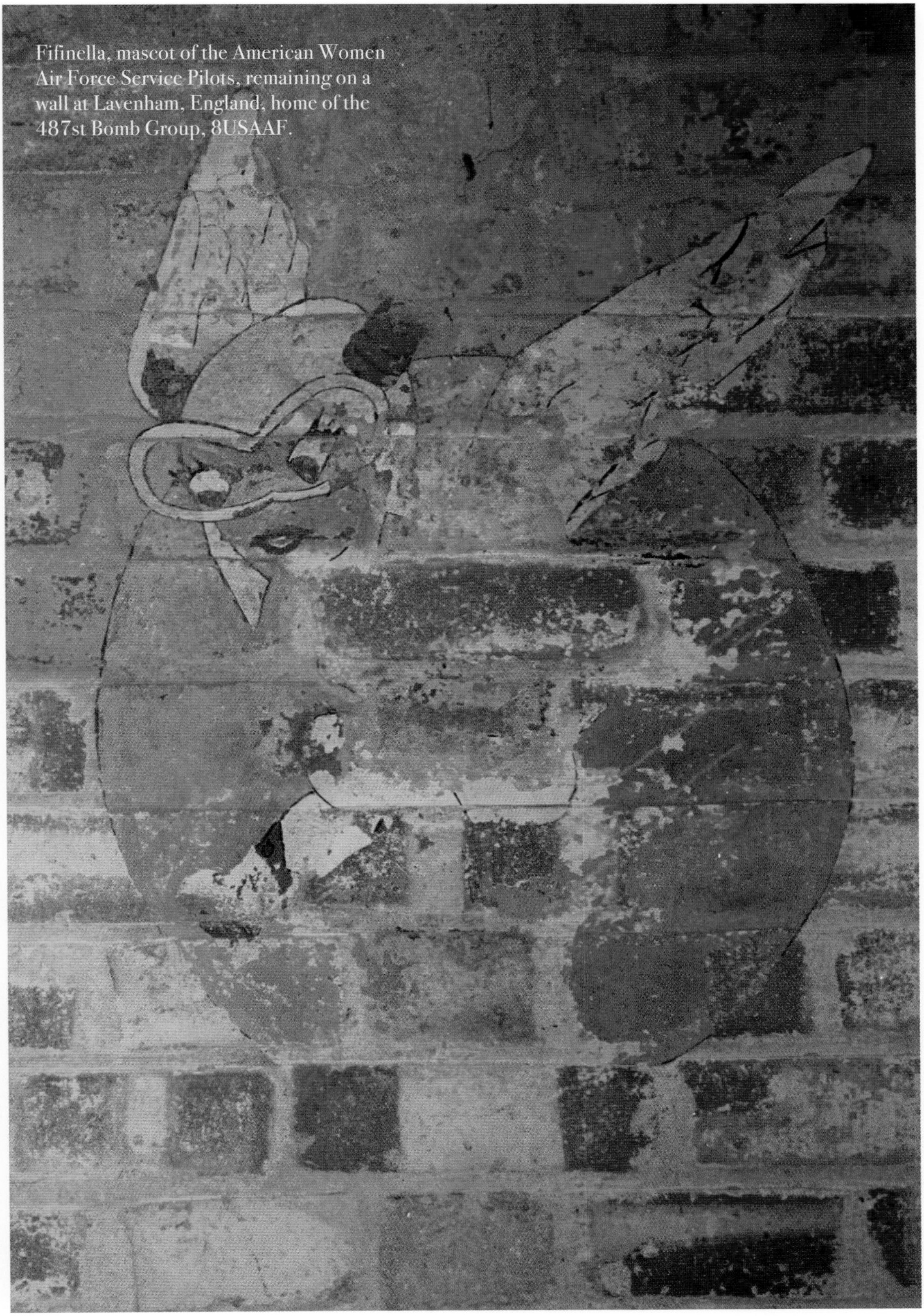

Fifinella, mascot of the American Women Air Force Service Pilots, remaining on a wall at Lavenham, England, home of the 487st Bomb Group, 8USAAF.

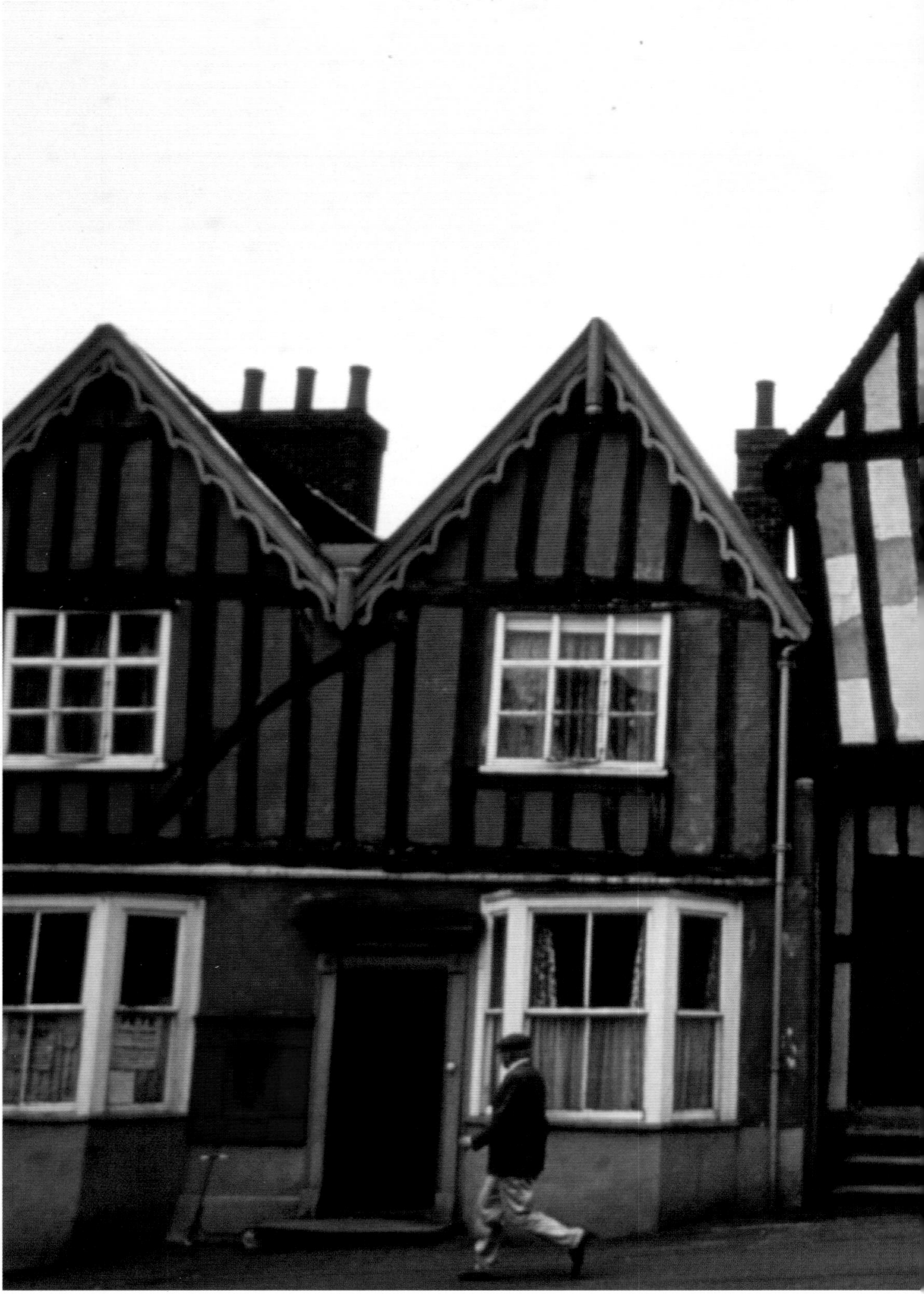

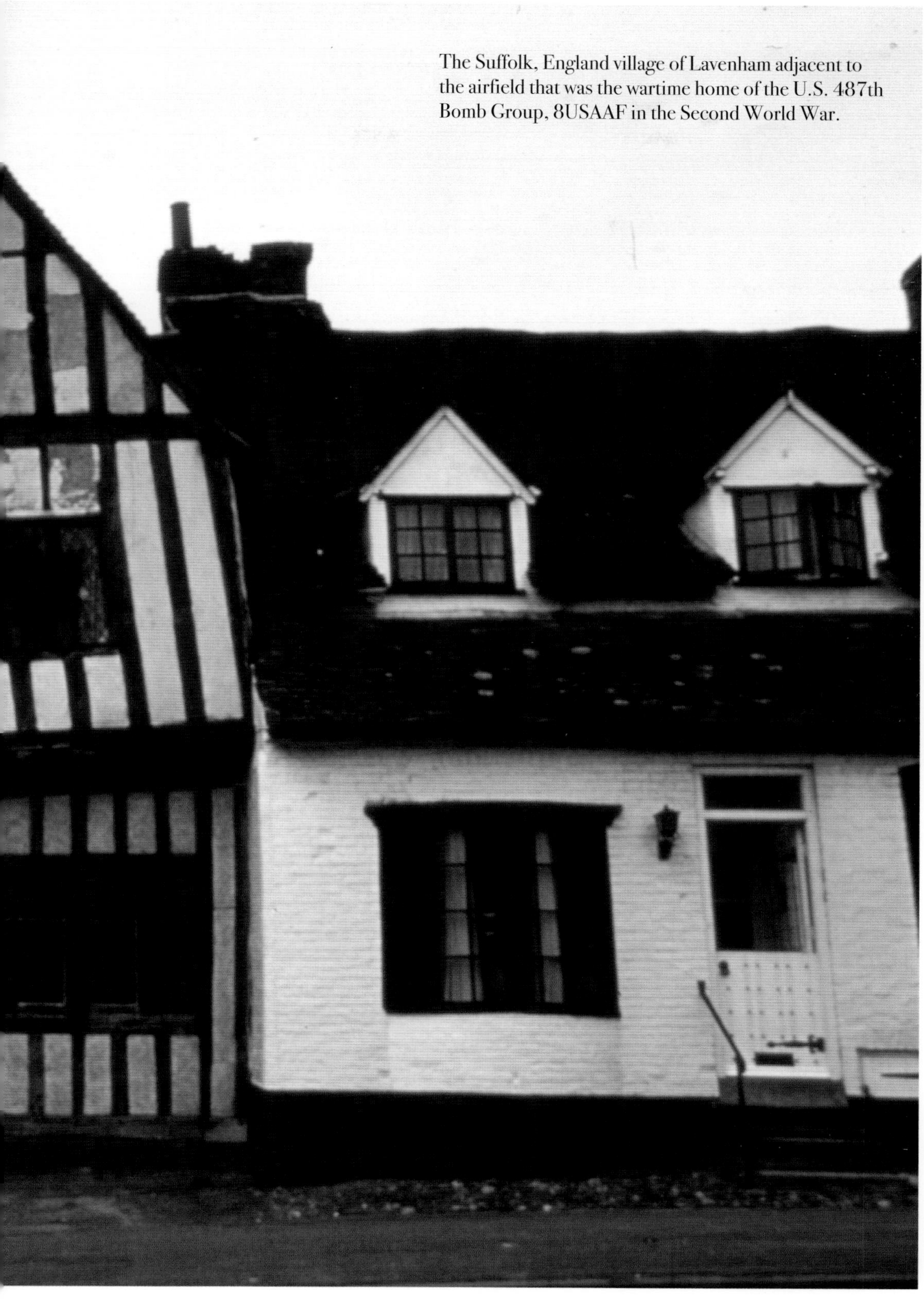

The Suffolk, England village of Lavenham adjacent to the airfield that was the wartime home of the U.S. 487th Bomb Group, 8USAAF in the Second World War.

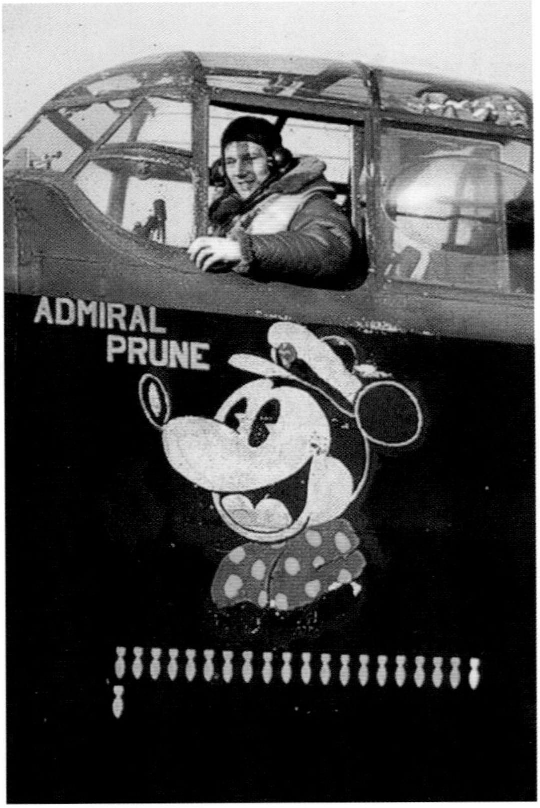
ADMIRAL
PRUNE

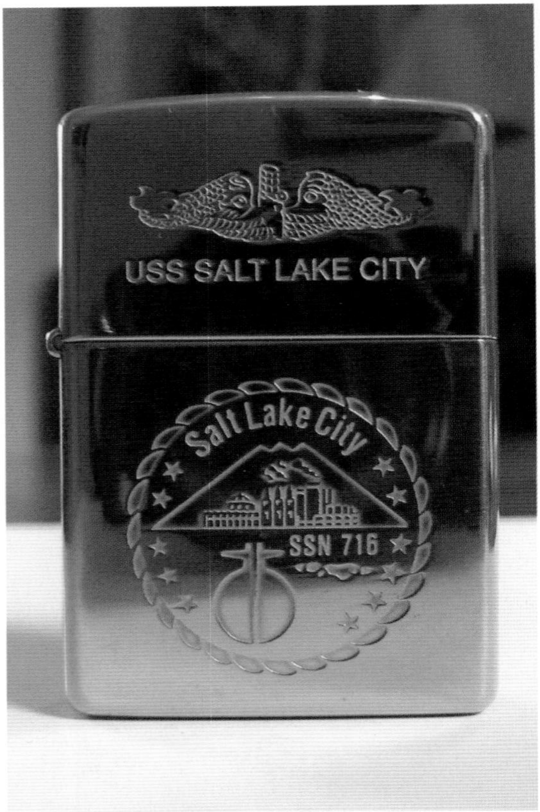
USS SALT LAKE CITY
Salt Lake City
SSN 716

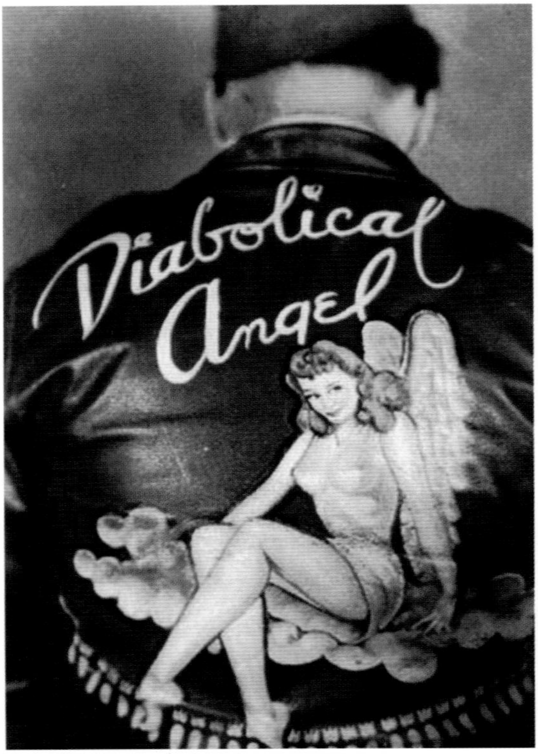
Diabolical
Angel

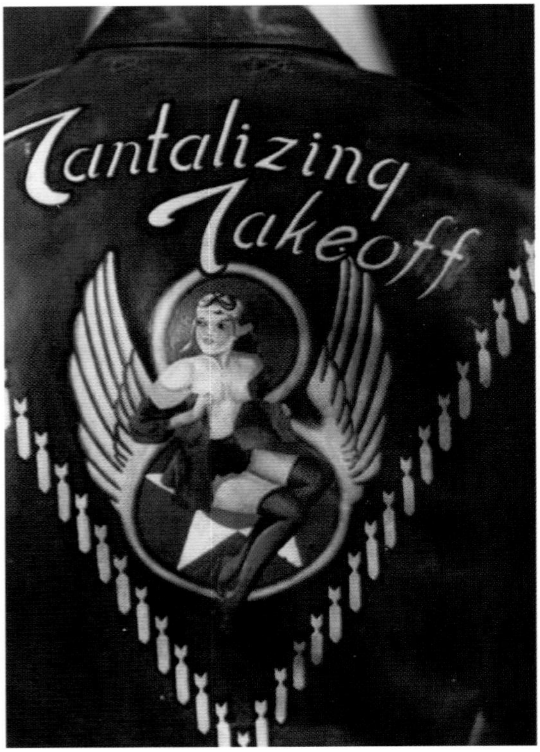
Tantalizing
Takeoff

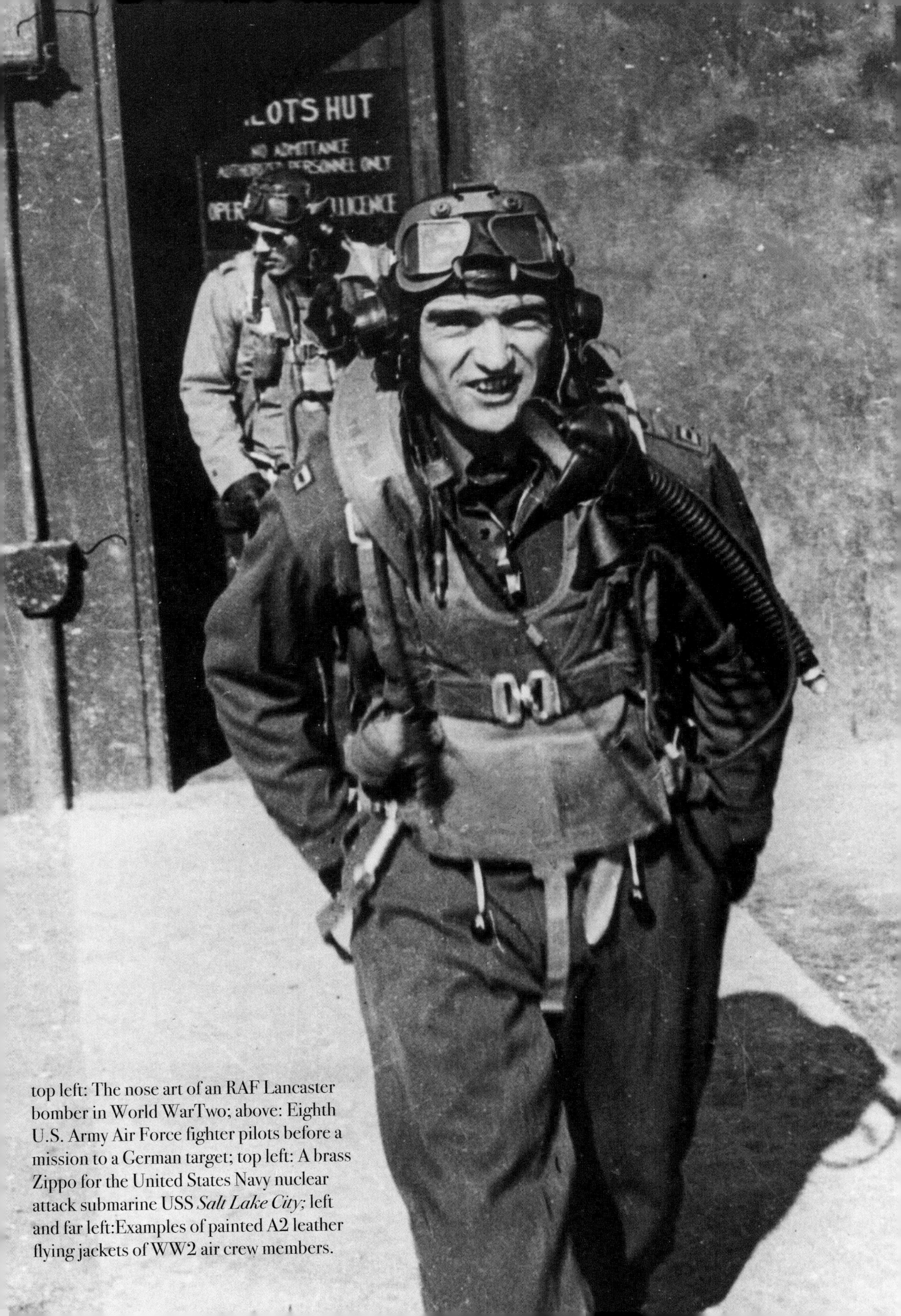
NO ADMITTANCE

top left: The nose art of an RAF Lancaster bomber in World WarTwo; above: Eighth U.S. Army Air Force fighter pilots before a mission to a German target; top left: A brass Zippo for the United States Navy nuclear attack submarine USS *Salt Lake City;* left and far left:Examples of painted A2 leather flying jackets of WW2 air crew members.

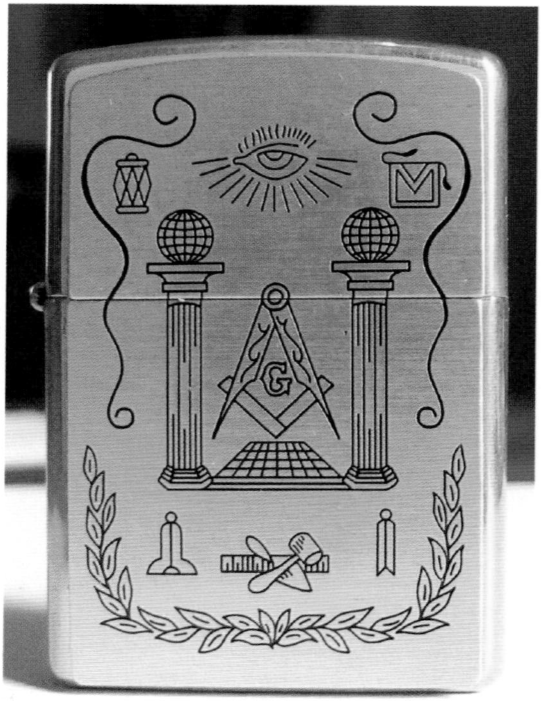

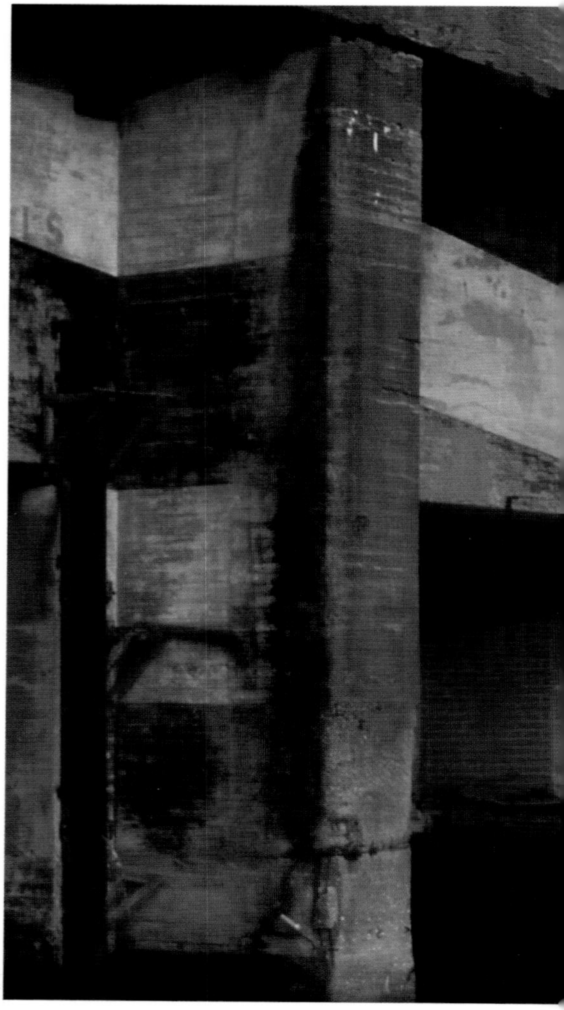

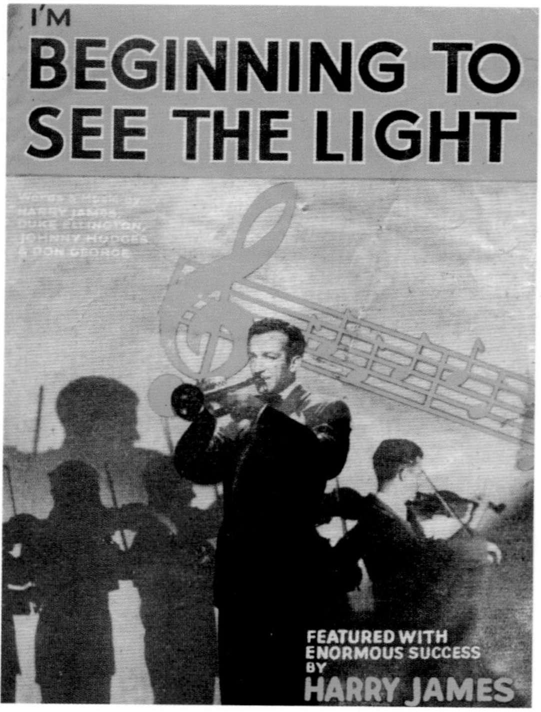
I'M
BEGINNING TO
SEE THE LIGHT
FEATURED WITH
ENORMOUS SUCCESS
BY
HARRY JAMES

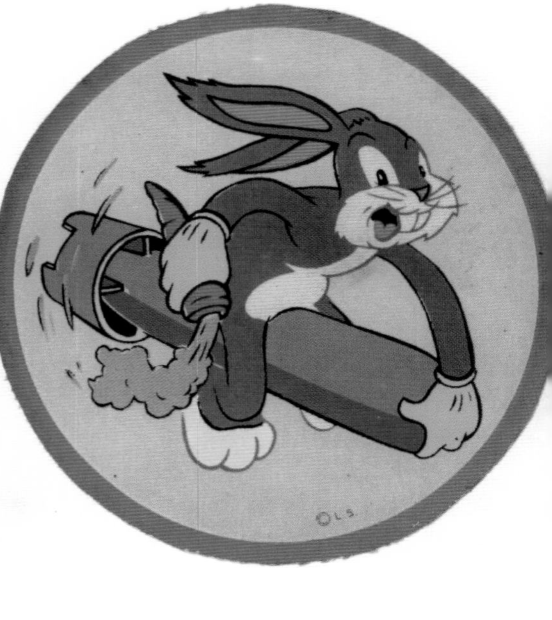

top: A Masonic Zippo; top right: The remaining German U-boat pen shelter at La Pallice on the Brittany coast of France; far right: A war worker's badge.

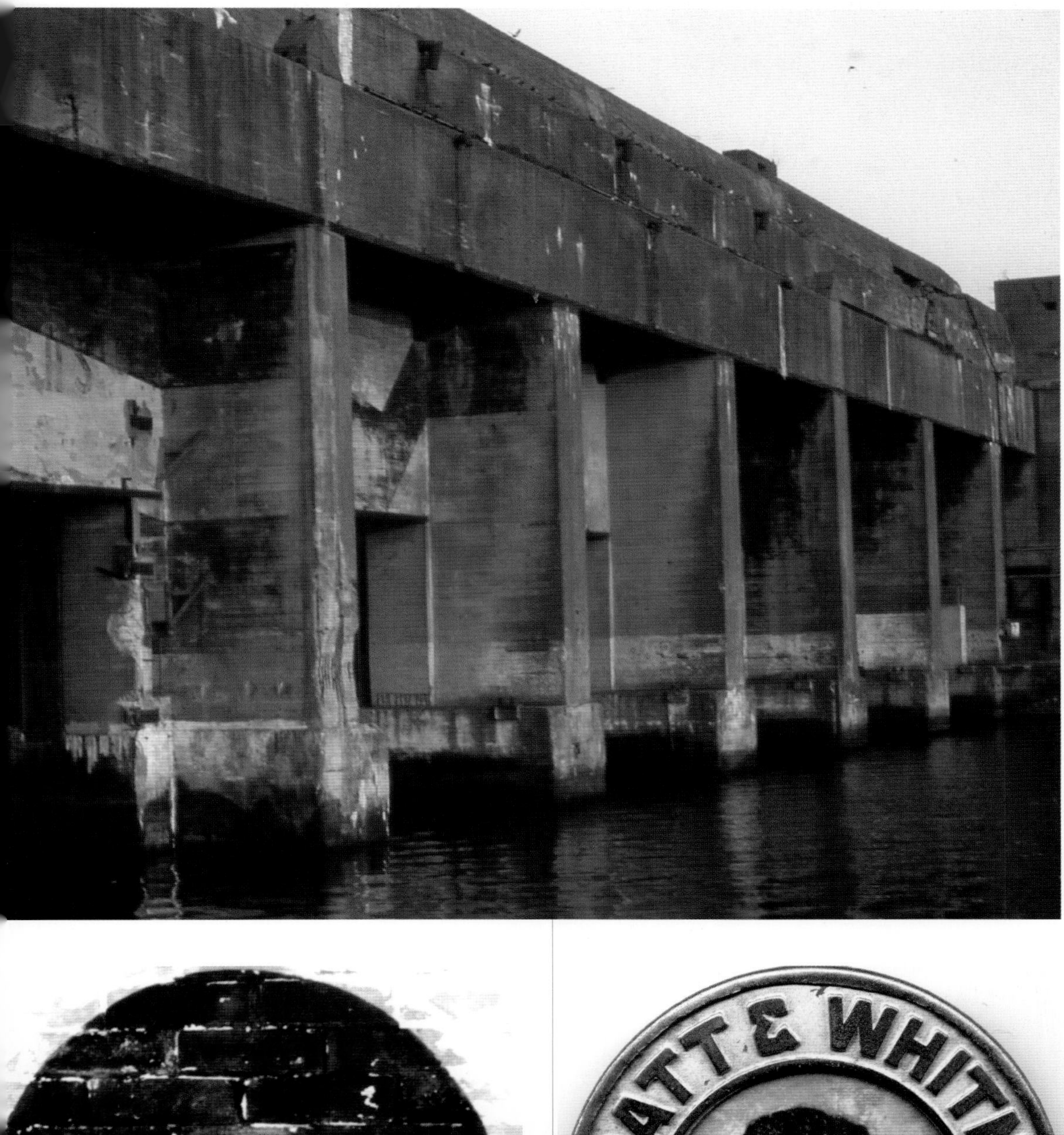

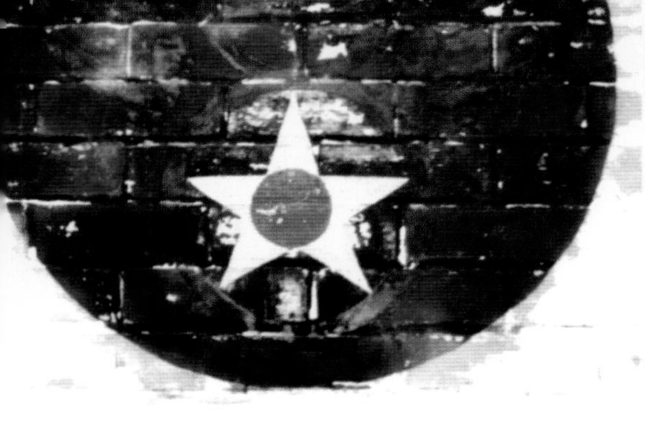

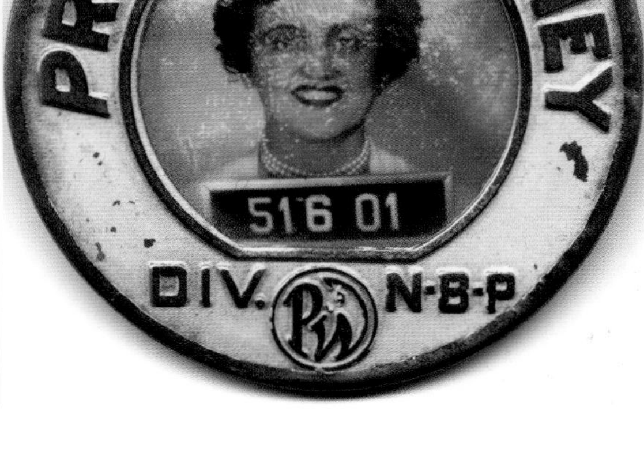
PRATT & WHITNEY
516 01
DIV.
N-B-P

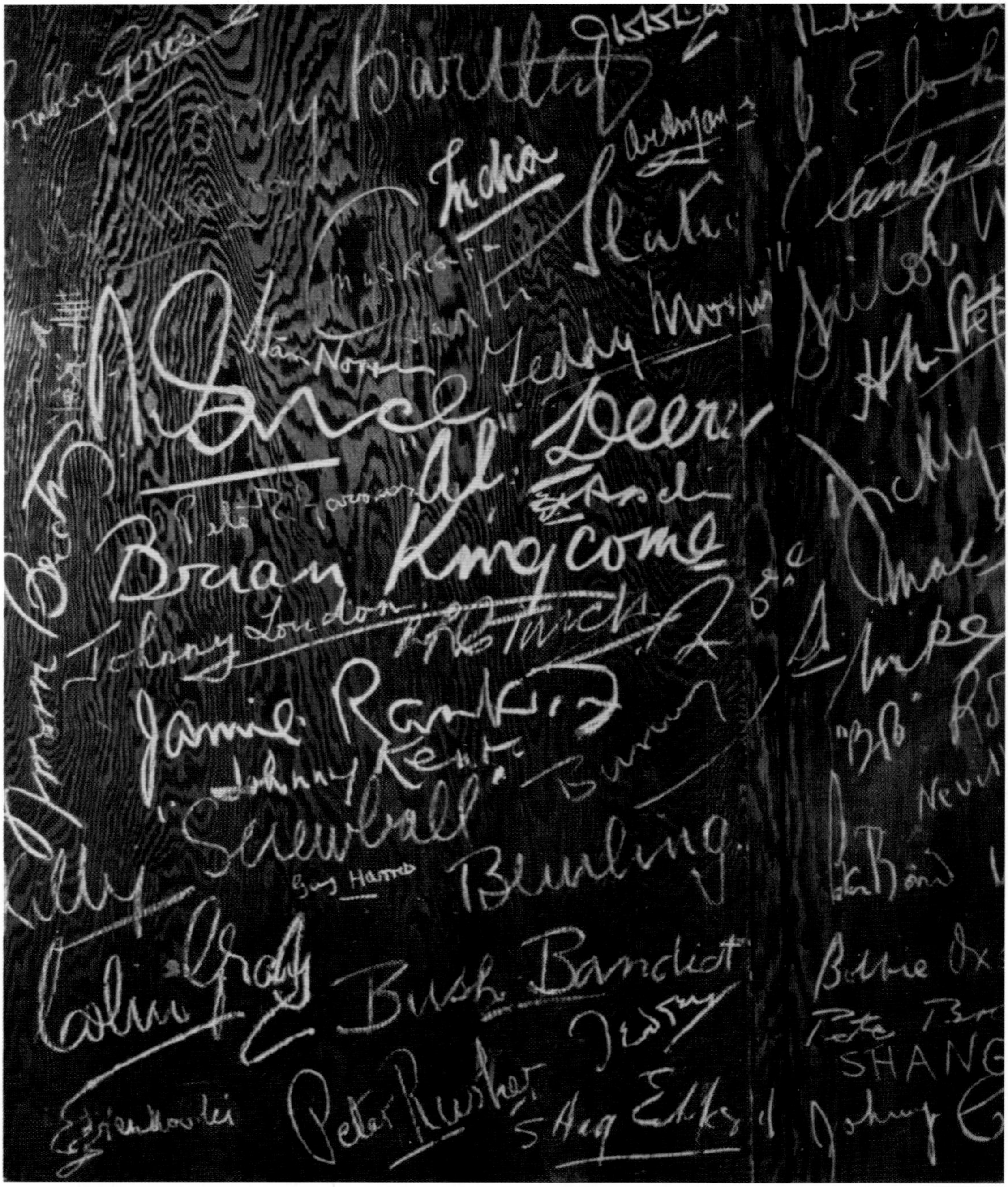
India
Brian Kingcome
Johnny London
Johnny Kent
Bush Bandit
Guy Harris
SHANG

above: The original chalk board of fighter pilots' signatures from the White Hart pub, Brasted, Kent, a frequent haunt of No 92 Squadron at nearby RAF Biggin Hill; right: A relaxing post-mission whisky before the routine operational interrogation.

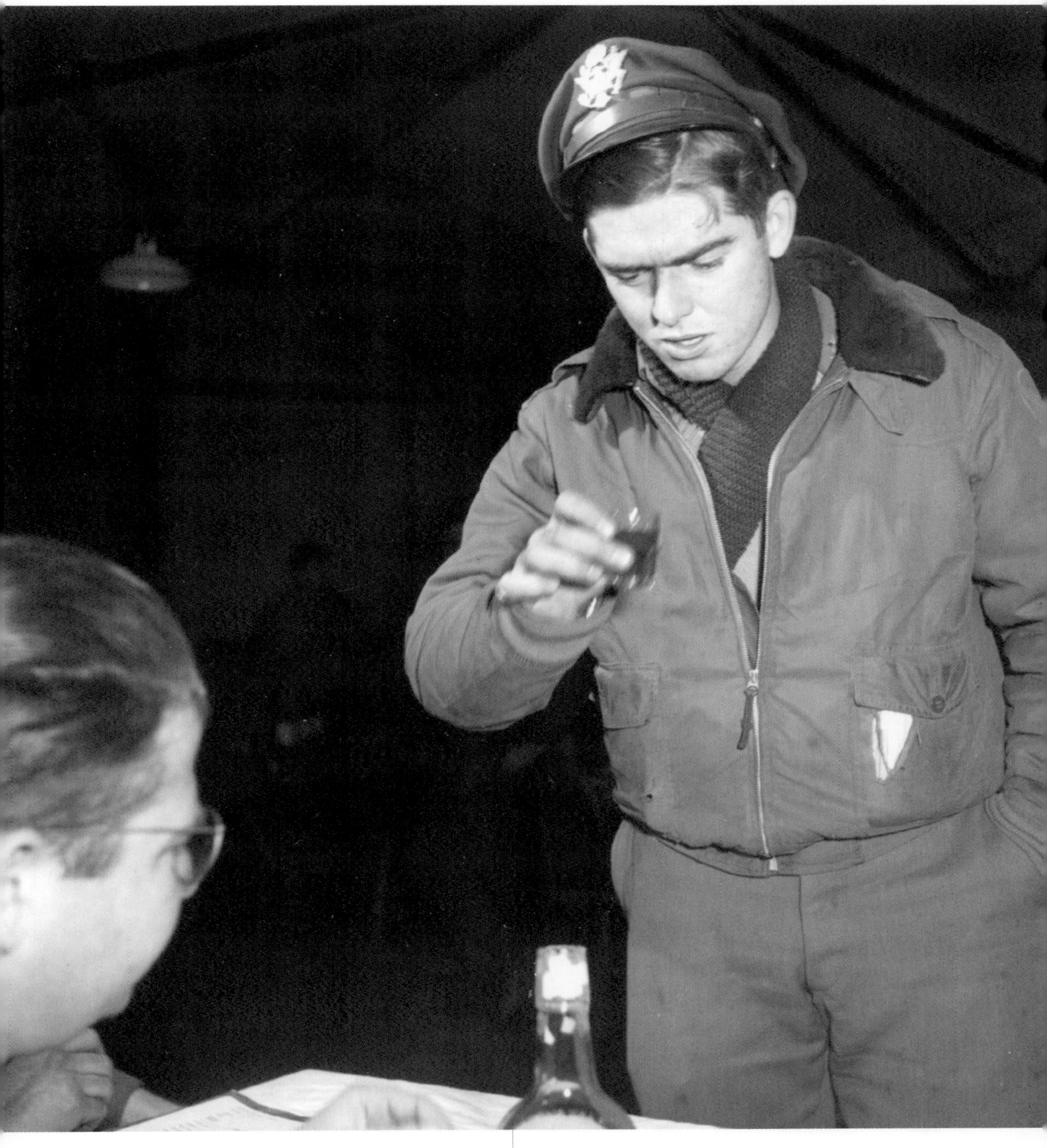

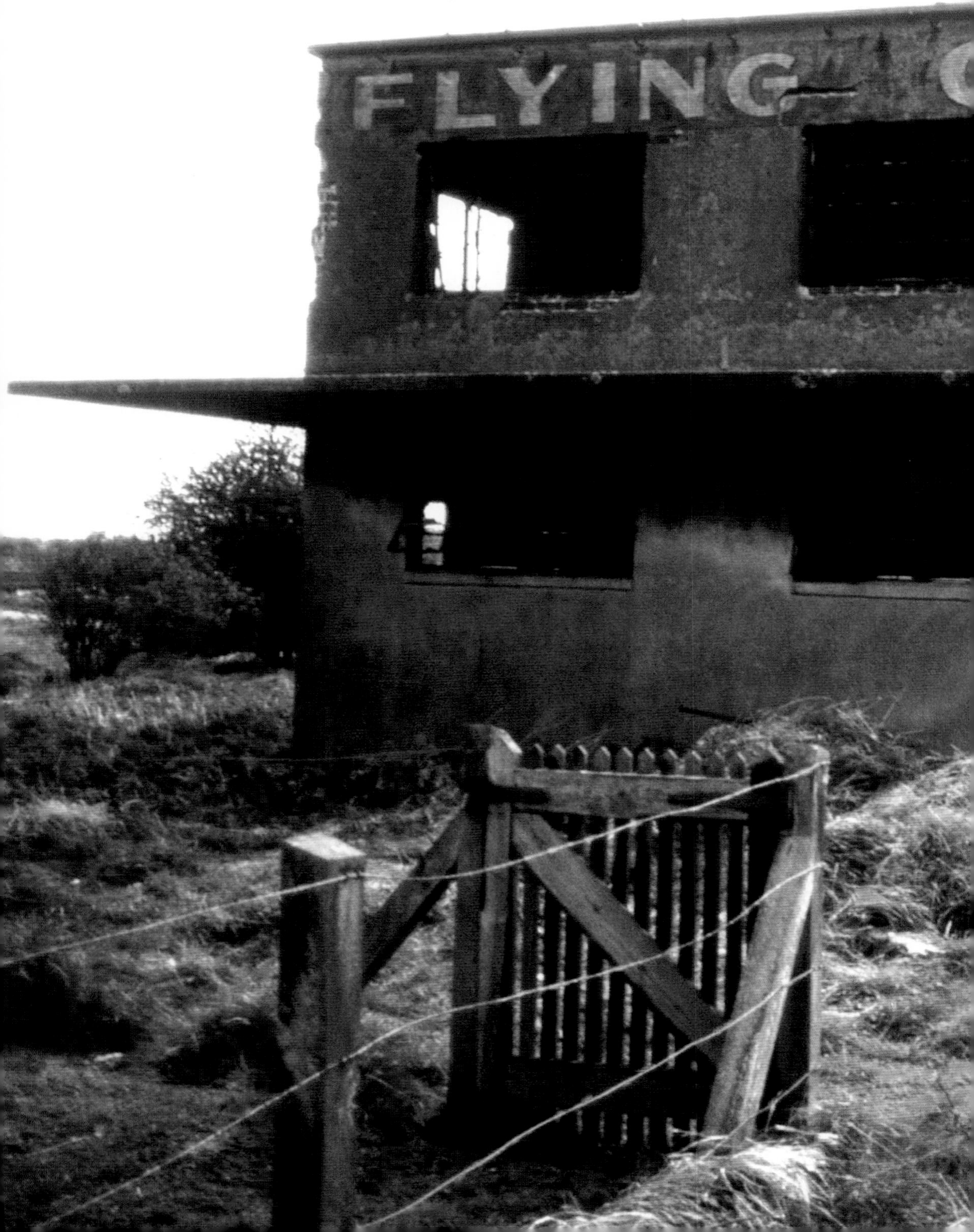
FLYING

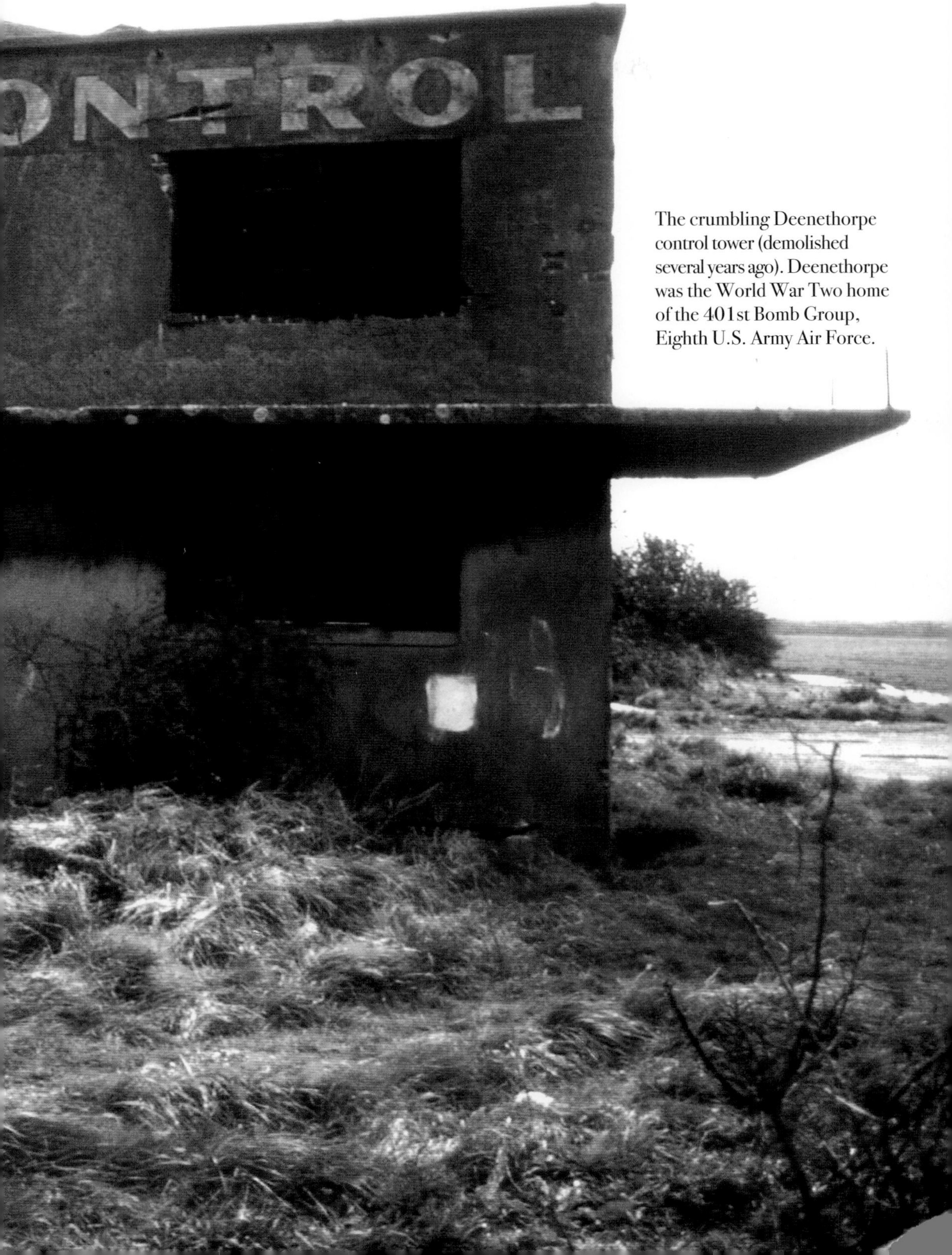
ONTROL

The crumbling Deenethorpe control tower (demolished several years ago). Deenethorpe was the World War Two home of the 401st Bomb Group, Eighth U.S. Army Air Force.

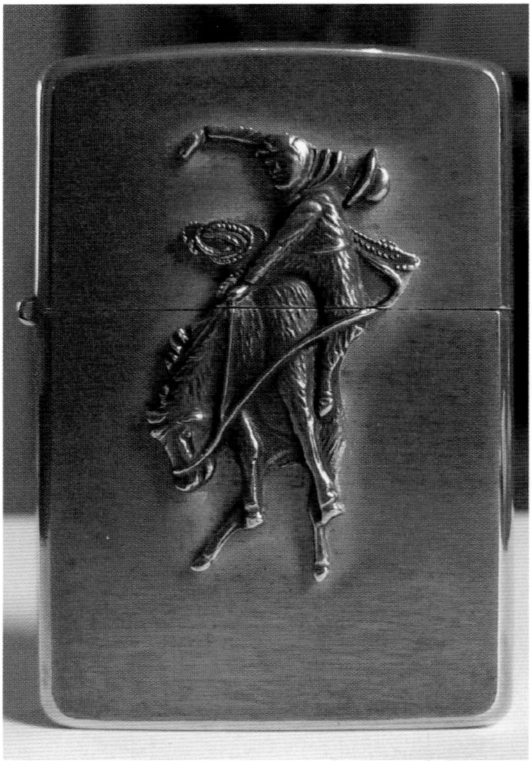

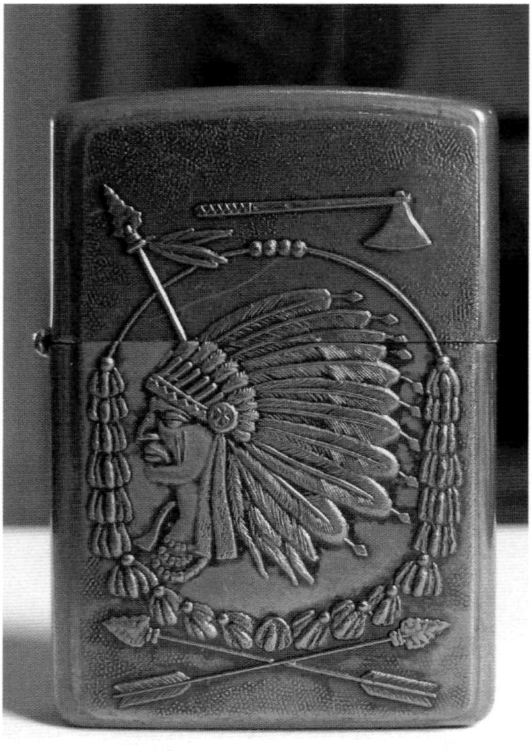

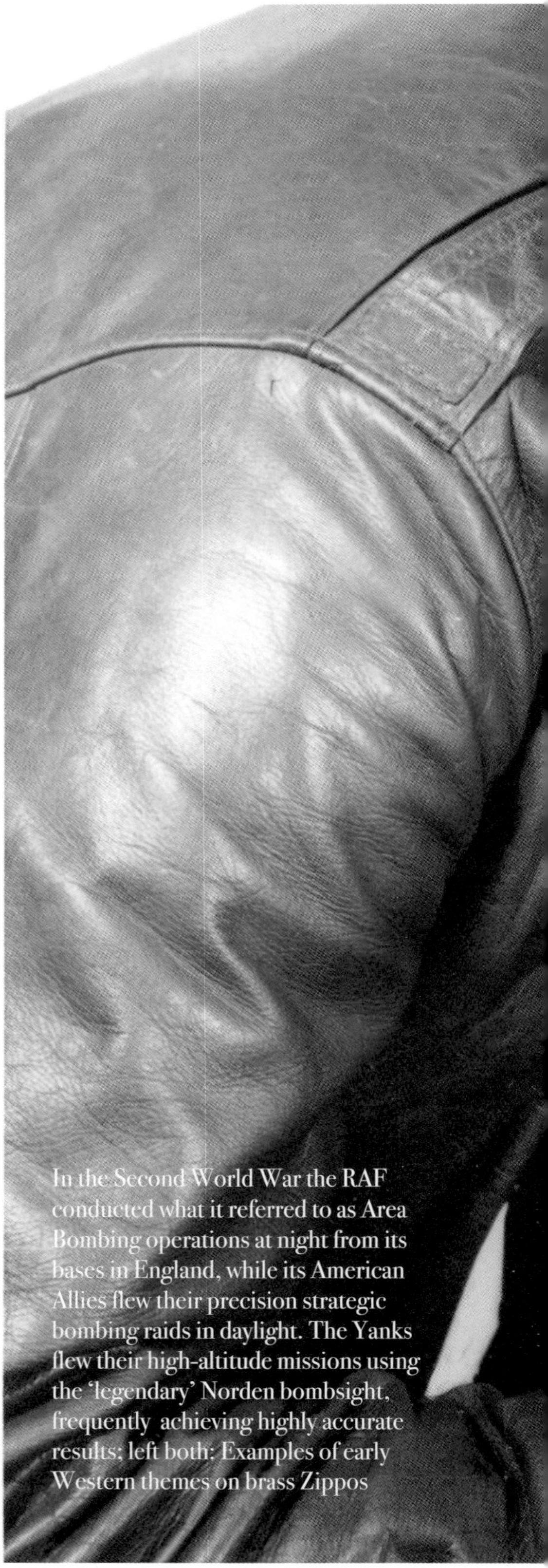

In the Second World War the RAF conducted what it referred to as Area Bombing operations at night from its bases in England, while its American Allies flew their precision strategic bombing raids in daylight. The Yanks flew their high-altitude missions using the 'legendary' Norden bombsight, frequently achieving highly accurate results; left both: Examples of early Western themes on brass Zippos

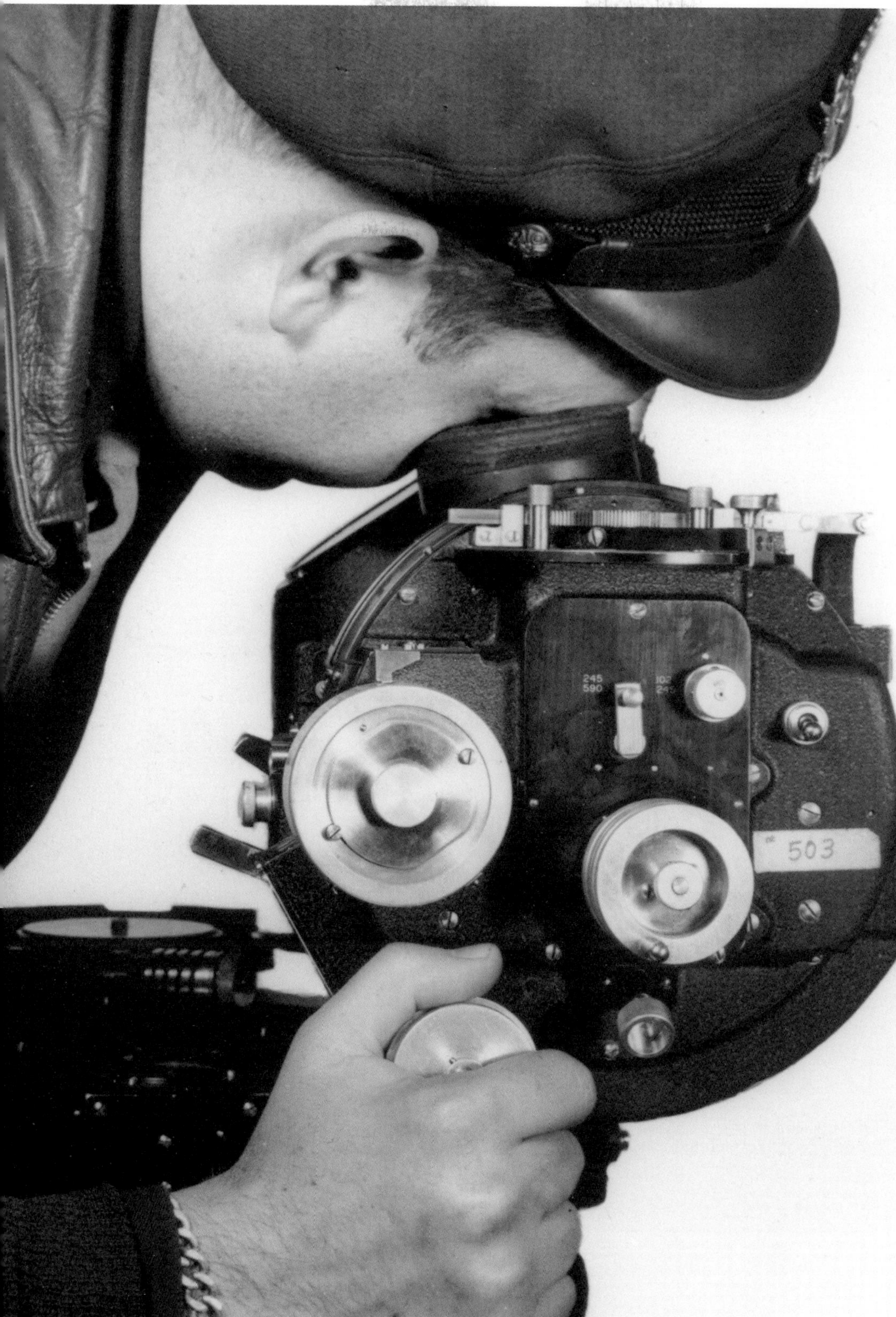
245
590
503

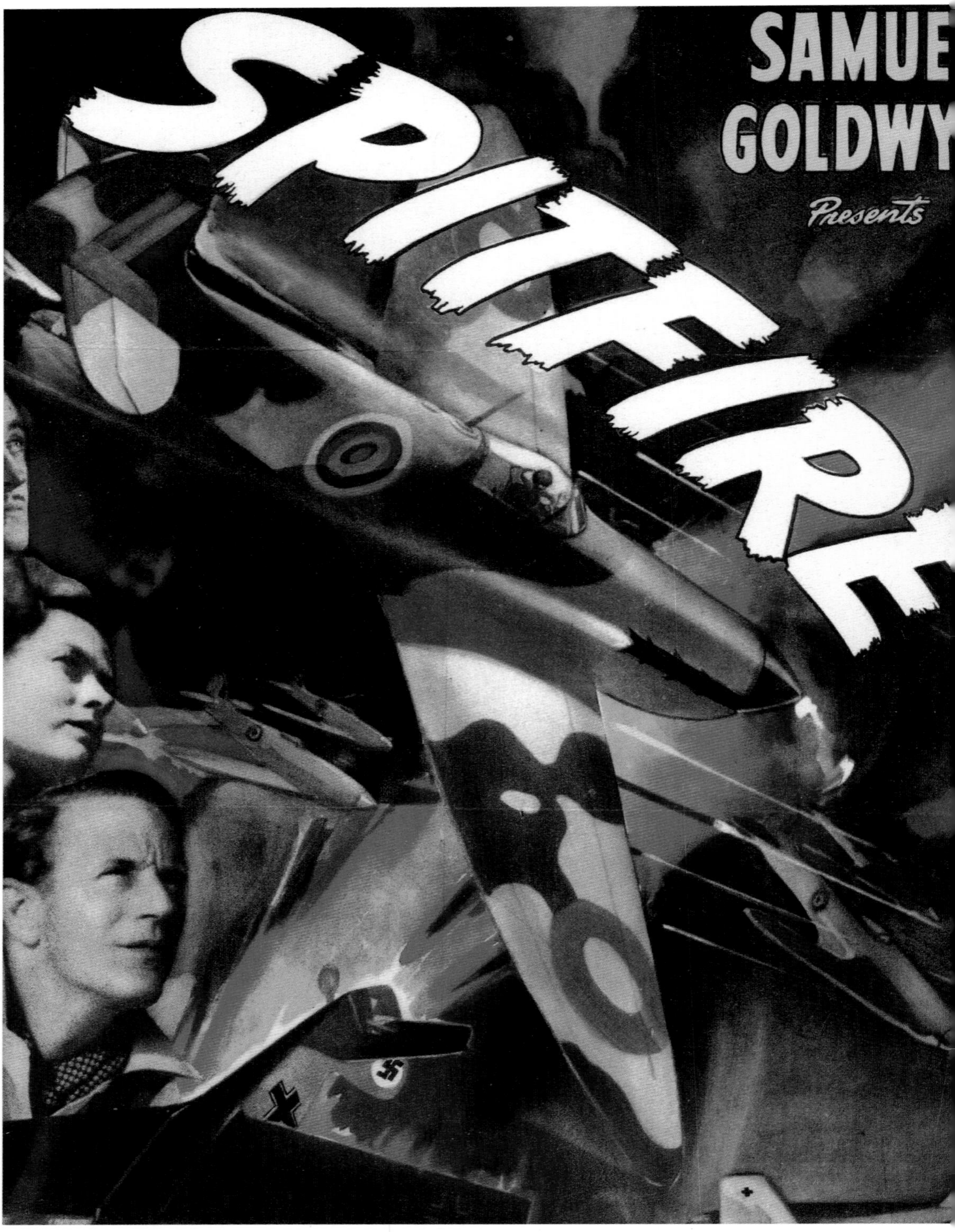
SAMUE
GOLDWY
Presents
SPITFIRE

above: A poster for *Spitfire,* the American title of the film *The First of the Few*, about Spitfire designer R.J. Mitchell; above right: wartime comics; right: A German U-boat commander on the deck of his sub.

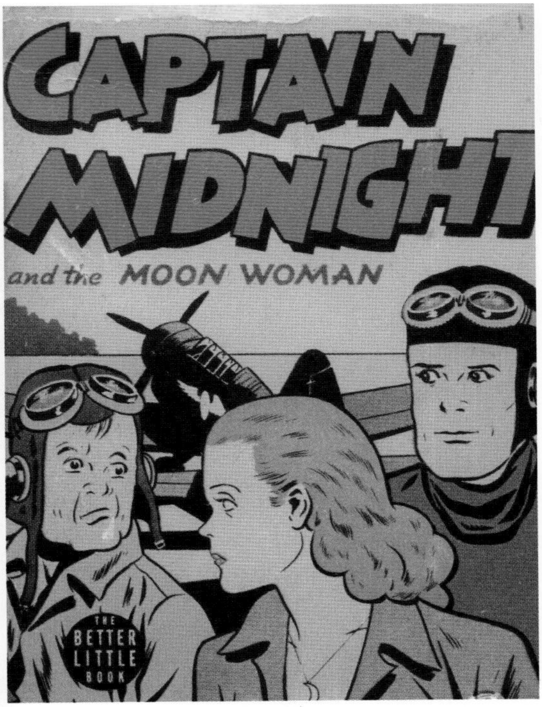
CAPTAIN MIDNIGHT
and the MOON WOMAN
THE BETTER LITTLE BOOK

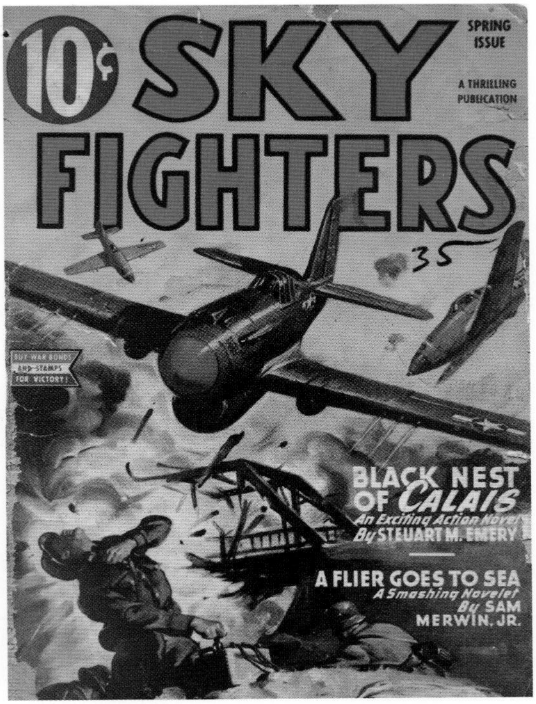
10¢
SKY FIGHTERS
SPRING ISSUE
A THRILLING PUBLICATION
BUY WAR BONDS AND STAMPS FOR VICTORY!
BLACK NEST OF CALAIS
An Exciting Action Novel
By STEUART M. EMERY
A FLIER GOES TO SEA
A Smashing Novelet
By SAM MERWIN, JR.

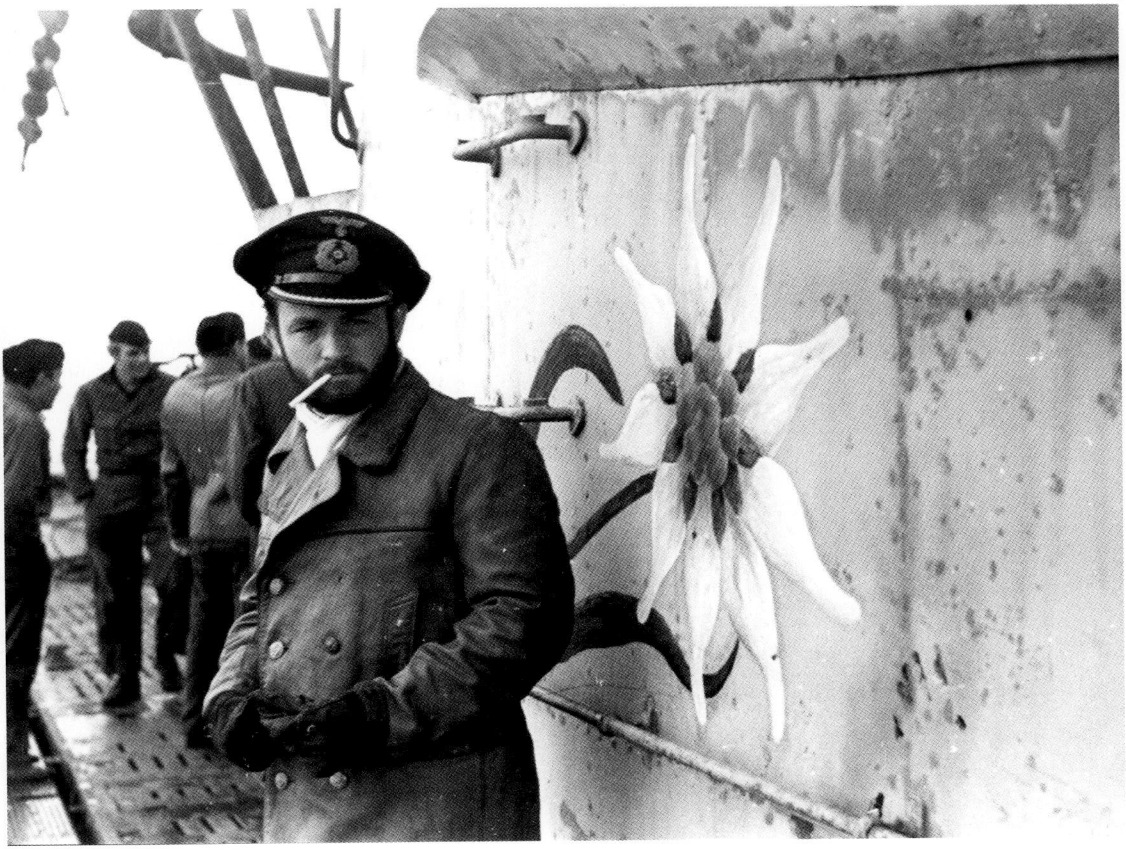

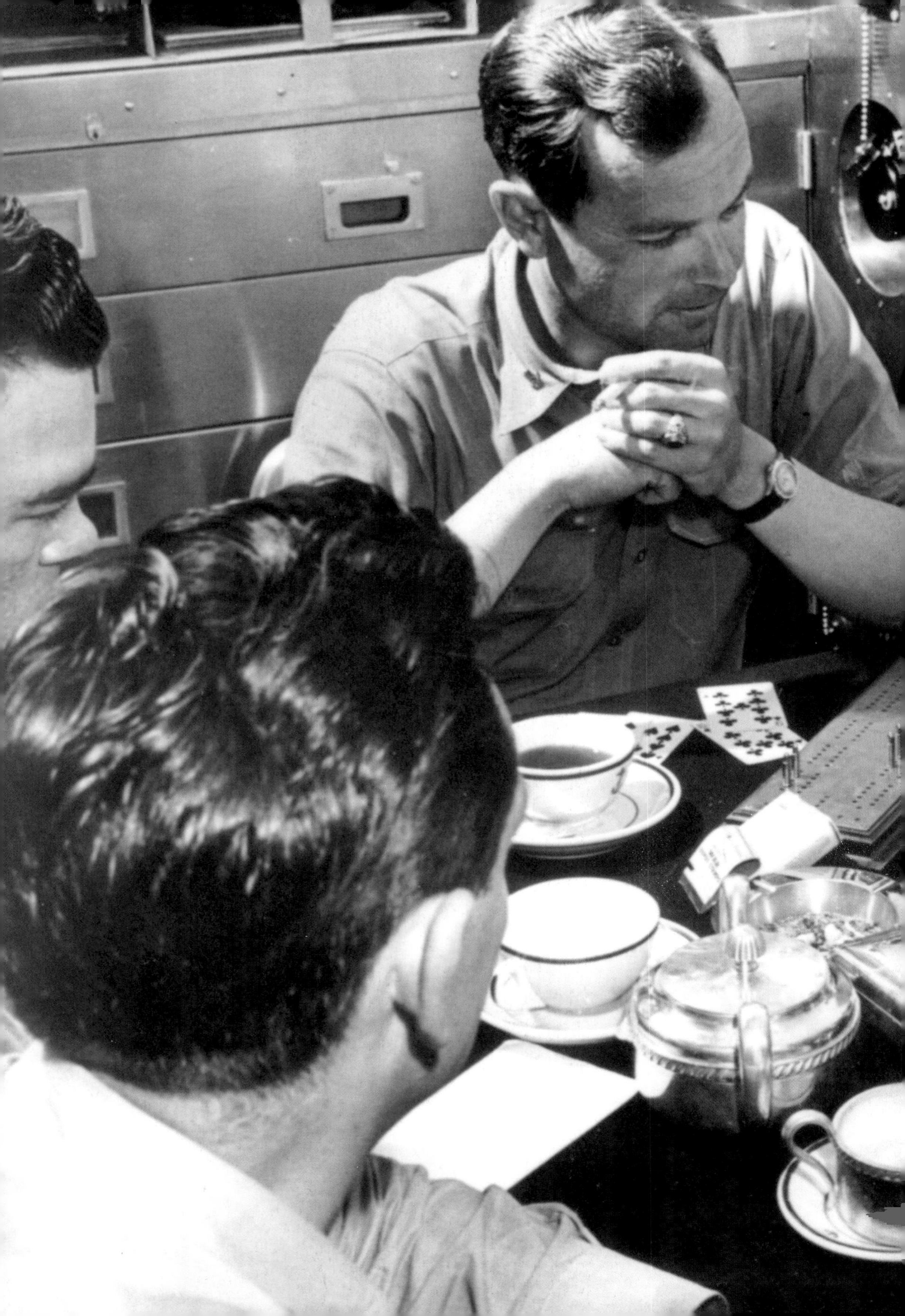

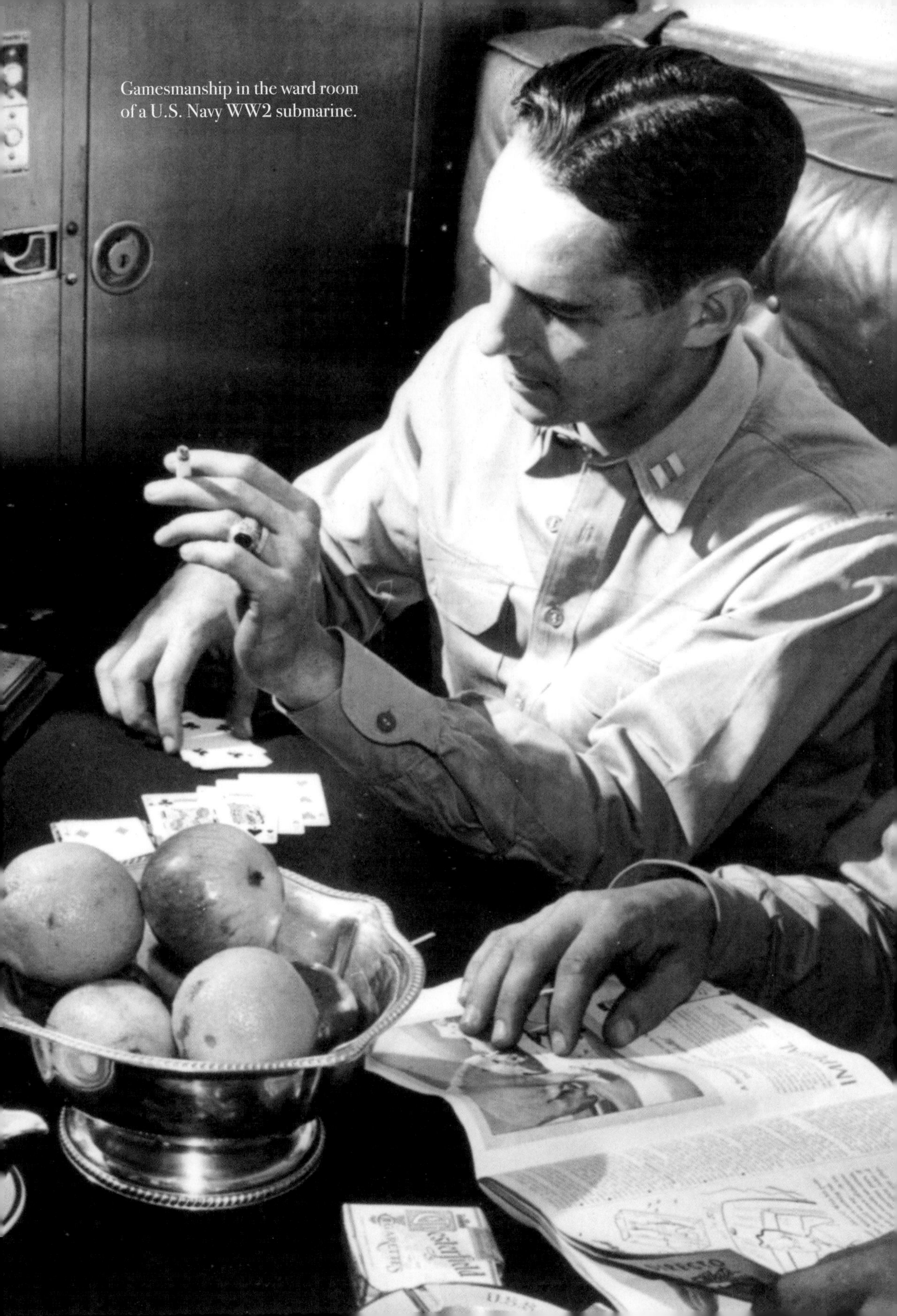

Gamesmanship in the ward room of a U.S. Navy WW2 submarine.

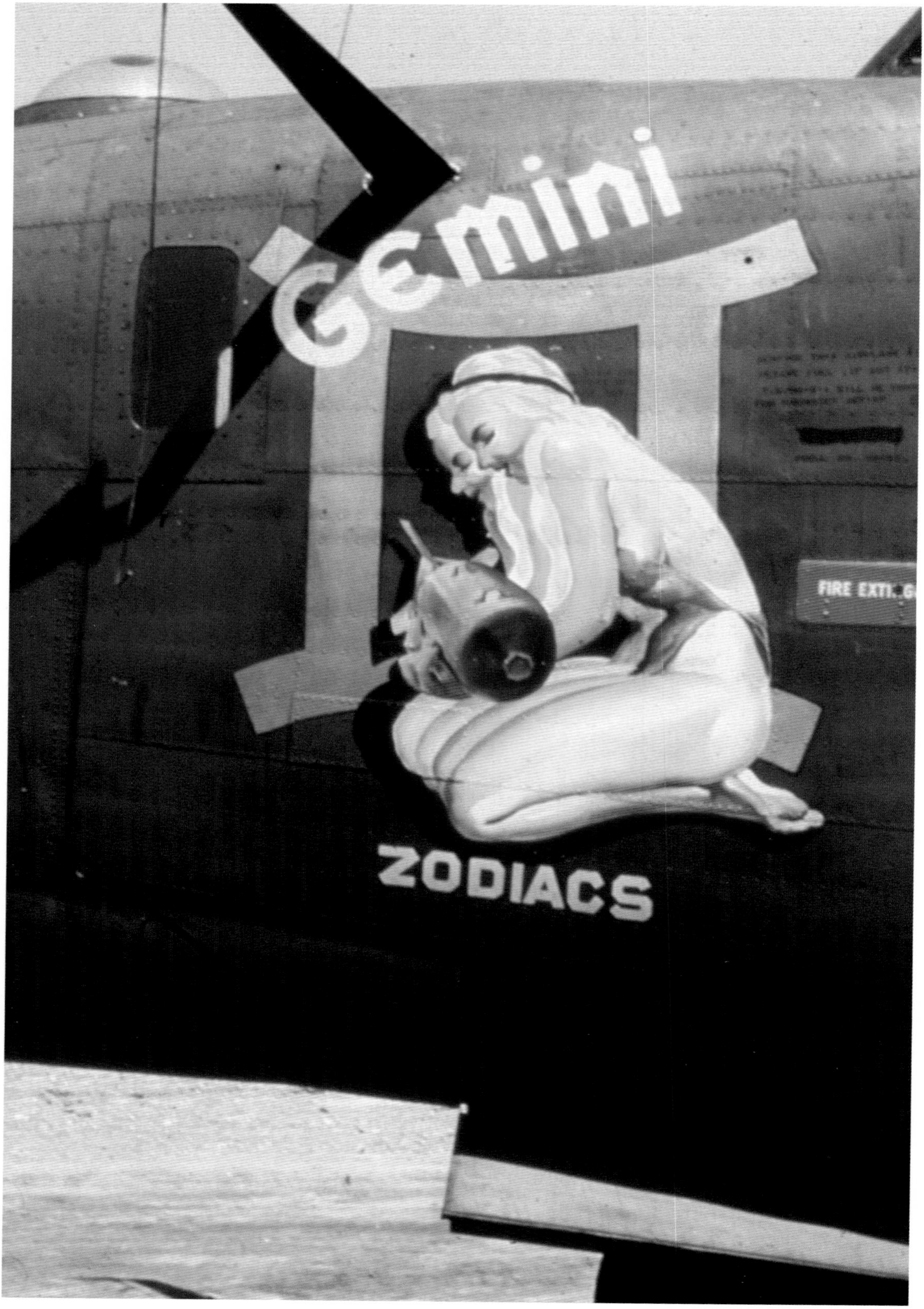
GEmini
ZODIACS
FIRE EXTI

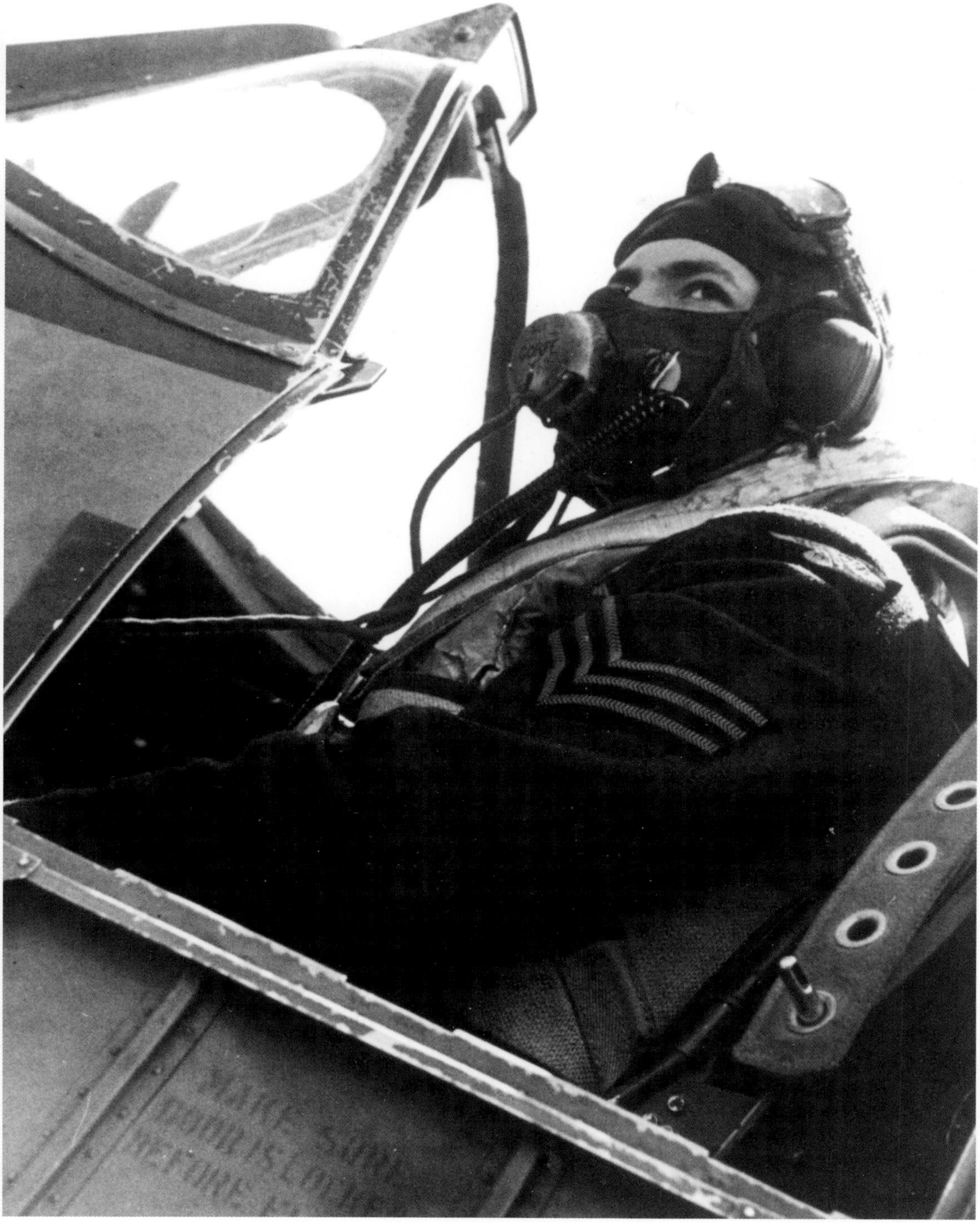

left: One of the Zodiac series of B-24 nose art paintings from artist and draftsman Philip Brinkman of the Sudbury-based 486th Bomb Group; above: An RAF sergeant pilot in the cockpit of his Supermarine Spitfire fighter.

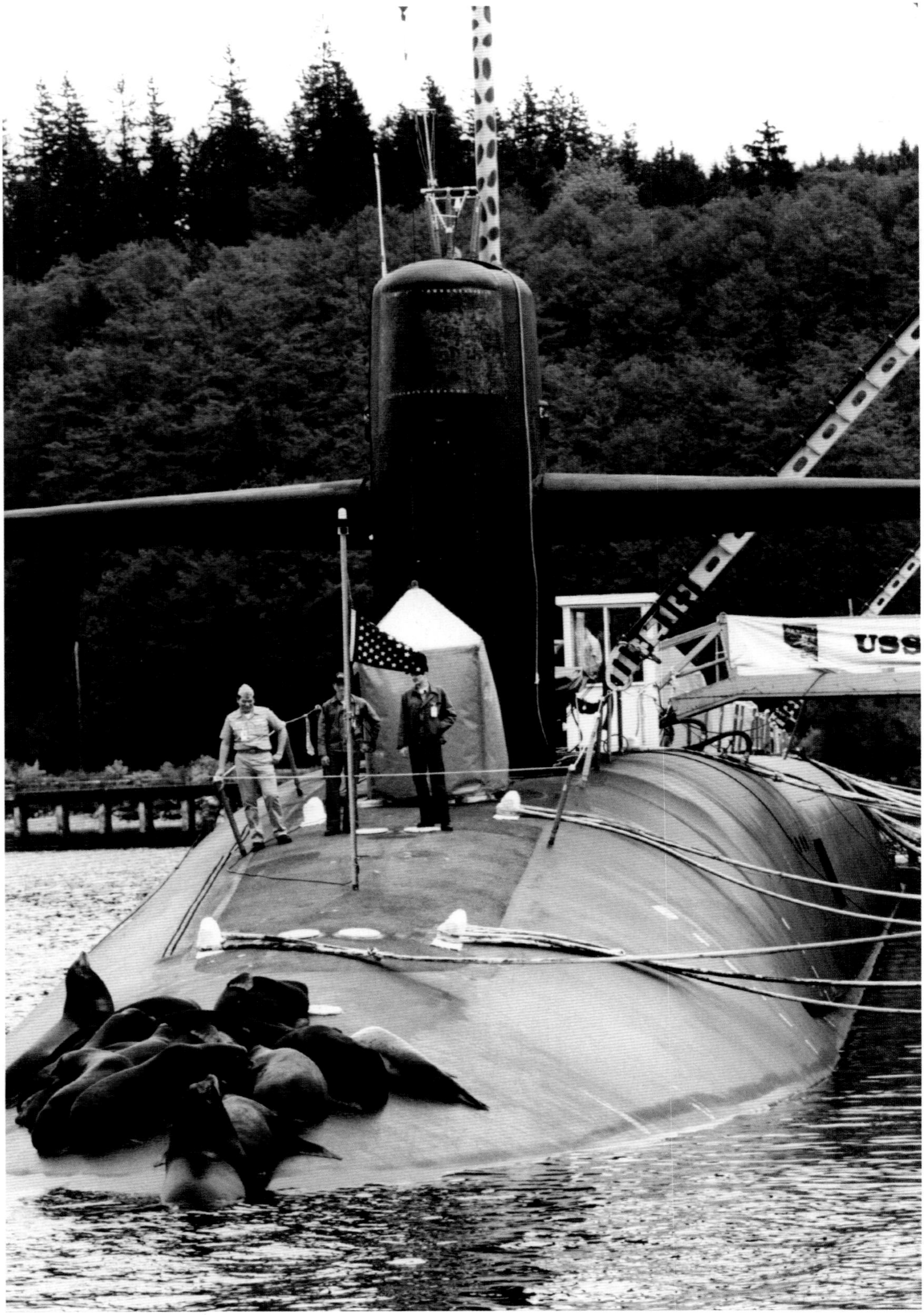
USS

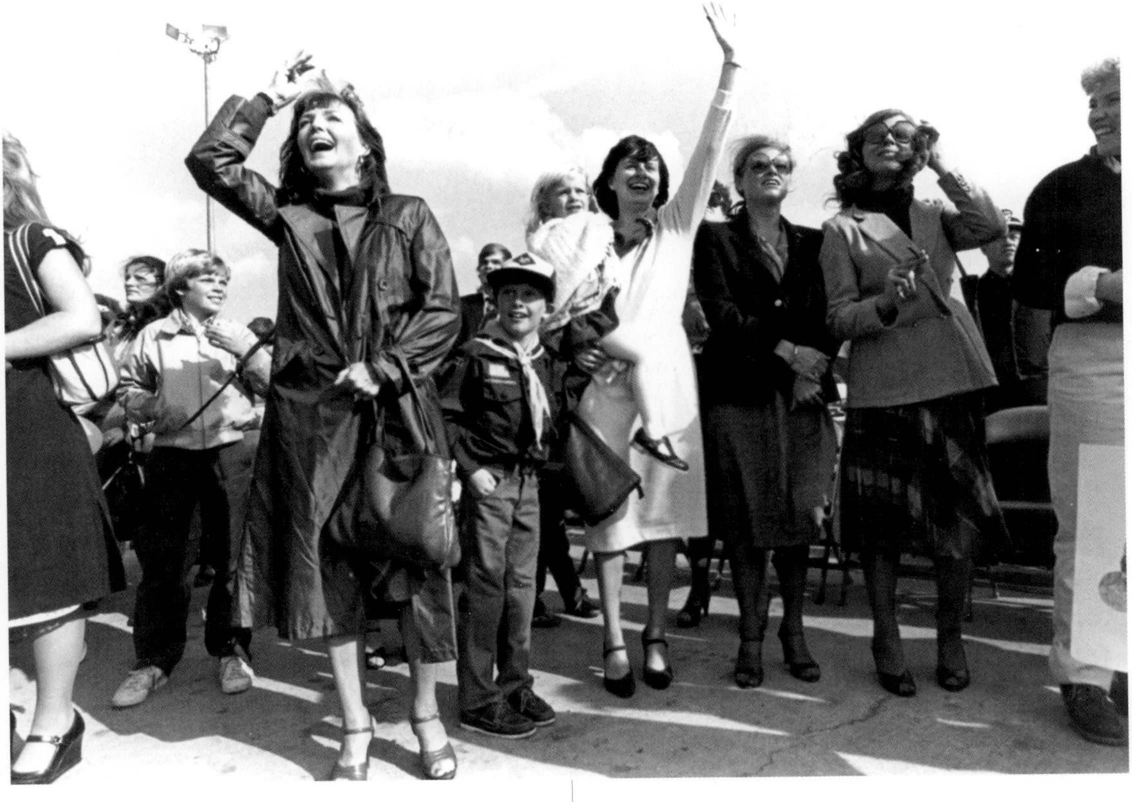

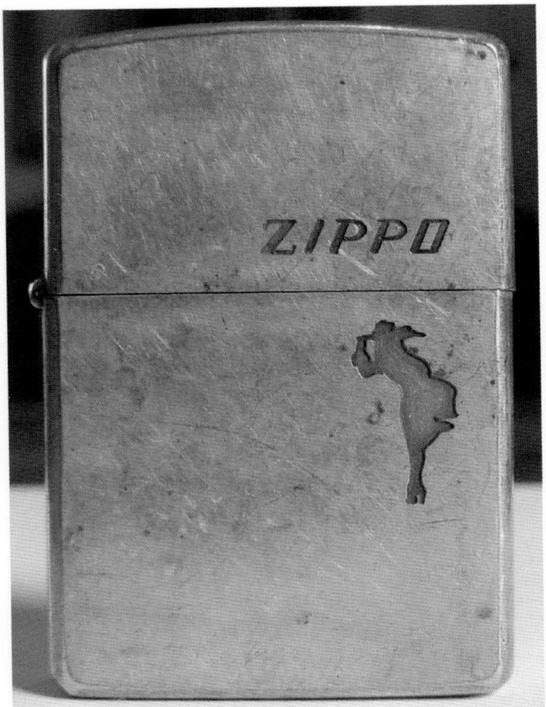
ZIPPO

far left: The USS *Nevada*, an *Ohio*-class nuclear-powered ballistic missile submarine in port at Bangor, Washington. The WASPs, was the Women Airforce Service Pilots, during the Second World War. The WASP originated before the United States' entry into the war, when Nancy Love lobbied for the opening of an American programme to allow women pilots to ferry warplanes from the plants where they were built, to the U.S. bases where they were needed. In the same period, one of the greatest female pilots of the time, Jackie Cochran, organized a group of women pilots for war transport service as part of the British Air Transport Auxiliary and, in late 1942 convinced the AAF commander, General Henry H. Arnold, to activate the Women's Flying Training Detachment which ultimately merged with Nancy Love's organization. In recognition of the WASP's many vital wartime achievements, United States President Barack Obama signed a bill in 2009 that awarded the Congressional Gold Medal to the WASP; left: Windy, the famous wind-swept symbol of Zippo; above: Farewells and Welcome Homes were commonplace in the military..

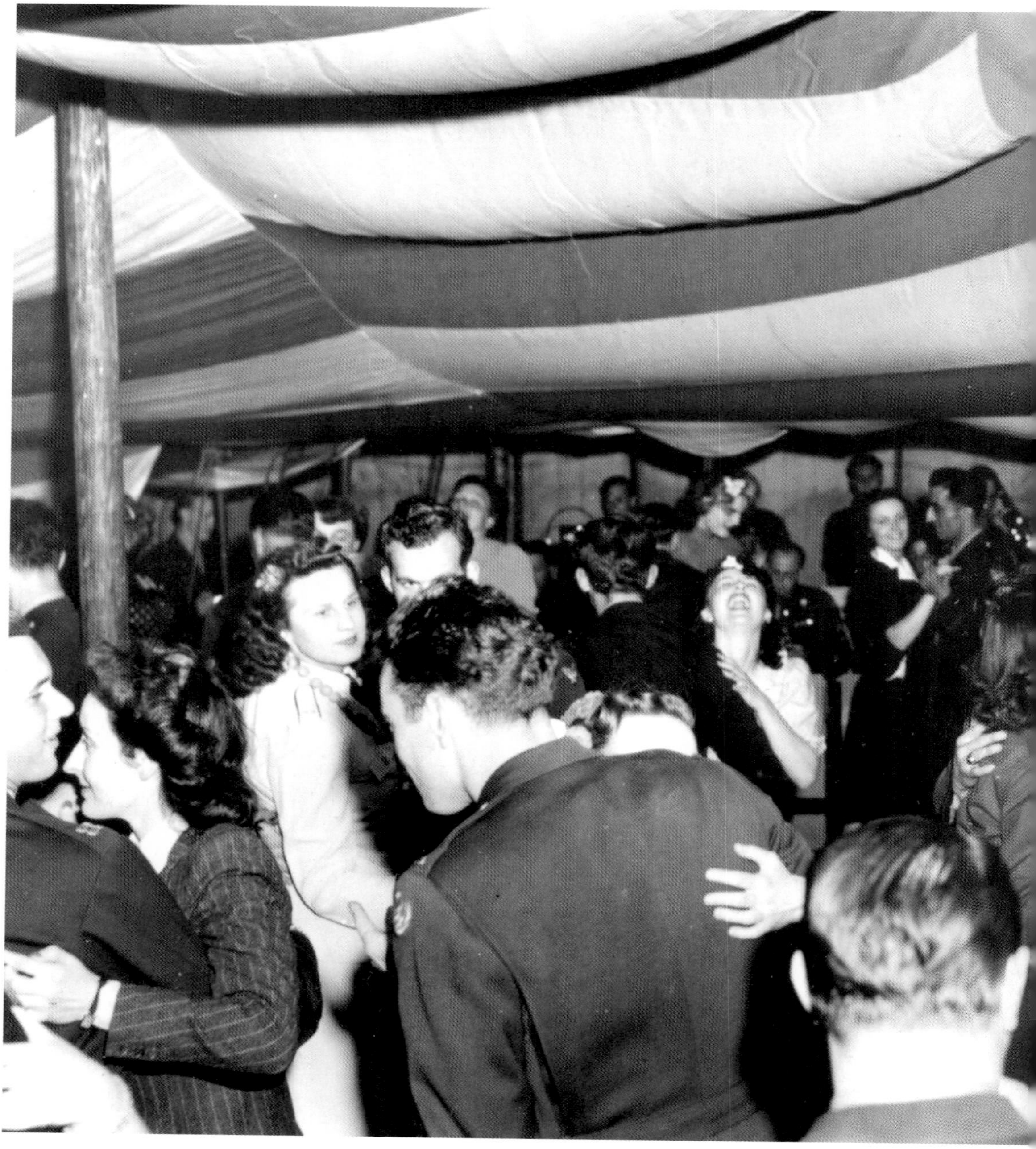

above: A dance at an American Eighth Air Force base in England; bottom right: Sheet music for the song *He Wears a Pair of Silver Wings*, a popular melody during the war years; top right: The world-famous American aviation pioneer Amelia Earhart.

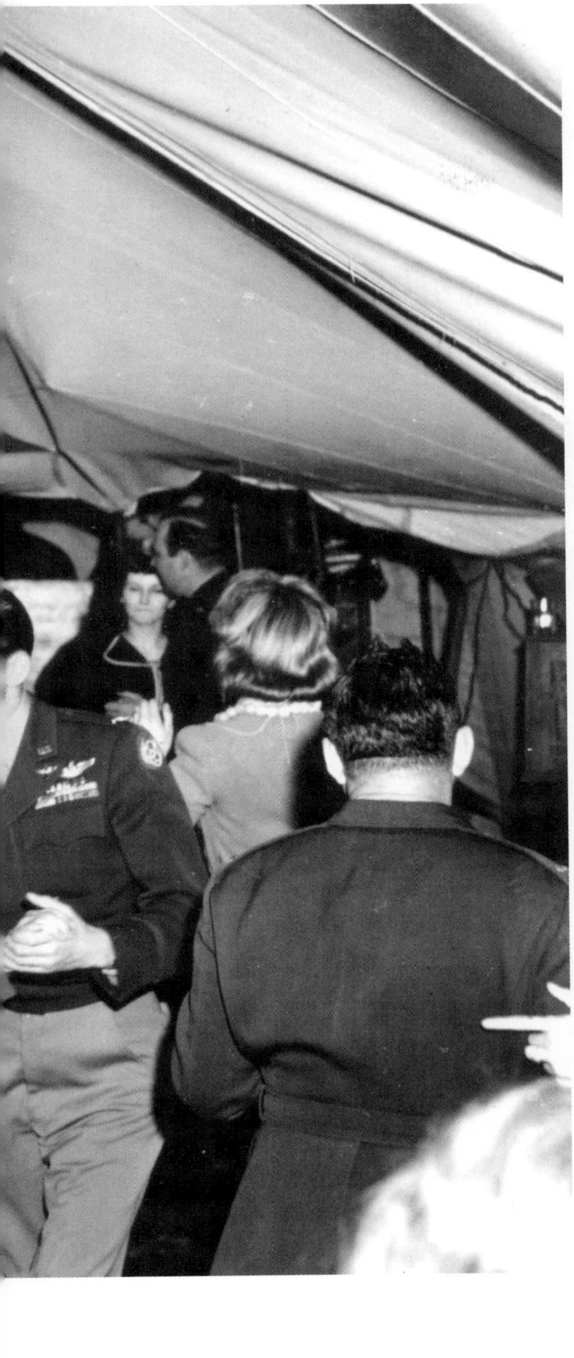

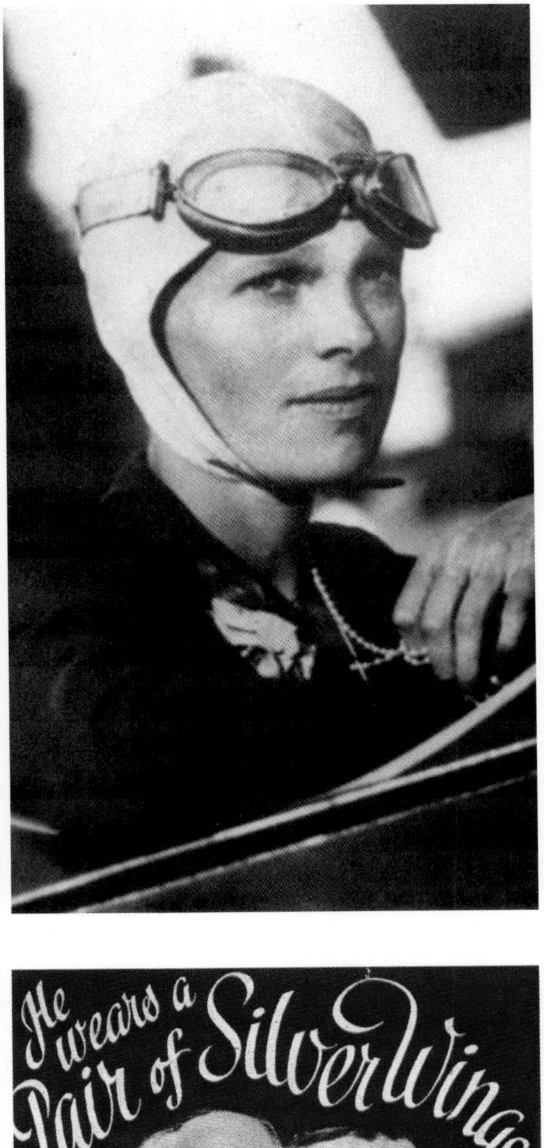

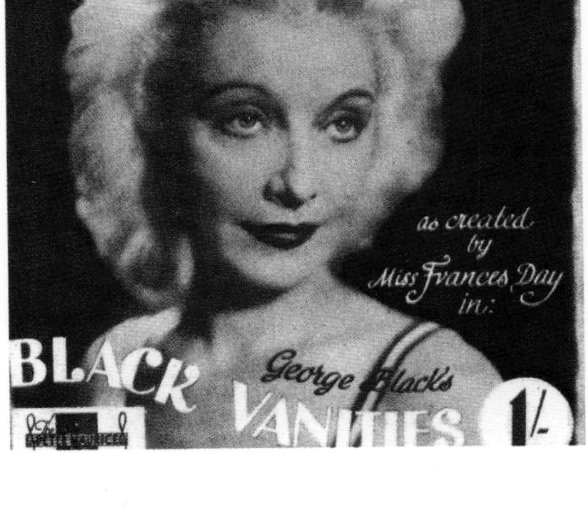
He wears a
Pair of Silver Wings
as created by Miss Frances Day in:
BLACK
George Black's
VANITIES
1/-

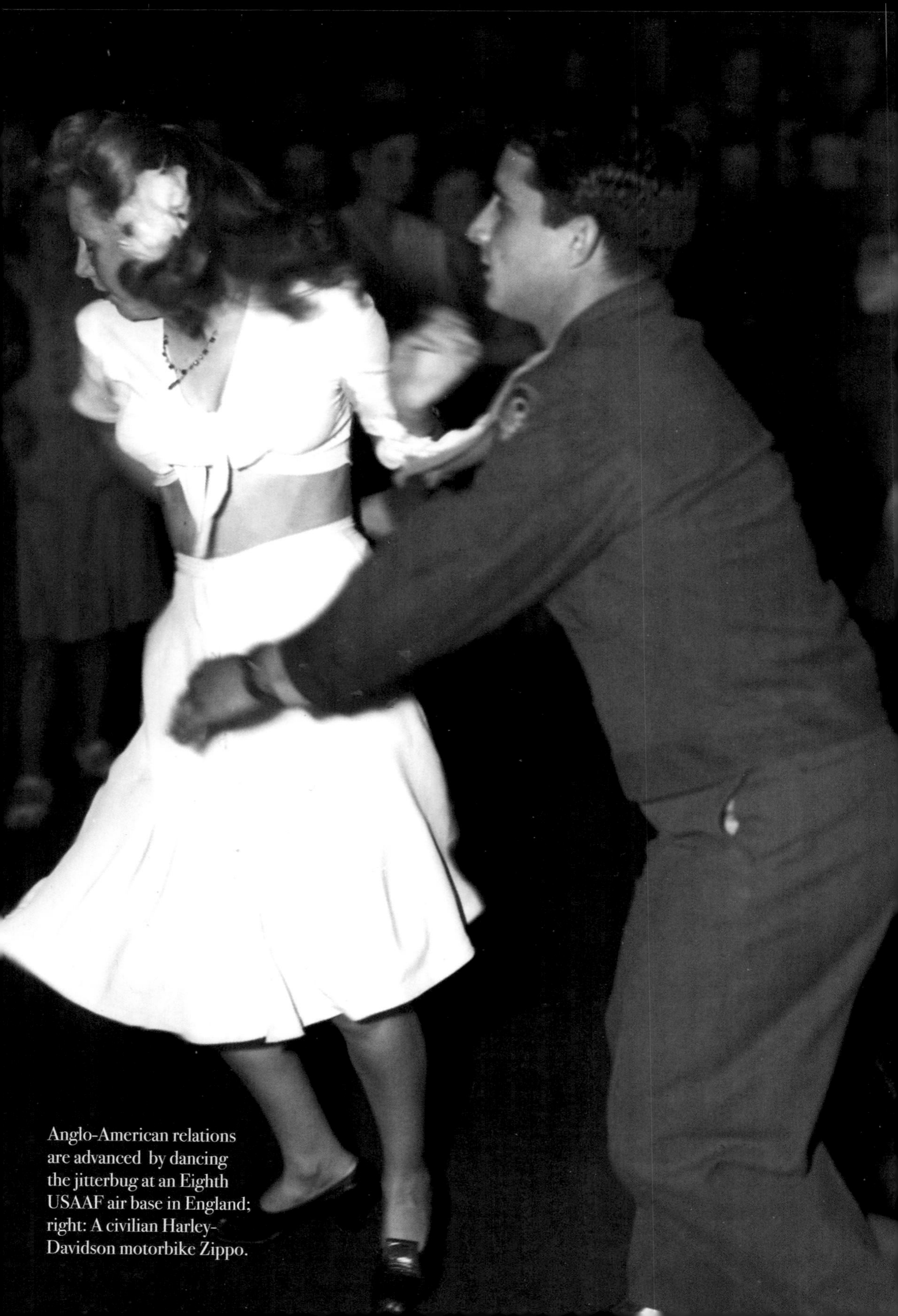

Anglo-American relations are advanced by dancing the jitterbug at an Eighth USAAF air base in England; right: A civilian Harley-Davidson motorbike Zippo.

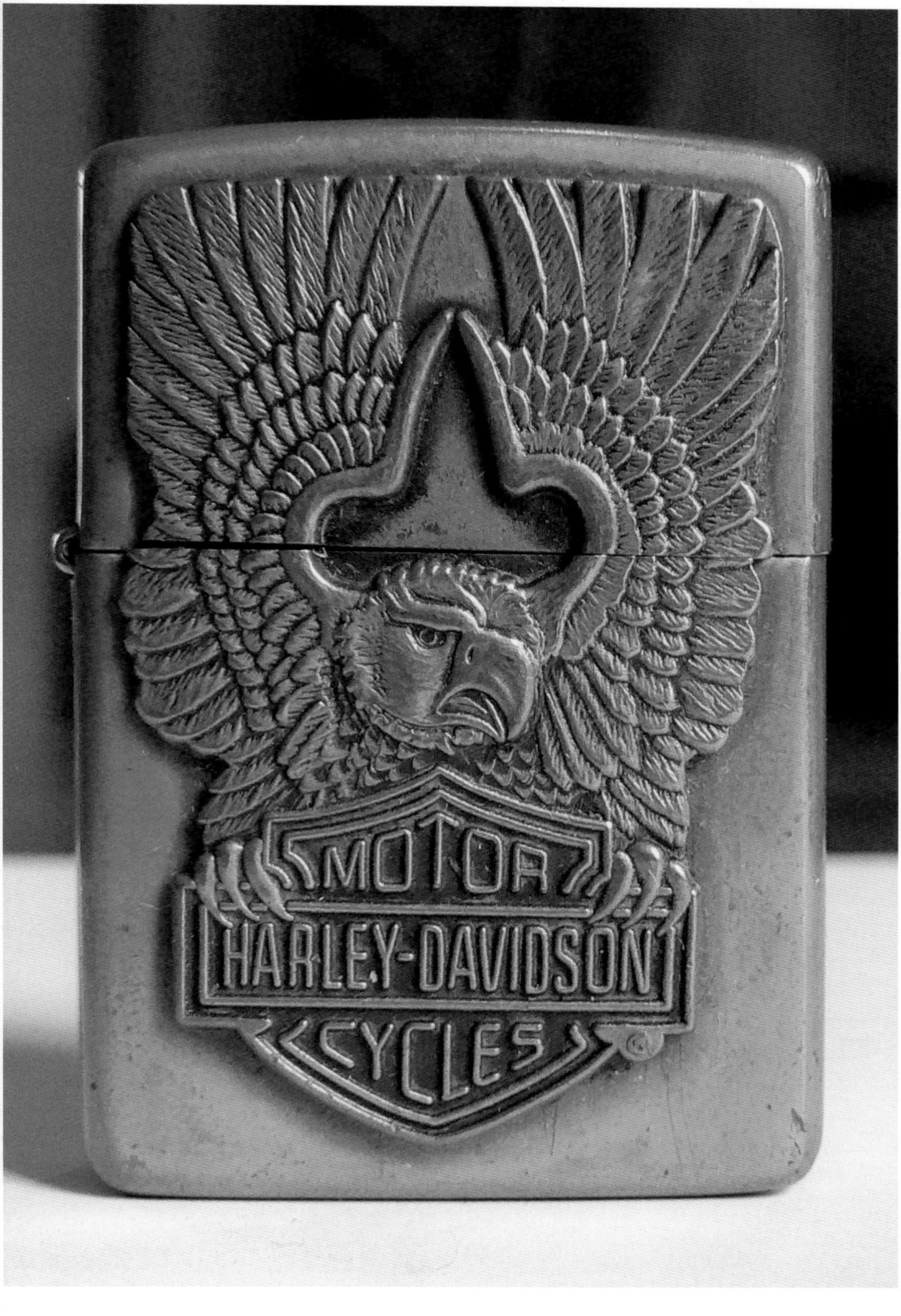
MOTOR
HARLEY-DAVIDSON
CYCLES

The Consolidated-Vultee B-24 Liberator bomber cockpit panel..

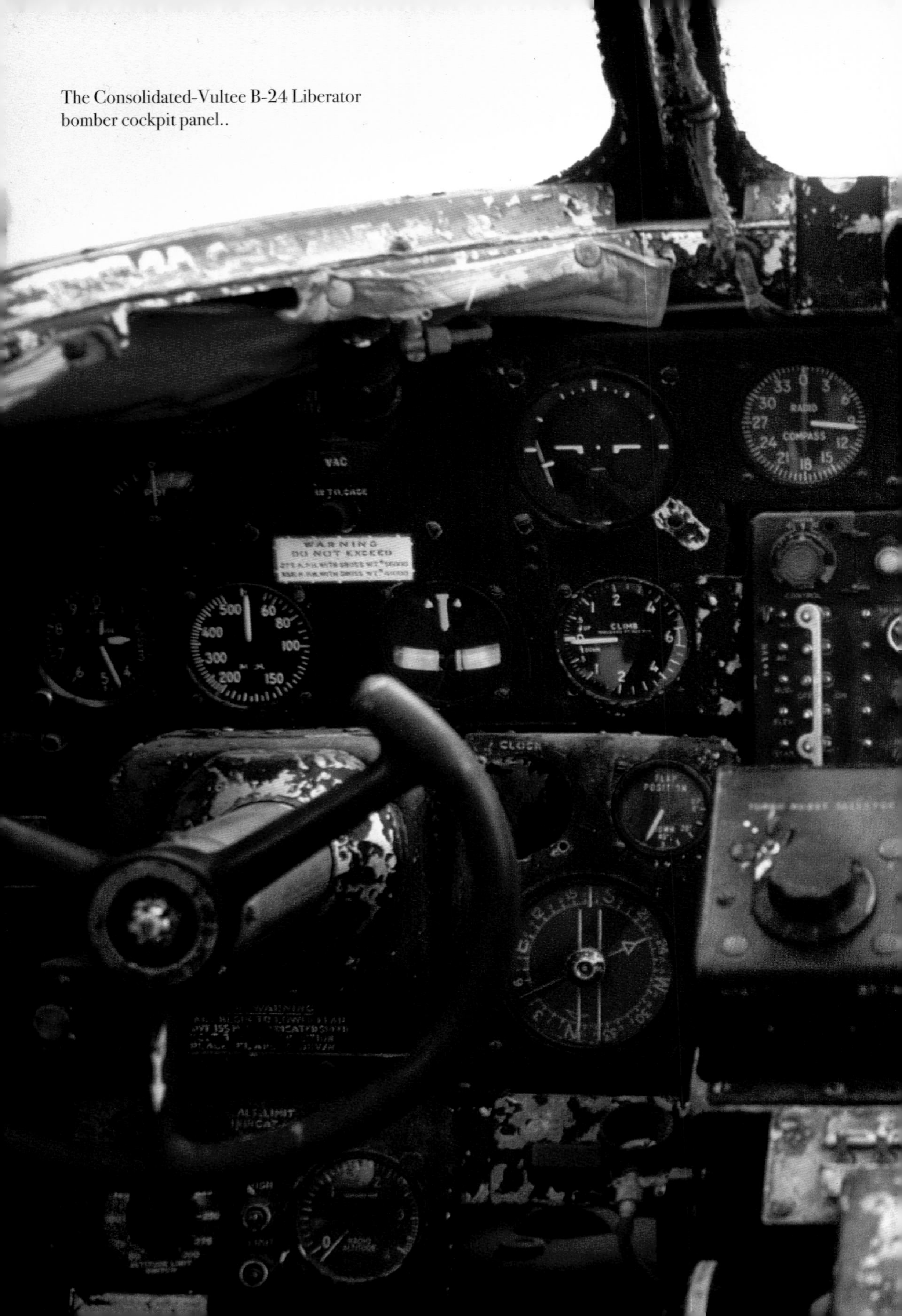
VAC
WARNING
DO NOT EXCEED
RADIO
COMPASS
CLIMB
FLAP POSITION

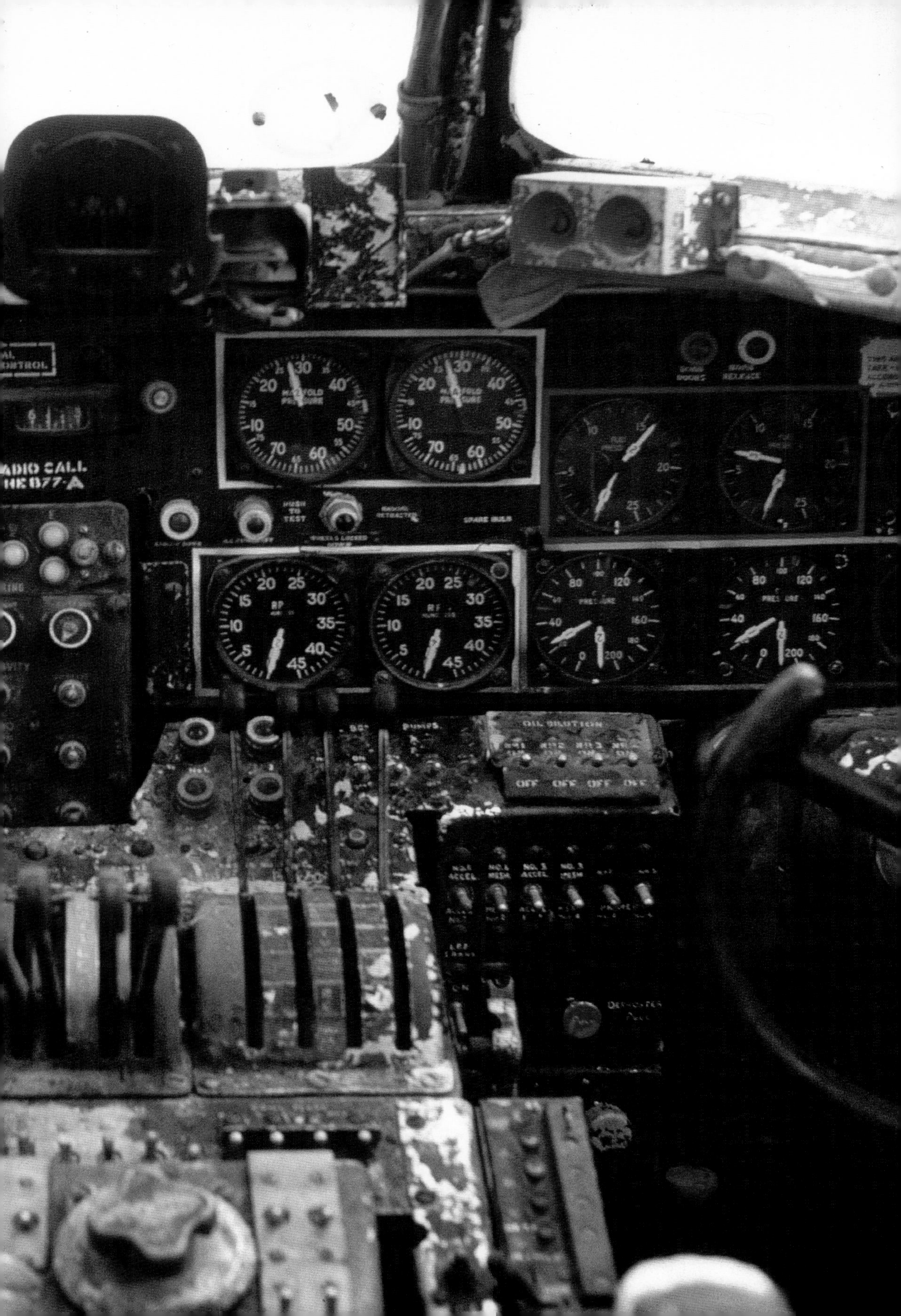
PUSH TO TEST
PUMPS
OIL DILUTION
OFF OFF OFF OFF
NO. 3 ACCEL

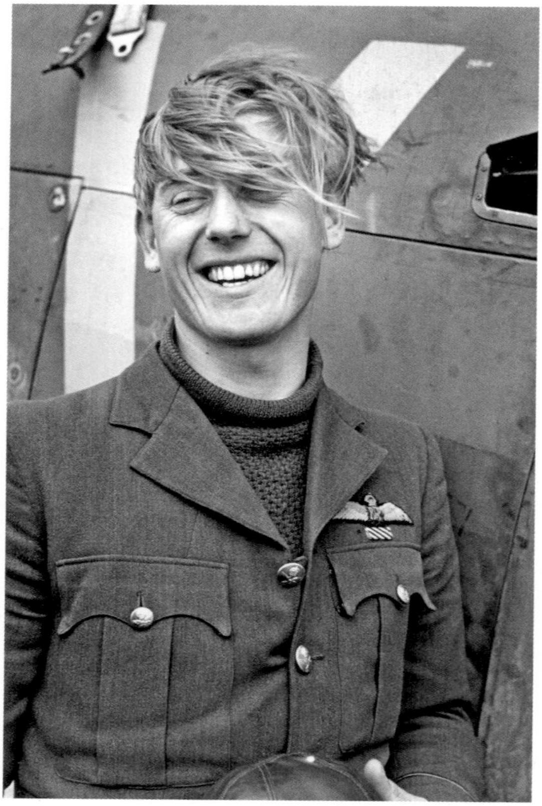

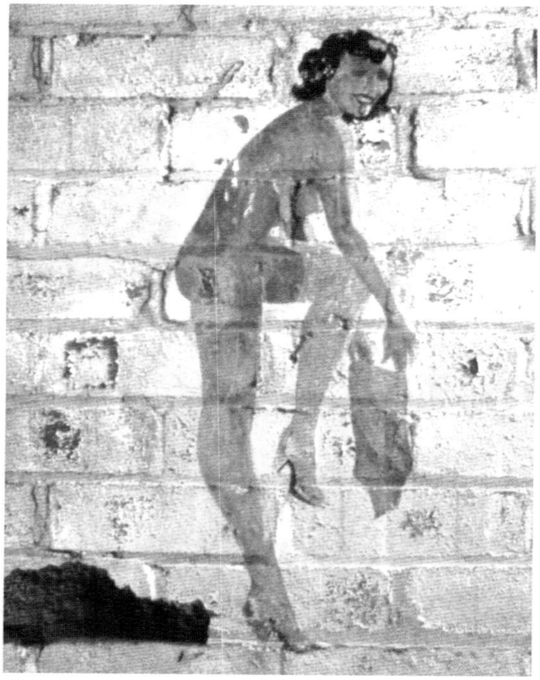

left: RAF Pilot Officer Albert Day Lewis; below: Members of the Women Auxiliary Air Force at Tangmere, West Sussexx; above: Shipdham wall art; right: A chow line at Deenethorpe, Northants.

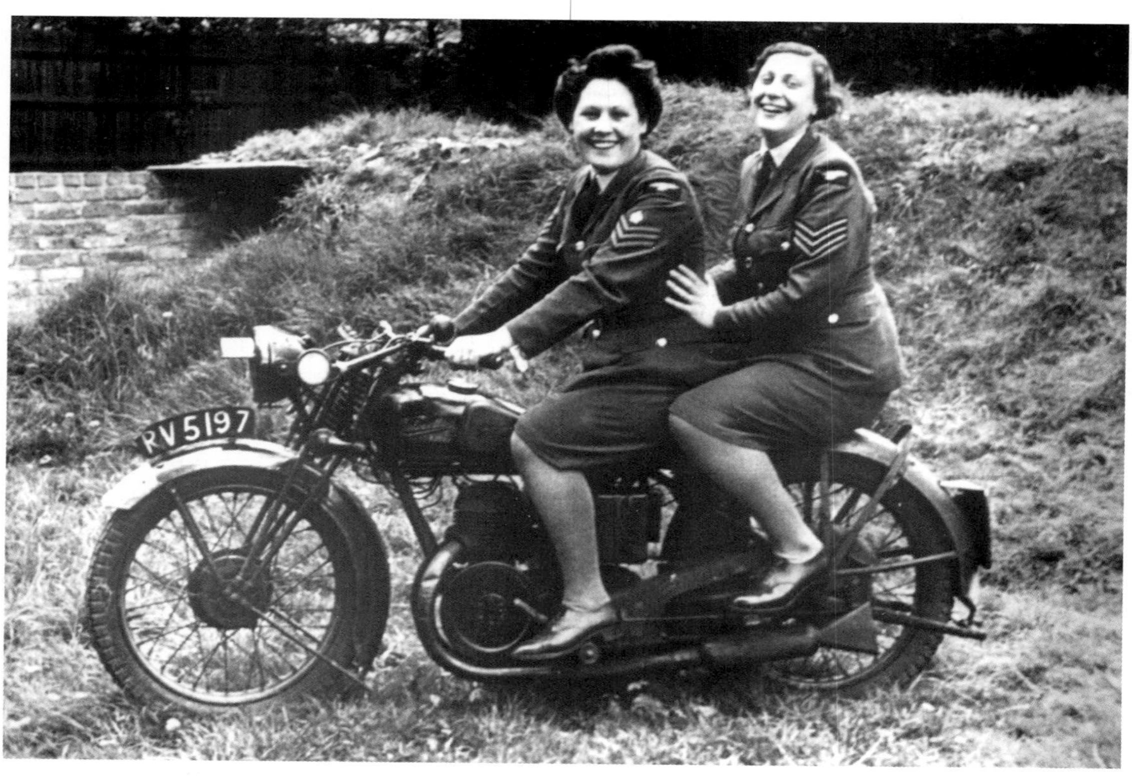
RV 5197

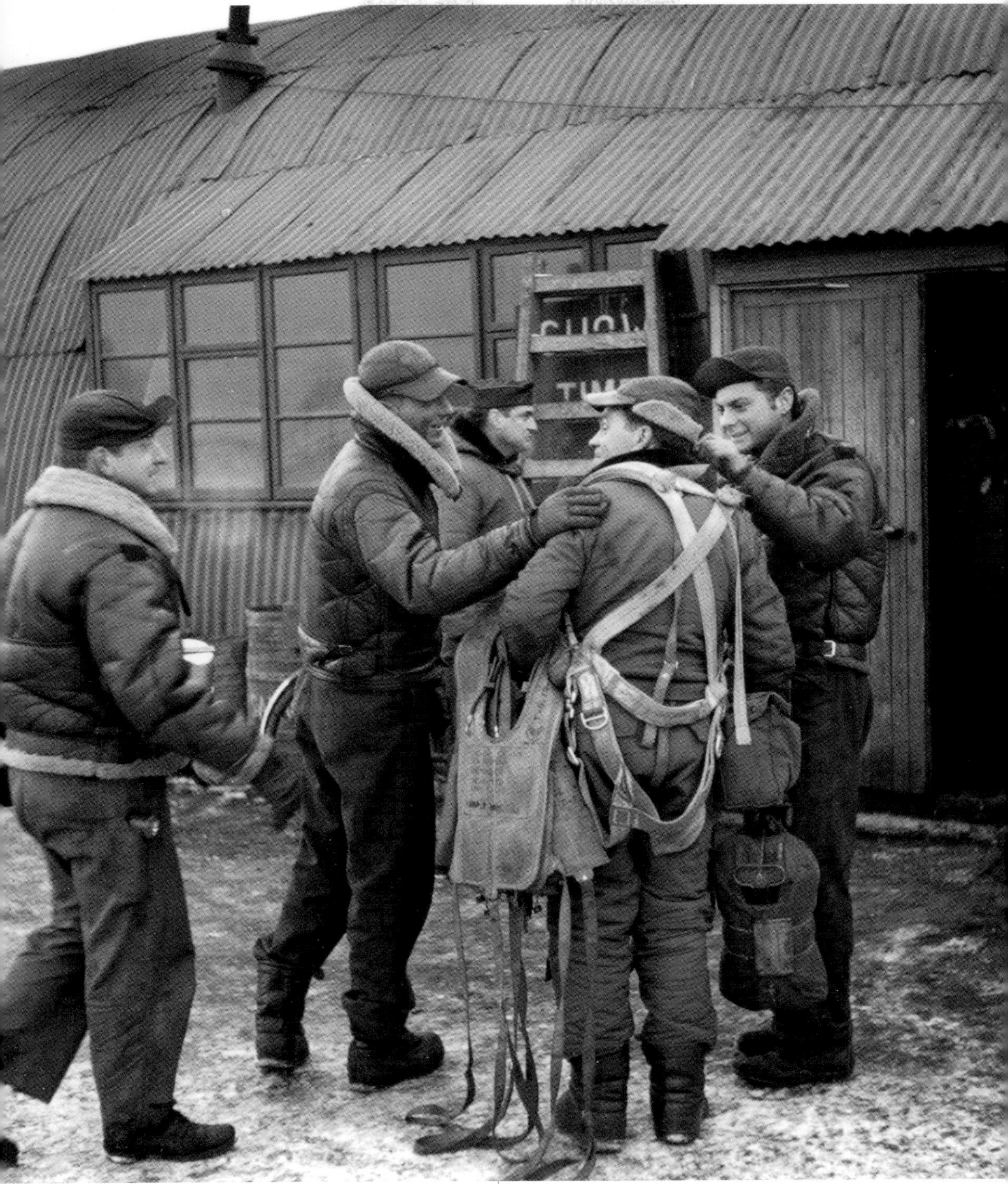

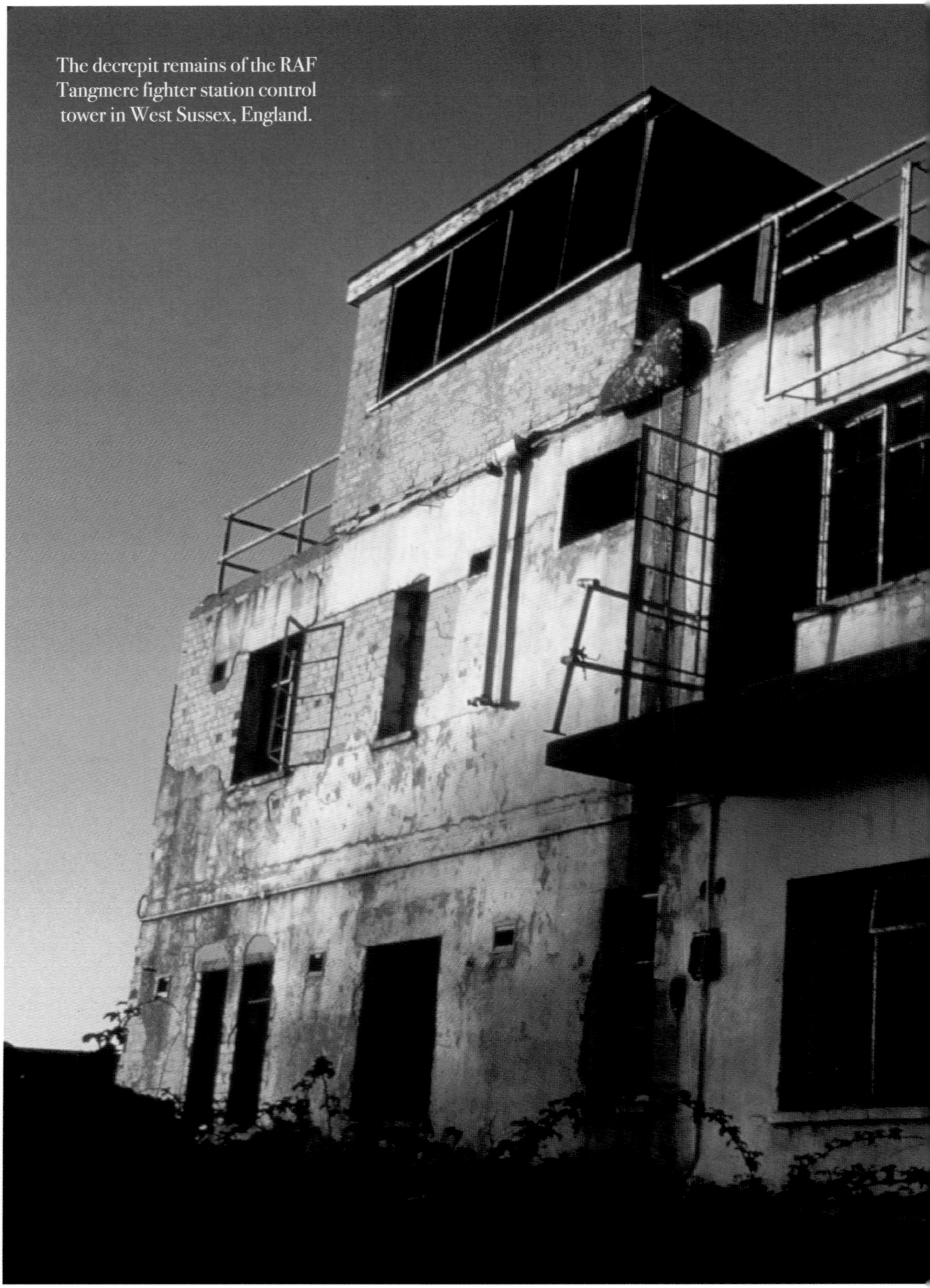

The decrepit remains of the RAF Tangmere fighter station control tower in West Sussex, England.

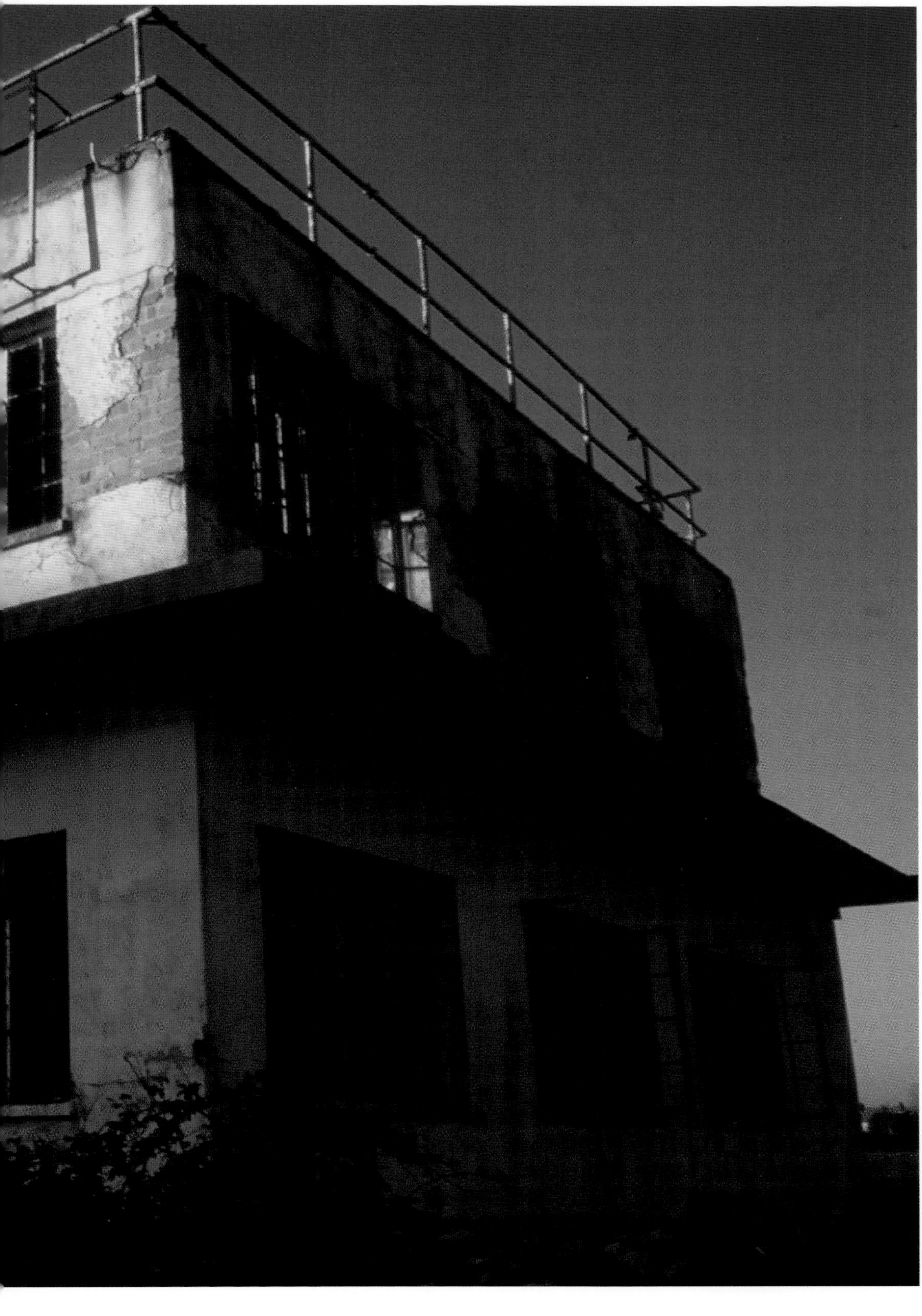

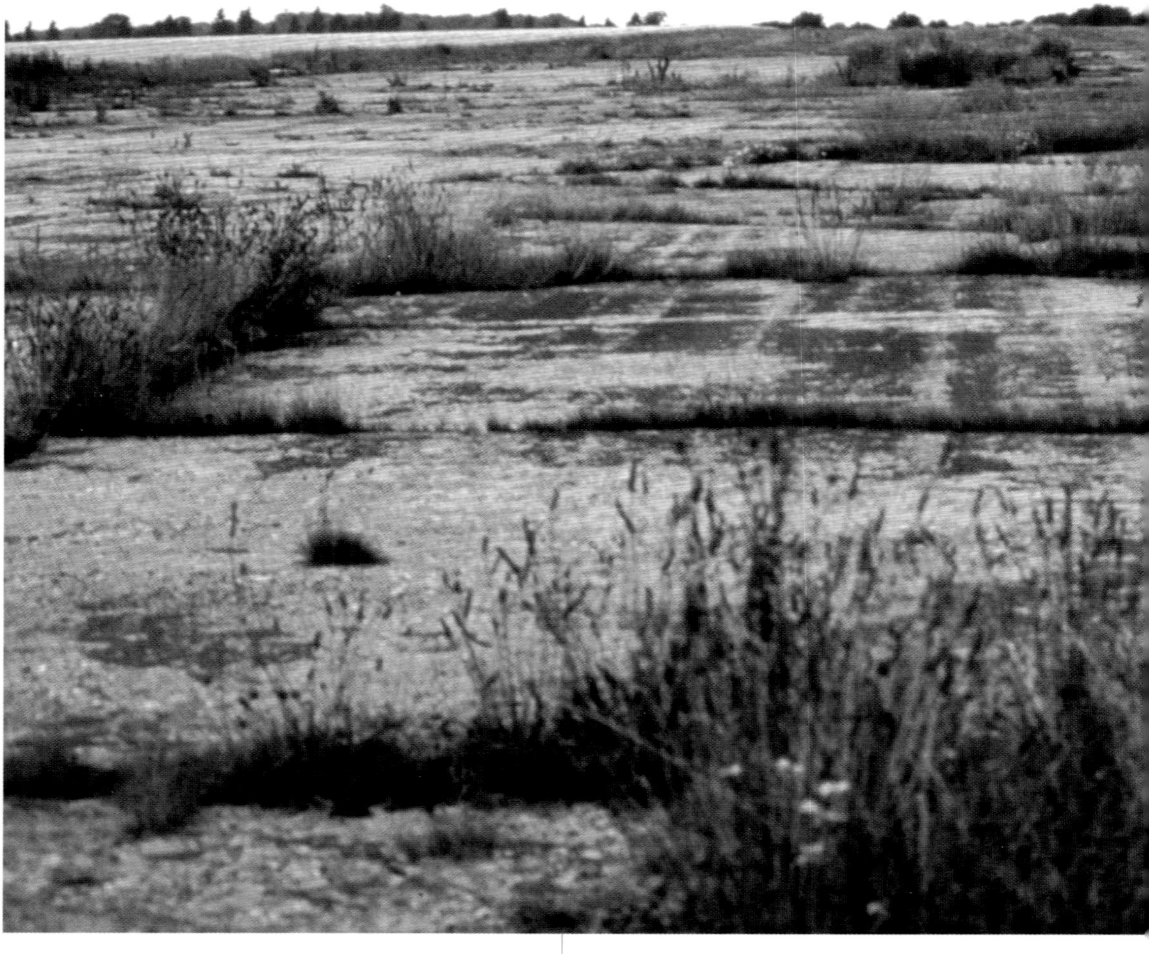

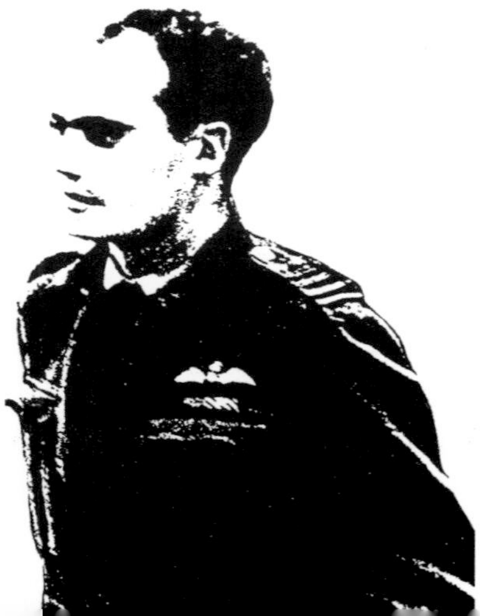

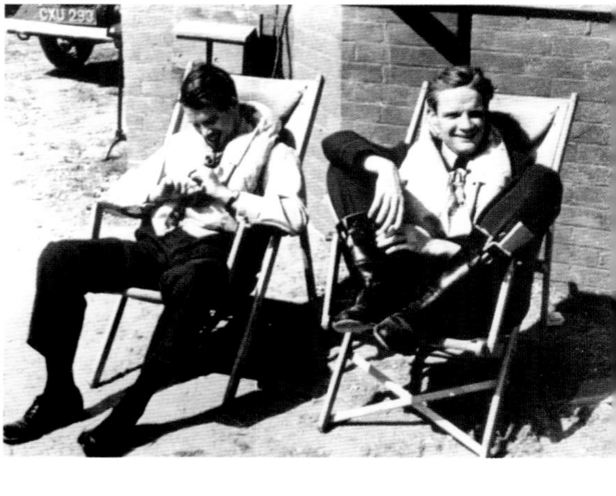
CXU 293

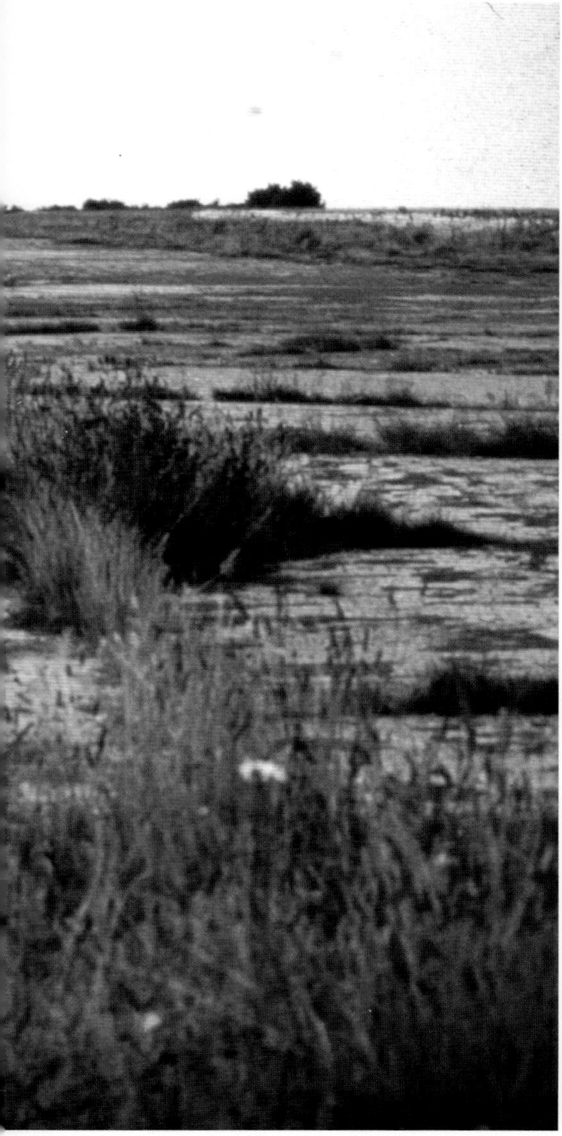

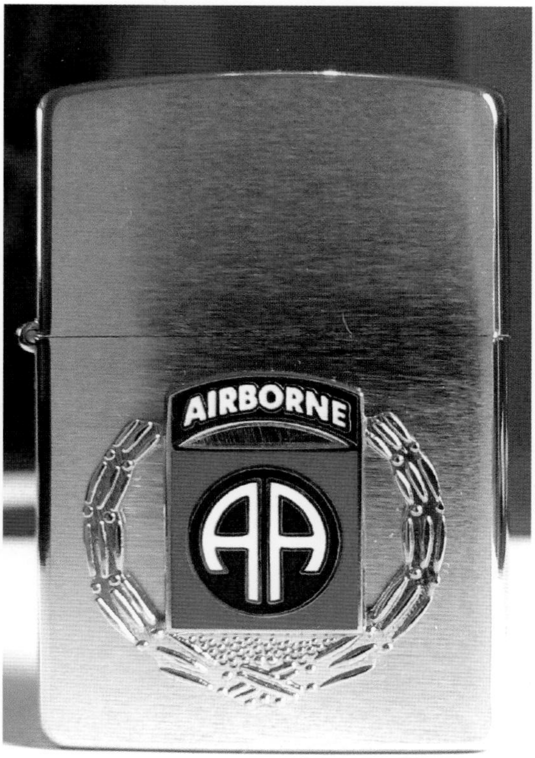
AIRBORNE
AA

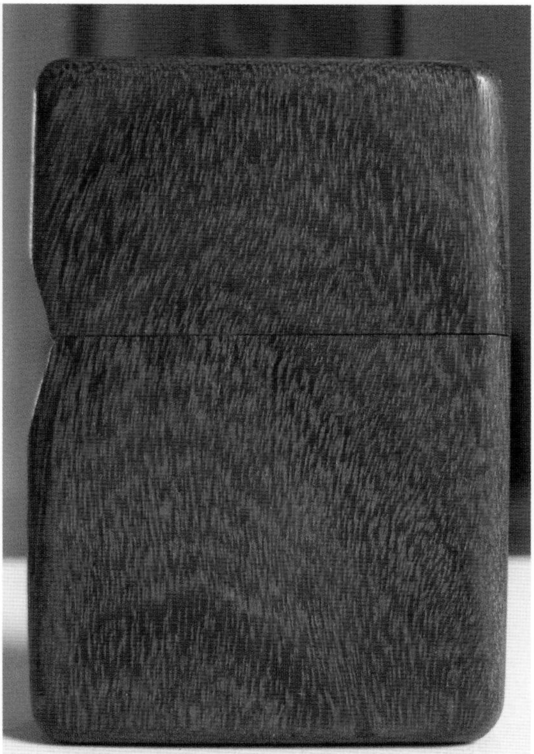

above: The former main runway of the 487th Bomb Group, Eighth Air Force airfield near the village of Lavenham, Suffolk, England; far left: Group Captain Brian Kingcome, No 92 Squadron, RAF in WWII; right: A wood-grain encased Zippo; left: RAF fighter pilots at their ease between combat sorties; at top: Honouring the U.S. Army 82nd Airborne Division.

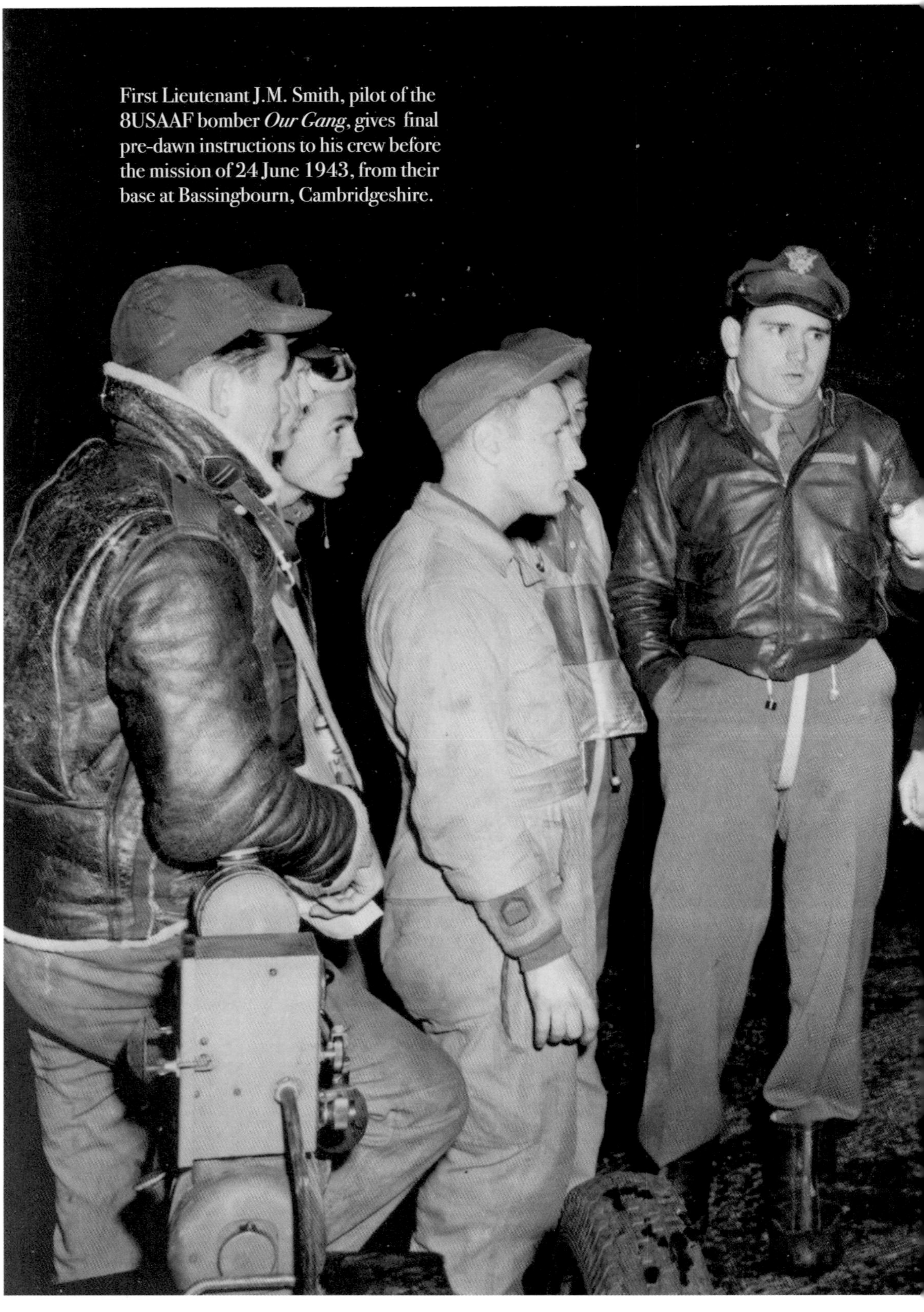

First Lieutenant J.M. Smith, pilot of the 8USAAF bomber *Our Gang*, gives final pre-dawn instructions to his crew before the mission of 24 June 1943, from their base at Bassingbourn, Cambridgeshire.

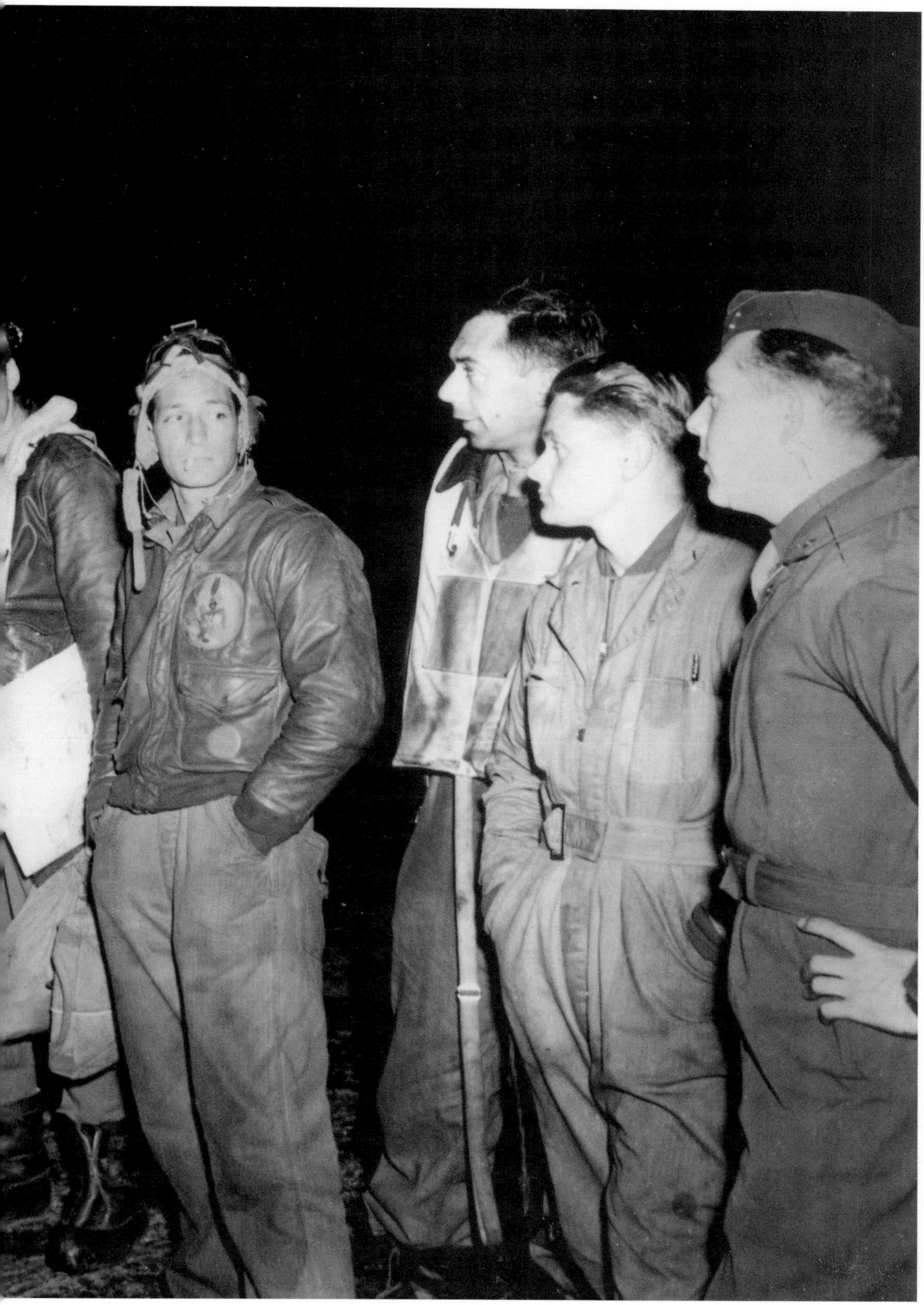

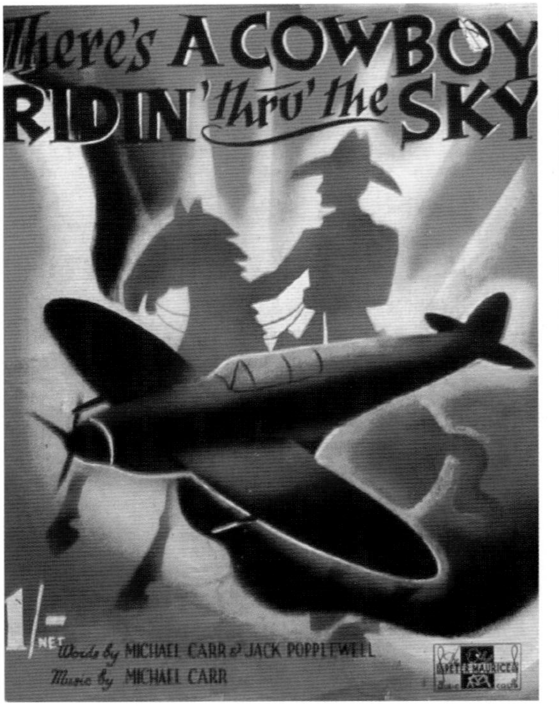
There's A COWBOY
RIDIN' thro' the SKY
1/- NET
Words by MICHAEL CARR & JACK POPPLEWELL
Music by MICHAEL CARR
PETER MAURICE

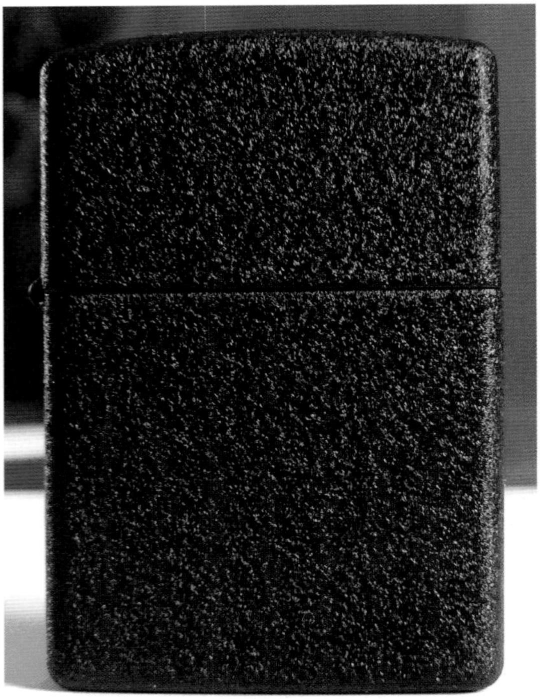

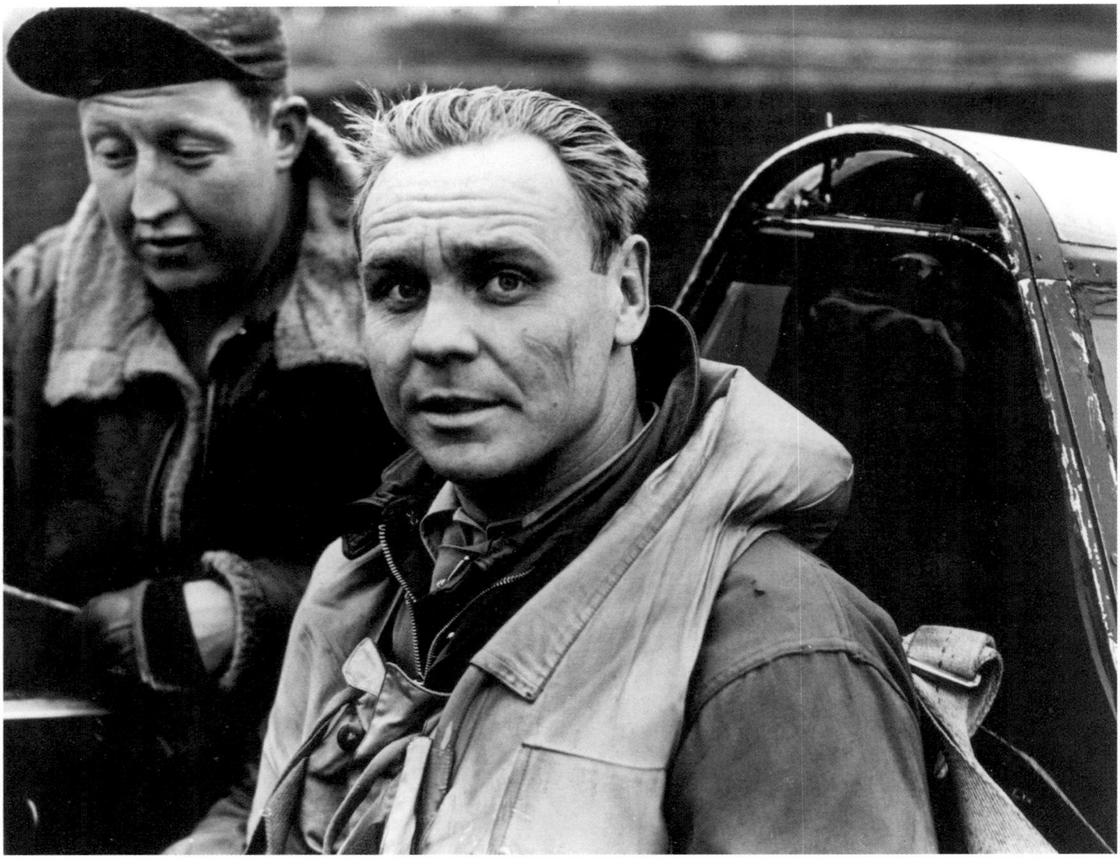

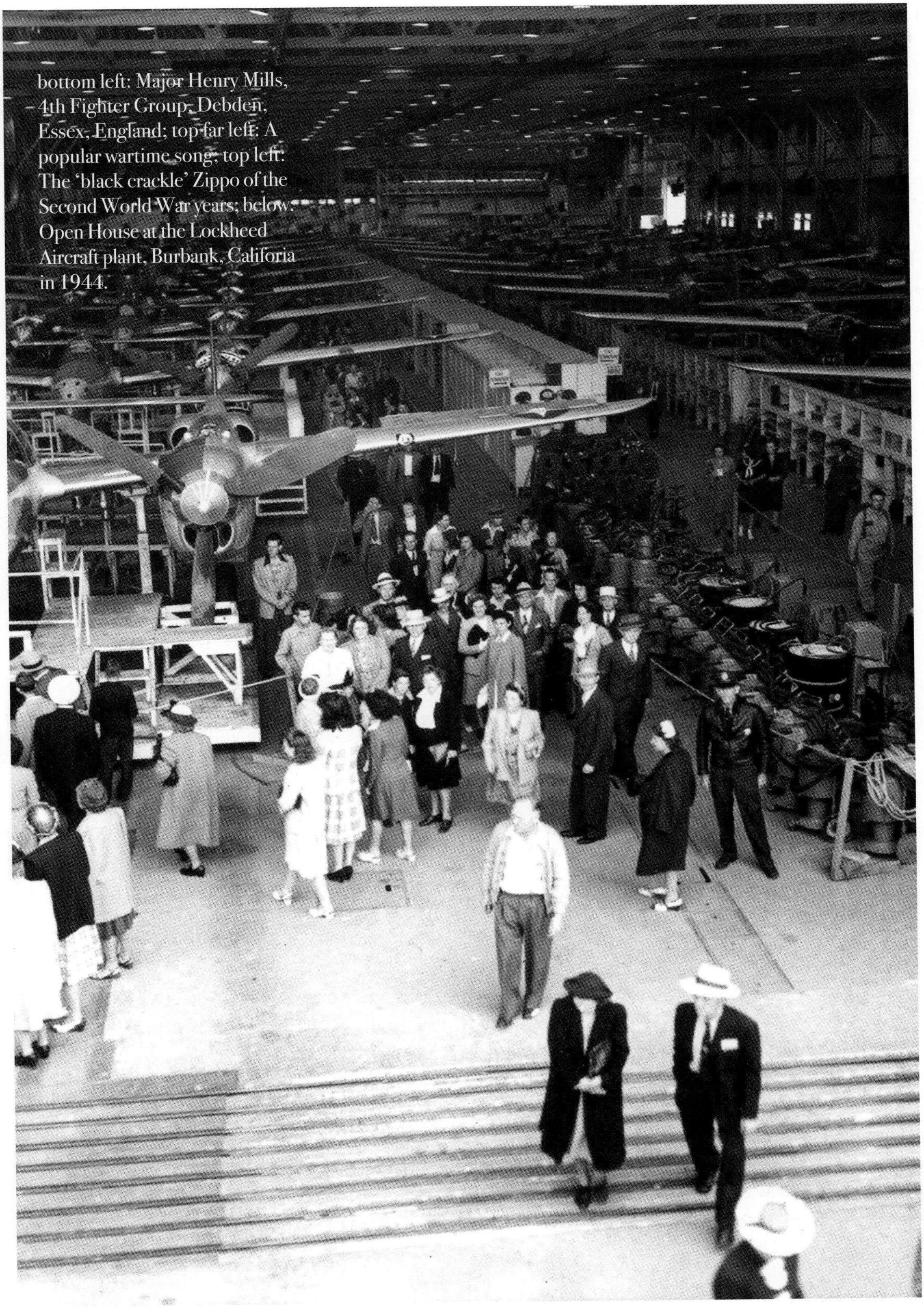

bottom left: Major Henry Mills, 4th Fighter Group, Debden, Essex, England; top far left: A popular wartime song; top left: The 'black crackle' Zippo of the Second World War years; below: Open House at the Lockheed Aircraft plant, Burbank, California in 1944.

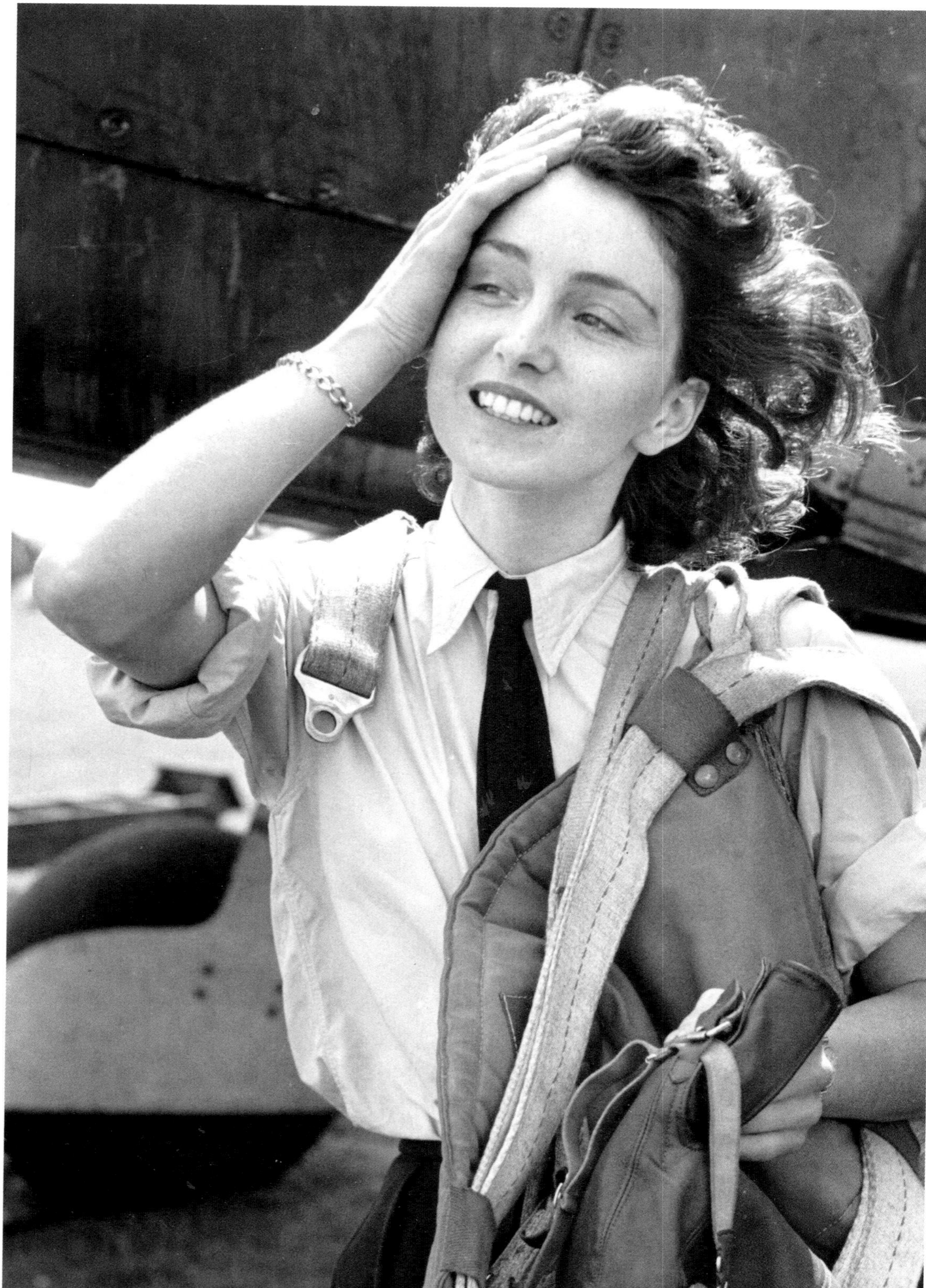

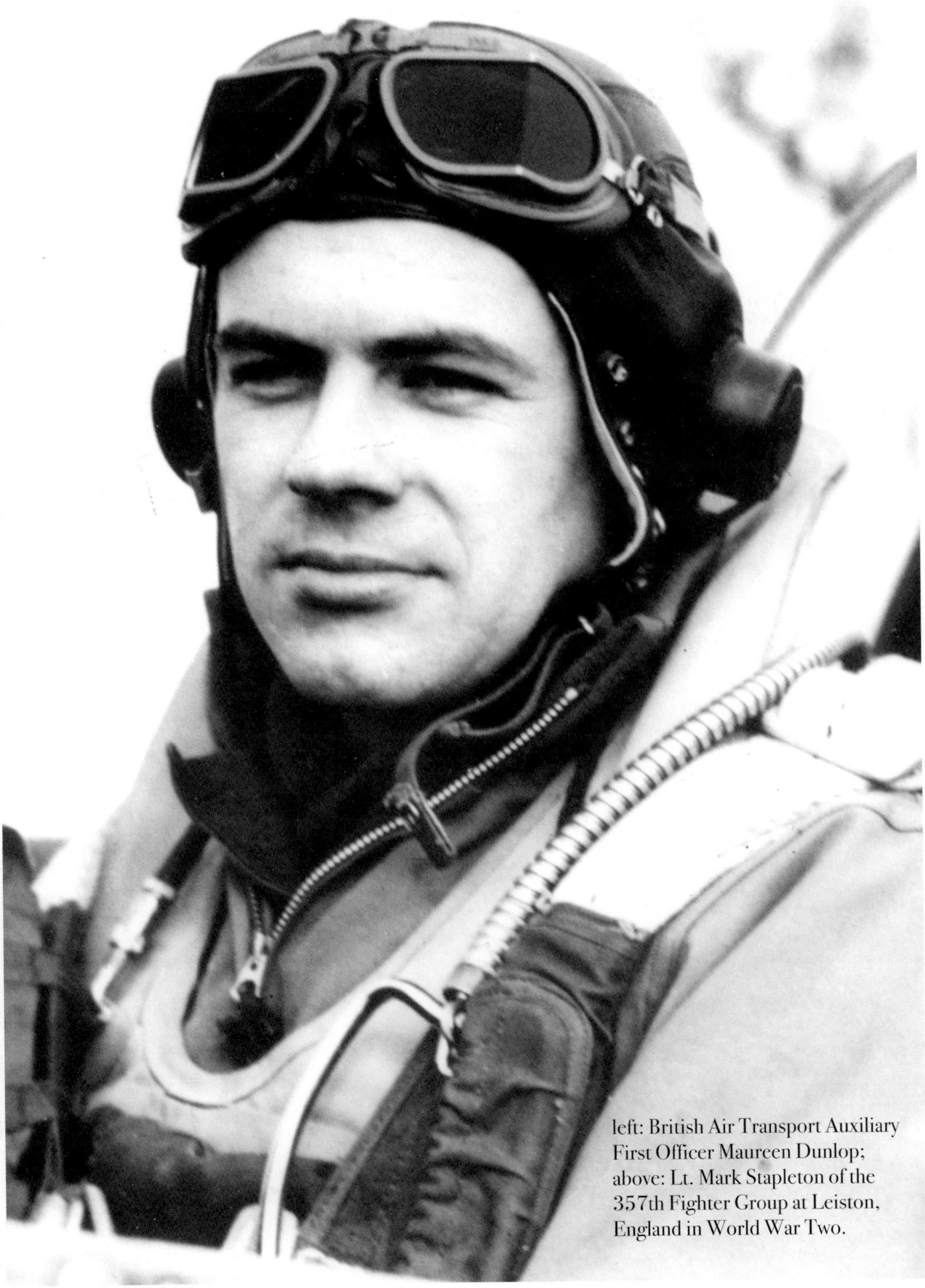

left: British Air Transport Auxiliary First Officer Maureen Dunlop; above: Lt. Mark Stapleton of the 357th Fighter Group at Leiston, England in World War Two.

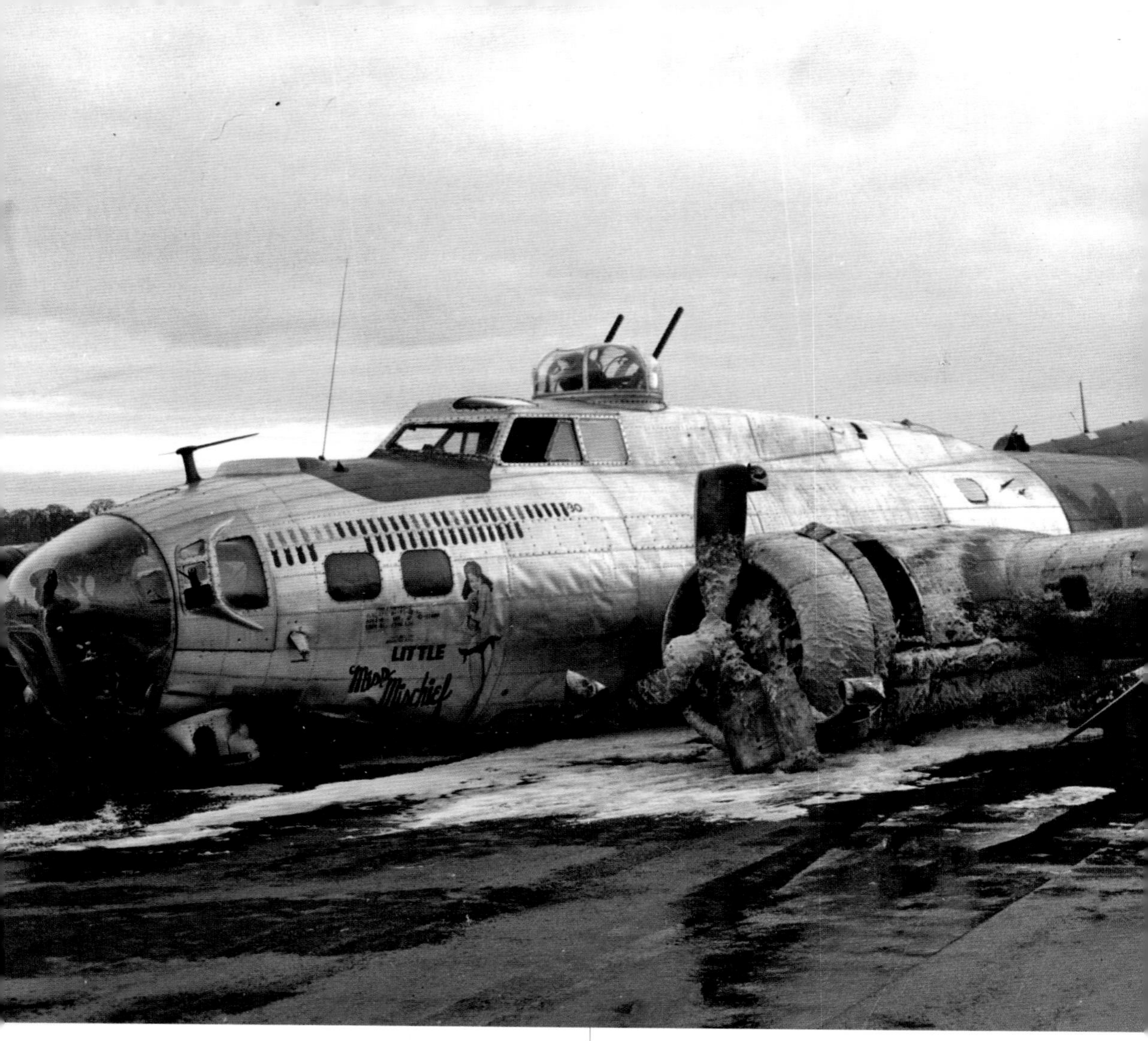
LITTLE
Miss Mischief

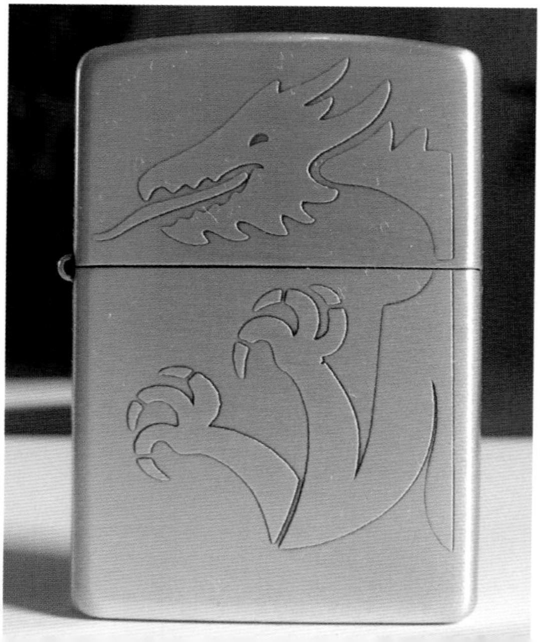

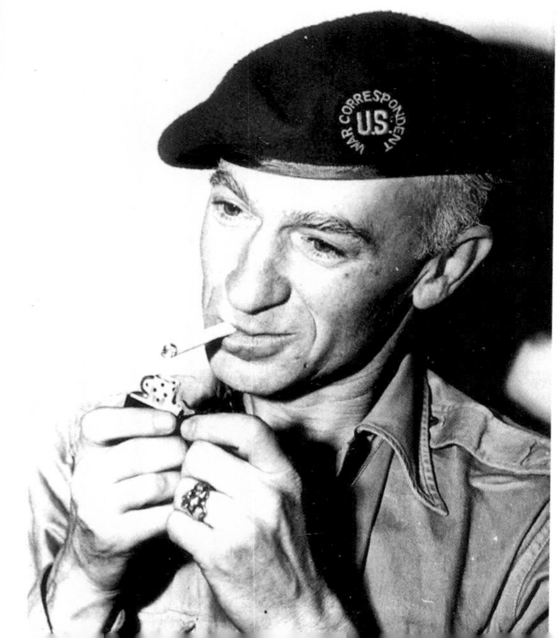
WAR CORRESPONDENT
U.S.

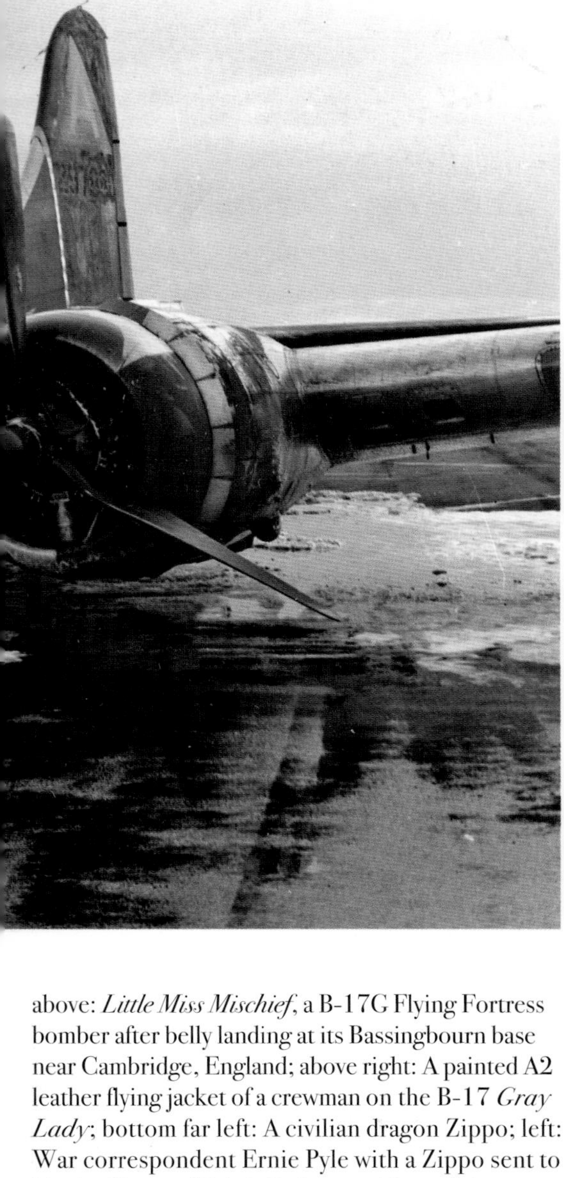

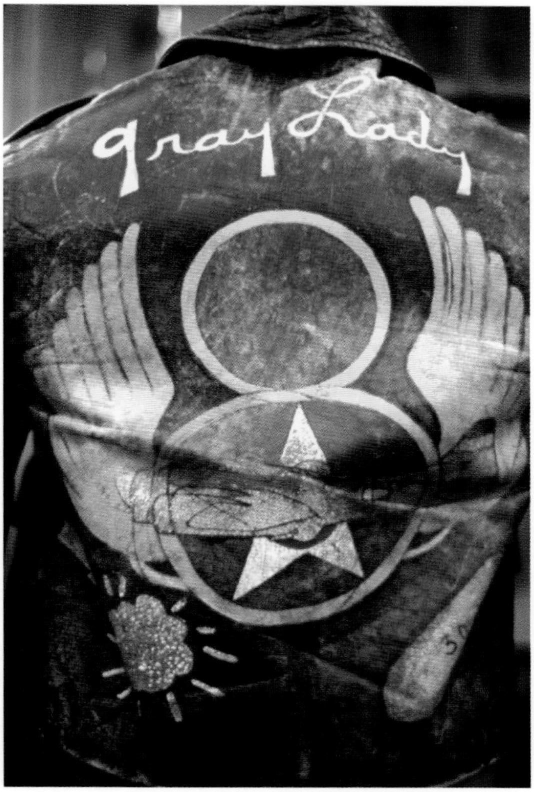
Gray Lady

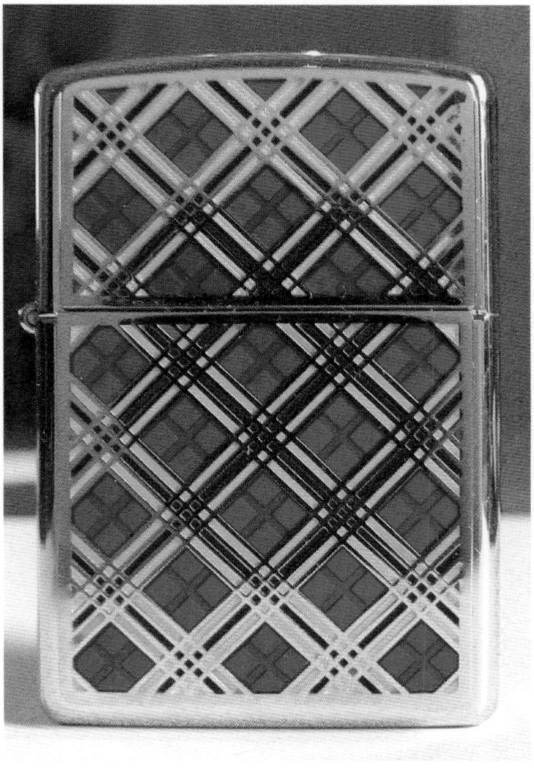

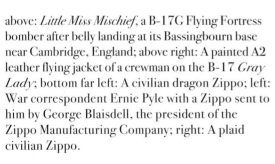

above: *Little Miss Mischief*, a B-17G Flying Fortress bomber after belly landing at its Bassingbourn base near Cambridge, England; above right: A painted A2 leather flying jacket of a crewman on the B-17 *Gray Lady*; bottom far left: A civilian dragon Zippo; left: War correspondent Ernie Pyle with a Zippo sent to him by George Blaisdell, the president of the Zippo Manufacturing Company; right: A plaid civilian Zippo.

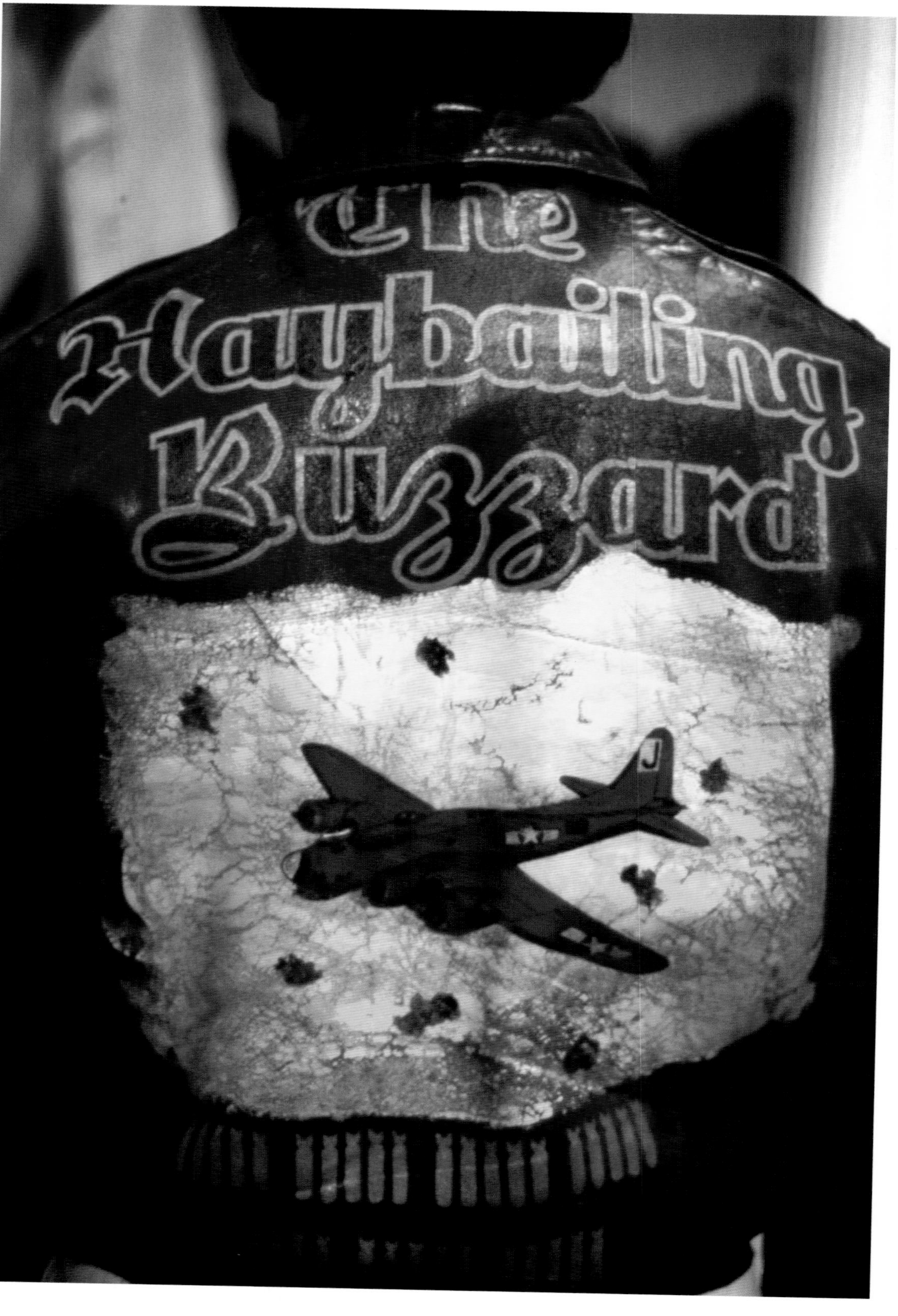
The
Haybailing
Buzzard
J

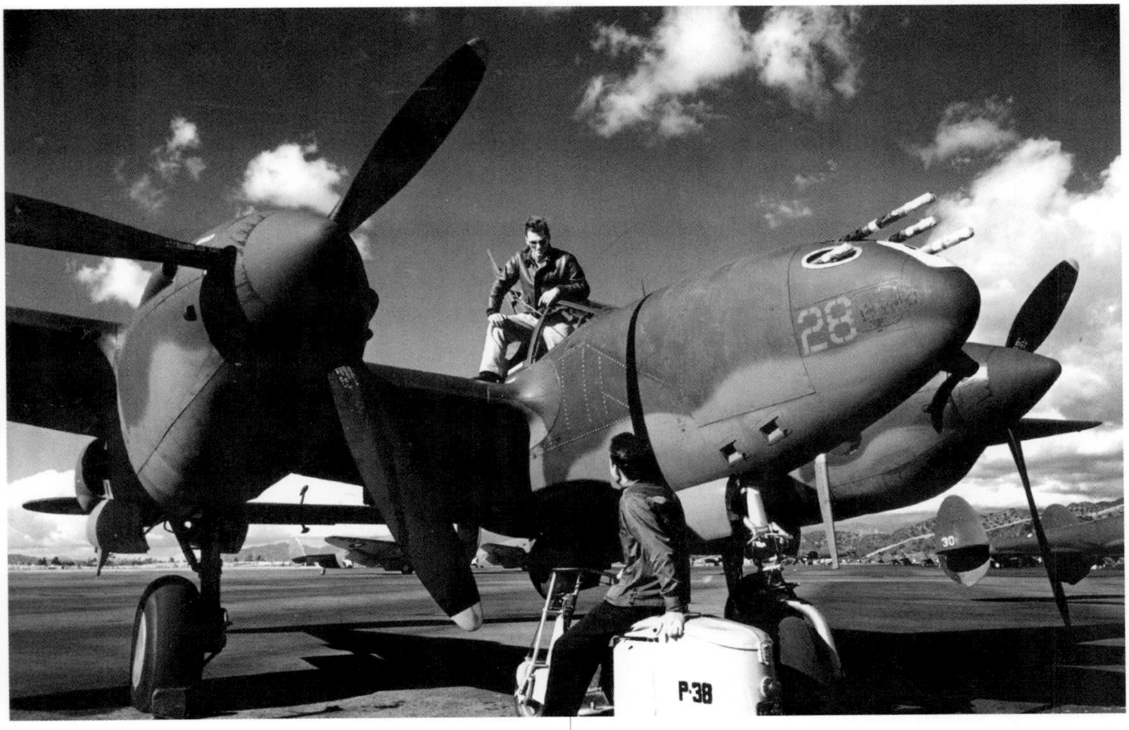
28
P-38

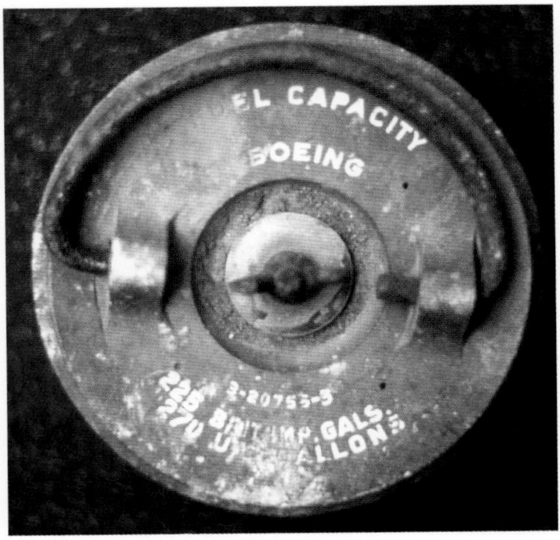
EL CAPACITY
BOEING

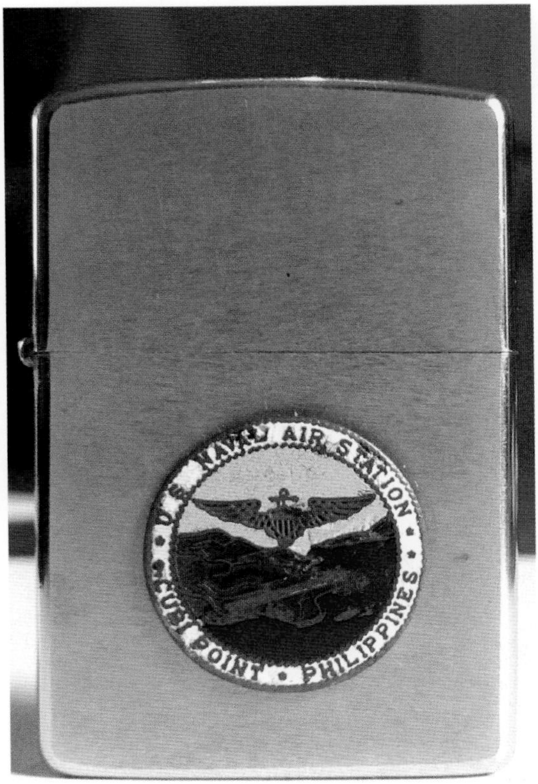
AIR STATION
PHILIPPINES

left: Painted A2 flying jacket of an airman with the 390th Bomb Group, Eighth USAAF, based at Framlingham, Suffolk, England; above: A B-17 bomber fuel filler cap found by the author near a hardstand at the former Grafton Underwood base, Northants; at top; A newly built Lockheed P-38 fighter at the Burbank, California plant; right: A U.S. Navy Zippo lighter for the Cubi Point Naval Air Station, Philippines.

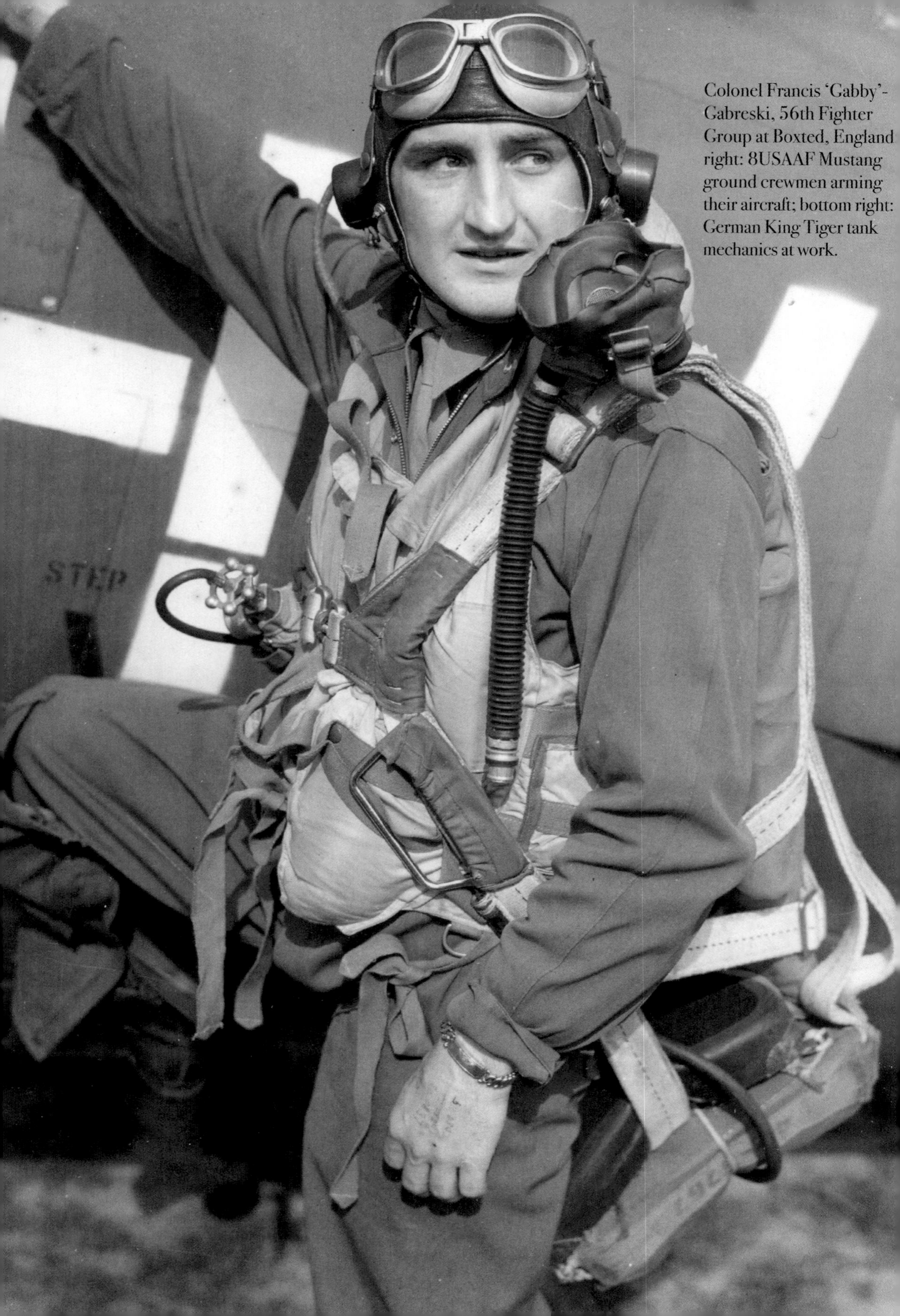
STEP

Colonel Francis 'Gabby'- Gabreski, 56th Fighter Group at Boxted, England right: 8USAAF Mustang ground crewmen arming their aircraft; bottom right: German King Tiger tank mechanics at work.

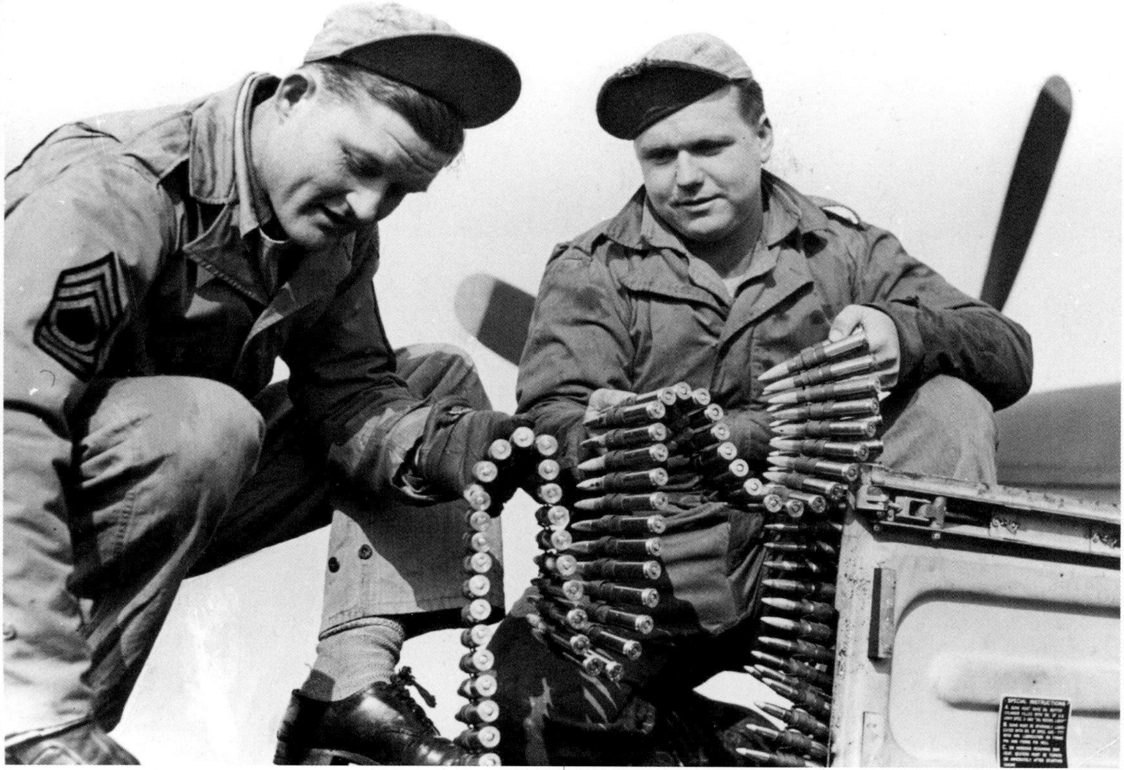
SPECIAL INSTRUCTIONS

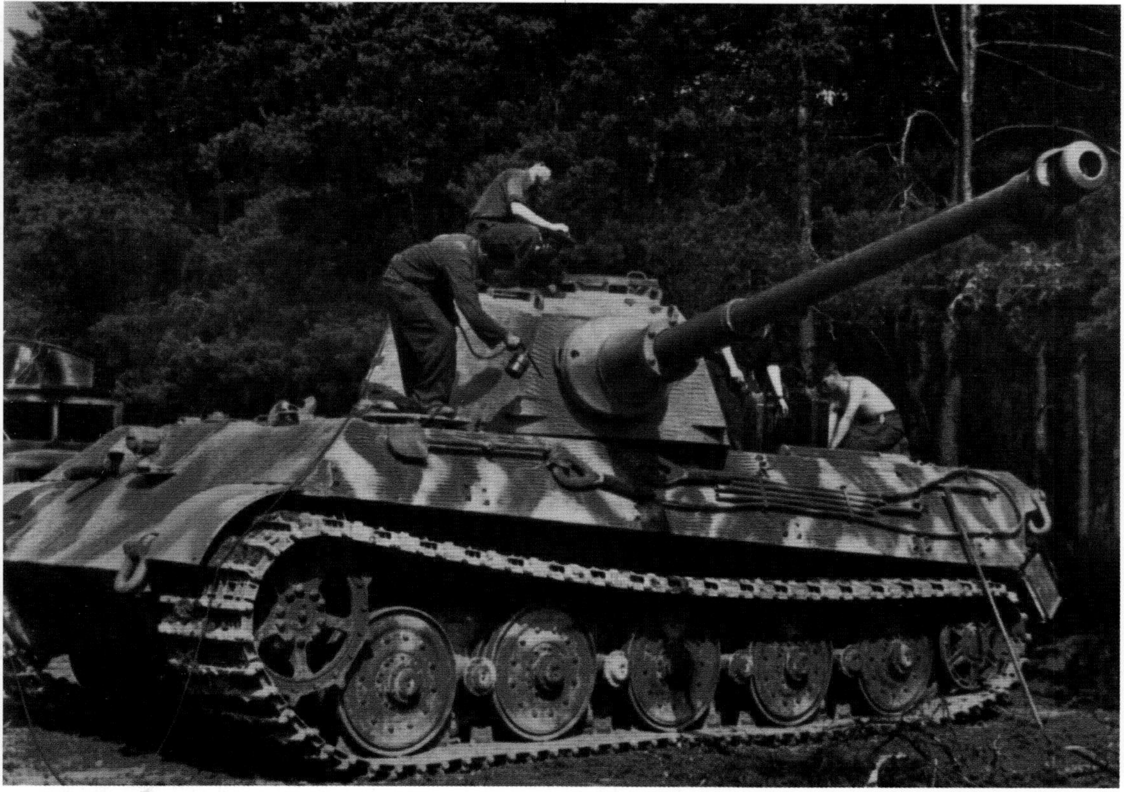

British Army tankies.

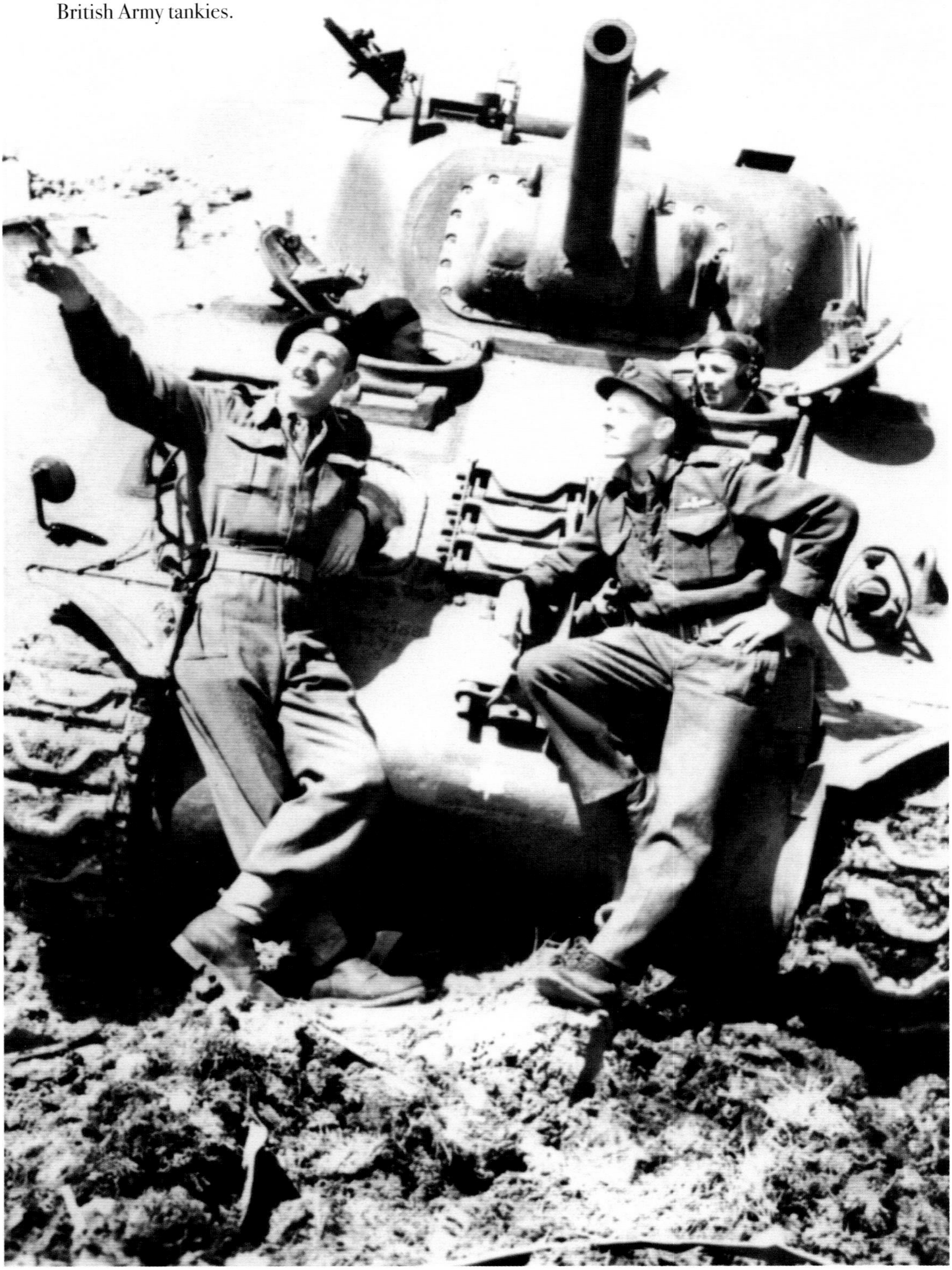

American journalist/war correspondent Ernie Pyle: 'While I was in Italy I had a letter from the president of the Zippo Company. It seems he is devoted to my column. It seems further that he'd had an idea. He had sent to our headquarters in Washington to get my signature, and then he was having the signature engraved on a special nickel-plated lighter and was going to send it to me as a gift.

'Pretty soon there was another letter. The president of the Zippo Company had had another brainstorm. In addition to my superheterodyne lighter he was going to send fifty of the regular ones to me to give to friends.

'I was amused at the modesty of the president's letter. 'You probably know nothing about the Zippo lighter,' he said.

"If he only knew how the soldiers coveted them! They'll burn in the wind, and pilots say they are the only kind that will light at extreme altitudes. Why, they're so popular I had three stolen from me in one year.

'Well, at last the lighter came, forwarded all the way from Italy. My own lighter was a beauty, with my name on one side and a little American flag on the other. I began smoking twice as much as usual just because I enjoyed lighting the thing.

'The fifty others went like hot cakes. I found myself equipped with a wonderful weapon for winning friends and influencing people. All fifty-one of us were grateful to Mr, Zippo.'

The great American war correspondent, Ernie Pyle was much admired and revered by ordinary troops the world over. He often accompanied them into action and had gained their trust with the authenticity of his writing. Another war correspondent and author, John Steinbeck, wrote of Pyle:

'There are really two wars and they haven't much to do with each other. There is a war of maps and logistics, of campaigns, of ballistics, armies, divisions and regiments— and that is General George C. Marshall's war. Then there is the war of the homesick, weary, funny, violent, common men who wash their socks in their helmets, complain about the food, whistle at the Arab girls, or any girls for that matter, and bring themselves through as dirty a business as the world has ever seen and do it with humour and dignity and courage—and that is Ernie Pyle's war.'

Late in the war, Pyle was asssigned aboard the aircraft carrier USS *Cabot* CVL-28, which, in March 1945 was sailing in the South Pacific. Having taken part in several operations in the war against Japan, the *Cabot* had recently been involved in support of operations off Luzon, Formosa, Indo-China and Hong Kong and was now on a secret assignment. Scuttlebutt had it that the ship was to be involved in a task of major importance and, knowing that Ernie Pyle was on board and reasoning that something big must be up, a young officer approached Pyle and tried to see if the war reporter could tell him where the ship was headed. Pyle was silent. Then he asked the officer for his lighter. The young man handed his Zippo to Pyle who took out a pocket knife and scratched something on the bottom of the lighter. He returned it with an admonition: 'Stick this in your pocket and promise not to look at it until the ship's sealed orders are opened in a half hour.' Soon enough the Bosun's pipe sounded 'attention to orders.' The officer took the Zippo from his pocket and read the word on the bottom—TOKYO.

On 18 April 1945, Ernie Pyle, probably

the most celebrated war correspondent of the Second World War, was killed while traveling in a jeep that was hit by Japanese machine-gun fire on the island of Le Shima in the battle for Okinawa. From *The Boston Globe* to Associated Press: '. . . a humble correspondent who artfully and ardently told the story of a war from the foxholes. From 1941 until his death, Pyle riveted the nation with personal, straight-from-the-heart tales about hometown soldiers in history's greatest conflict.' Of Ernie Pyle, the U.S. President Harry S. Truman said: 'Pyle told the story of the American fighting man as the American fighting men wanted it told.' American soldiers on Le Shima erected a plaque there reading: AT THIS SPOT THE 77TH INFANTRY DIVISION LOST A BUDDY. ERNIE PYLE. 18 APRIL 1945.

George Blaisdell of Zippo had lighters engraved to be given as gifts to the crew of the USS *Cabot* in Ernie Pyle's memory .

Ernie Pyle is today remembered as one of the best-known high-achieving Allied war correspondents of all time. For several years he wrote a column that appeared in 400 daily and 300 weekly newspapers worldwide. In 1940 he reported from London on the Battle of Britain and the Blitz. From there he moved on to cover the Allied operations in North Africa, Sicily, Italy and France. In that time he commented on the phenomenon of the Zippo among battlefield troops: 'The Zippo lighter is in great demand here. I truly believe that the Zippo is the most coveted thing in the army.'

U.S.troops landing at Omaha Beach, Normandy, on D-Day, 6 June 1944.

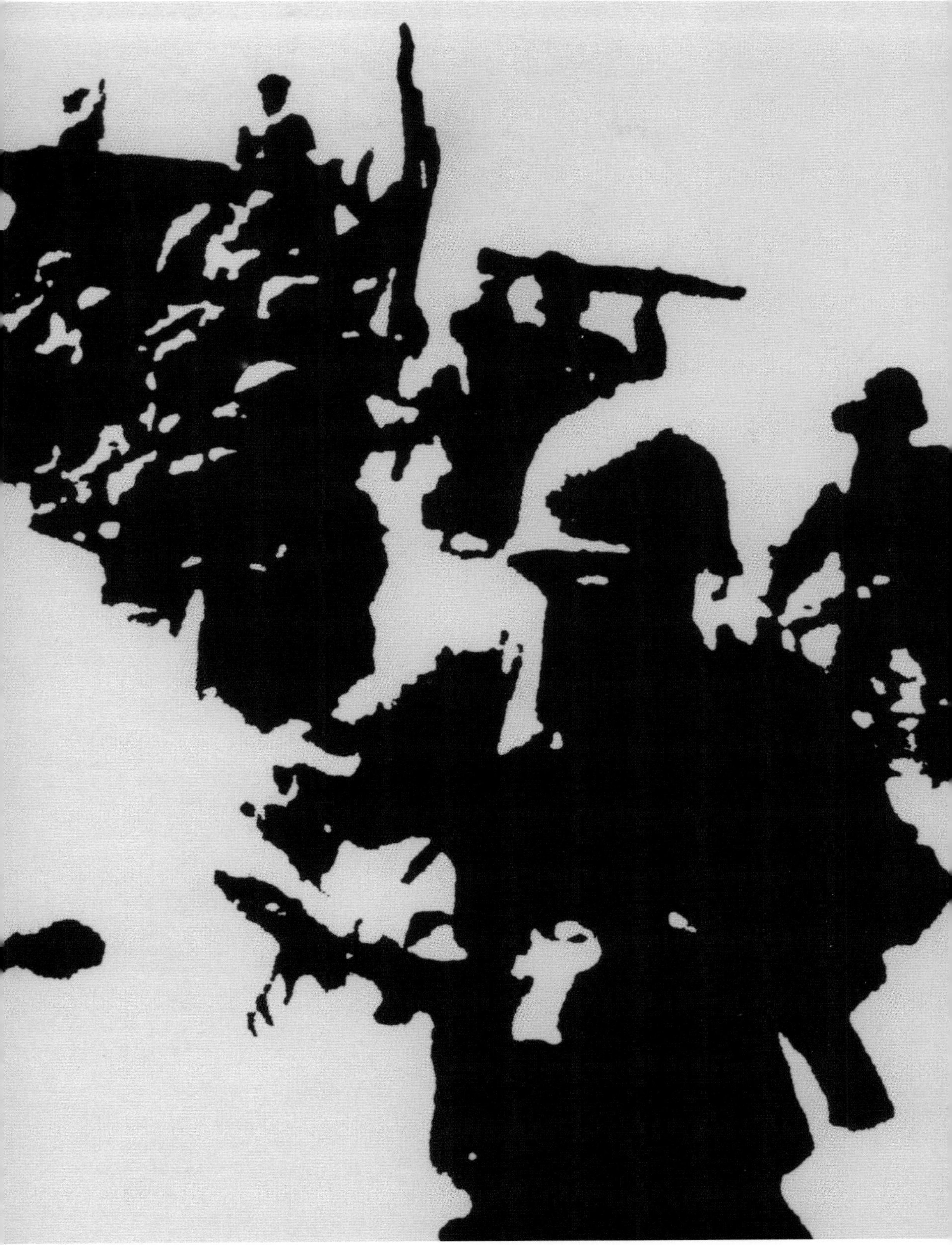

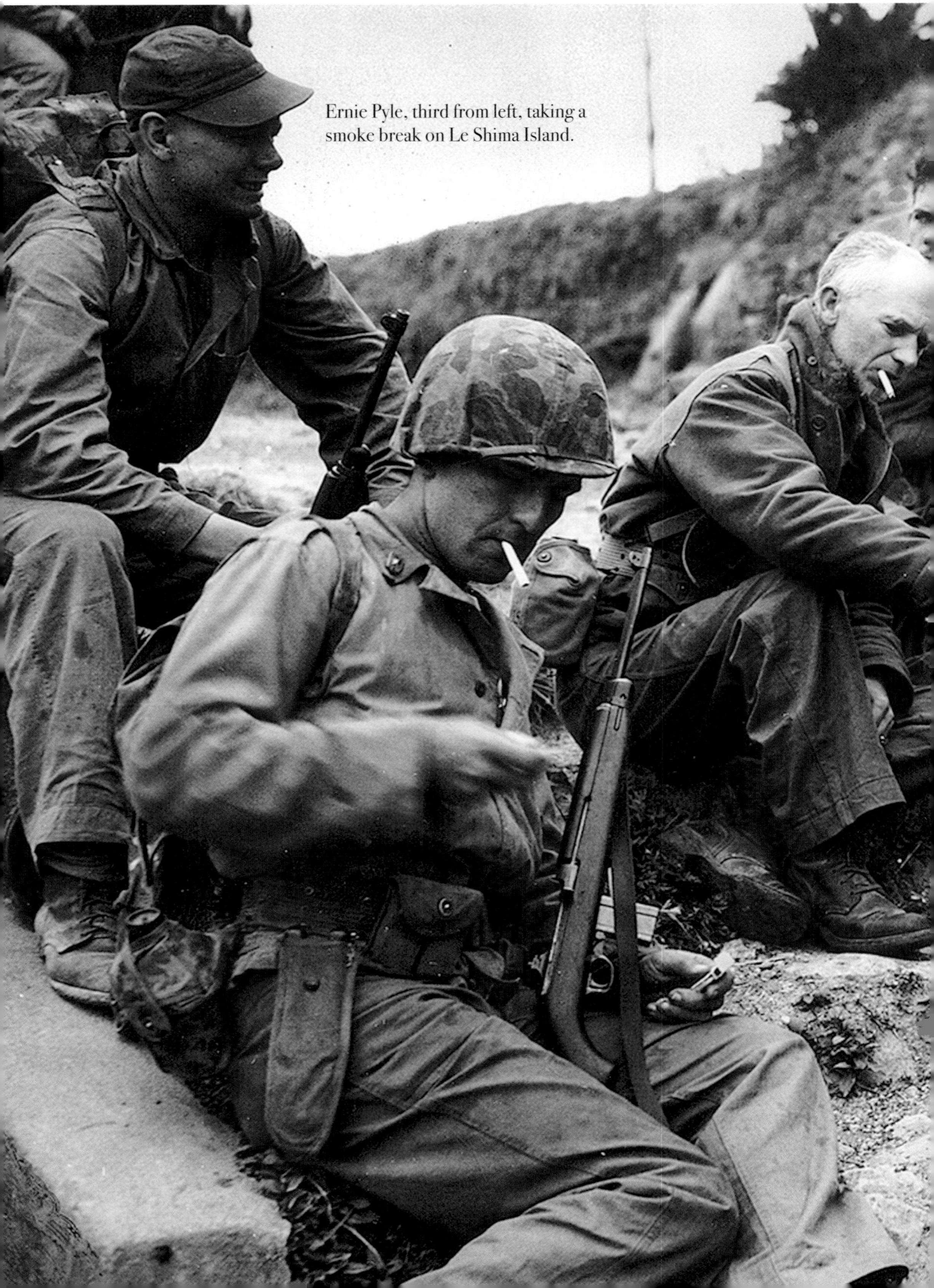

Ernie Pyle, third from left, taking a smoke break on Le Shima Island.

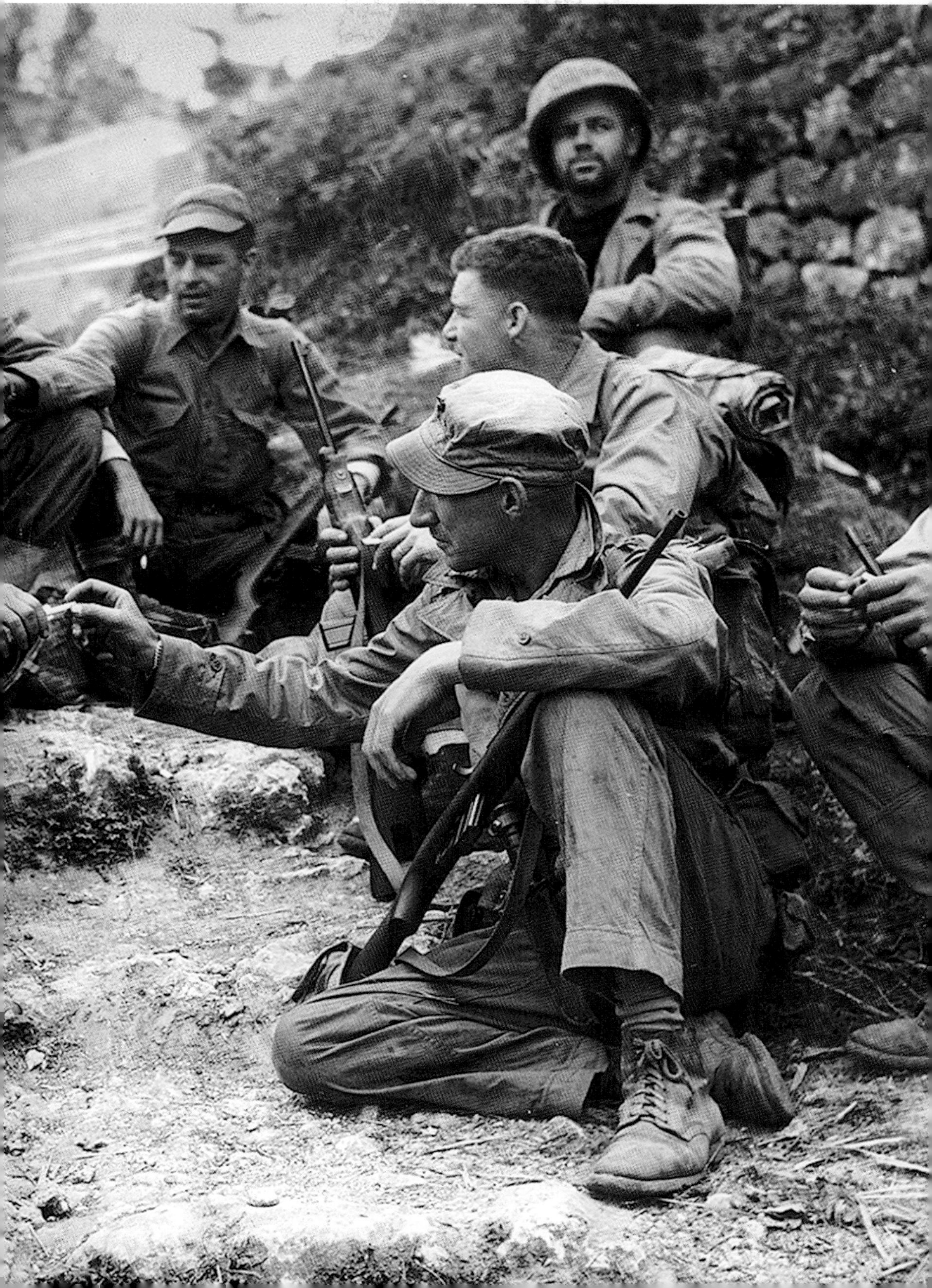

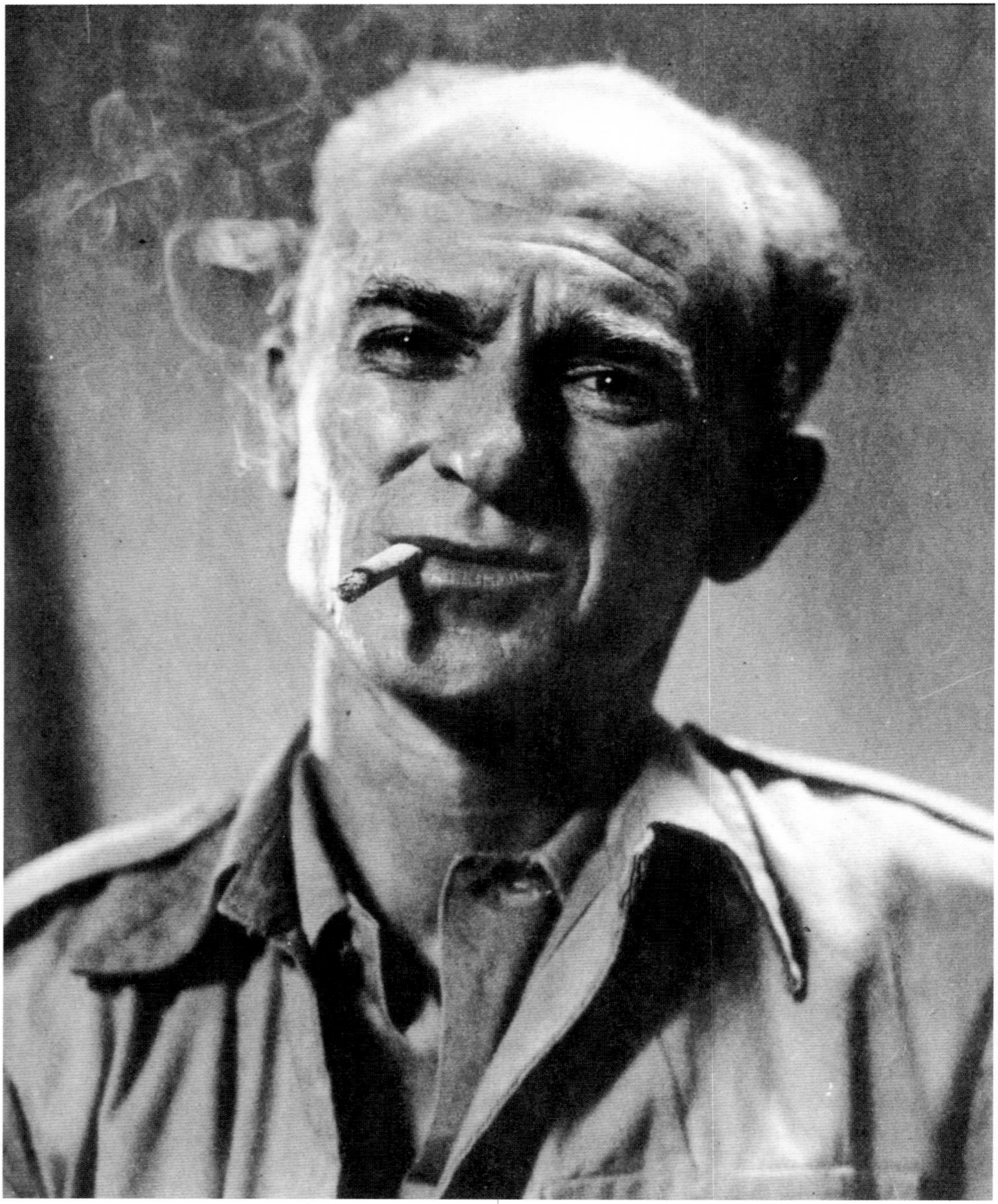

above: Forty-three-year-old Ernie Pyle was a world-renowned war correspondent and journalist in the Second World War; right: Fashion photographer Toni Frissell volunteered her talent during WWII to the American Red Cross in England and worked for the U.S. Eighth Army Air Force there as well. Her image is of a wounded airman of the Eighth Air Force being taken from the B-17 bomber that had carried him to an enemy target where he suffered a severe injury during aerial combat. He is being escorted to a waiting Army ambulance that will take him into the care of skilled doctors and clinicians.

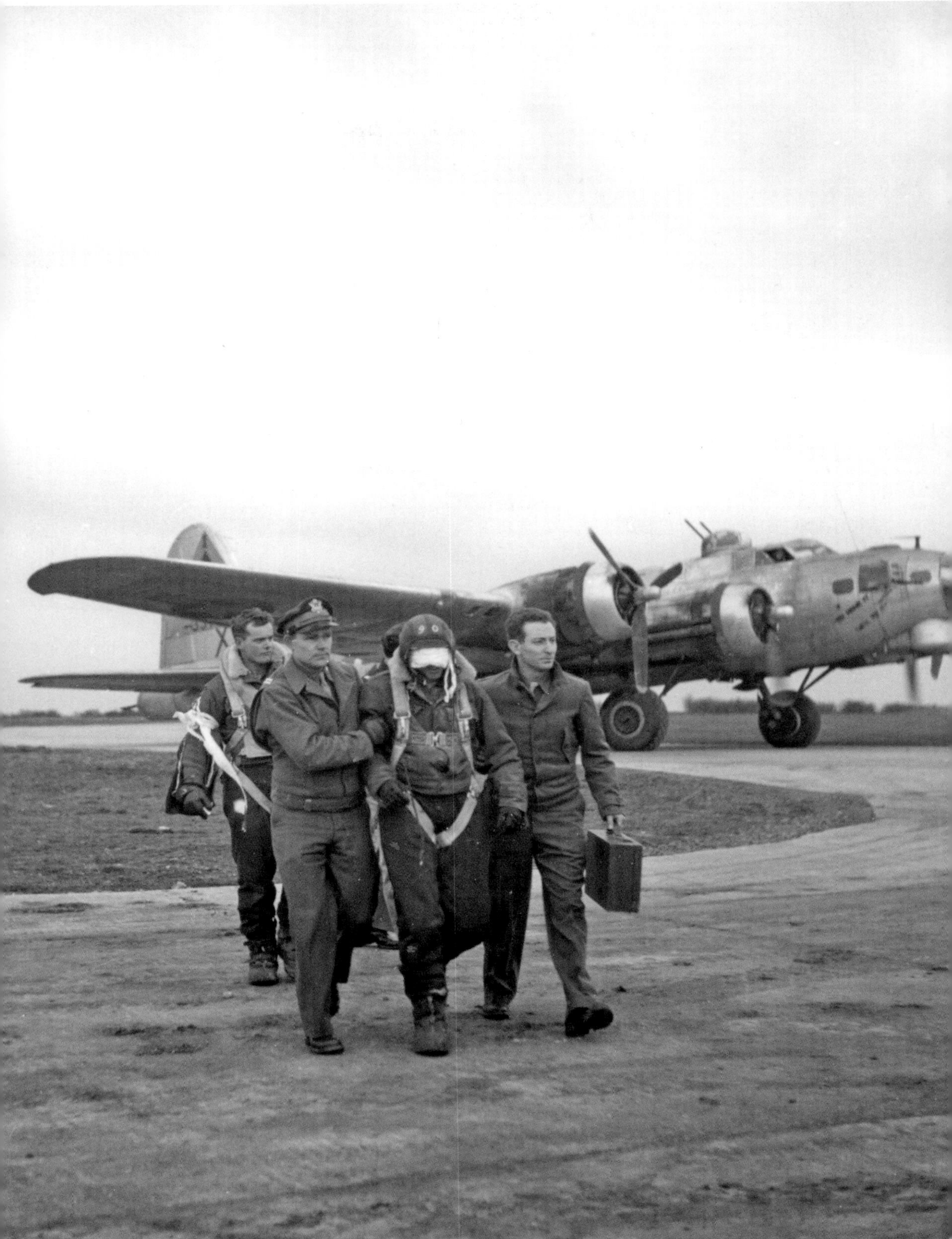

In 1954 the celebrated, unique American journalist and war correspondent Edward R. Murrow said about the former British wartime Prime Minister Sir Winston Churchill: 'He mobilized the English language and sent it into battle to steady his fellow countrymen and hearten those Europeans upon whom the long dark night of tyranny had descended.'

Through much of his life Ed Murrow was a heavy smoker, reportedly going through three packs, or around sixty cigarettes, a day. Ironically, it was *See It Now*, a show he hosted on the CBS television network, which was the first tv programme to report about the link between smoking and cancer. It was during that particular show that Murrow stated: 'I doubt I could spend a half hour without a cigarette with any comfort or ease.' He would develop lung cancer and die two years later at the age of 57. His friend and colleague Eric Sevareid, another of the great American wartime journalists, said of Murrow: 'He was a shooting star and we will live in his afterglow a very long time.'

Ed Murrow famously delivered a powerful wartime radio broadcast series during the 1940-41 bombing of Britain. The programme was called *This Is London*. It added greatly to his war reporting celebrity and, in a sincere reference to the nightly visits of the German bombers to the British capital, he ended each installment with the catchphrase 'Good night, and good luck.' It is believed that Murrow flew on more than twenty Allied combat missions to enemy targets in continental Europe during the war. He knew something about the luck part of that experience, a knowledge expressed in the many riveting broadcasts he recorded in those war-torn skies.

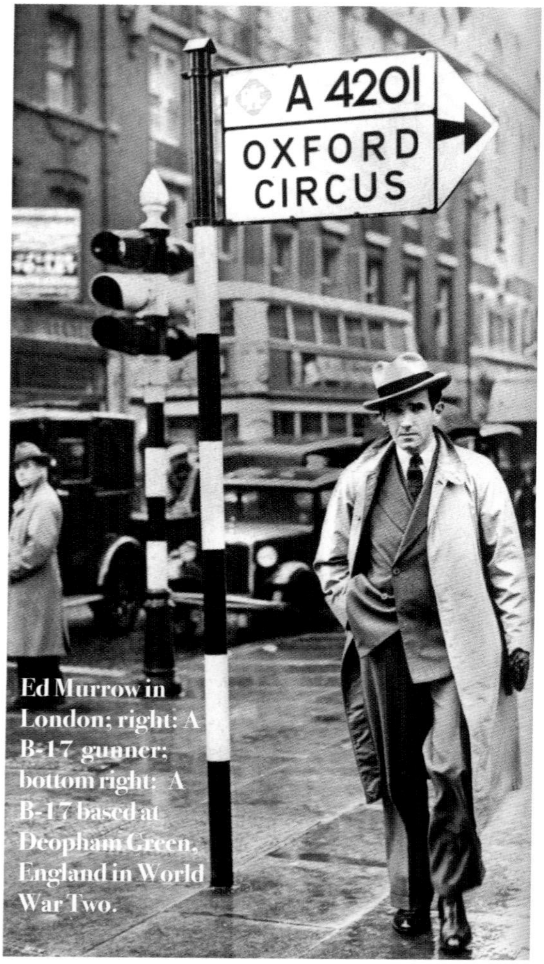
A 4201
OXFORD
CIRCUS
Ed Murrow in London; right: A B-17 gunner; bottom right: A B-17 based at Deopham Green, England in World War Two.

In the war years Ed Murrow resided in a Hallam Street flat in central London. Today, one of the traditional blue historic plaques appears on the facade identifying it as 'the wartime home of the American broadcaster and war correspondent Edward R. Murrow'.

Murrow continued to bring his uniquely vivid descriptive reports from London for most of the war. In April 1945 he and fellow war correspondent Bill Shadel were among the first war reporters to enter the German concentration camp at Buchenwald where he described what he saw in chilling terms:

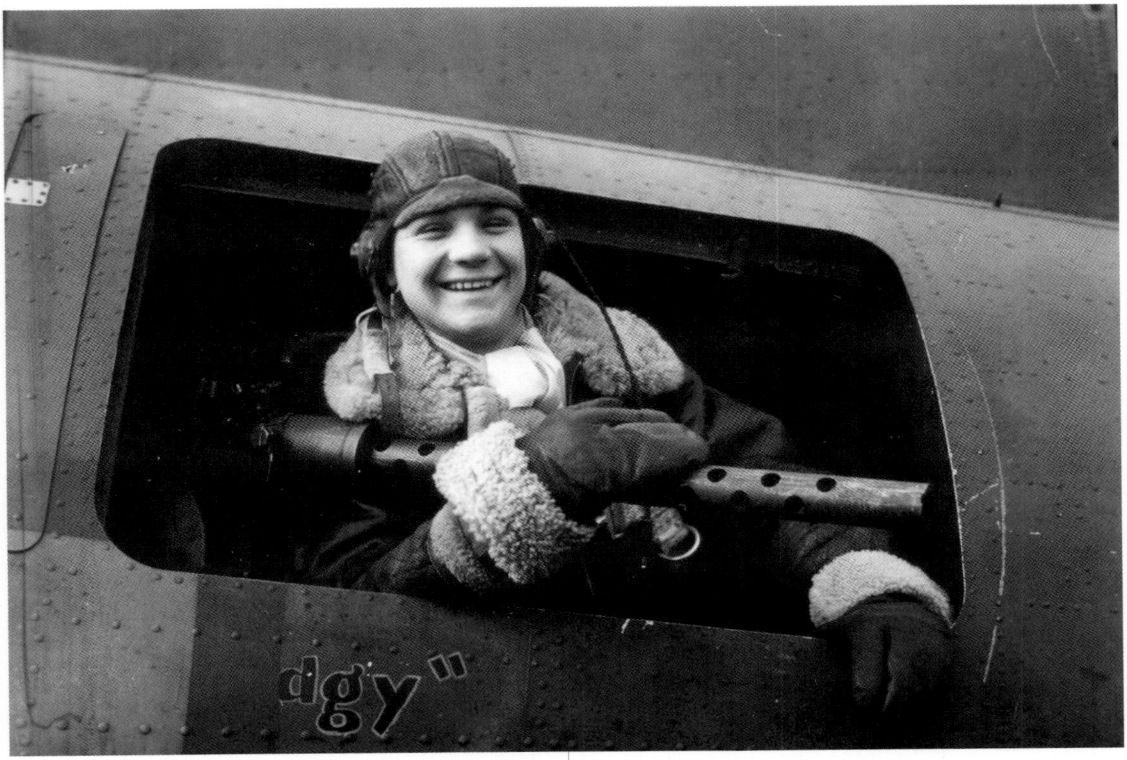

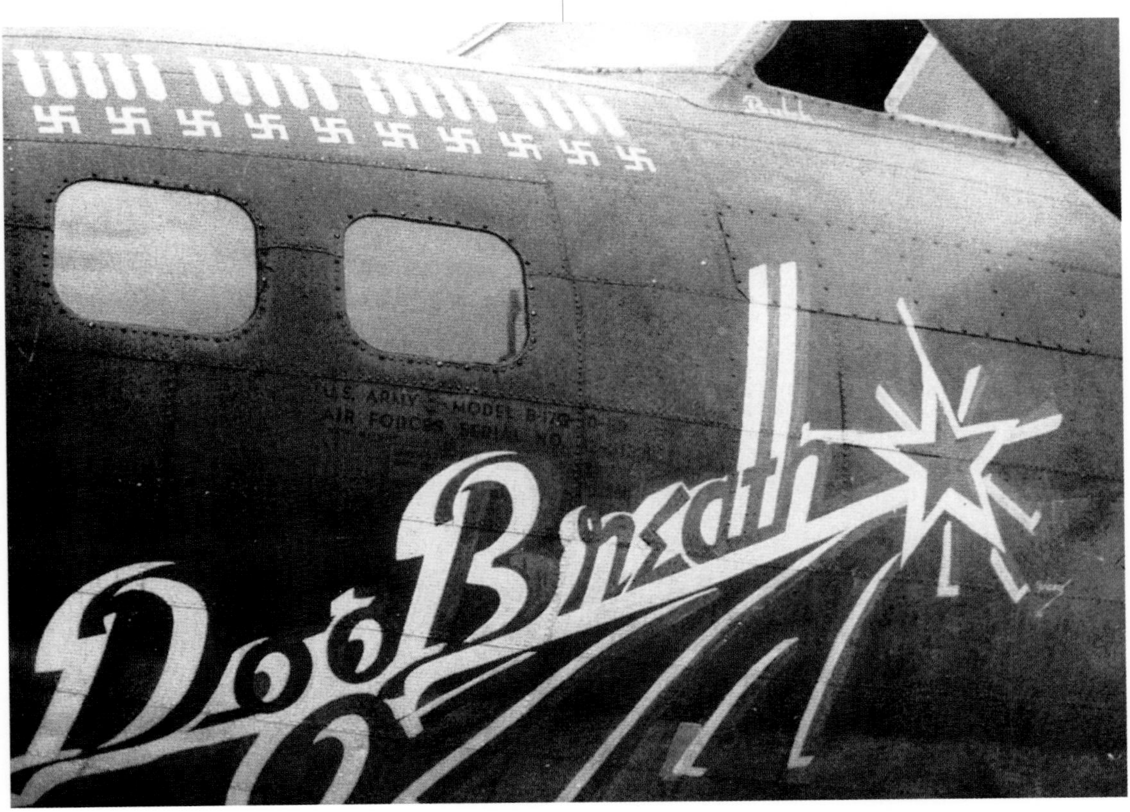
Dog Breath

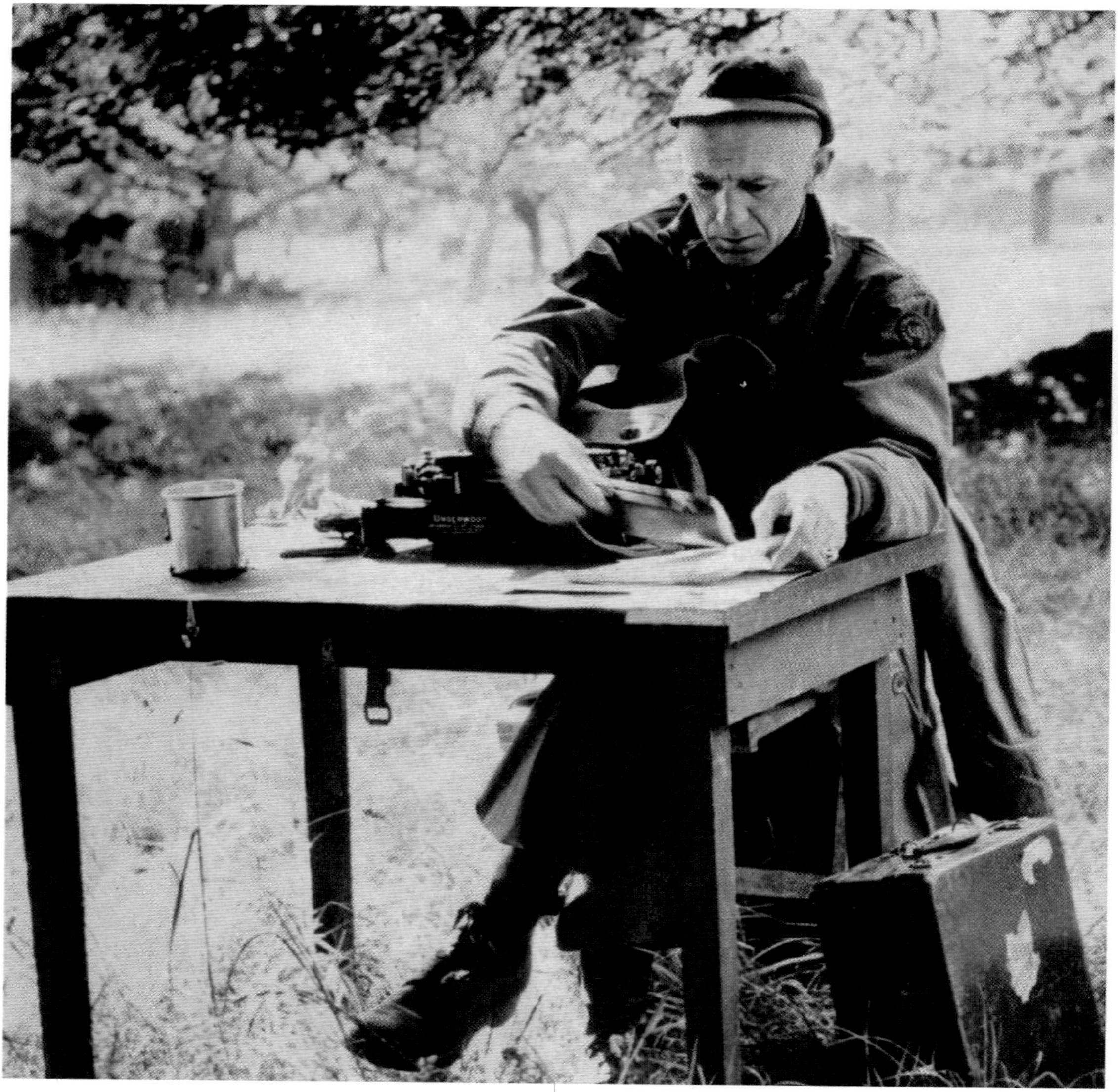

'I pray you to believe what I have said about Buchenwald. I have reported what I saw and heard, but only part of it. For most of it I have no words . . . . If I've offended you by this rather mild account of Buchenwald, I'm not in the least sorry.' –from an extract of Edward R. Murrow's Buchenwald report, 15 April 1945.

above: The American war correspondent Ernie Pyle at work in a Normandy apple orchard a few months after the D-Day invasion in 1944; right: The Queen meets an 8AF bomber crew on their base in 1943.

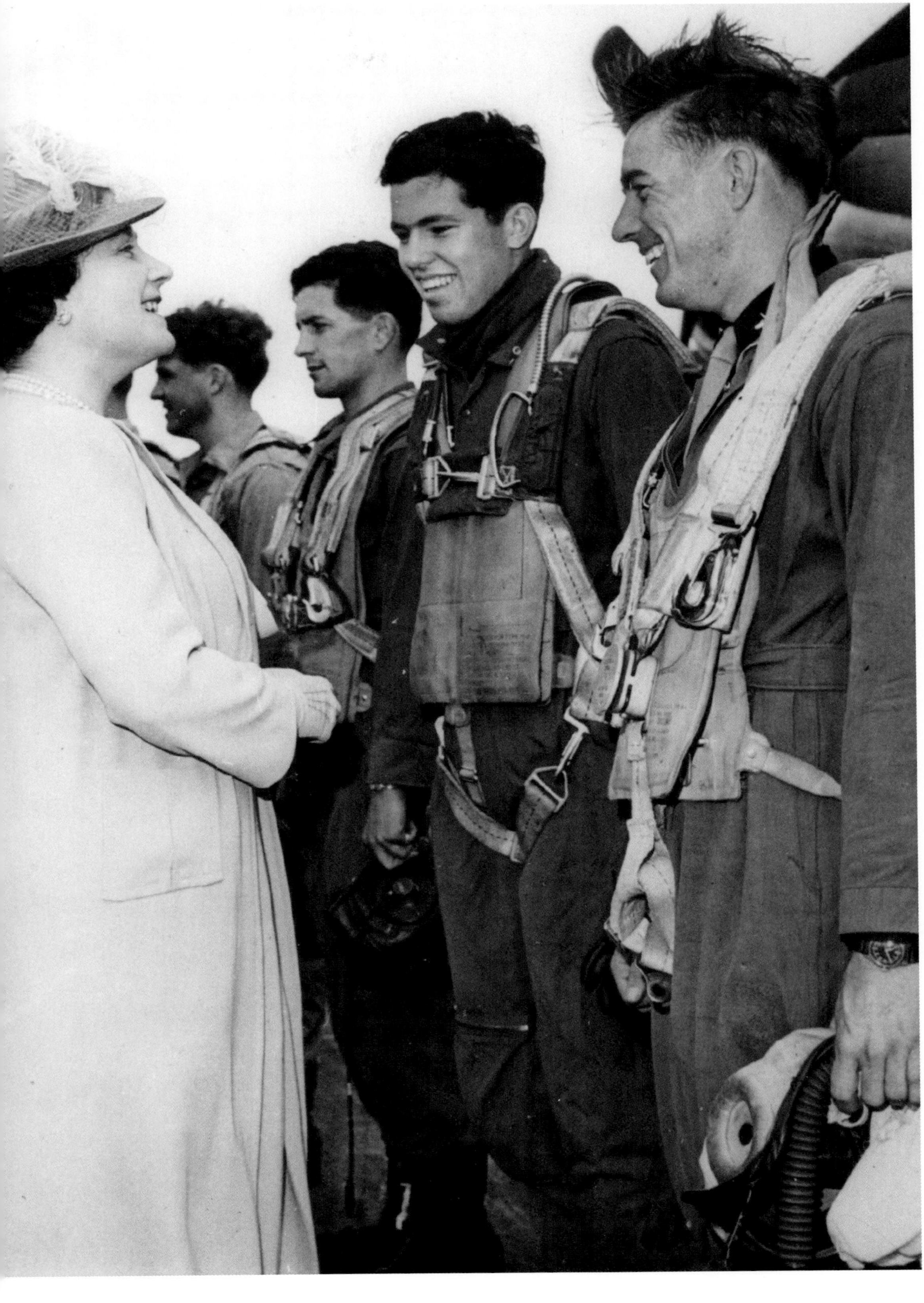

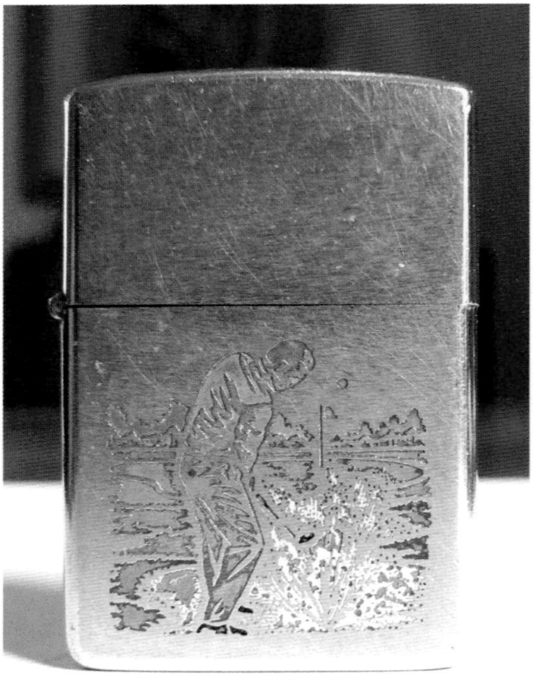

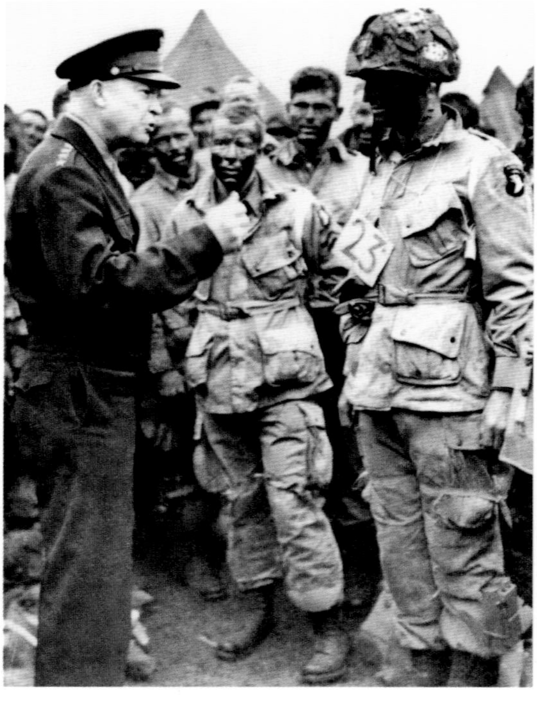

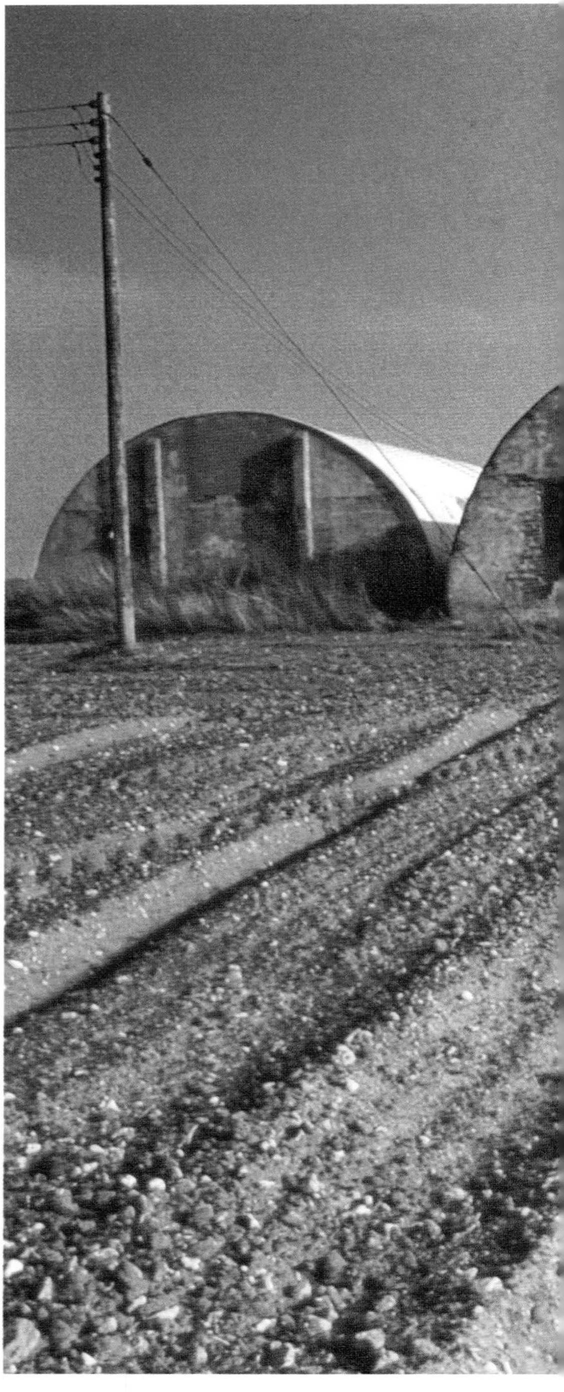

above: General Dwight D. Eisenhower talks with members of the U.S. 101st Airborne Division before the D-Day invasion drops on inland Normany;

top left: One of a series of sports-related Zippos that have featured lighters showing golf, fishing, shooting and other favourite sporting activities.

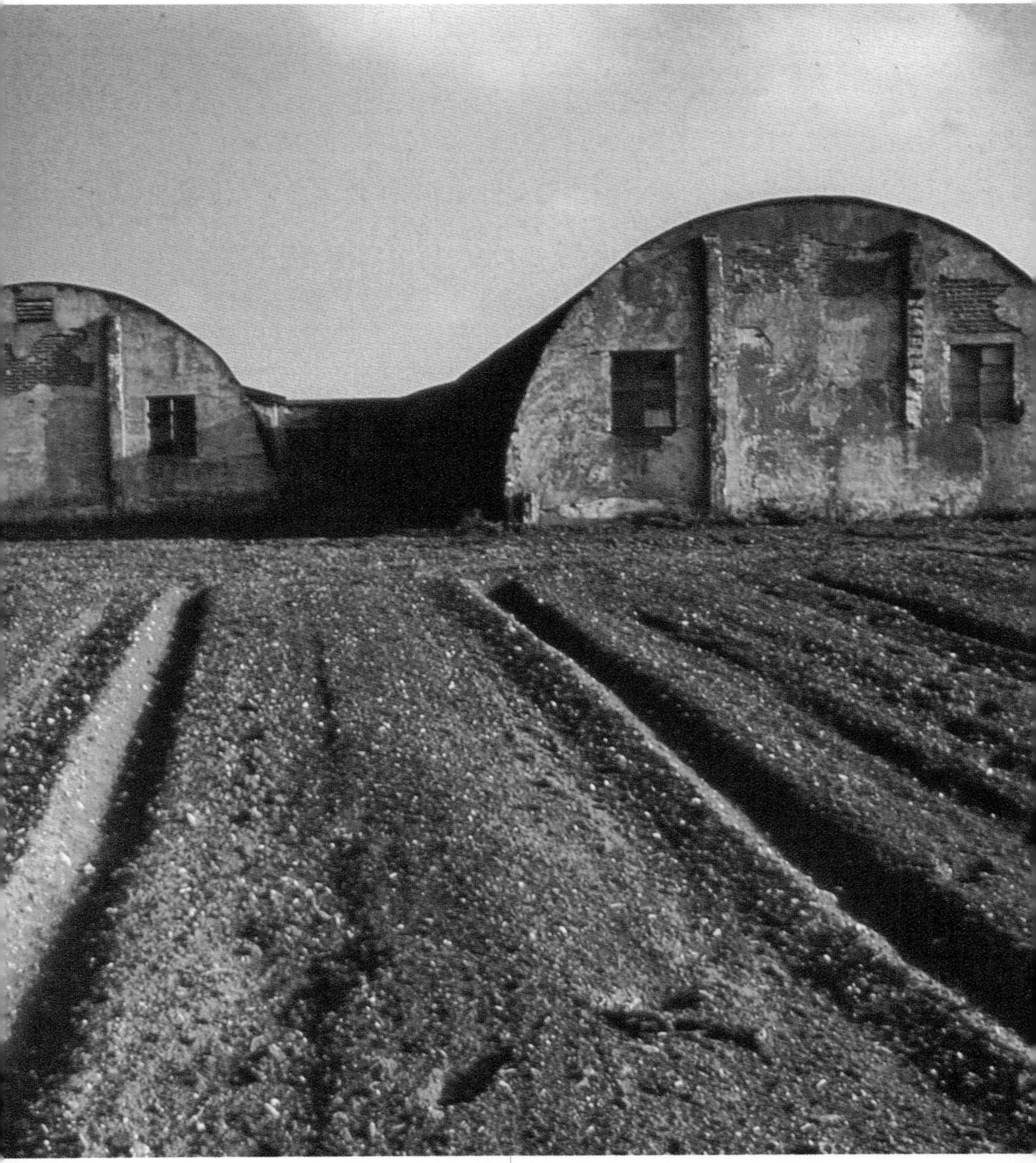

A trio of Nissen huts at Steeple Morden, the WW2 base of the 355th Fighter Group, Eighth U.S. Army Air Force in the Second World War.

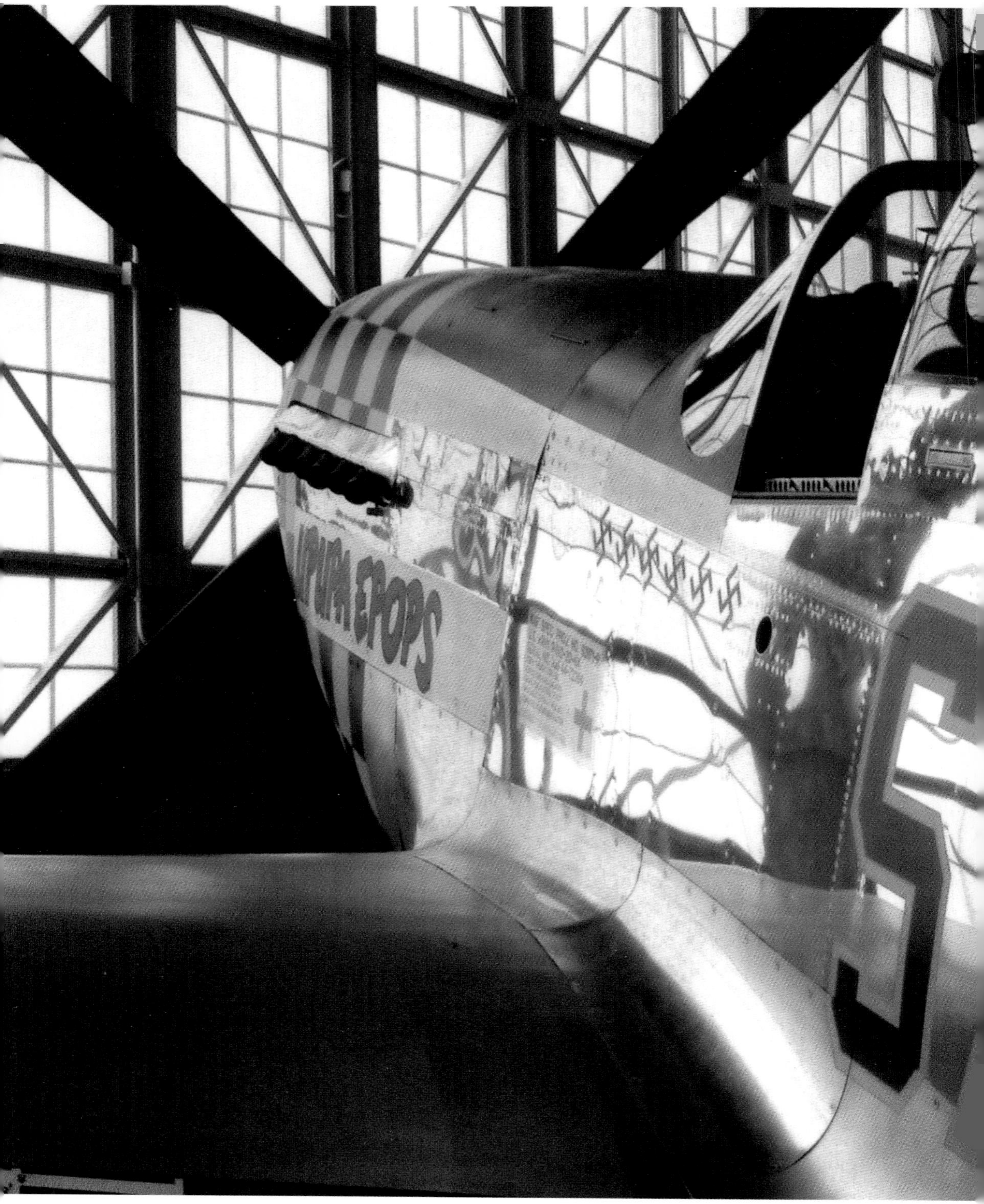
EPOPS

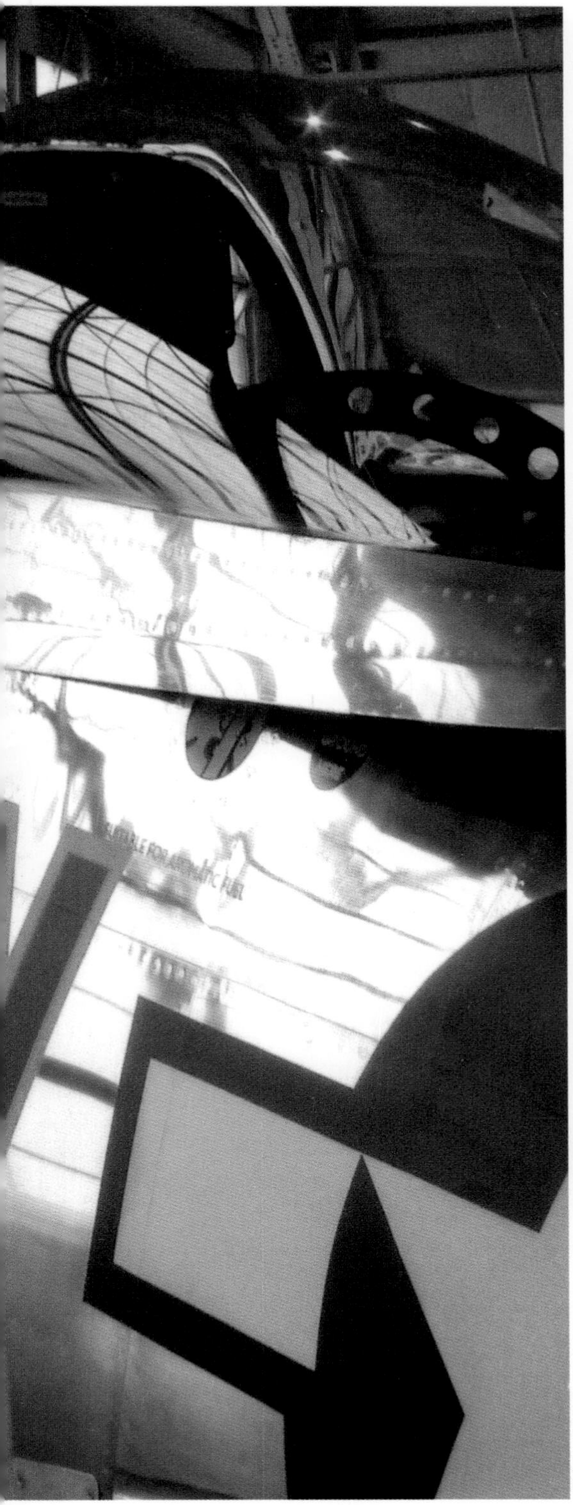

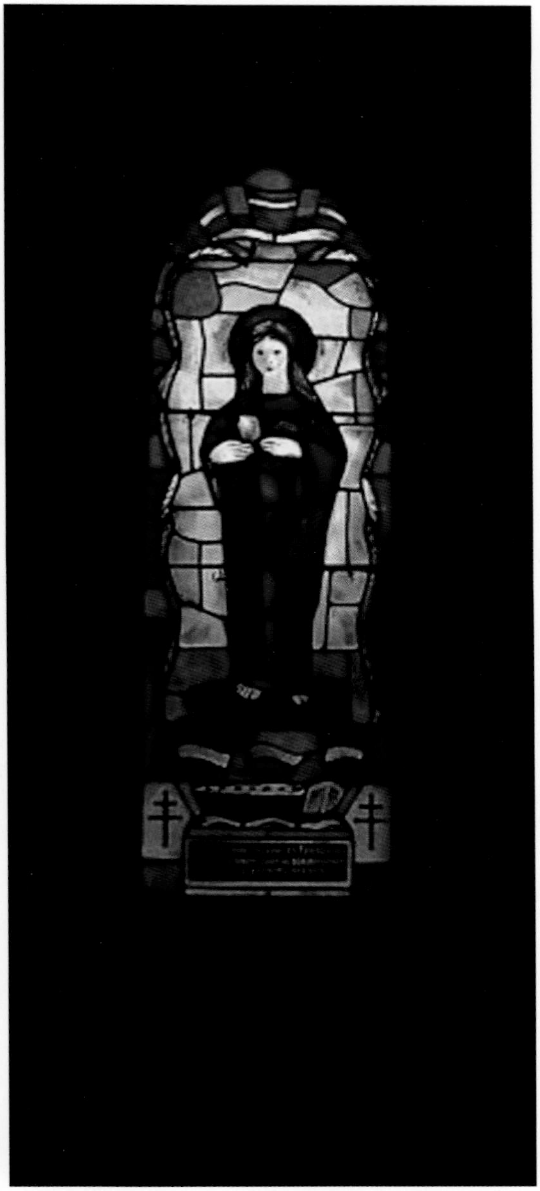

above: A commemorative D-Day stained-glass window in a church near one of the Normandy invasion beaches; left: A pristine P-51D Mustang fighter immaculately restored to museum-quality condition in America.

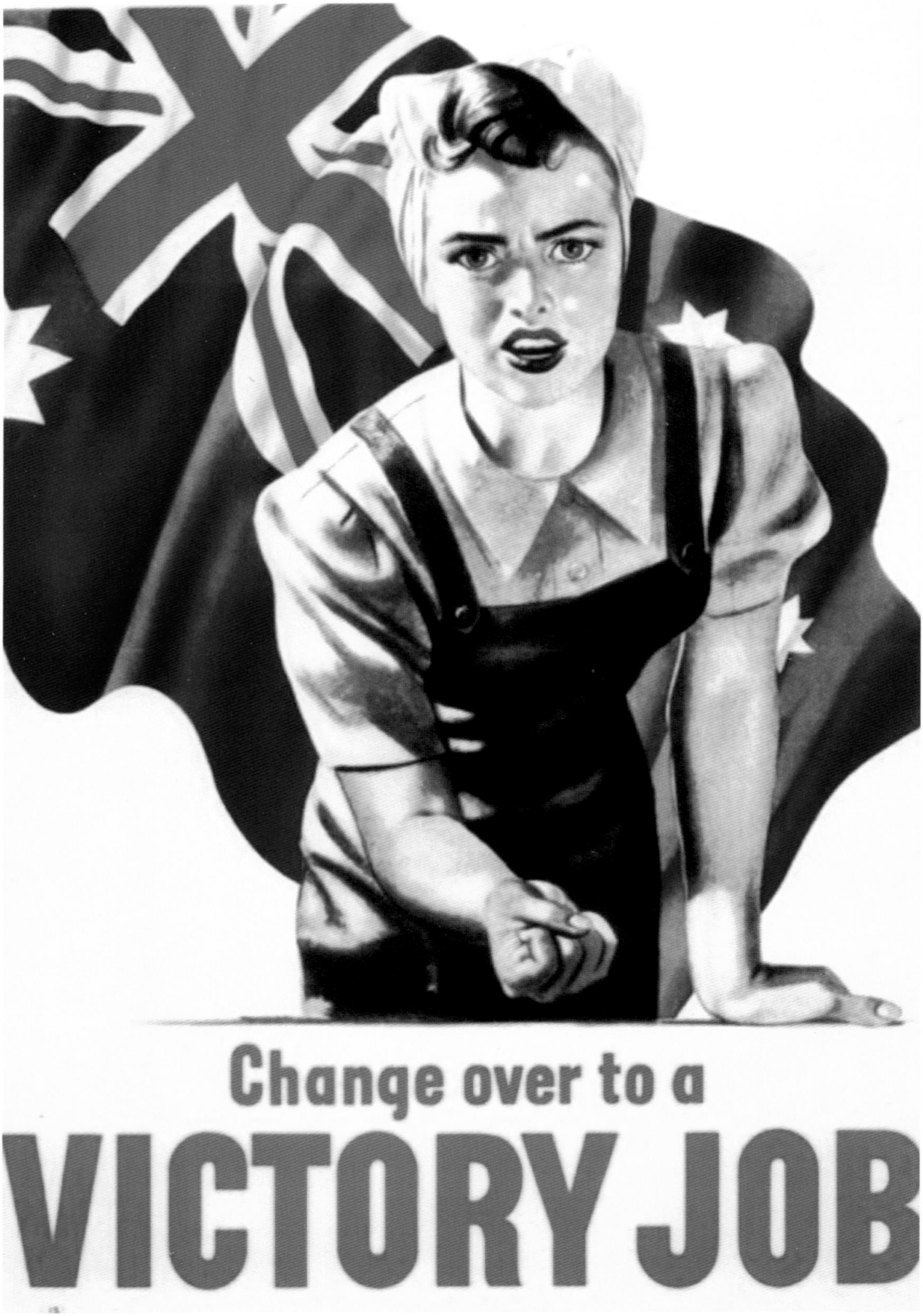
Change over to a
VICTORY JOB

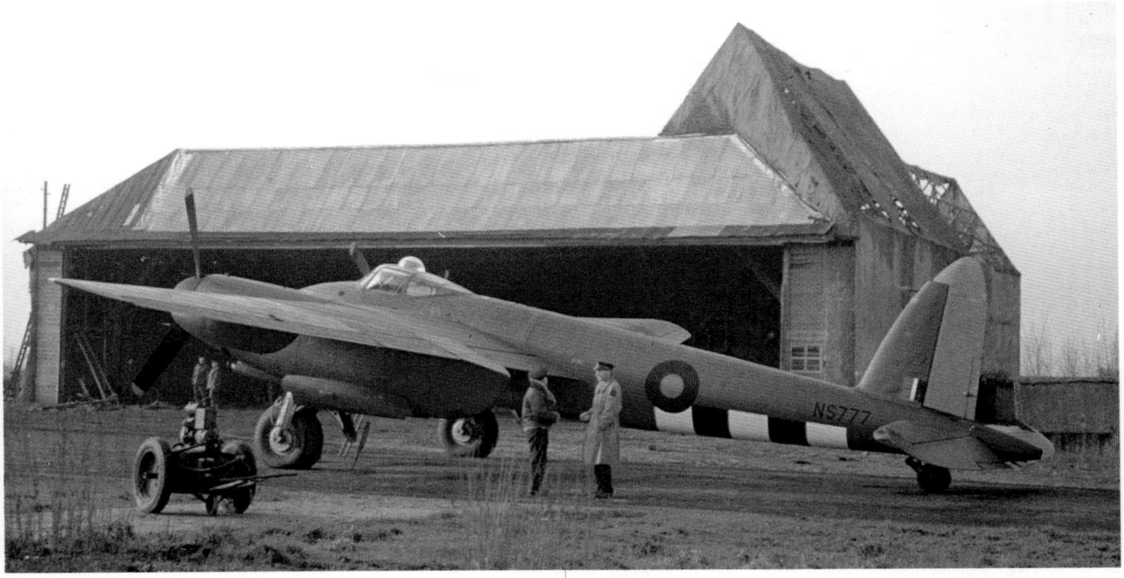
NS777

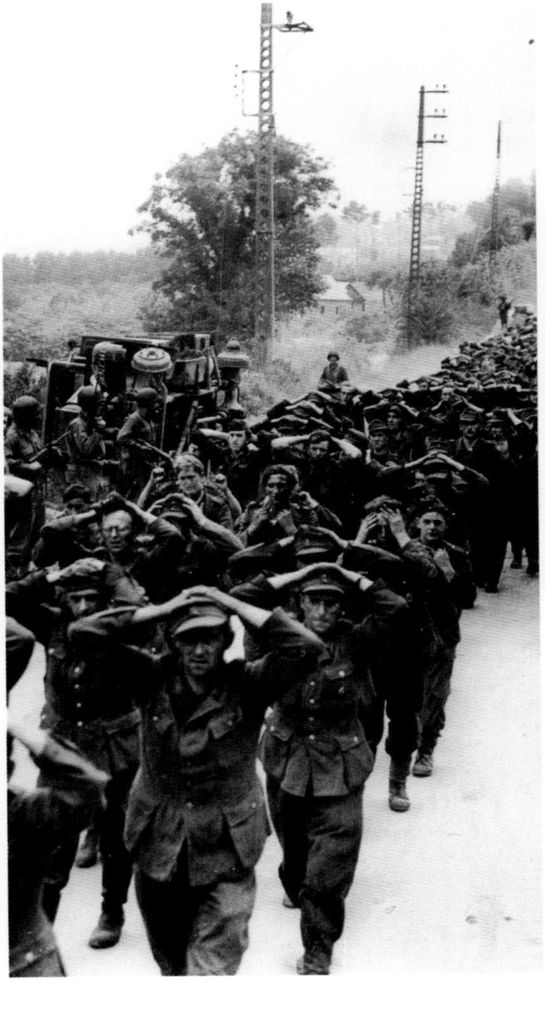

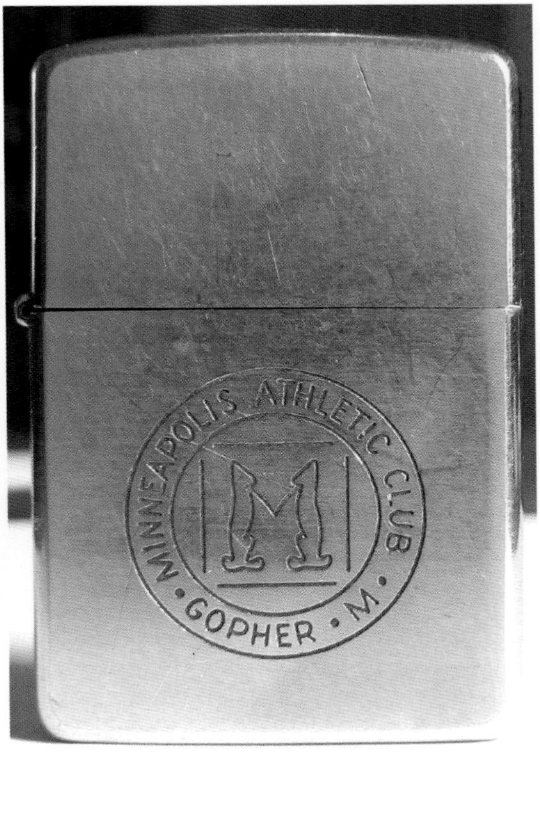
MINNEAPOLIS ATHLETIC CLUB
M
GOPHER · M ·

above: A Zippo lighter made for the Minneapolis Athletic Club; top: An RAF Mosquito bomber; left: German prisoners of war on the march behind a Normandy beachhead.

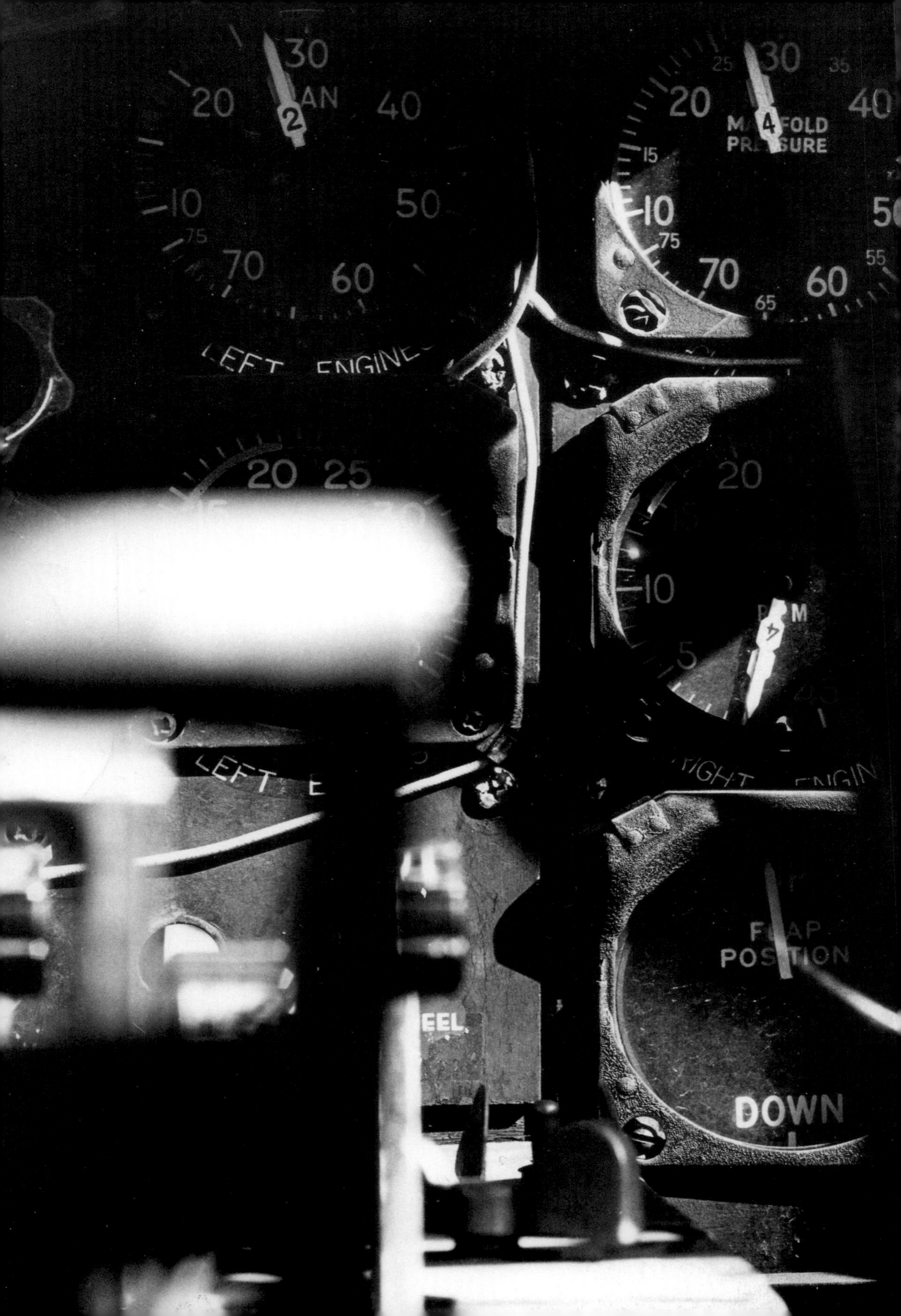
DOWN

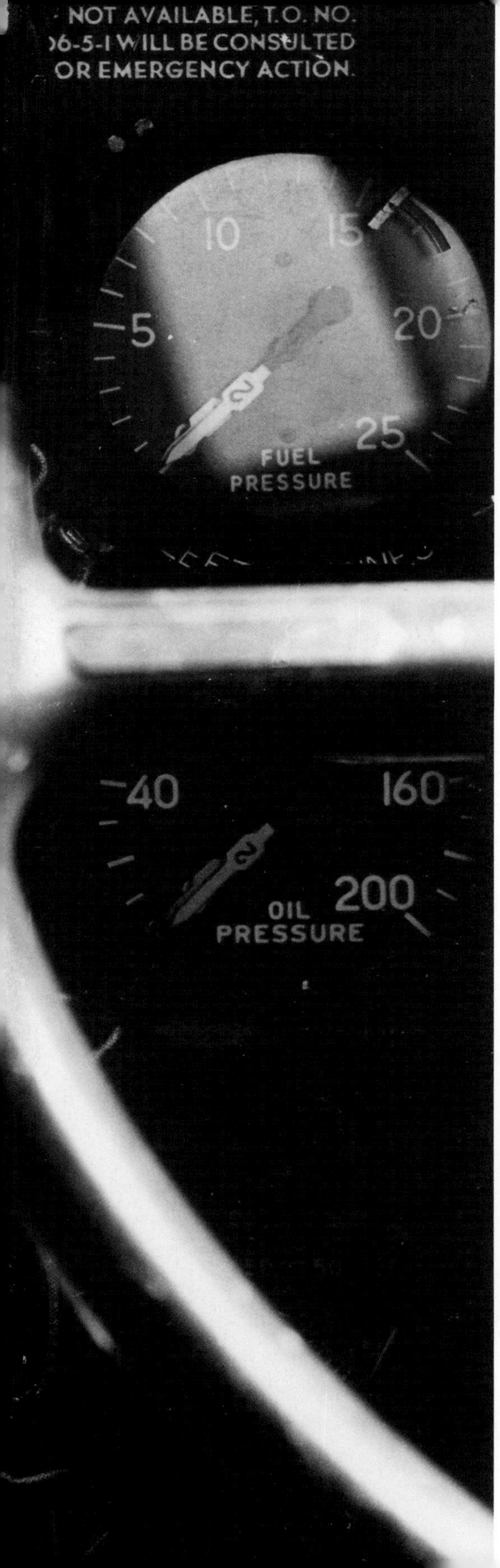
NOT AVAILABLE, T.O. NO.
WILL BE CONSULTED
OR EMERGENCY ACTION.
FUEL
PRESSURE
OIL
PRESSURE

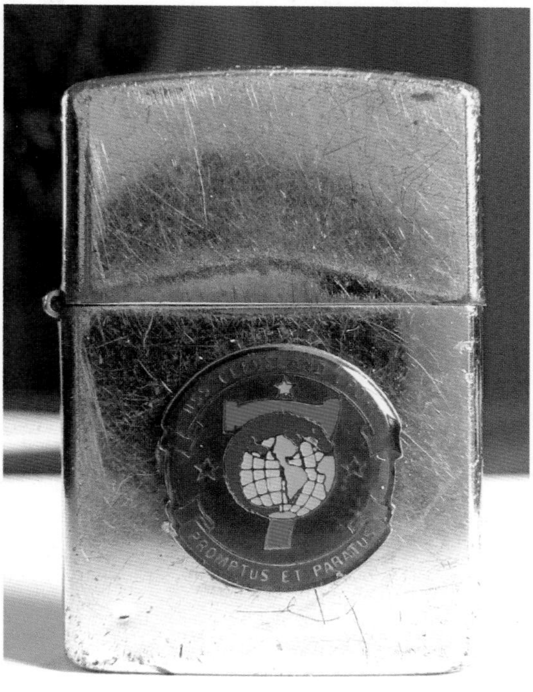
PROMPTUS ET PARATUS

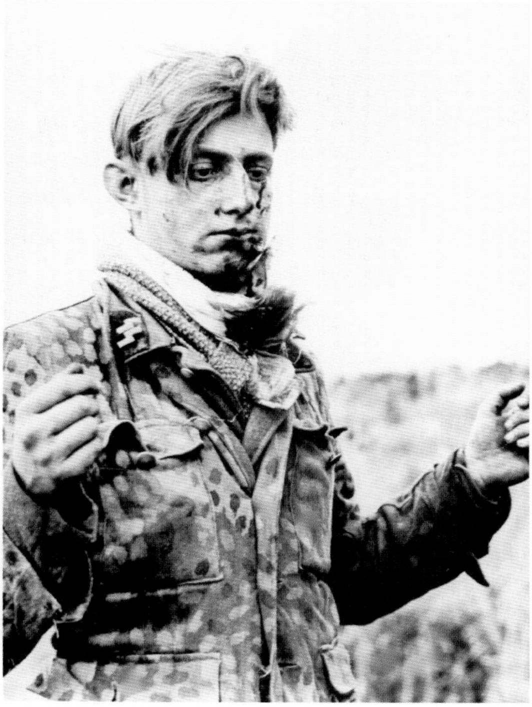

left: Part of a B-17 bomber cockpit instrument panel; top: A U.S. Navy Zippo for the USS *Cleveland*; A wounded and captured German soldier in France.

Referred to by aviation writer Roger Freeman as 'the premier fighter leader of his day'. Hubert 'Hub' Zemke had commanded the Eighth Air Force's 56th and 479th fighter groups. Hub was leading Mustang fighters escorting a force of B-24 bombers in an attack on an oil target in central Germany on 30 March 1944 when weather conditions were threatening. Turbulence suddenly threw his P-51 into a violent spin. He struggled to recover while the plane continued to gain airspeed and was heading straight down. The visibility was nil.

In the next few seconds the Mustang parted company with one wing. Still strapped in his seat, Hub had lost his flying helmet, goggles and oxygen mask and was in considerable pain from blows to his head, right shoulder and leg. Years later Hub recalled the events of that March day.

Shocked and dazed, he hung in his parachute harness. The descent seemed interminable. Somehow the parachute had opened and he was aware and greatly concerned that it was taking him down through the cloud base and that he was roughly 400 feet above the earth and coming down so fast he had almost no time to observe the area where he would be landing. He was just able to pull his knees up and ready himself for the violent impact that, when it came, cleared his mind. Now he was reviving, breathless and miserably aware of his cold, soaking wet clothes. He knew he had never taken a wallop in his boxing days like the one he had just experienced, but was grateful to have come down in a shallow, marshy area of heavy grass and wet scrub. His first thought was safety and the shelter of a pine forest only 100 yards away, but what he had just been through had exhausted him so that when he had reached the shelter

of the trees he could only sit, catch his breath and begin to consider his situation. The cold and wet chilled him and his teeth chattered uncontrollably. He lit a cigarette and thought about what to do. He began to relax and gradually the tremors stopped and he was able to take stock of the injuries he had incurred during the disintegration of his Mustang. The severe pain of his head, leg and shoulder kicked in furiously and his swelling right eye began to close.

His first priority was to shed his G-suit and dispose of it under a nearby bush. The awful agony of his damaged shoulder was eased some as he quickly fashioned a sling from one of his parachute panels. He then hid the remains of the 'chute and focused on lighting a small fire to warm up and stop his teeth chattering. He seemed quite alone there and doubted that such a little fire would attract any attention. He gathered some twigs and branches and used his Zippo lighter to make a very nice and comforting blaze.

Calmed, he began to inventory the assets in his pockets that might be of use in his travels. They amounted to his two dog tags on a chain, a knife, his U.S. Government wrist watch, the Zippo lighter, a pack of cigarettes and a little escape kit. As he surveyed the contents of the kit he discovered a very small but promising dime-store compass and various other items, the most welcome being a traditional silk escape map which he immediately put to use.

Now Hub was thinking that his plane had probably come down somewhere to the east of the German city of Hannover. He reasoned that Holland or Belgium were a few hundred walking miles to the west. Oh, what a happy thought. His fellow pilots were returning to base now to a welcoming fire, a drink or three and a wholesome dinner at the club.

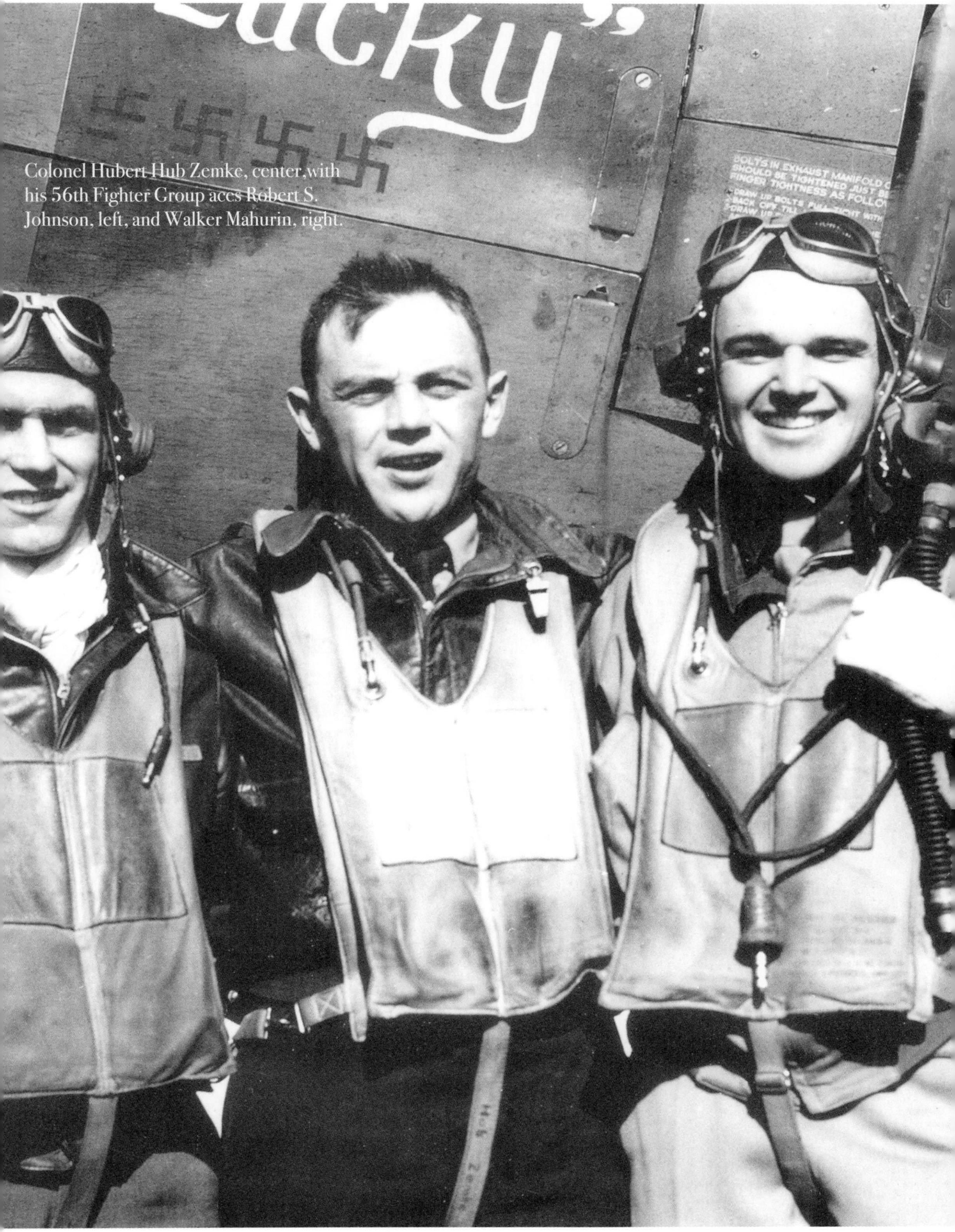

Colonel Hubert Hub Zemke, center, with his 56th Fighter Group aces Robert S. Johnson, left, and Walker Mahurin, right.

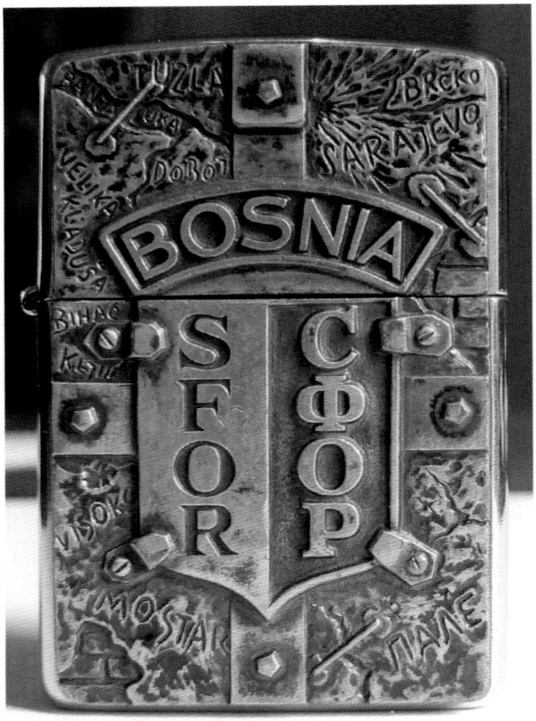
TUZLA
SARAJEVO
BOSNIA
SFOR
СФОР
VISOKO
MOSTAR
ПАЛЕ

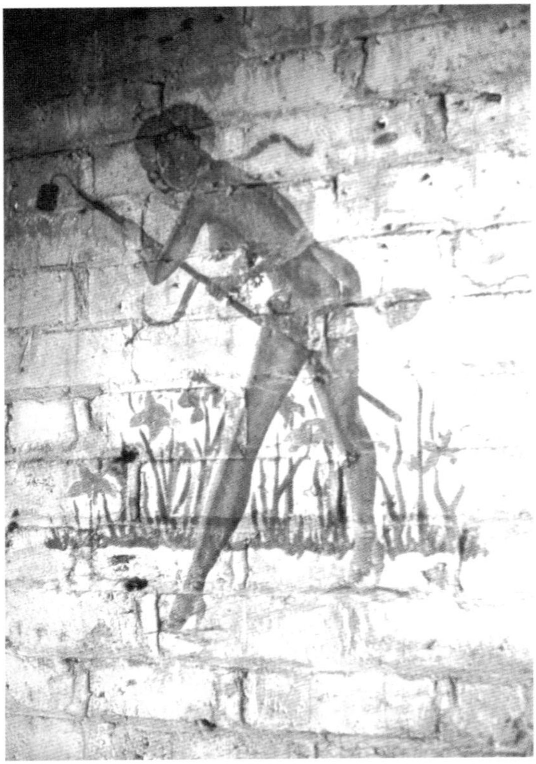

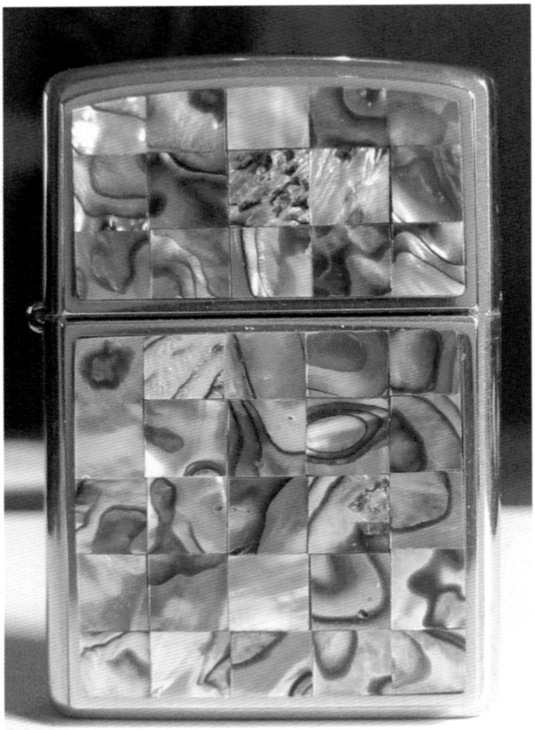

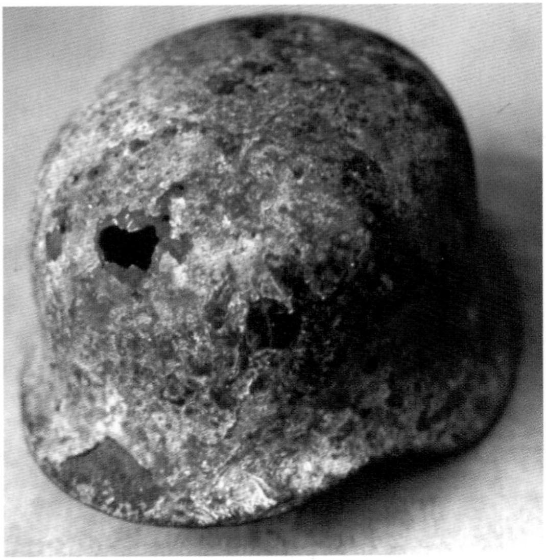

top left: A Zippo relating to the Bosnia war in 1992; top: Eighth U.S.Army Air Force wall art on the former B-24 base at Shipdham, England; left: A Mother-of-Pearl Zippo; above: A German army helmet found on one of the Normandy1944 D-Day invasion beaches.

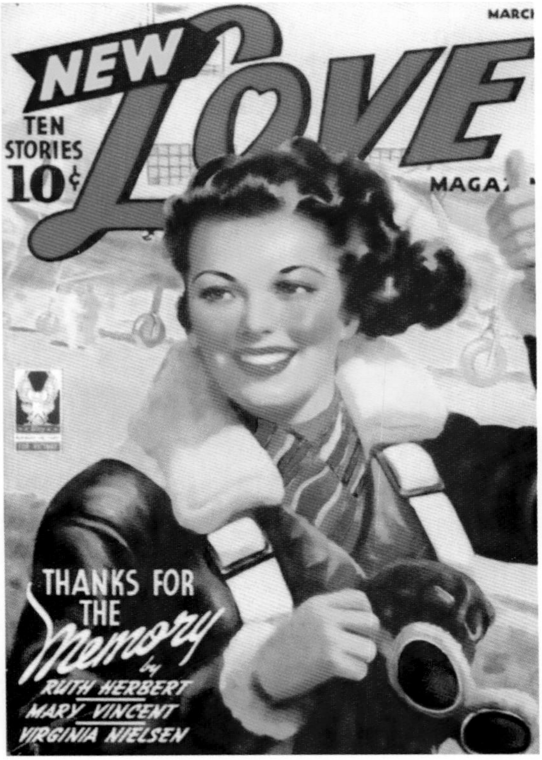
MARCH
NEW LOVE
TEN STORIES 10¢
MAGAZ
THANKS FOR THE Memory
by
RUTH HERBERT
MARY VINCENT
VIRGINIA NIELSEN

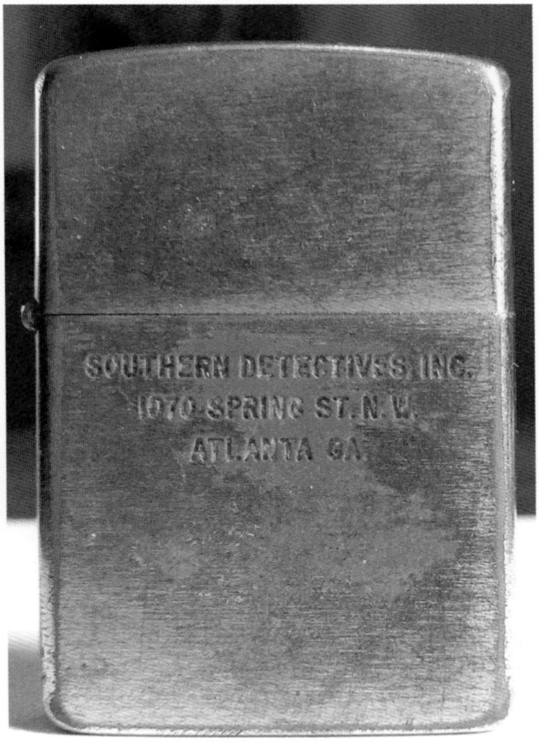
SOUTHERN DETECTIVES, INC.
1070 SPRING ST. N.W.
ATLANTA GA.

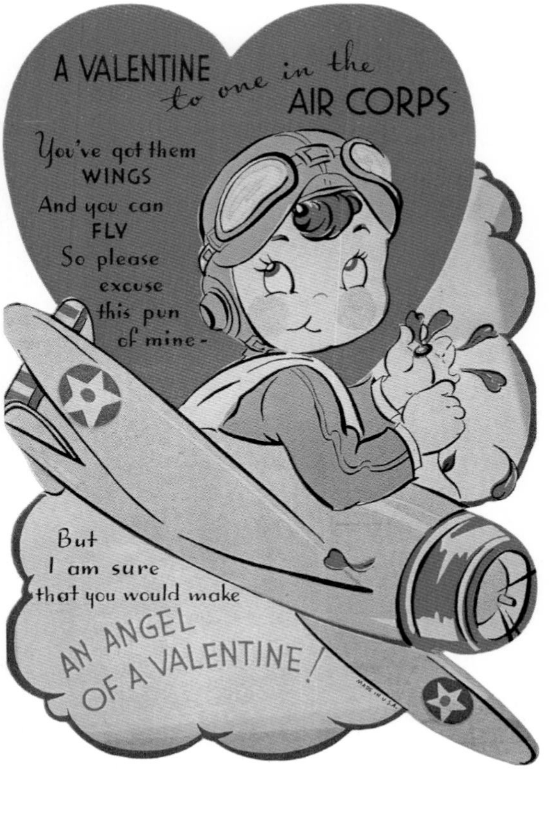
A VALENTINE to one in the AIR CORPS
You've got them WINGS And you can FLY So please excuse this pun of mine-
But I am sure that you would make
AN ANGEL OF A VALENTINE!

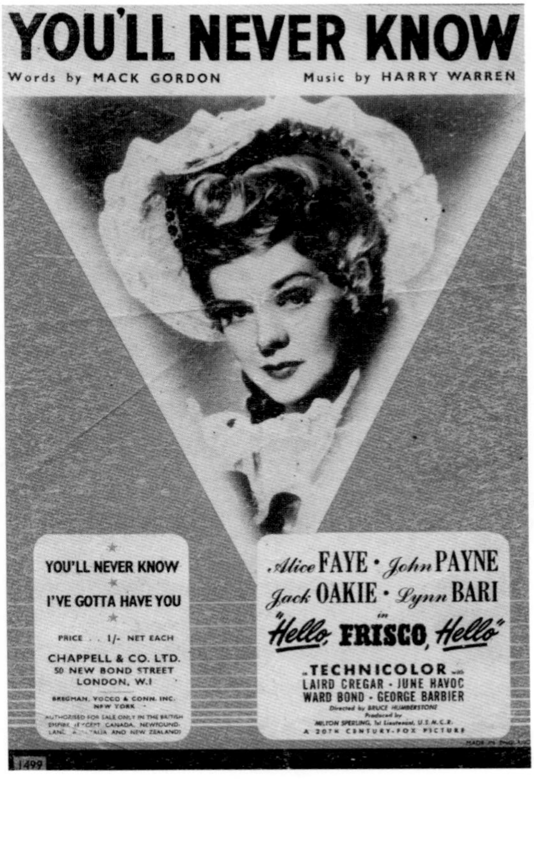
YOU'LL NEVER KNOW
Words by MACK GORDON
Music by HARRY WARREN
YOU'LL NEVER KNOW
I'VE GOTTA HAVE YOU
PRICE . . 1/- NET EACH
CHAPPELL & CO. LTD.
50 NEW BOND STREET
LONDON, W.1
Alice FAYE · John PAYNE
Jack OAKIE · Lynn BARI
in
"Hello, FRISCO, Hello"
in TECHNICOLOR with
LAIRD CREGAR · JUNE HAVOC
WARD BOND · GEORGE BARBIER
A 20TH CENTURY-FOX PICTURE

In the Second World War, when the Zippo Manufacturing Company was forced by the government reclassification of brass as a strategic metal, to use steel and a 'black crackle' paint surface on the lighter casing, it received an unexpected response from American soldiers in various combat zones. The GIs expressed their appreciation to the company for its application of the black crackle finish and the resulting benefit it provided in not reflecting light as older shiny metal-finished lighters did. The new ones thus avoided the attentions of enemy snipers.

Another aspect of the personable little lighter was the sleek deco styling, providing a perfect display surface for the owner to extend the First World War tradition of engraving or otherwise embellishing lighters by affixing a coin, medallion or some other decoration that served to represent something about that owner. That tradition had also applied to pre-war Zippos of 1936-41 vintage, many of which were still in regular use during the Second World War years.

On the U.S. home front, where the aircraft of war were being designed and built for the Allied fighting men, the companies involved, including Boeing, Grumman, Lockheed, Beechcraft, Bell, Consolidated, Northrop, North American and Republic had their logos applied to Zippos to promote their products in the war effort. In addition to these primary aeroplane makers, other participants in the manufacture of weapons and equipment for the Allied war effort included Goodyear, General Electric, Westinghouse, General Motors, Allison, Chance Vought and Piper, all were promoted on Zippos during the war.

After the entry of the United States into the Second World War, an army of another sort began to appear in some of the war zones including Britain. There some of the bomber and fighter groups of the American Eighth and Ninth Air Forces were seen to be personalizing their aircraft with images of familiar cartoon characters such as Mickey Mouse, Donald Duck, Pluto, Bugs Bunny, Woody Woodpecker, Mighty Mouse and Popeye. Soon these characters were also showing up on the Zippos of the crewmen in the air groups in England, and later in Italy, North Africa, and out in the Pacific islands.

After the end of the Second World War, on 2 September, 1945, the battleship USS *Missouri* was selected as the site for the unconditional surrender ceremony of Japan, an official and formal event in which General Douglas MacArthur, together with other representatives of the United States and its Allied nations, met to receive surrender documents from officials of the Japanese Government. The event marked the closure of the Second World War.

A plaque on the deck of the USS *Missouri* demarcates the location of the surrender ceremony and reads:
ON THIS SPOT ON 2 SEPTEMBER 1945 THE INSTRUMENT OF FORMAL SURRENDER OF JAPAN TO THE ALLIED POWERS WAS SIGNED, THUS BRINGING TO A CLOSE THE SECOND WORLD WAR. THE SHIP AT THAT TIME WAS AT ANCHOR IN TOKYO BAY.

Major Pierce McKennon of the 4th Fighter Group, Debden, England, with *Ridge Runner*, his P-51 Packard-Rolls-Royce-powered Mustang aircraft.

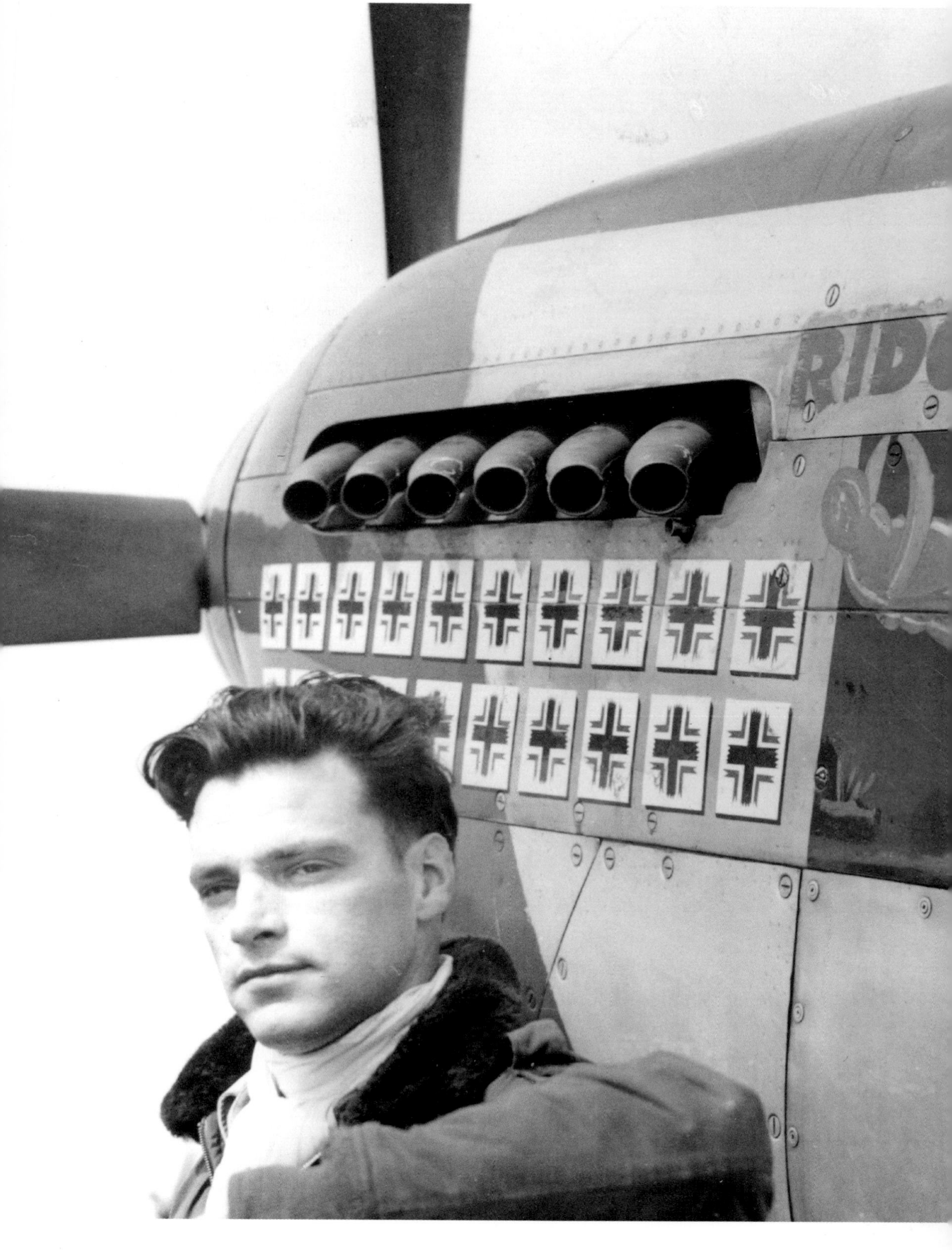
RID

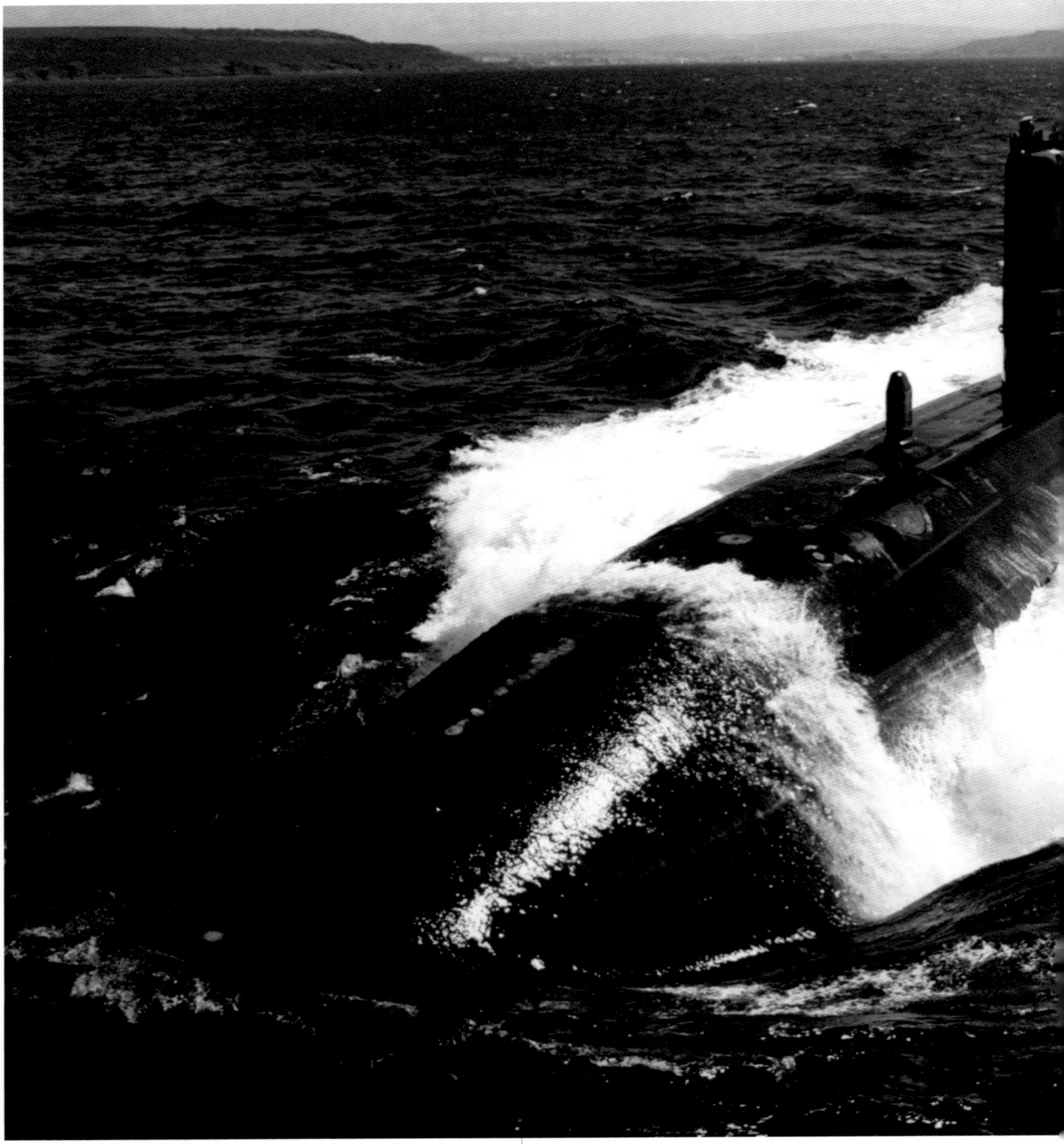

The Royal Navy Trafalgar-class nuclear-powered cruise-missile submarine HMS *Turbulent* had a speed of more than thirty knots submerged. She was armed with up to thirty weapons including Tomahawk cruise missiles and Spearfish torpedoes. *Turbulent* was commissioned in April 1984 and in service until July 2012.

More than 2.5 million people died as a result of a war which began on 25 June 1950, when forces of North Korea supported by those of the Soviet Union and China invaded South Korea which had the backing of the United States and the United Nations. It was the time of the Cold War. North Korea was a Socialist state led by a communist, Kim Il Sung, and the anti-communist South Korea was governed by Syngman Rhee.

Ultimately, twenty-one countries comprised the UN fighting force with fully ninety per cent of the personnel being Americans.

In only a few months the South Koreans and their American allies were overwhelmed and all but defeated, soon forcing them to withdraw to a rear area known as the Pusan Perimeter. Then, in the autumn of 1950, they managed to mount a counter-offensive in the form of an amphibious landing at Incheon, trapping a large number of North Korean troops. And in October, soldiers of the United Nations forces were able to move into the north and push up towards the Yalu River on the Chinese border. That action soon led to the entry of the Chinese People's Volunteer Army into the fight, causing a withdrawl by the UN forces back across the Yalu and the 38th Parallel in December. The battle turned into a war of attrition with Seoul, the capitol of South Korea, changing hands four times until the ground fighting ended in July 1953. Before the war's end, however, U.S. bombers flew a punishing bombing campaign against the north and the world witnessed the first air combat by jet fighters as North American F-86 Sabres took on the MiG-15s of the North Korean Air Force in air battles that saw the Americans establish a kill ratio of ten to one over their adversaries.

Zippo went to war again in Korea, in the pockets of UN soldiers, sailors and airmen of twenty-one participating countries and once again proved a hugely popular and reliable companion and for many a lucky talisman, as well. Over the years the Zippo company has been gifted with lighters that were said to have stopped bullets and saved lives in such conflicts. What a lucky charm.

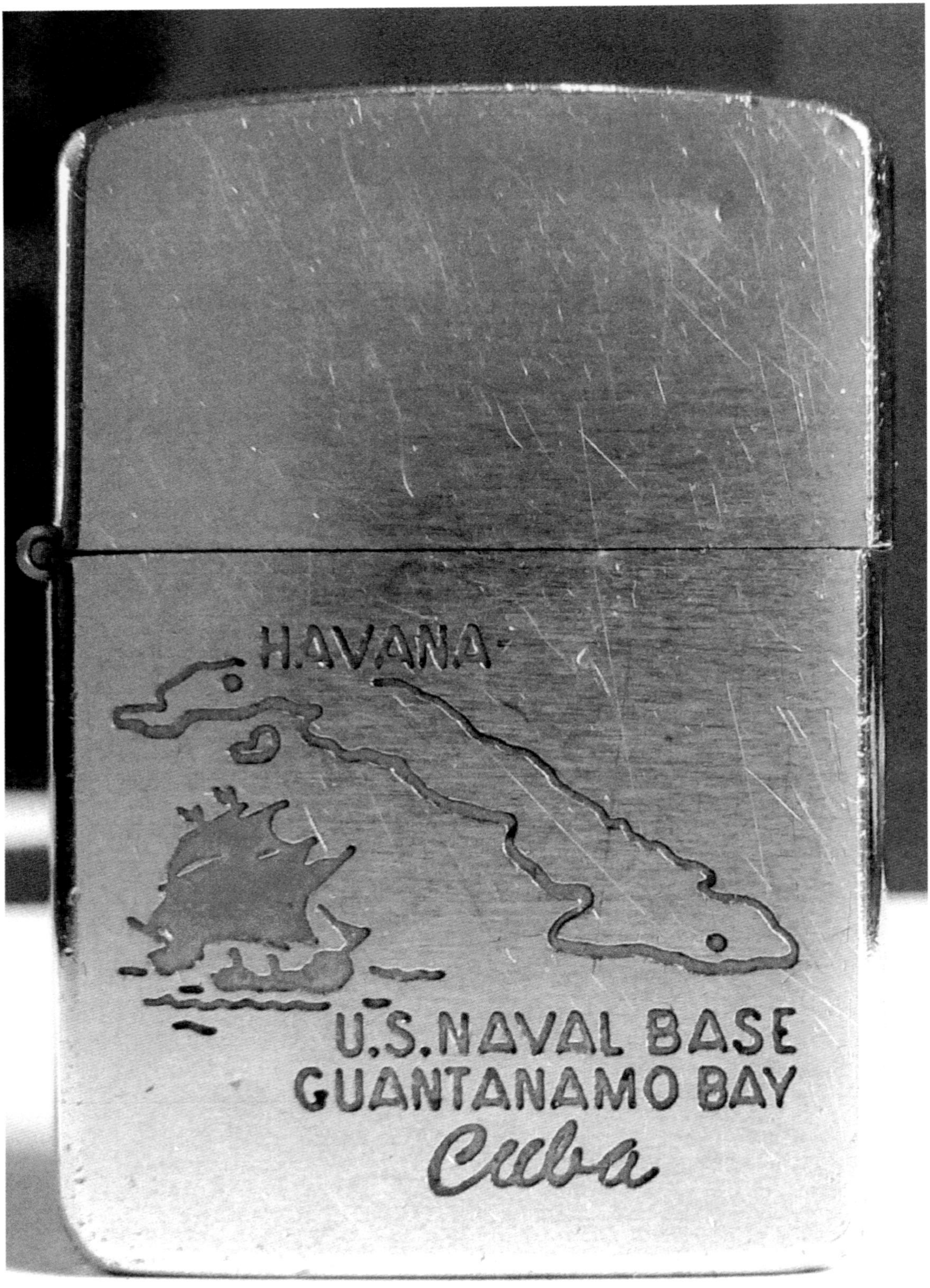
HAVANA
U.S. NAVAL BASE
GUANTANAMO BAY
Cuba

Evidently, cigarette smoking did not actually begin until after the end of the American Civil War. During that conflict, it is known that the use of chewing tobacco was common among the men and cigars were enjoyed mainly by the officers. Beginning in the First World War, the American tobacco industry first started to 'recruit' military personnel through the distribution of free cigarettes to the servicemen, and later saw the inclusion of cigarettes into their rations.

History has shown how society in general has moved away from the use of cigarettes since the 1964 Surgeon General's report on smoking and health, which linked cigarette smoking with lung cancer and heart disease as well as lung and laryngeal cancer in men and a probable cause of lung cancer in women, and the most important cause of chronic bronchitis. In her introduction to *The Health Consequences of Smoking—50 Years of Progress Report* of the Surgeon General Executive Summary 2014, Kathleen Sebelius, U.S. Secretary of Health and Human Services stated: 'Fifty years after the release of the first Surgeon General's report warning of the health hazards of smoking, we have learned how to end the tobacco epidemic, and what steps must be taken if we truly want to bring to a close one of our nation's most tragic battles—one that has killed ten times the number of Americans who died in all of our nation's wars combined.

'In the United States, successes in tobacco control have more than halved smoking rates since the 1964 landmark Surgeon General's report came out. Americans' collective view of smoking has been transformed from an accepted national pastime to a discouraged threat to individual and public health. Strong policies have largely driven cigarette smoking

out of public view and public air space. Thanks to smokefree laws, no longer is smoking allowed on airplanes or in a growing number of restaurants, bars, college campuses and government buildings.' In its campaign to increase the smoking of cigarettes by U.S. military personnel after the United States' entry into the First World War in 1917, the American tobacco industry sought to promote cigarette use as a means of psychologically escaping the battlefield situations they found themselves in and a morale booster to boot. Apparently soldiers then, and later in the Second World War, mostly felt that a smoke in those often terrible conditions helped to calm their nerves and get them through the stresses and dangers they faced. They felt that a cigarette lightened the inevitable hardships of war. By the time of the Second World War, popular American magazines were even featuring colour ads for cigarette brands in which a 'medical doctor' appeared to endorse the claim of a health benefit for a particular cigarette brand.

Some American tobacco companies during the Second World War maintained an effort to get soldiers smoking in those war years by providing free cigarettes, supporting the inclusion of those smokes in their rations. The American military services continued to include cigarettes in the rations until 1975 despite increasing evidence of adverse health effects from their use.

left: .Guantanamo Bay detention camp is a U.S. Navy prison facility located on the Cuban coast.

This is believed to be No 9 Squadron at RAF Bardney, Lincolnshire, in the Second World War. Here, bomber crews are waiting to be transported to their aircraft on hardstands around the perimeter of the airfield.

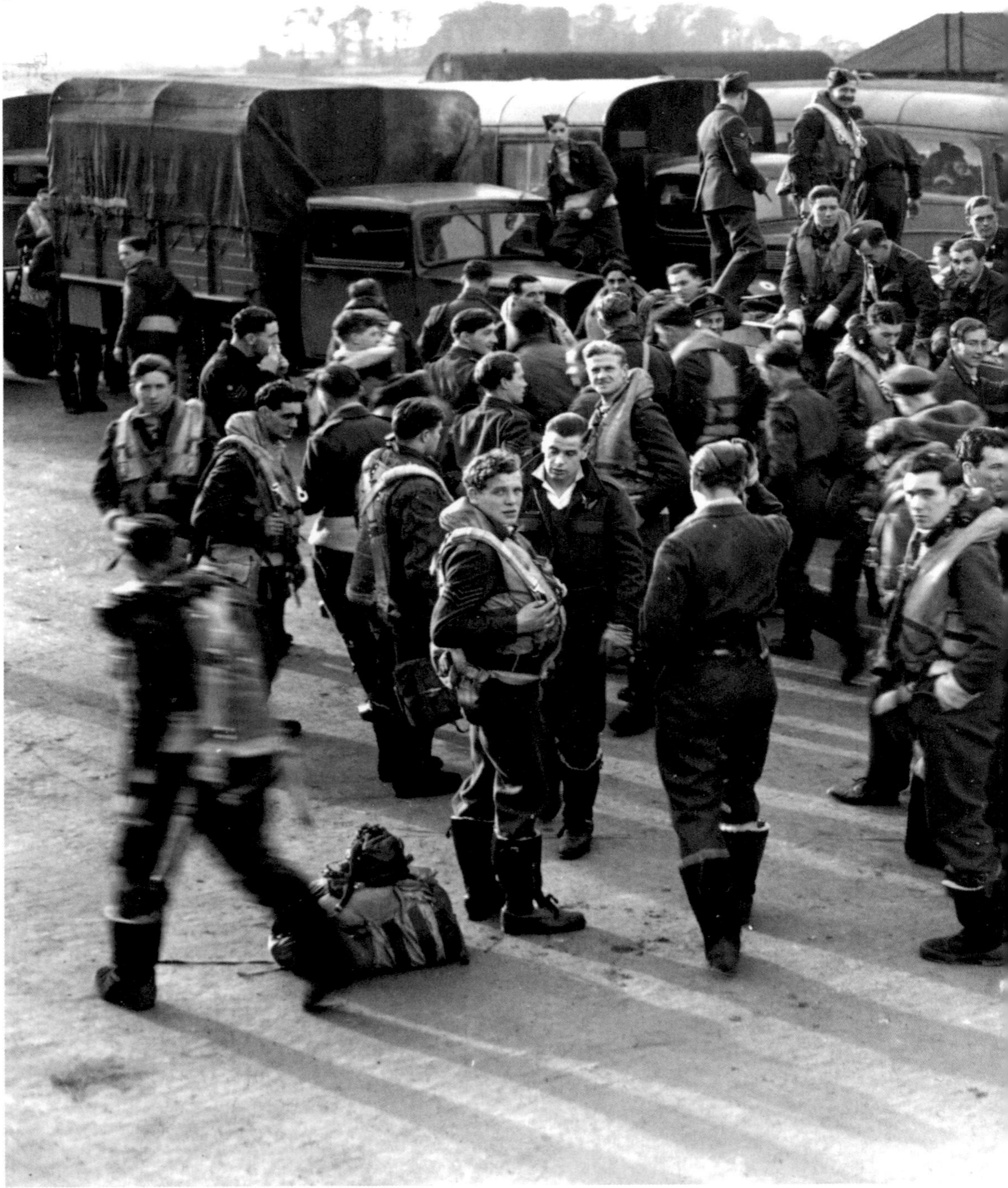

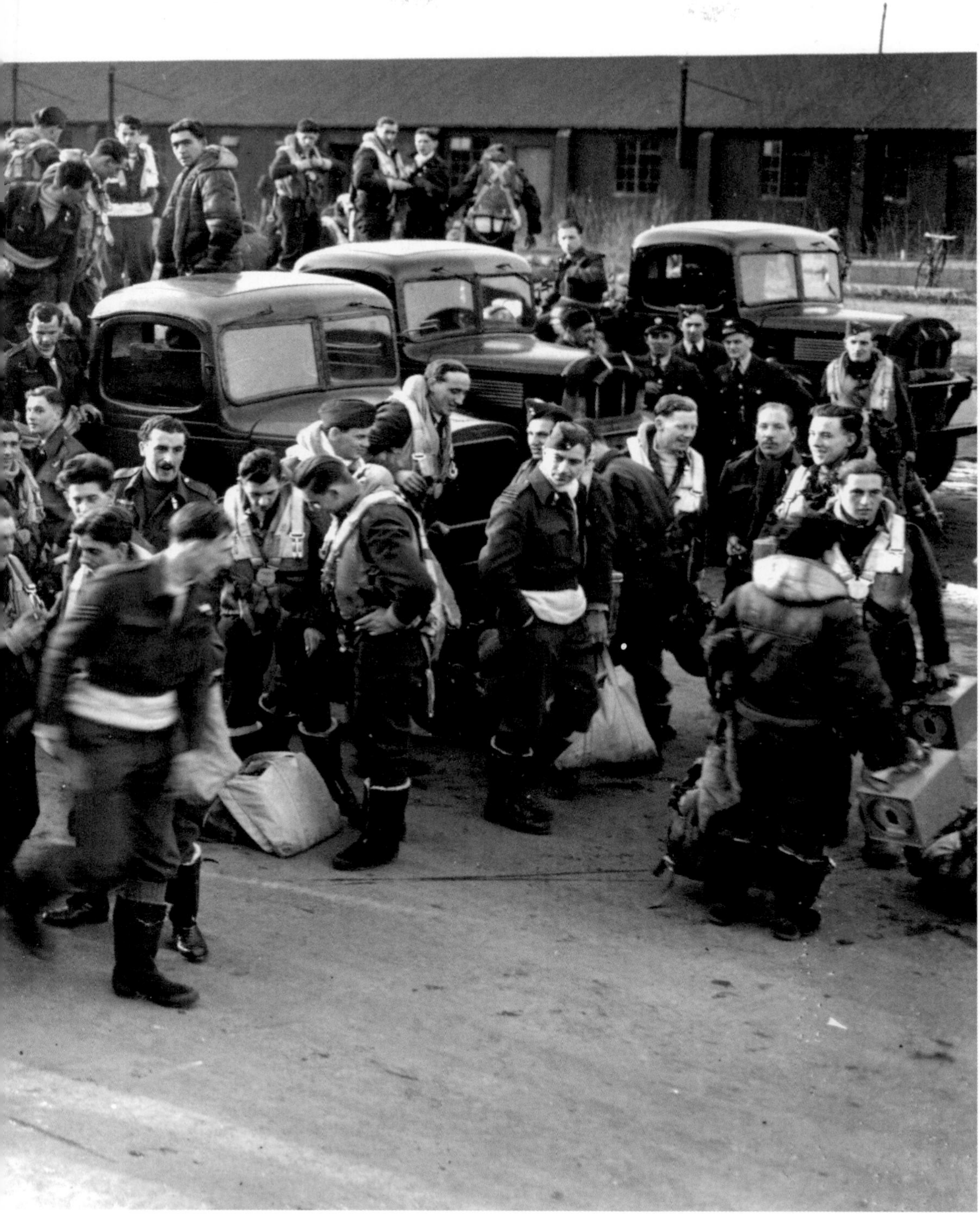

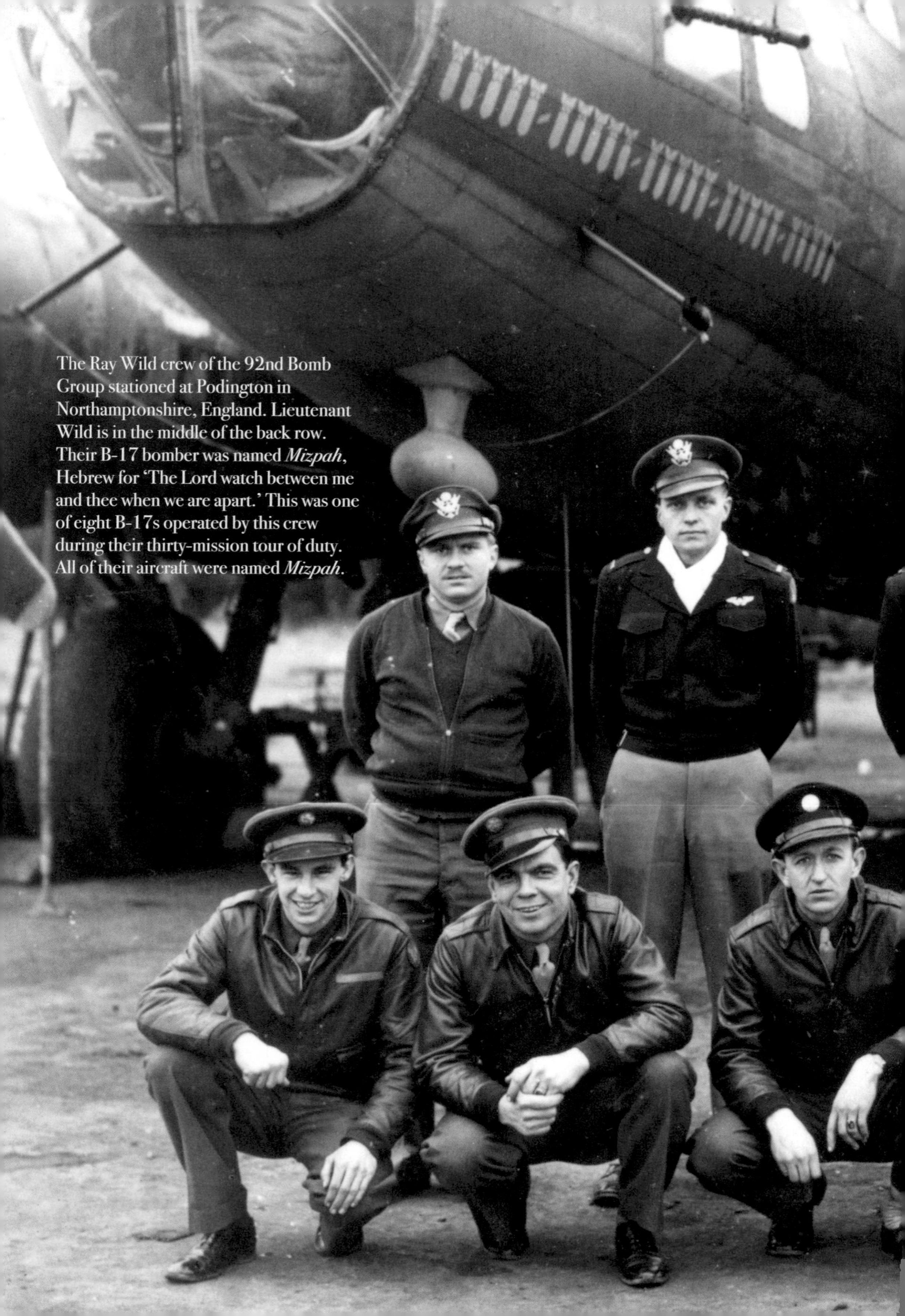

The Ray Wild crew of the 92nd Bomb Group stationed at Podington in Northamptonshire, England. Lieutenant Wild is in the middle of the back row. Their B-17 bomber was named *Mizpah*, Hebrew for 'The Lord watch between me and thee when we are apart.' This was one of eight B-17s operated by this crew during their thirty-mission tour of duty. All of their aircraft were named *Mizpah*.

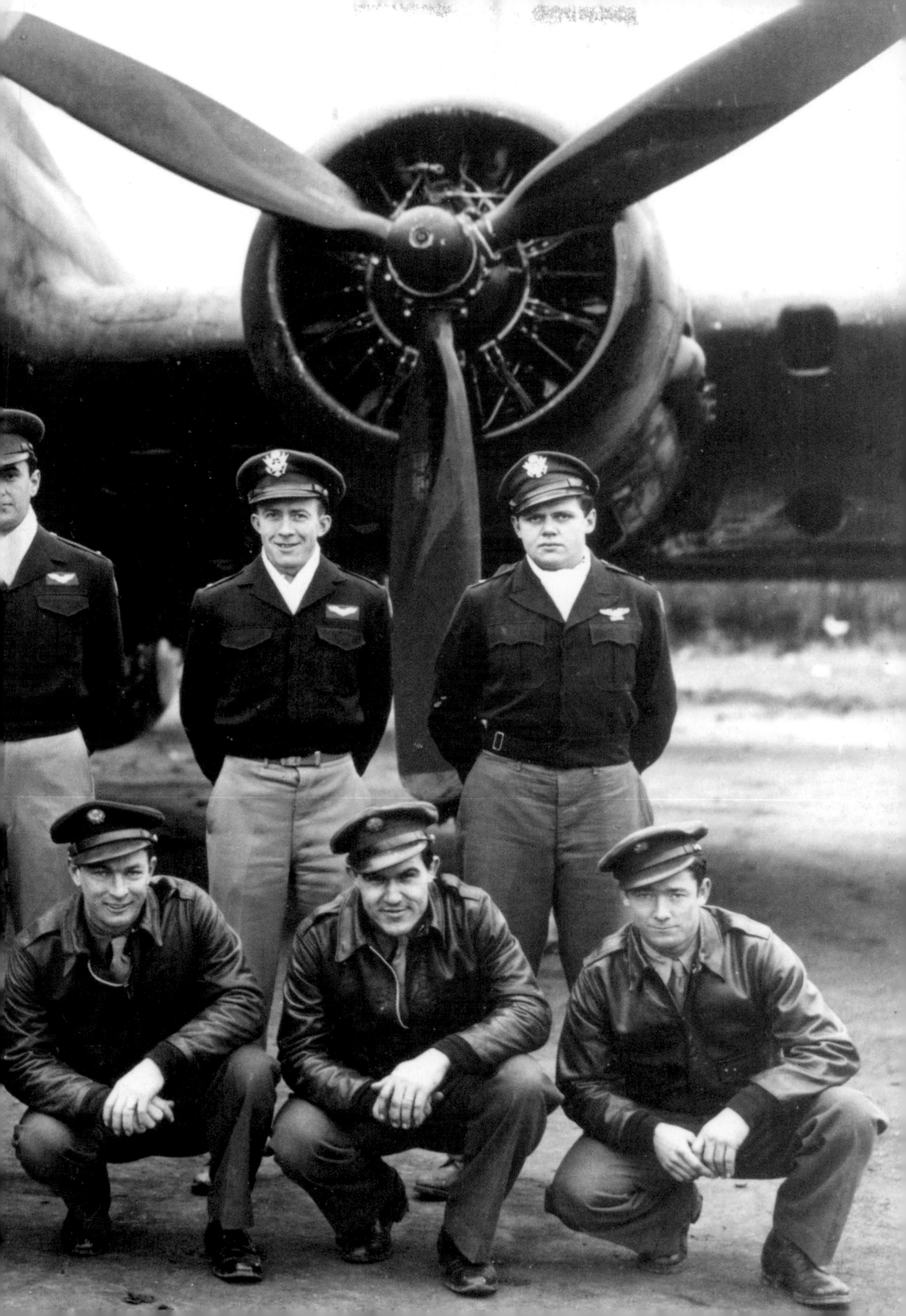

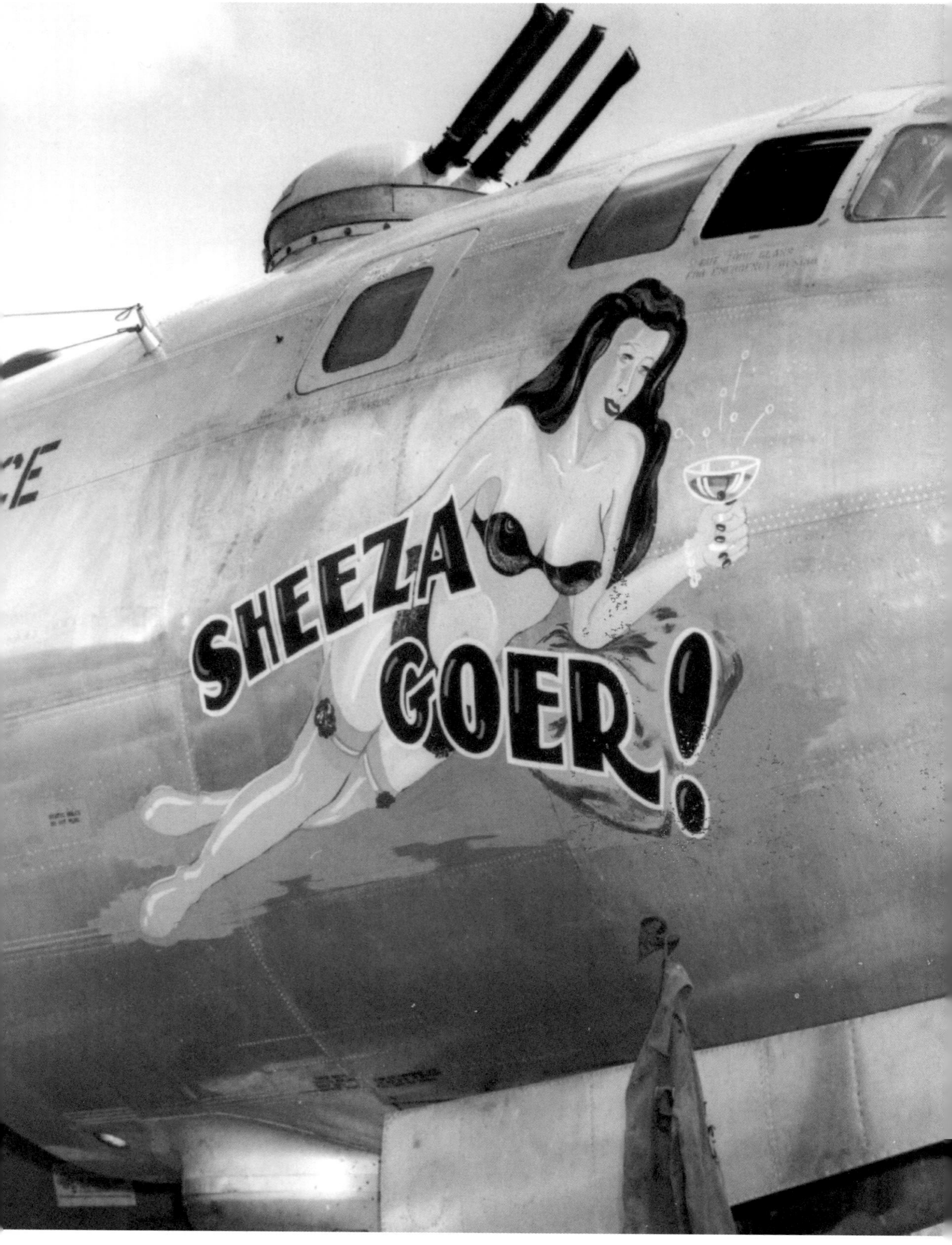
SHEEZA
GOER!

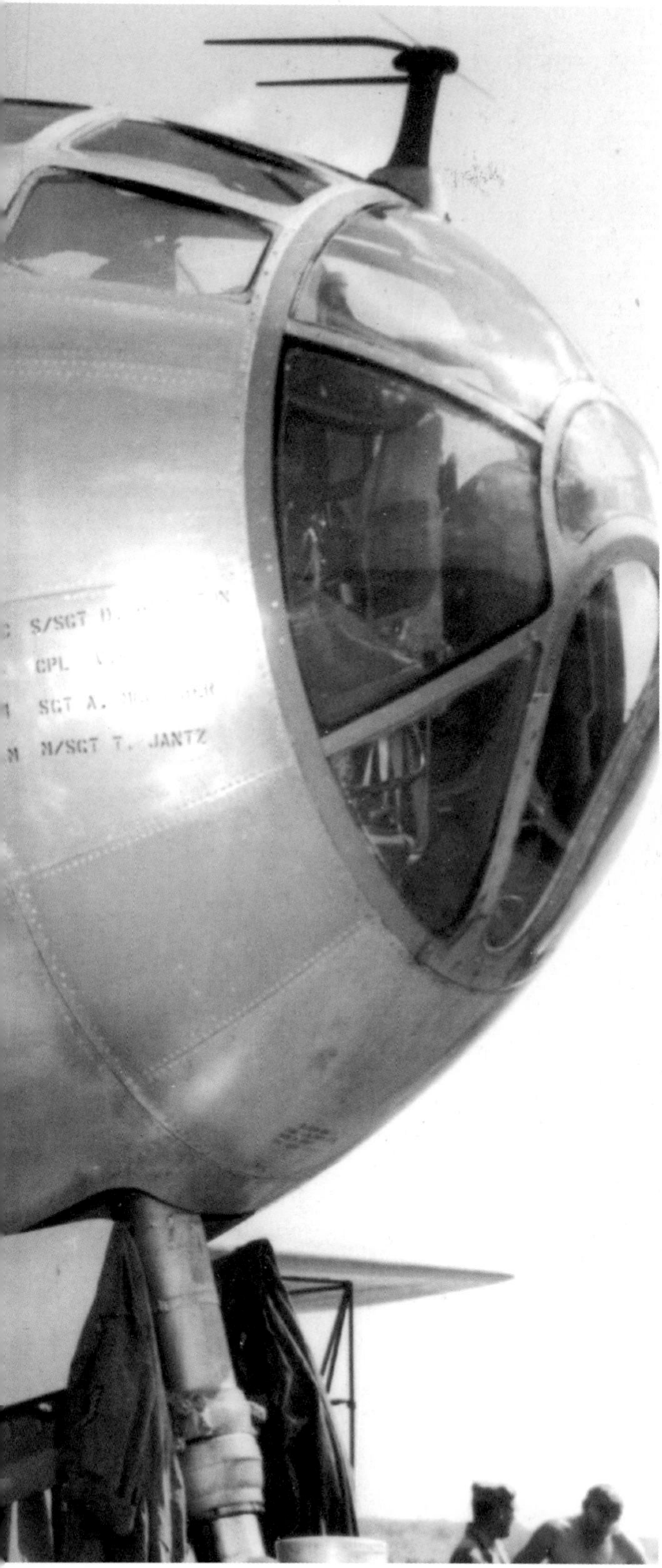
S/SGT
CPL
SGT A.
M/SGT T. JANTZ

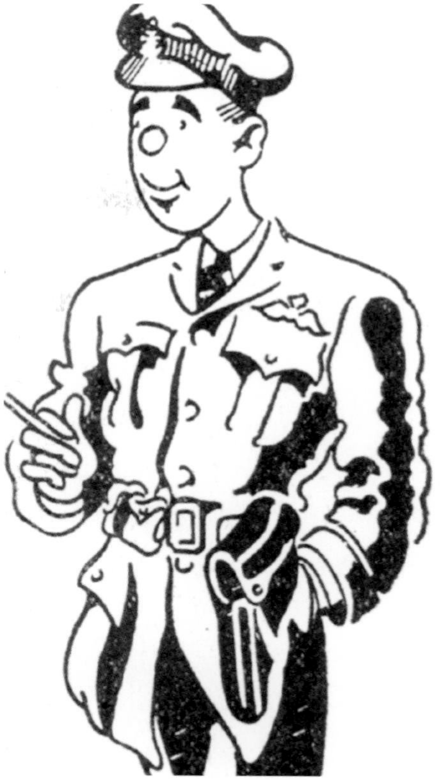

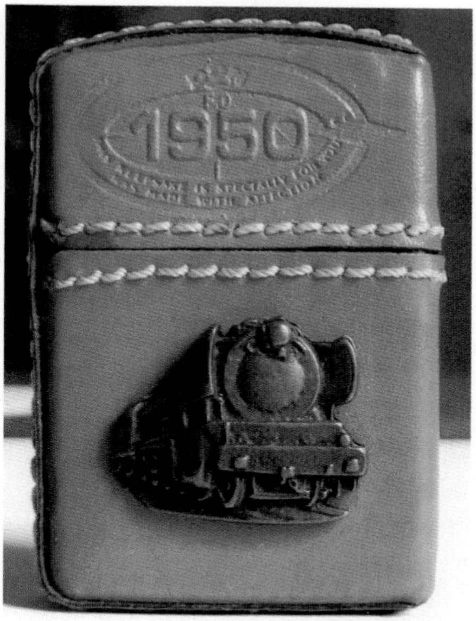
1950

left: A Boeing B-29 Superfortress heavy bomber similar to the USAAF aircraft that dropped the atom bombs on Hiroshima and Nagasaki, Japan, leading to the end of the war in 1945; above: A railway Zippo.

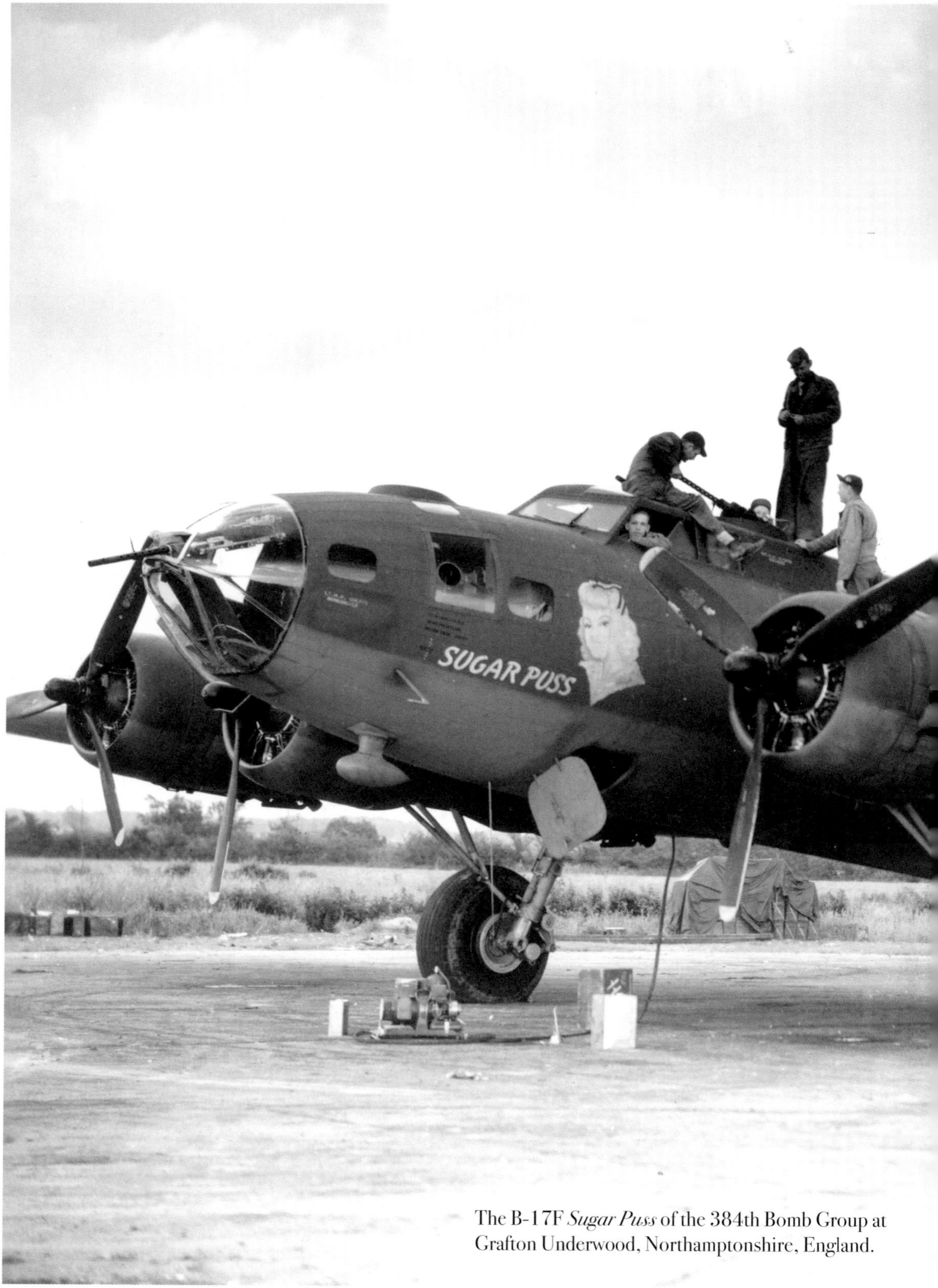
SUGAR PUSS

The B-17F *Sugar Puss* of the 384th Bomb Group at Grafton Underwood, Northamptonshire, England.

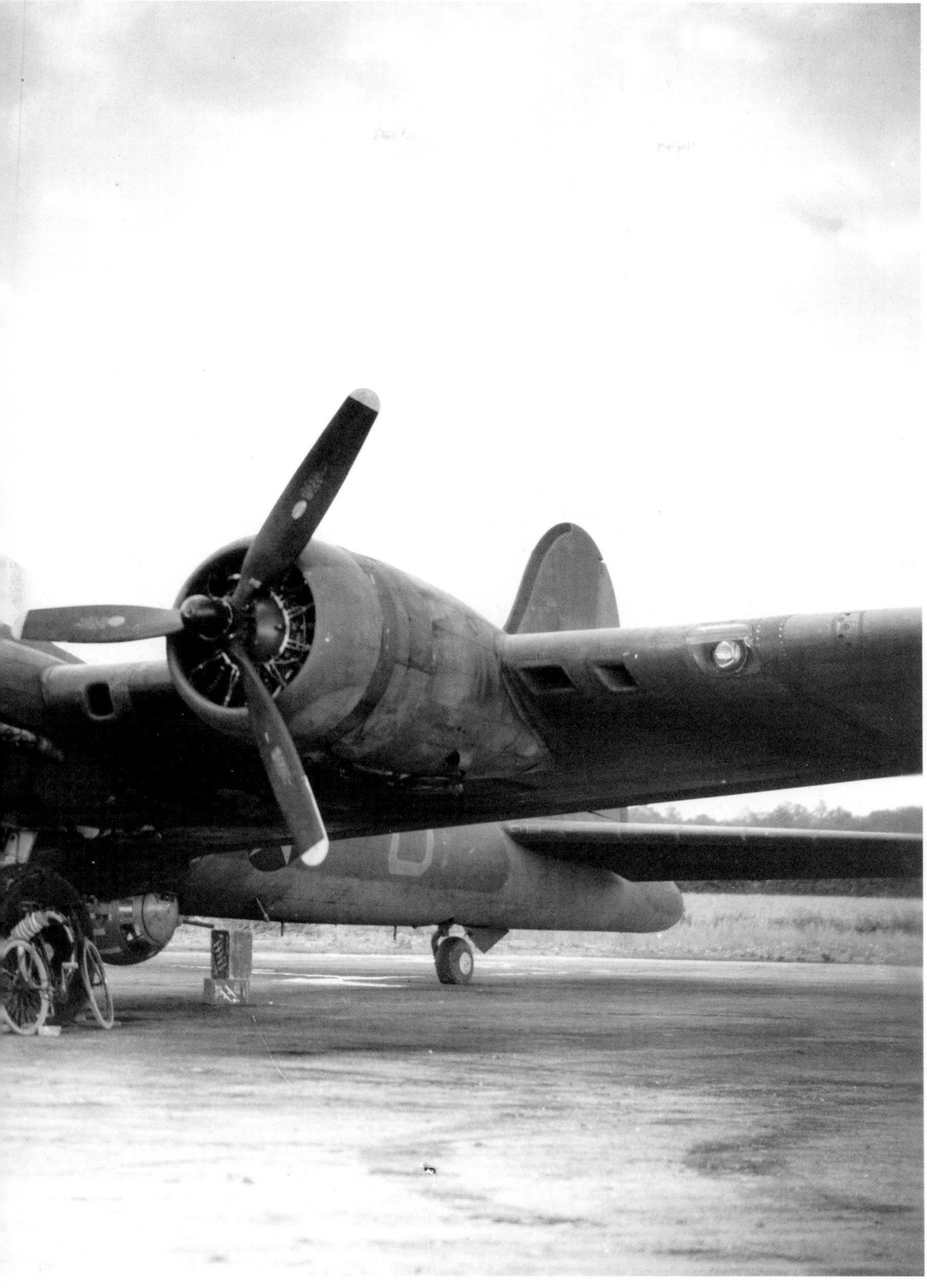

The B-17 bomber *Jerry Jinx* and her 303rd Bomb Group crew at their Molesworth, England base.

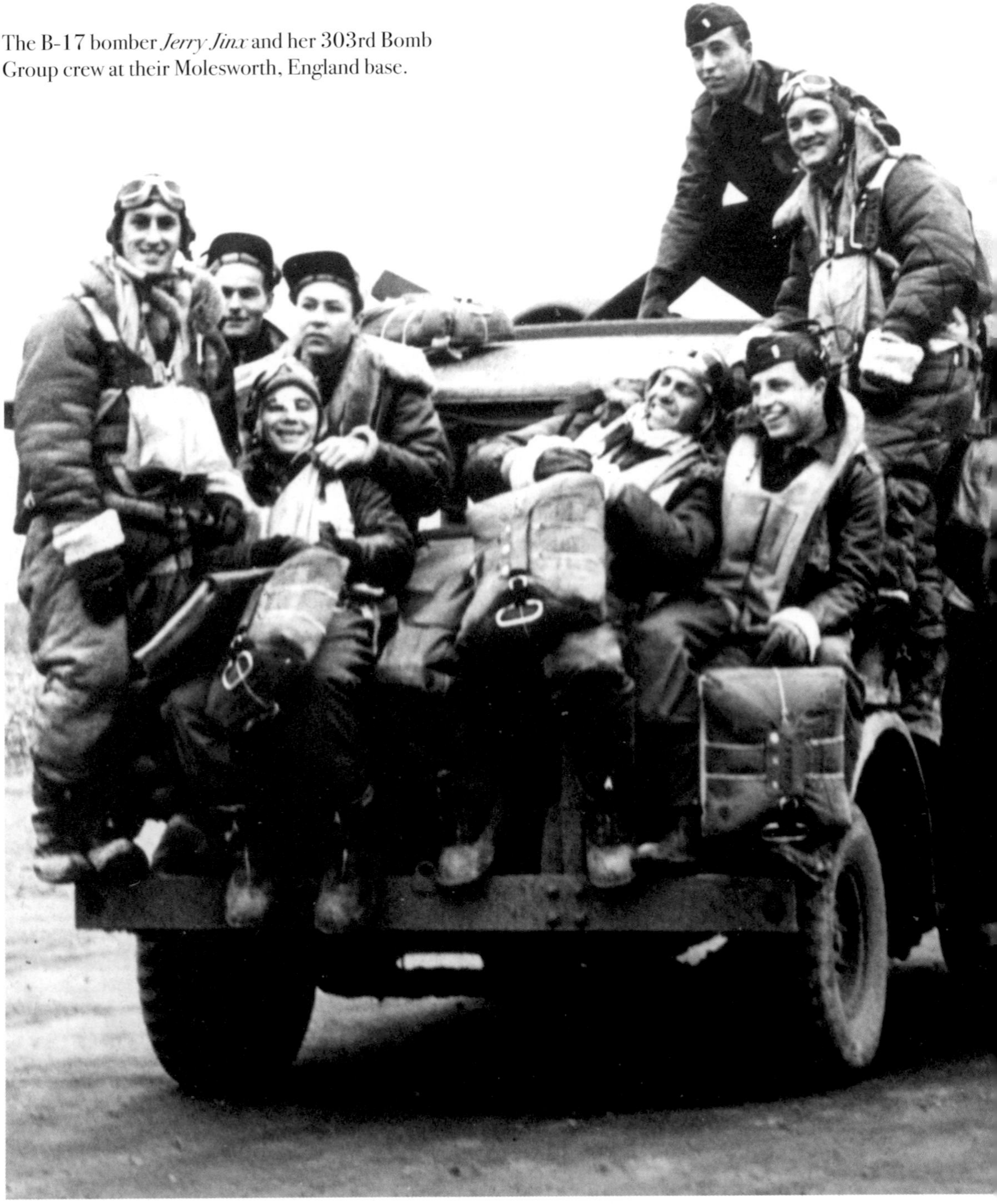

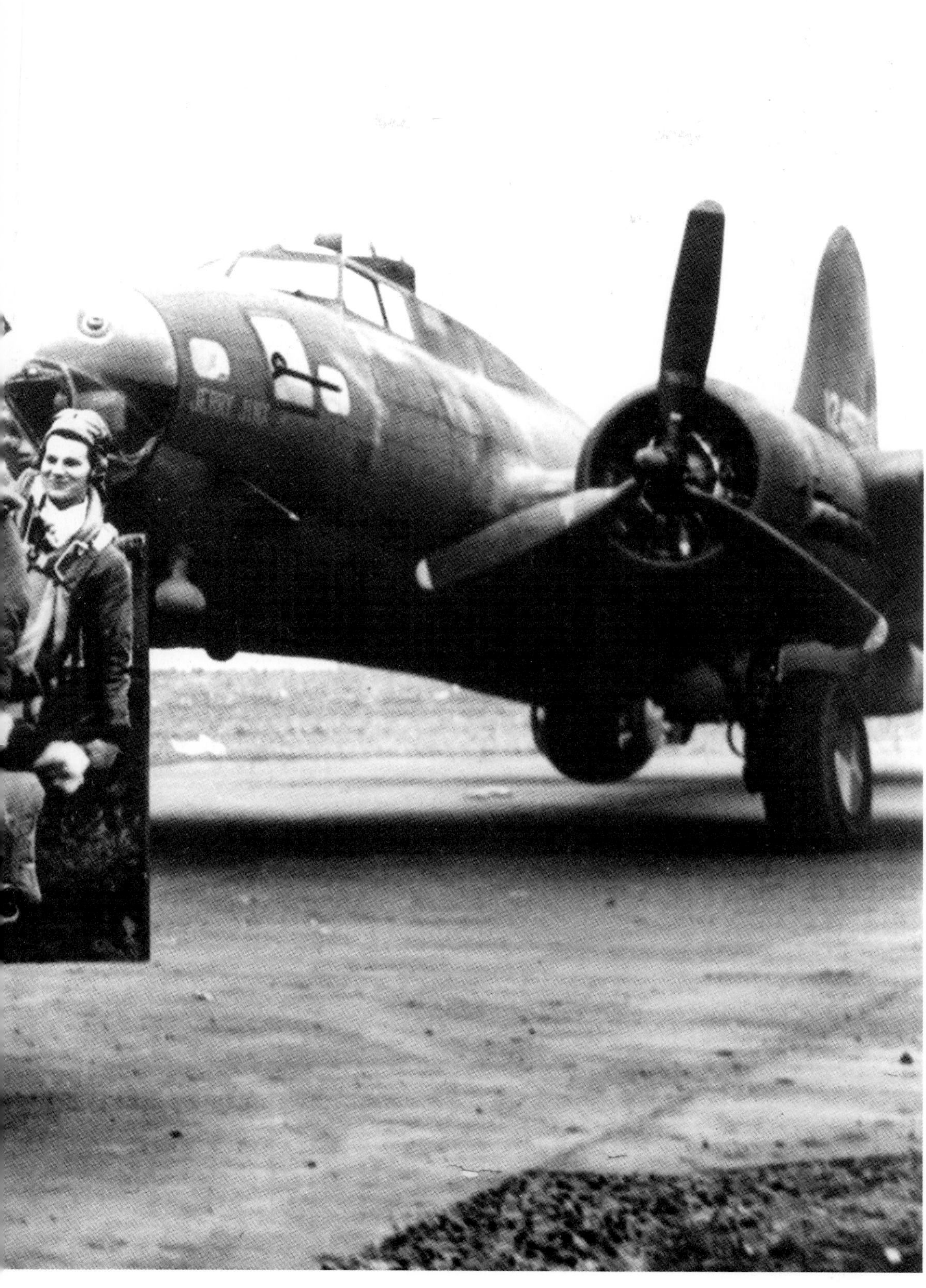
JERRY JINX

With the end of the war in 1945, English well-wishers turned out to wave goodbye to American air crews who had come over to do their bit for the Allied victory.

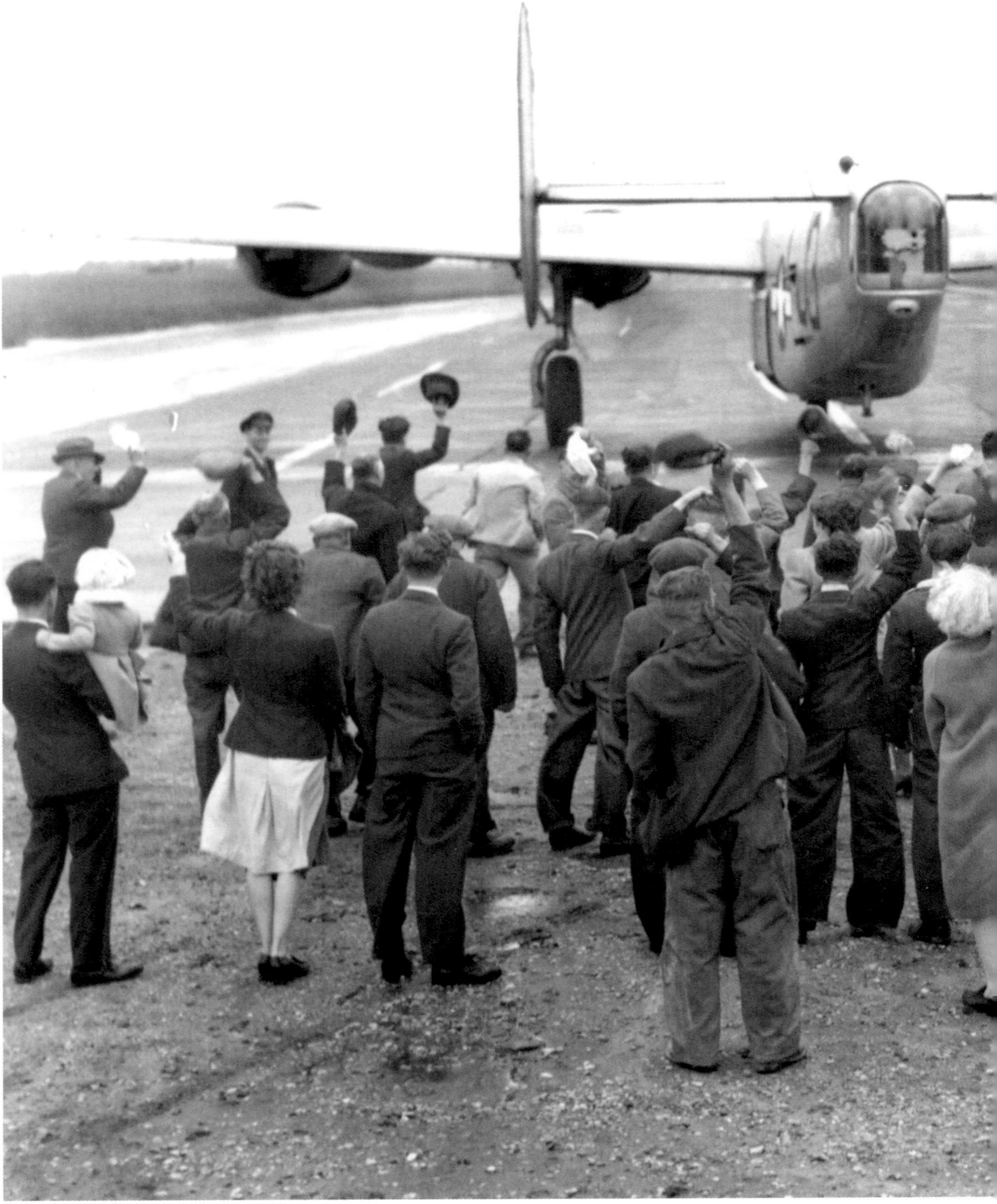

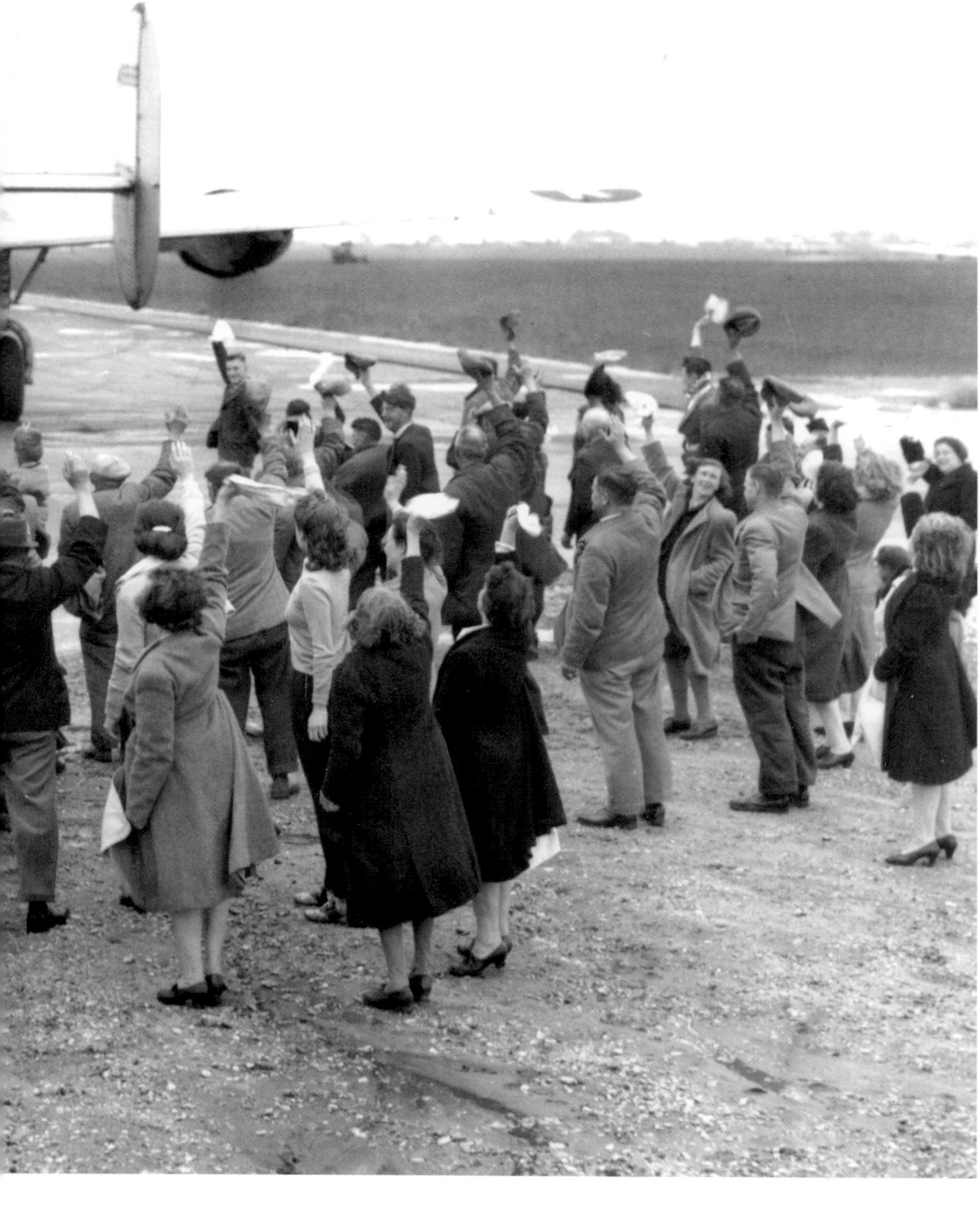

Sometimes referred to as the Second Indo-China War, the Viet Nam conflict lasted from November 1955 until 30 April 1975 and the fall of Saigon. It had officially been a struggle between North and South Viet Nam with the north being aided by China, the Soviet Union and other communist allies. South Viet Nam had the support of the United States, South Korea, the Philippines, Australia, Thailand and other anti-Communist nations. Under the administration of President John F. Kennedy, the American involvement in the Viet Nam War escalated from about 1,000 military advisors in 1959 to nearly 16,000 in 1963. By the following year there were 24,000 such advisors in South Viet Nam. Passage of the Gulf of Tonkin Resolution by the U.S. Congress authorized President Lyndon B. Johnson to dramatically increase the U.S. military presence in Viet Nam. He then increased American troop levels to 184,000 leading to significant annual increases in troops. By late in 1966, despite the introduction of large scale air superiority, search and destroy missions-and a massive strategic bombing campaign against North Viet Nam and Laos by the U.S., the American Secretary of Defense Robert McNamara, who had been one of the key architects of the Viet Nam War, was starting to have doubts about the outcome. By 1975 the main Spring Offensive and the fall of Saigon had brought the end of the war.

The presence of Zippo in Viet Nam was huge. Along with it came the often ugly proliferation of imitators; a range of crude, rude, and lewd fakes that swere brandished by the many unfortunates who had landed in that awful, winless war locale.More than 58,000 U.S. military personnel died in the Viet Nam conflict and in its aftermath came a new period of isolationism and resentment by the American public of any involvement in overseas conflicts. It was reminiscent of the feeling present in the years between the First and Second World Wars.

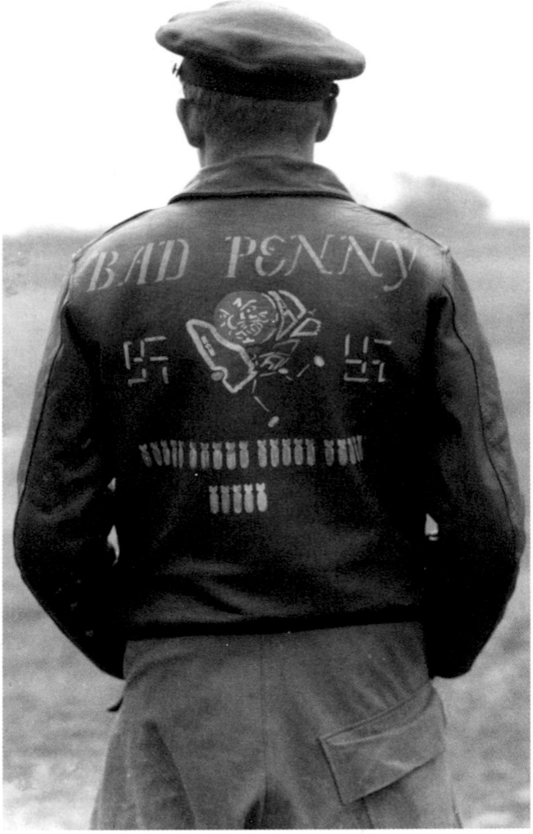
BAD PENNY

above: A crew member of a B-17 Flying Fortress bomber named *Bad Penny*, part of the 8USAAF 401st Bomb Group at Deenethorpe, England in WW2; right: War workers building tail assemblies for Vickers-Supermarine Spitfire fighter aircraft.

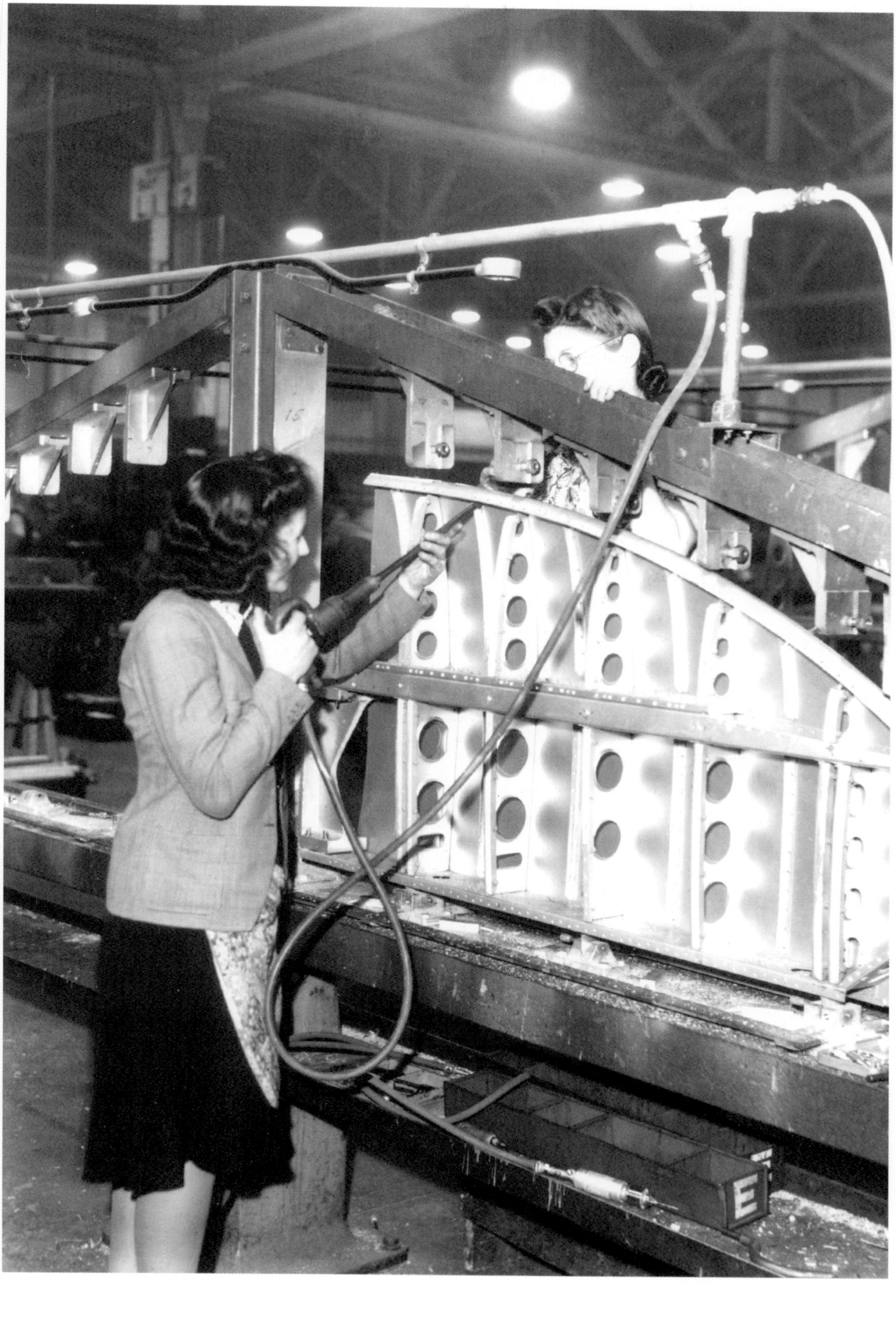

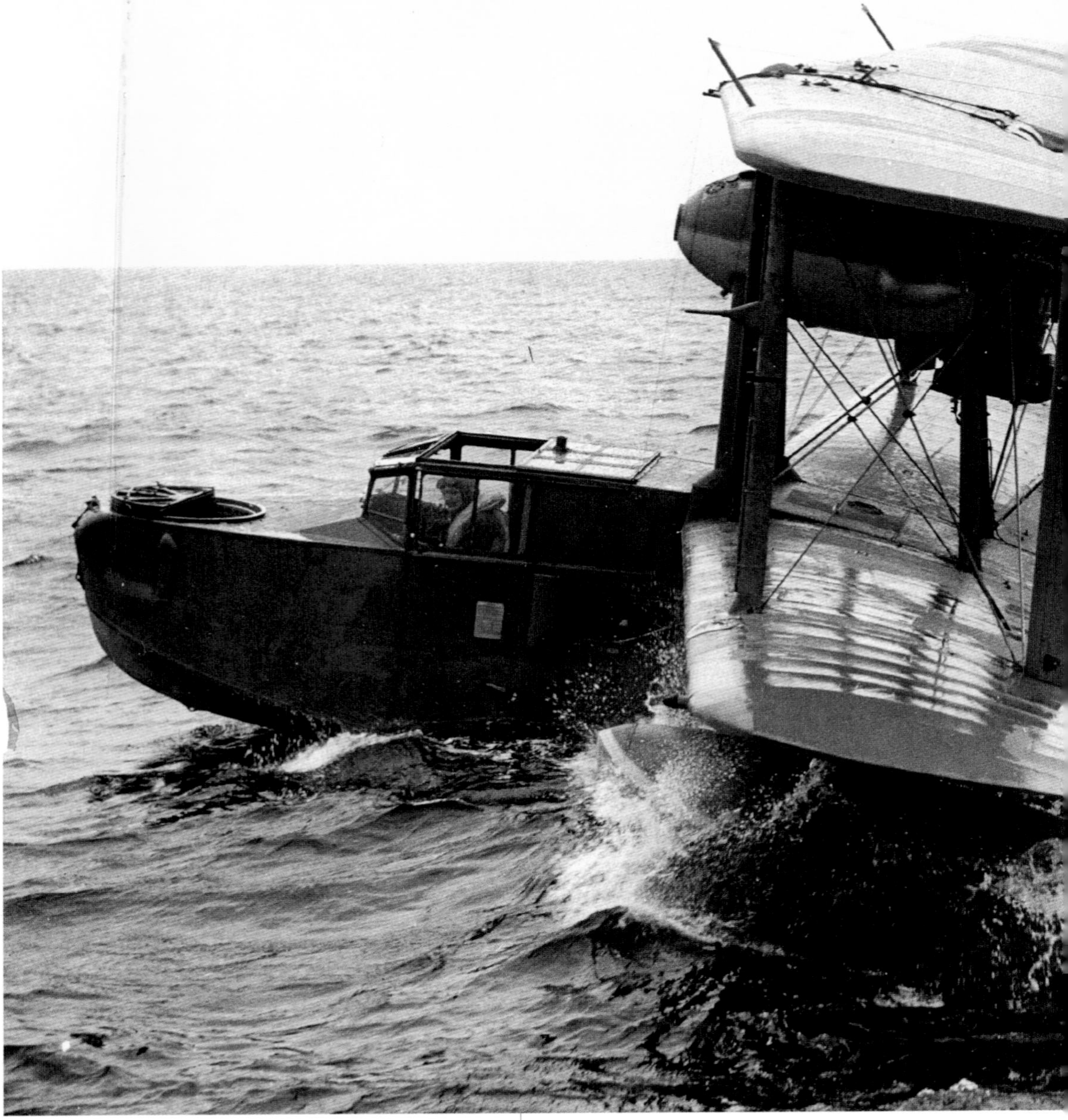

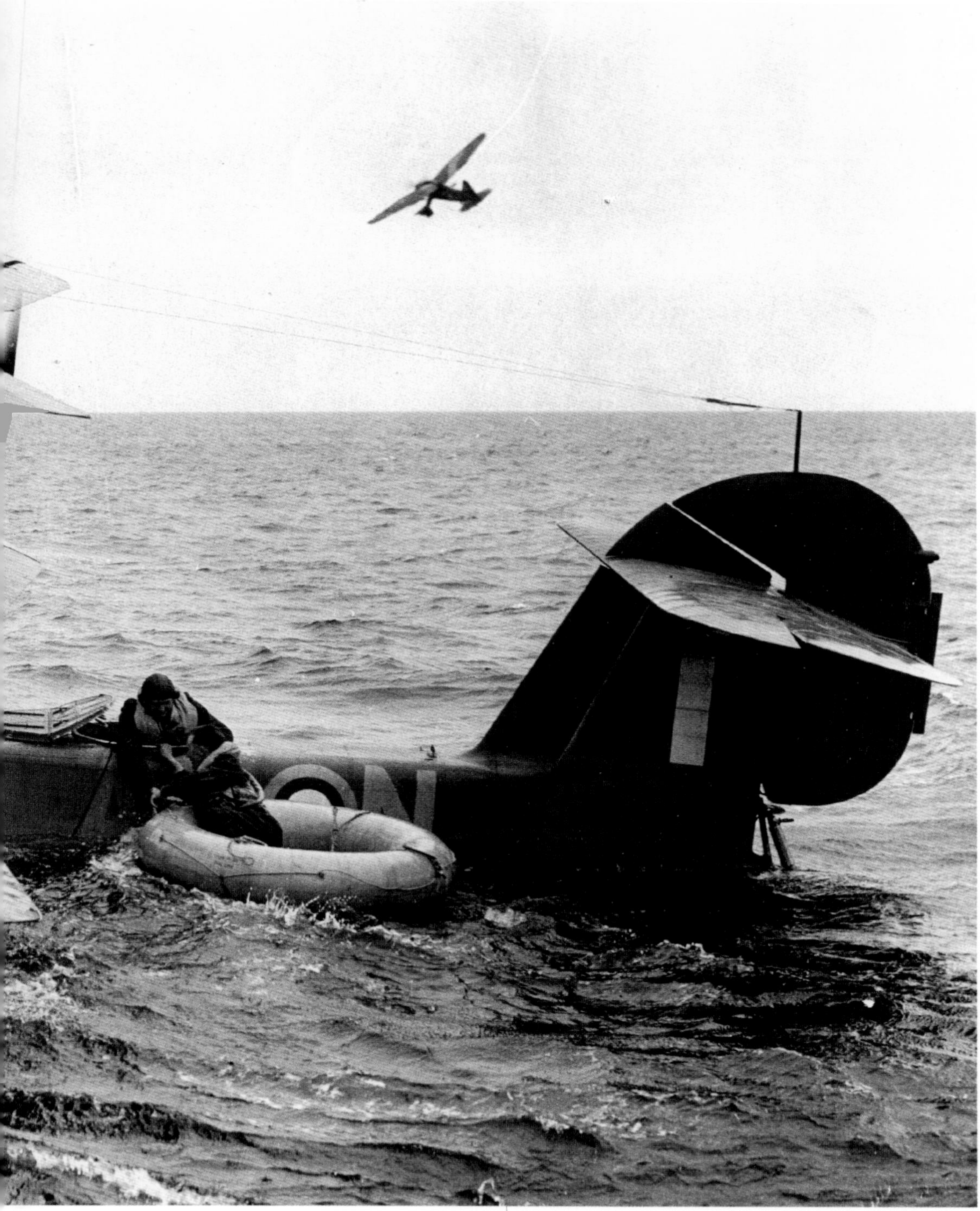

above: An RAF Walrus flying boat crew rescuing a downed pilot off the English coast, with a Westland Lysander aircraft in the background.

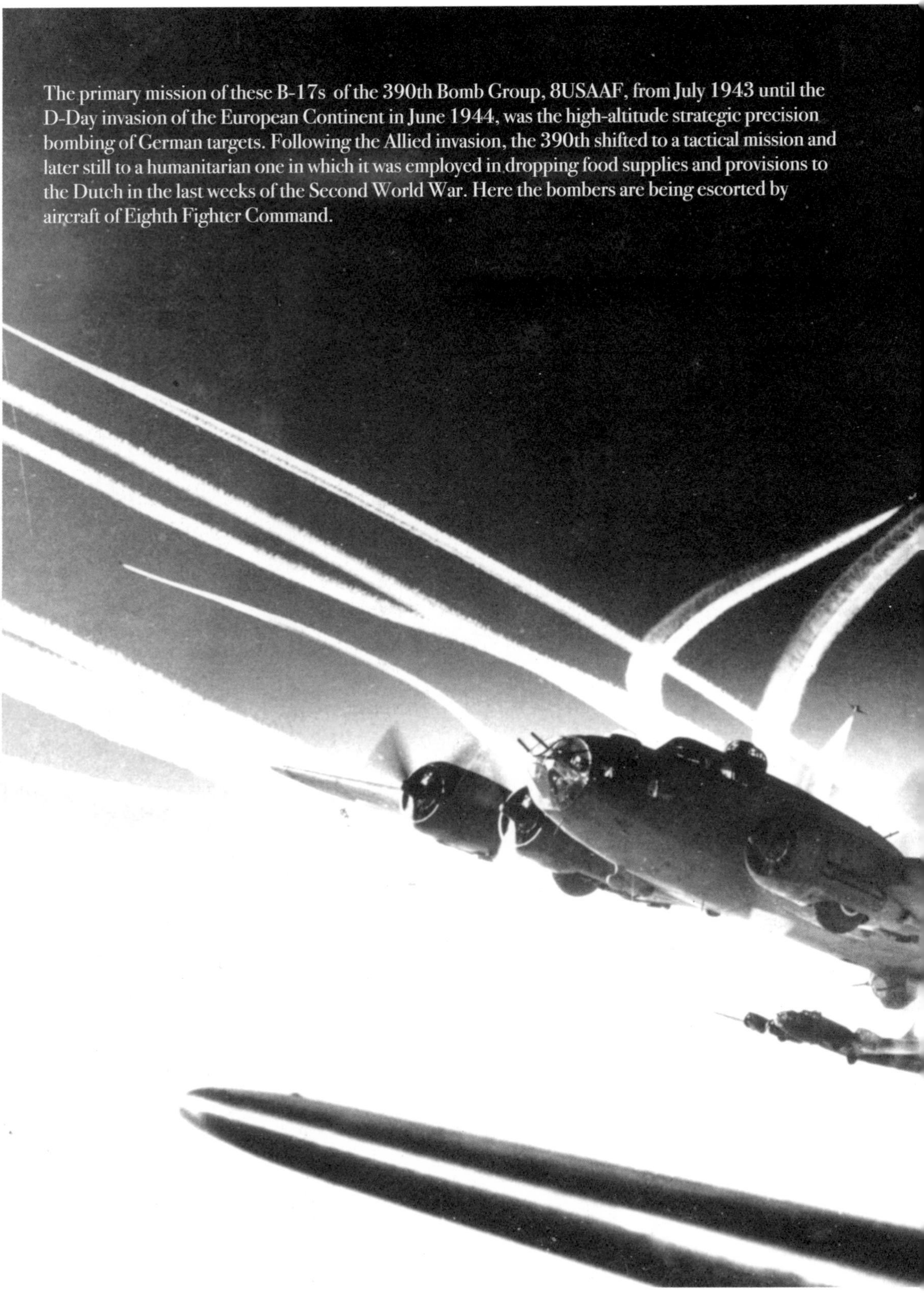

The primary mission of these B-17s of the 390th Bomb Group, 8USAAF, from July 1943 until the D-Day invasion of the European Continent in June 1944, was the high-altitude strategic precision bombing of German targets. Following the Allied invasion, the 390th shifted to a tactical mission and later still to a humanitarian one in which it was employed in dropping food supplies and provisions to the Dutch in the last weeks of the Second World War. Here the bombers are being escorted by aircraft of Eighth Fighter Command.

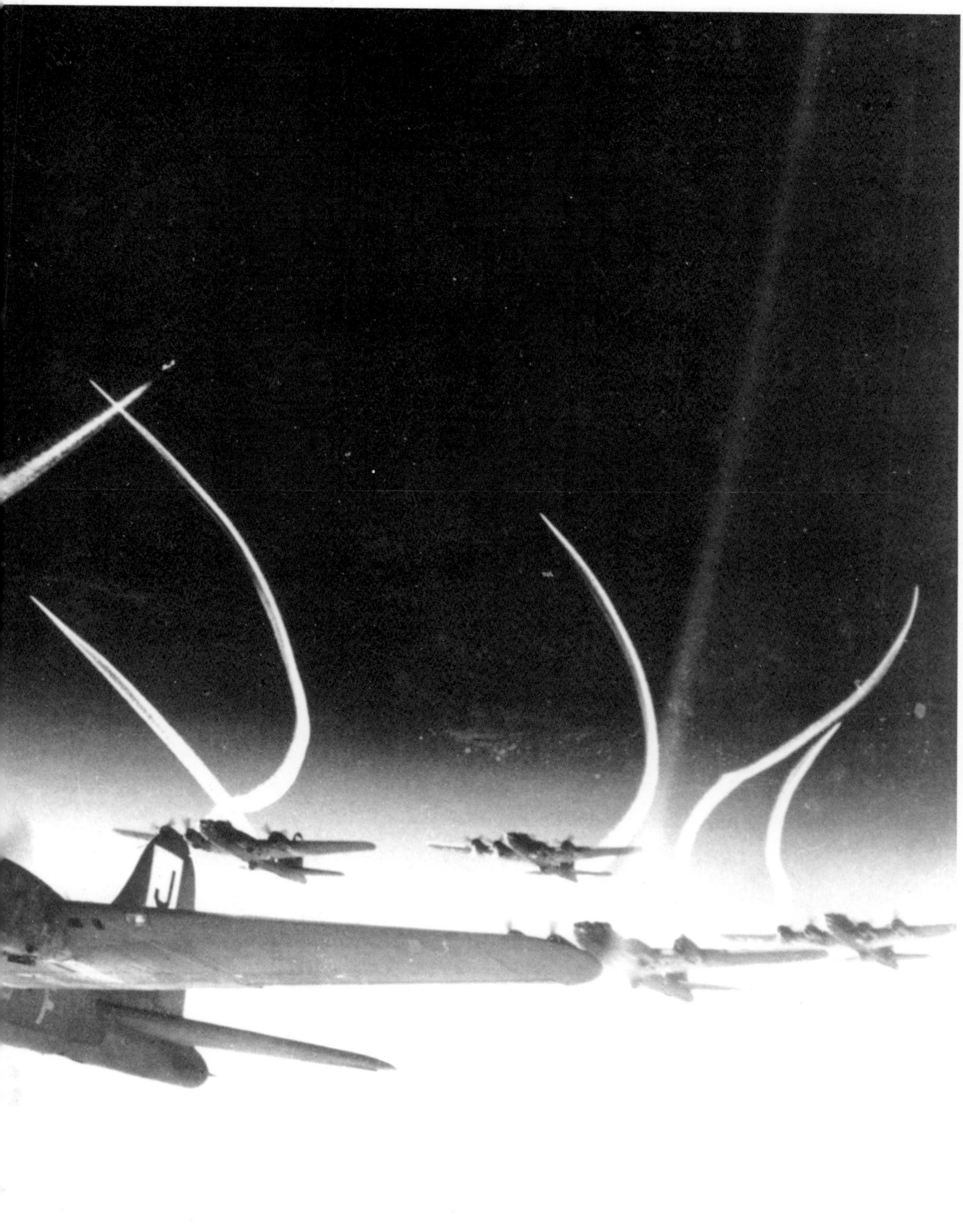

PICTURE CREDITS

Photographs by the author are credited: PK; photographs from the collection of the author are credited: AC; photographs from the United States National Archives are credited: NARA; photographs courtesy of the Zippo Manufacturing Company are credited: Zippo; photographs courtesy the Degolyer Library—Southern Methodist University are credited: Degolyer Library—SMU. Front cover: AC; back cover: all PK; 2-3: NARA; 4: top Zippo, bottom PK; 7: AC; 8: Zippo; 10: both AC; 11: both AC; 12: top left PK, top right AC, bottom AC; 13: all AC; 14: top PK; 15: AC; 16: AC; 17: both AC; 18: top left AC, bottom left AC, all others PK; 19: top both AC, bottom both PK; 20-21: AC; 22: AC; 24-25 AC; 26: AC; 27: AC; 28: Toni Frissell; 29: both PK; 30: top NARA, bottom PK; 31: top both PK, bottom both AC; 32: AC; 33: both PK; 34: both Bundesarchiv; 35: both PK; 36: Mark Brown-USAF; 37: AC; 38: AC; 39: PK; 40: courtesy Jack Currie; 2: AC; 43: AC; 44: USAF Museum; 45: both AC; 46: top AC 46: bottom PK; 47: PK; 48-49:Zippo; 50: both PK; 51: AC; 52: PK; 53: Bundesarchiv; 54-55: AC; 56: top AC, bottom left AC, bottom right: PK; 57: all AC; 58: AC; 59: AC; 60-61: AC; 62: PK; 63: top both PK, bottom courtesy Fred Kaplan; 64: top left PK, bottom AC; 65: PK; 66-67: AC; 68-69: PK; 69: far right both PK; 70-71: U.S. Coast Guard; 72: Degolyer Library-SMU; 73: PK; 74: both AC, courtesy J.P. Benamou; 76: both AC; 77: Degolyer Library-SMU; 78: AC; 79: PK; 80-81: AC; 82-83: all PK; 84: all AC; 85: AC; 86: AC; 87: top both PK; 87: bottom courtesy Fred Kaplan; 88: top left AC, bottom Frank Wootton; 89: NARA; 90: AC; 91: top courtesy Merle Olmsted, bottom both PK; 92: all AC; 93: Bundesarchiv; 94: AC, bottom left AC; 95: Degolyer Library—SMU; 96: NARA; 97: both PK; 98: AC; 99: top PK, bottom AC;100: top PK, bottom left AC, bottom right PK; 101: AC; 102: AC; 103: top AC, bottom AC, far right AC; 104: both PK; 105: Toni Frissell; 106: top left AC, all others PK; 107: PK; 108: Degolyer Library-SMU, bottom both PK; 109: PK; 110-111: PK; 112: top left and bottom both AC, top right PK; 113: AC; 114: top PK, bottom both AC, top PK; 115: bottom both AC; 116: PK; 117: Toni Frissell; 118-119: PK; 120: left both PK; 120-121: NARA; 122: AC; 123: top both AC, bottom Bundesarchiv; 124-125: NARA; 126: Mark Brown-USAF; 127: AC; 128: U.S. Navy; 129: top AC; 130-131: NARA; 131: both AC; 132: AC; 133: PK; 134-135: PK; 136: top left AC, top right PK, bottom courtesy M. Kaplan;

137: Toni Frissell; 138-139: PK; 140-141: PK; 140: bottom both AC; 141: both PK; 142-143: NARA; 144: top left AC, top right PK, bottom AC; 145: AC;146: AC; 147: courtesy Merle Olmsted; 148-149: top NARA; 148: bottom left PK, bottom right Zippo; 149: both PK; 150: courtesy Dave Hill; 151: top AC, bottom both PK; 152: NARA; 153: both AC; 154: courtesy J.P. Benamou; 156-157: AC; 158-159: AC; 160: AC; 161: Toni Frissell; 162: AC;163: both AC; 164: Zippo; 165: NARA; 166: top PK, bottom NARA; 166-167: PK; 168-169: PK; 169: PK; 170: AC; 171: top AC, bottom left courtesy J.P. Benamou, bottom right PK; 172: PK; 173: top PK, bottom courtesy J.P. Benamou; 175: AC; 176: top left AC, top right PK, bottom both PK; 177: top left AC, top right PK, bottom both AC; 179: Degolyer Library-SMU; 180-181: Royal Navy; 182: PK; 184-185: AC; 186-187: courtesy Ray Wild; 188-189: AC;189: top AC, bottom PK; 190-191: AC; 192-193: NARA; 194-195: AC; 196: AC; 197: Vickers; 198-199: AC:200-201 AC; 203: both AC; 204-205: courtesy Quentin Bland; 205: PK; 207: NARA.

BIBLIOGRAPHY

Avi R. Baer/Alexander Neumark/*Zippo An American Legend*/Running Press. 1999
Robert Capa/*Slightly Out of Focus*/Henry Holt/1947
Arthur A. Durand/*Stalag Luft III*/Touchstone/1988
Roger A. Freeman/*Zemke's Wolf Pack*/Crown/1989
Roger A. Freeman/*Zemke's Stalag*/Airlife/1991
John Gunther/*D-Day*/Hamish Hamilton/1944
Harris Lewine/*Good-Bye To All That*/McGraw Hill/1970
Linda Meabon/*Zippo Manufacturing Company*/Arcadia Publishing/ 2003
Edward R. Murrow/*This Is London*/Simon & Schuster/1941
Ernie Pyle/*Brave Men*/Popular Library/1964
Ernie Pyle/*Ernie Pyle in England*/Robert M.McBride/1941
Raff/*Behind The Spitfires*/Methuen & Co/1941
Curt Riess/*They Were There*/G.P. Putnam's Sons/1944
John Steinbeck/*Bombs Away*/The Viking Press/142
Bert Stiles/*Serenade to the Big Bird*, W.W. Norton/1952

right both: Among the most popular of the Zippos are those of this sports series.

ACKNOWLEDGMENTS

My thanks to Margaret Mayhew for her consultation on the development of this book. The compatability of our working relationship stems from our strong mutual interest in the 1940s, nearly all things art deco, and our many years of enthusiastically exploring the remains of the Second World War in England and elsewhere. To my old chum Eric Holloway for all the skill, creative problem-solving, consideration and sensitivty he has lent to so many books of mine over the years. Special thanks to: the Air Transport Auxiliary, Allison Engines, Beth and David Alston, Virginia Bader, Malcolm Bates, Jean Pierre Benamou, The Boeing Company, the British Army, the British Merchant Navy, Bundesarchiv, Robbie Collin, Convair, Jack Currie, Al Deere, *The Daily Telegraph* (London), The Degolyer Library-Southern Methodist University, Eagle pub-Cambridge, England, Flying Fortress pub-Rougham, England, Flying Heritage and Combat Armor Museum, Roger A. Freeman, Toni Frissell, General Electric, Alex Henshaw, John Hersey, Claire Kaplan, Fred Kaplan, Joseph Kaplan, Neal Kaplan, Alex Kershaw, Adolph Malan, Eric Marsden, Steve McQueen, Edward R. Murrow, the United States National Archives and Records Administration, Michael O'Leary, Merle and Margreth Olmsted, Geoffrey and Pauline Page, Alice and John Pawsey, Ernie Pyle, Alan and Sandra Reeves, Republic Aviation, Mark Ritchie, Rolls-Royce, Andy Rooney, Royal Air Force, Royal Australian Air Force, Royal Canadian Air Force, Royal Navy, San Diego Aerospace Museum, William L. Shirer, Tangmere Aviation Museum, D.R. Turley-George, 20th Century Fox, United States Air Force, United States Air Force Museum, United States Air Force Academy Library, United States Coast Guard, United States Marine Corps, United States Navy, The White Hart public house-Brasted, England, Ray Wild, Women Airforce Service Pilots (WASP), Hubert Zemke, Zippo Manufacturing Company-Karen Snow and Shirley Evers.

Acknowledgement to the following for the use of previously published material: Quentin Bland, Holt, Rinehart & Winston Inc for a brief Zippo excerpt from *Brave Men* by Ernie Pyle; *The Daily Telegraph* for excerpts from the 2 April 2016 article, 'How Smoking Became Film's Last Taboo'—© Robbie Collin /the Telegraph Media Group Limited 2020; W.W. Norton & Company Inc for a brief excerpt from *Serenade to the Big Bird* by Bert Stiles, published in 1952.

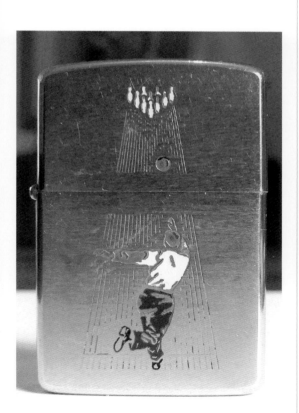

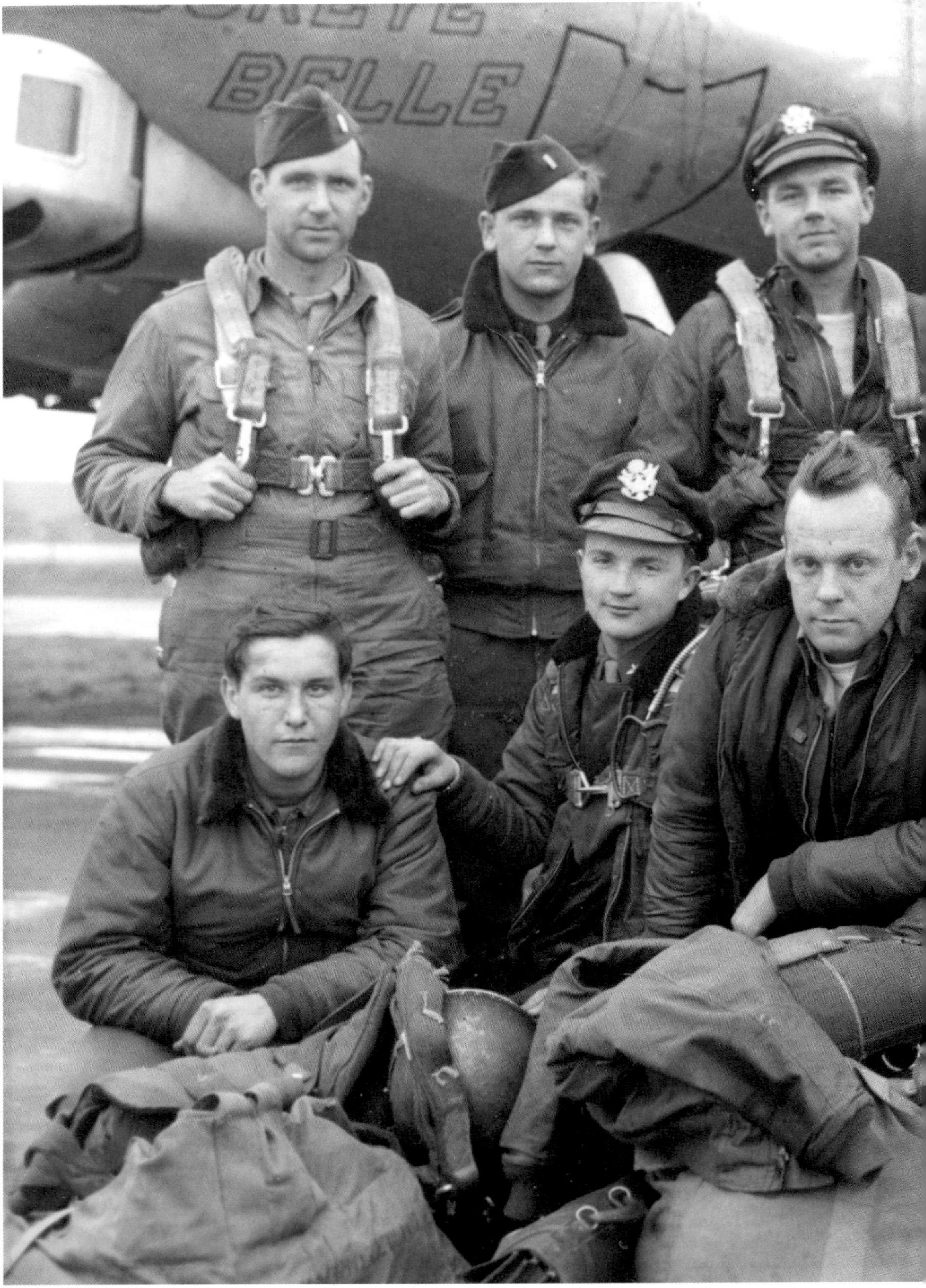
BELLE

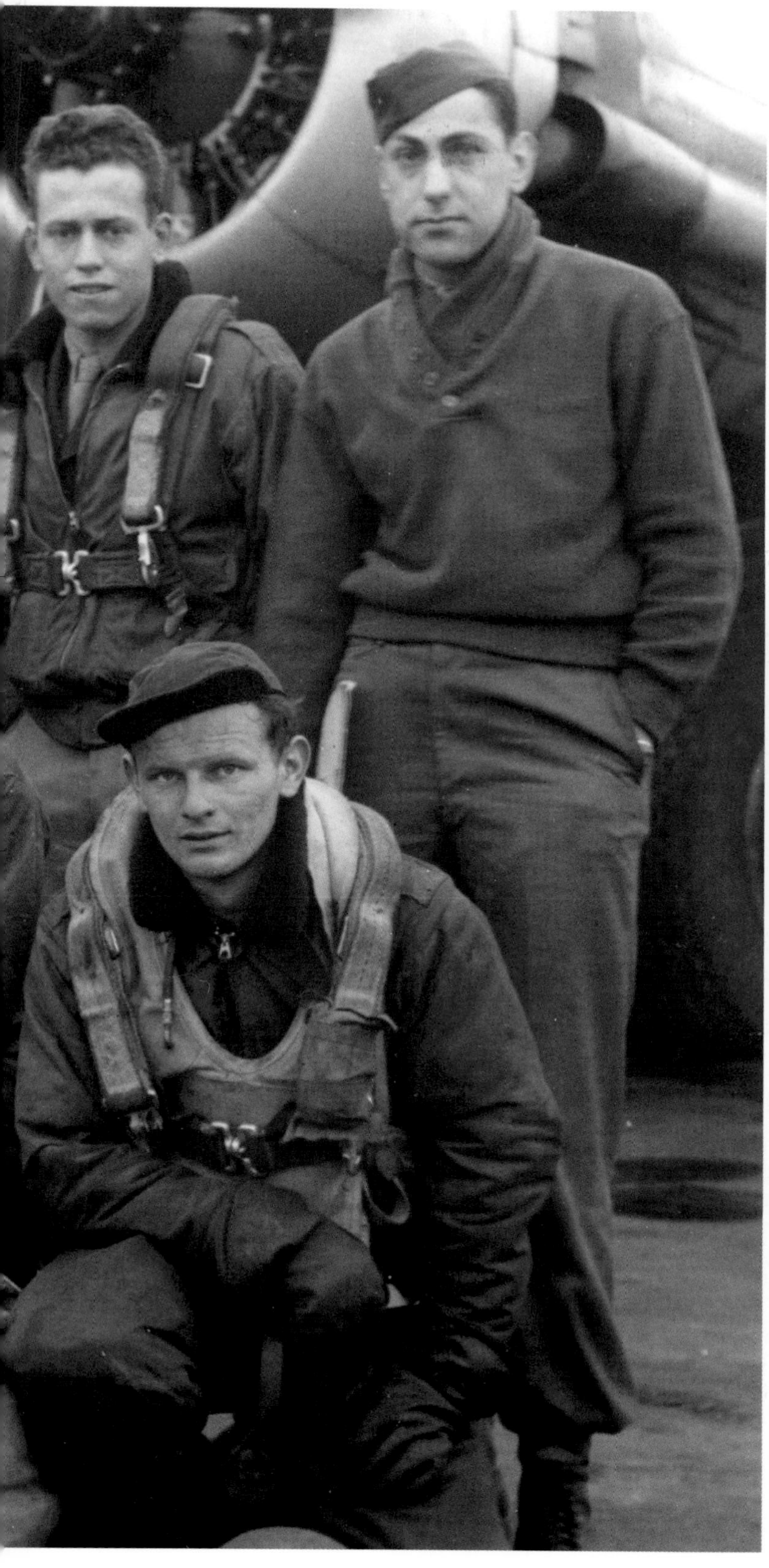

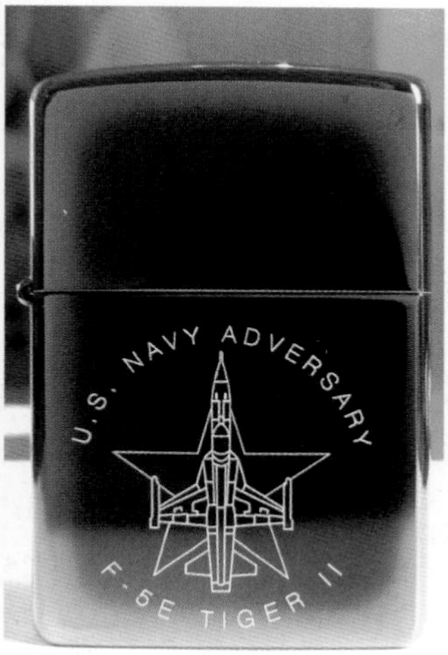
U.S. NAVY ADVERSARY
F-5E TIGER II

left: Nine of the ten-man crew of *Buckeye Belle*, a B-17 bomber of the 384th Bomb Group at their Grafton Underwood base in Northamptonshire, England; above: A Zippo of a U.S. Navy Adversary Squadron.

INDEX

Michigan, USS, Zippo, 91
Mickey Mouse, 178
Middleton, Drew, 50
MiG-15, 181
Miller, Glenn, 104
Mills, Henry, 144

Credited with 17.33
kills in aerial combat,
Colonel Vermont
Garrison of Mount
Victory, Kentucky,
was one of only seven
Americans to achieve
ace status in both the
Second World War
and the Korean War.